THE
ENGLISH
ECSTASY

THE ENGLISH ECSTASY

How England Rose to Greatness 1558-1649

Includes Bonus Section on Francis Bacon

WILL DURANT

foreword by Richard Smoley

MAPLE SPRING PUBLISHING

Published 2025 by Maple Spring Publishing

This work was originally published in *The Age of Reason Begins* by Will Durant in 1961.

The bonus section on Francis Bacon was originally published
in *The Story of Philosophy* by Will Durant in 1926.

Book design by Jason Snyder

Library of Congress Cataloging-in-Publication Data is available upon request

ISBN: 979-8-3505-0222-0

10   9   8   7   6   5   4   3   2   1

CONTENTS

CHAPTER III

ON THE SLOPES OF PARNASSUS
1558–1603
71

CHAPTER IV

WILLIAM SHAKESPEARE
1564–1616
97

CHAPTER V

MARY QUEEN OF SCOTS
1542–87
123

BONUS

FRANCIS BACON
249

ENDNOTES
288

Foreword

by Richard Smoley

THE PHENOMENON OF THE BRITISH EMPIRE is unique in world history. How did this small island come to rule a full quarter of the globe? No other empire can match this achievement: the closest was the empire of the Mongols in Asia in medieval times.

The story of the British Empire, which takes us into the eighteenth and nineteenth centuries, is out of the scope of this volume. But it does tell us about the turning point in English history: when it transformed from an outlier among the powers of Europe—insignificant compared to Spain, France, and the Holy Roman Empire—to the richest of them all, and if not the most powerful, then certainly on a scale comparable to that of its European rivals. This "English ecstasy," as Durant terms it, included not only political and economic success but some of the greatest cultural achievements of the human spirit—crowned by the genius of Shakespeare and Francis Bacon.

The contents of this volume are taken from *The Age of Reason Begins*, first published in 1961 as part of his monumental series The Story of Civilization. In language as fresh as clear today as it was then, Durant describes and explains this remarkable turning point, which was the era he discusses here: from the accession of Elizabeth I as queen of England in 1558 to the deposition and execution of King Charles II in 1649.

As always, Durant tells his story capably, succinctly, insightfully, and with wit, so there is no point in my attempting to recapitulate it. All the same, I think there is value in setting some context for this "English ecstasy." It is important to understand what came both before and after.

Although no exhaustive account of medieval and early modern English history is possible here, some salient points can be made. The first is that in the fourteenth and fifteenth centuries, England was continually submersed in two major conflicts: the Hundred Years' War and the Wars of the Roses. Again without going into details, we can focus on two crucial facts.

The first is that these struggles were almost entirely dynastic in nature. The centerpiece of the medieval European state was the monarch, so who got to be monarch was of the utmost importance. Each king's death plunged the nation into uncertainty. He might be lucky and have a living male heir, who under most circumstances would be proclaimed king in his father's stead. But this did not always happen, even when there was a male heir, especially if he was an infant or a child.

Many times there was no legitimate son who could inherit the crown without dispute. This uncertainty plunged the nation into crisis: other members of the dynasty (legitimate or illegitimate), distant relatives, and the rulers of neighboring countries all contended for the throne. These squabbles—which often led to bloody conflict—characterize the two great wars of England's preceding centuries.

The second key fact about these convulsions can be summed up by their dates. The Hundred Years' War, which was mostly about the claims of English kings to various regions of France, lasted from 1337 to 1453. (In brief, England lost.)

The name of the Wars of the Roses comes from the white rose, the symbol of the house of Lancaster, and the red rose, the symbol of the house of York, both of whom laid claim to the throne. These wars took place from 1455 to 1485. They ended in the latter year, when Henry Tudor, of the house of Lancaster, defeated and killed King Richard III at the battle of Bosworth Field.

In short, from 1337 to 1485—very close to 150 years—England was submerged in costly and bloody conflicts, which were almost entirely over claims to a throne or a piece of territory and secondarily (if at all) over any benefits the subject peoples might enjoy from victory.

After the fall of Richard III in 1485, Henry Tudor reigned as Henry VII, beginning the long and mostly peaceful reign of the Tudor dynasty. Henry VII is remembered as a capable monarch, but his fame has been eclipsed by that of his much more colorful son, Henry VIII, who reigned from 1509 to 1546—a long time for a king to sit on the throne, then or now.

Henry VIII launched the second trend that affected the era covered in this book. The Protestant Reformation began with the Ninety-Five Theses of Martin Luther in 1517, which questioned many of the most important claims of the Catholic church. At the beginning, Henry was on the side of the church. He even wrote a short treatise opposing Luther, which led Pope Leo X to bestow on him the title "Defender of the Faith."

Henry did not live up to this title—at least not from the Catholic point of view. He had grown impatient with his queen, the Spanish Catherine of Aragon, because she was unable to give him a male heir. Infatuated with a lady at court, Anne Boleyn, he asked the pope (now Paul III) for a dispensation for a divorce on a technicality so he could remarry, but the pope, fearful of Spanish arms, refused to grant it.

At this point, in 1533, Henry broke with the Catholic church once and for all—a breach that has never been repaired. Along with some sympathetic bishops, he proclaimed the autonomy of the English church, with himself as its de facto head. To this day, the English monarchs are, at least titularly, heads of the Church of England.

Henry's decision had fiscal advantages. Church property in England was now effectively in his hands. He ordered the dissolution of the monasteries (some of which were actively destroyed), appropriated their wealth, and enabled a number of nobles to share in the spoils.

The public reaction to Henry's move was ambivalent. Parliament supported him (even restoring his title "Defender of the Faith" in 1534), but many of his subjects did not. Thus began a struggle over religious allegiance which colored English history for the next 120 years, pitting those who remained loyal Catholics to those who submitted to the Church of England—making them Protestants. Into the mix went the Puritans, who maintained that the Protestants had not done enough to expel the Roman elements from the church.

Henry died in 1547 and was succeeded by his only legitimate son (by his third wife, Jane Seymour), who ruled as Edward VI. Ten years old when he was crowned, he showed great promise as a monarch, being both vigorous and intellectually gifted. Unfortunately, he did not get to enjoy his reign for long, dying of tuberculosis in 1553. Since he had not reached the age of sixteen, he left no son to replace him, but he was the only legitimate son Henry had.

The ensuing ambiguity led to yet another dynastic struggle that, in this case, was settled quickly with the accession of Henry's eldest daughter, Mary, to the throne.

Mary was the offspring of Henry's first marriage, to Catherine of Aragon. As we have seen, Henry's divorce from Catherine led to his split with the church of Rome. Mary, following her mother, remained a devout Catholic and was determined to return her domain to the Catholic faith. This move was widely unpopular, in the first place with the nobility, who had profited from the seizure of church property, and secondly with Protestants.

Mary reinforced her attempt to reestablish Catholicism by her unpopular decision to marry King Philip II of Spain (Spain was a bulwark of Catholicism). She promulgated strict laws against "heresy"—that is, anything and anyone not conforming to the Catholic faith—and persecuted those who would not submit. Some 300 dissenters were burned at the stake during her five-year reign, giving her the sobriquet by which she remains best known to history: Bloody Mary.

Mary hoped that her marriage to Philip of Spain would bless her with a male heir, but it did not. Vexed by a series of false pregnancies and increasingly poor health, she died in 1558, at the age of forty-two.

Resigned to the fact that she would have no male successor, Mary left the throne to her half-sister, Elizabeth Tudor, daughter of Henry VIII through Anne Boleyn. As Durant tells us, the dying Mary sent the crown jewels to her sister. Elizabeth was crowned in 1558.

Durant's account picks up at this point, so there is no need to go further into it here. He does admirable duty with Elizabeth's stellar qualities. To this day, she can be reckoned as the greatest monarch England has ever had.

Nor is there any need here to go into the history of the years 1558—Elizabeth's accession—to 1649, the year of the deposition and execution of King Charles I: the climactic, and final, event of the English Civil War. Again, Durant tells the story in his inimitably concise and insightful fashion.

But there is some value in saying a few words about the aftermath. As Durant shows, the English Civil War of 1642–49 pitted supporters of the king versus a Parliament that was dominated by republican-minded Puritans. Led by the indomitable Oliver Cromwell, they were victorious.

The subsequent years—1649 to 1658—are known in English history as the Protectorate, with the nation governed by Parliament, led by Oliver Cromwell as Lord Protector. It was the zenith of the Puritan dominance of England.

Although Cromwell was never crowned king and never wanted to be, his death in 1658 created yet another crisis in succession. His son Richard was installed as Lord Protector in his place, but (a rarity in world history) after eight months Richard realized he was not up to the job and resigned. Parliament voted to restore the monarchy, bestowing it upon Charles II, the legitimate son of Charles I. He was crowned in 1660: a moment known to history as the Restoration. With that twelve-year interruption, the Stuart dynasty ruled England from 1603 (the accession of James I) to 1688, when a disgruntled Parliament, exasperated by Charles II's son, James II, who sought to bring the nation back to the Catholic church, expelled him from the throne and gave it to a Dutch prince, the Protestant William of Orange. Since then, all British monarchs are, and have had to be, Protestant.

These are the bare facts of the history that both precedes and succeeds Durant's account, but some further observations can be made. Durant speaks of the lusty, exuberant "merrie England" of the sixteenth and early seventeenth centuries, which was brought to heel by the repressions of the Puritans of the Protectorate. The accession of Charles II reversed the mood yet again, and the Restoration period (dated to his reign, from 1660 to 1685) reverted to merriment and license. As Durant points out, this period gave us "the bawdiest dramas in modern literature" (at least up to his time of writing; he might have a different opinion if he were alive today).

These reversals pose yet another of the many unanswered questions of history: what provokes these shifts of national mood, which are not matters of mere fashion but of a shift in the mindsets of generations? During the time Durant covers here, the influence of the monarch was great—Elizabeth was tolerant of sensual indulgences, her own and others'—but what explains the rise of Puritanism, which was not modeled or supported by her or any other English monarch?

We can see these reversals recur later in English history. The Restoration set a mood for the nation that persisted through the eighteenth century—the lusty, rollicking England of Fielding and Richardson—into the early nineteenth century, when, in the reign of Victoria, a somber, repressive, antisensual mood took hold of the nation again. It permeated the national mentality until the swinging England of the 1960s (a happier time for that nation, which was not immersed in war, than for the U.S., mired in Vietnam).

There is really only one explanation for these long-lasting reversals, although it is a vague and unsatisfactory one: the Newtonian law, whereby for every action there is an equal and opposite reaction. This law is evident for anyone watching a pendulum, but we are not dealing with pendulums here; we are dealing with the spirit of a nation over generations. How could some Newtonian law apply in this context? One can suspect that no matter how many dates and facts are assimilated or how many socioeconomic statistics are piled up, these historical forces will not be easily explained.

Bacon and the Problem of Induction

Just as Shakespeare—to whom Durant does rich justice—is the great literary luminary of this period, Francis Bacon is the great philosophical luminary. He is by far the greatest thinker that the English nation has given to the human race.

Again, this volume presents a great deal of material on Bacon, both from Durant's *Story of History* and his *Story of Philosophy*, so I think any attempt to cover the same ground would be pointless. Rather I would like to focus on Bacon's greatest contribution to Western thought. In many respects, he was the first and most influential proponent of the scientific method as it is known today.

In Bacon's time—and this had been true throughout the Dark Ages and the Middle Ages—knowledge was understood as knowledge of tradition. This attitude was no doubt influenced by Christianity, which placed the authority of the Bible as the centerpiece of its knowledge. Knowledge was, in the first place, knowledge of the Bible: learning what was in it, what agreed with it and what did not. In the second place, knowledge consisted of the learning of the authorities from classical antiquity: Galen in medicine and Aristotle in philosophy, including natural philosophy and logic. This was not necessarily unwise, because, given the enormous collapse of learning after the fall of the western Roman Empire in 476, there were no authorities who knew better or could teach anything more. Indeed Aristotle formulated the principles of formal logic with such excellence that the discipline made no real advances until the nineteenth century.

But the restless minds of Bacon's era were beginning to chafe under this bit. Better and more precise instrumentation made it possible to, for example, measure the movements of the planets with more precision, casting doubt on the geocentric view of the solar system that had prevailed up to that point.

Even more crucially, the methods of acquiring knowledge were starting to seem increasingly inadequate. As Bacon saw, at that time, knowledge proceeded for the most part deductively. *Deductive reasoning* starts with certain premises accepted as true and working out their logical consequences. The classic example is the syllogism. This example goes back to Aristotle:

All men are mortal.

Socrates is a man.

Therefore Socrates is mortal.

If the first two premises are true, the conclusion is necessarily true. There can be no further debate about the matter.

In fact, you don't even need to know what you are talking about specifically. You could just as well say:

All A's are B.

All B's are C.

Therefore all A's are C.

Hence this kind of reasoning is called *a priori*, which is Latin for "from the prior." Prior to what? To actual experience. It doesn't even matter whether A, B, or C even exist. You are reasoning from premises that you have already granted to be true.

Obviously deductive reasoning is extremely useful, and we rely on it all the time. But it has at least one problem: where do you get the premises to begin with? Do you just make them up? Do you get them from Galen or Aristotle?

Up to a point, reliance on the deductive approach was satisfactory, but by Bacon's time, it no longer was. He advocated the complete reversal of this approach. He realized that in addition to deductive reasoning, which worked out the implications of certain propositions, you need some way to come up with those propositions to begin with. You do so, Bacon said, exactly the opposite way: you start with observations, you notice certain common elements in them, and you use those to formulate your principles. Durant writes:

> Philosophy has been barren so long, says Bacon, because she needed a new method to make her fertile. The great mistake of the Greek philosophers was that they spent so much time in theory, so little in observation. But thought should be the aide of observation, not its substitute. "Man," says the first aphorism of [Bacon's] *Novum Organum*, as if flinging a challenge to all metaphysics, "Man, as the minister and interpreter of nature, does and understands as much as his observations on the order of nature . . . permit him; and neither knows nor is capable of more." . . . Ultimately, our troubles are due to dogma and deduction; we find no new truth because we take some venerable but questionable proposition as an indubitable starting-point, and never think of putting this assumption itself to the test of observation or experiment.

With this call was born experimental science as we know it. Bacon himself did not excel in this respect. Durant points out that Bacon's "conclusion that heat is a form of motion constitutes one of his few specific contributions to natural science."

This process of taking a certain collection of facts and drawing a general conclusion from them is called *inductive reasoning* (which, as we can easily see, is the opposite of deductive reasoning). It is *a posteriori*, "from what comes after"—after observation.

The eighteenth-century philosopher David Hume expressed the principle thus: "I have found that such an object has always been attended with such an effect, and I foresee, that other objects, which are, in appearance, similar, will be attended with similar effects."

Deductive and inductive reasoning are the pillars of knowledge, in science and in many other disciplines. But as philosophers have long seen, certain problems arise. Inductive reasoning works like this: you see lots of ravens—raven after raven—and you conclude that all ravens are black. This is uncontroversial until somebody asks, "How do you know that the next raven you come across won't be white?"

This question has proved notoriously difficult to answer, but it casts some light on how Bacon's influence has shaped the thought of later centuries.

The problem becomes more acute if you throw causation into the mix. Everyone uses causal thinking all the time, and it is impossible to imagine living an ordinary life without it. I let go of my keys; they drop on the floor. I do this over and over, and I conclude that my dropping the keys causes them to fall. Or rather, the fact that I let go of my keys is inevitably followed by their falling on the floor. Causality is another underlying assumption of the scientific method.

So far this is simple enough, but as usual, it gets complicated. The English philosopher Bertrand Russell expressed it wittily: "The man who has fed the chicken every day throughout its life at last wrings its neck instead, showing that more refined views as to the uniformity of nature would have been useful to the chicken." Or as investors read in every mutual fund prospectus, "past performance does not guarantee future results."

Russell hits on one key problem: uniformity. Every raven you have ever seen is black, but what happens if you come across an albino? In this case, it's not a huge problem: you just reformulate your conclusion: all ravens are black except for albinos. But the solution isn't always that easy.

The principles of induction and uniformity are the mainstays of science, but both are harder to validate philosophically than is generally realized. Indeed Hume famously argued that the principle of uniformity cannot be proved rationally (for reasons that are too complex to go into here).

Where does this leave science? I often wonder what would be the case if the uniformity principle did not apply across the entire universe. After all, we are dealing with distances that are nearly inconceivable to the human mind: why should we assume that natural laws that apply to our little corner of the cosmos should apply everywhere?

Consider this. We see galaxies that are light-years, light-centuries, and light-millennia away. How do we know how far they are? By the law of the red shift: "The wavelength of the light is stretched, so the light is seen as 'shifted' towards the red part of the spectrum," as I learn from the website of the European Space Agency. But how do we know that the red-shift principle works the same way with light that may come to us from millions or billions of years ago?

Similarly with the age of the universe. Like most people, I have read the well-known statement that the universe is 13.8 billion years old, when the big bang ostensibly occurred. But I find this claim difficult to understand. A year is the time it takes the earth to go around the sun. But what was a year billions of years before there was an earth or a sun to go around it?

Maybe we don't know the real age of the universe. On this matter, a NASA website says it is determined by the age of the oldest stars (but how do we know that?) and by the Hubble constant, "a measure of the current expansion rate of the universe." Note the use of "constant" here: we are still with the principle of uniformity.

Unfortunately, NASA goes on to tell us, "If we compare the two age determinations, there is a potential crisis. If the astronomers who estimate that $1/H_0$ [the Hubble constant] is as small as 10 Billion years are correct, then the age of the Universe would be shorter than the age of its oldest stars. This contradiction implies that either the Big Bang theory is incorrect or that we need to modify general relativity by adding a cosmological constant."

Why, then, does science continue to rely on the principles of induction and uniformity? The answer is maddeningly circular: because they have worked up to this point.

The problems here, particularly that of causation, are of immense interest to me, I cannot go any further into them than here, but I have explored some of them in my book *The Dice Game of Shiva*.

Personally I find many of the basic premises behind the scientific method as shaky, perhaps, as Hume did. Once this is more firmly grasped, it is likely to create a scientific revolution that will overshadow every one that came before it. But that is a much larger issue. The point here is not to grope for some kind of ultimate solution, which may well never be found. It is to suggest how we owe the whole scientific enterprise—its insights and discoveries as well as its conundrums—to the genius of Francis Bacon. Durant is a superb guide to him.

RICHARD SMOLEY, a graduate of Harvard and Oxford universities, is the author of fourteen books, including *The Dice Game of Shiva: How Consciousness Creates the Universe*; *Forbidden Faith: The Secret History of Gnosticism*; and *Seven Games of Life and How to Play*.

CHAPTER I

THE GREAT QUEEN

1558–1603

I. The Uses of Adversity

On November 17, 1558, a courier galloped into the court of the royal palace at Hatfield, thirty-six miles north of London, and announced to Elizabeth Tudor that she was Queen of England. Her half-sister Queen Mary, of pitiful fame, had died in the dark of that morning. In London the Parliament, receiving the news, cried out, "God save Queen Elizabeth! Long may she reign over us!"—not dreaming that it would be forty-five years. The churches, though foreboding trouble, thrilled the air with the clangor of their bells. The people of England, as they had done for Mary, spread festive tables in the streets, and that evening they colored the sky with bonfires of eternal hope.

By Saturday the nineteenth the leading lords, ladies, and commoners of the realm had gathered at Hatfield to vow their allegiance and feather their nests. To them, on the twentieth, Elizabeth spoke right royally:

My Lords: The laws of nature move me to sorrow for my sister; the burden that has fallen upon me maketh me amazed; and yet, considering I am God's creature ordained to obey His appointment, I will thereto yield; desiring from the bottom of my heart that I may have assistance of His grace to be the minister of His heavenly will in the office now committed to me. And as I am but one body materially considered, though by His permission a body politic to govern, so shall I desire you all, my lords, chiefly you of the nobility, every one in his degree and power, to be assistant to me; that I with my ruling, and you with your service, may make a good account to Almighty God, and leave some comfort to our posterity on earth.[1]

On the twenty-eighth, clad in purple velvet, Elizabeth rode through London in public procession to that same Tower where, four years earlier, she had been a prisoner awaiting death. Now, on her route, the populace acclaimed her, choruses chanted her glory, children tremblingly recited to her the little speeches of homage they had memorized, and "such shooting of guns as never was heard afore" heralded a reign destined to abound, beyond any English precedent, in splendor of men and minds.

Twenty-five years of trials had tempered Elizabeth to mastery. It seemed, in 1533, good fortune to have been fathered by Henry VIII, but it was dangerous to have been born of Anne Boleyn. The disgrace and execution of the mother fell within the child's forgetful years (1536); yet the pain of that somber heritage outlived her youth and yielded only to the balm of sovereignty. An act of Parliament (1536) declared Anne's marriage null, making Elizabeth illegitimate; coarse gossip debated the girl's paternity; in any case, to most Englishmen she was the daughter of adultery. Her legitimacy was never re-established in law, but another act of Parliament (1544) confirmed her right, after her half-brother Edward and her half-sister Mary, to succeed to the throne. During Edward's rule (1547–53) she adhered to the Protestant worship; but when Catholic Mary acceded, Elizabeth, preferring life to consistency, conformed to the Roman ritual. After Wyatt's Rebellion (1554) had failed to unseat Mary, Elizabeth was accused of complicity and was sent to the Tower; but Mary judged her guilt unproved, and released her to live under surveillance at Woodstock. Before Mary died she recognized her sister as her successor and sent her the jewels of the Crown. We owe Elizabeth's reign to the kindliness of the "bloody" Queen.

Elizabeth's more formal education was overwhelming. Her famous tutor, Roger Ascham, boasted that "she talks French and Italian as well as she does English, and has often talked to me readily and well in Latin, moderately in Greek."[2] She had a daily stint of theology and became expert in Protestant dogma; but her Italian teachers seem to have transmitted to her something of the skepticism they had imbibed from Pomponazzi, Machiavelli, and Renaissance Rome.

She was never sure of her crown. Parliament (1553) had reaffirmed the invalidity of her mother's marriage to her father; state and Church agreed that she was a bastard; and English law, ignoring William the Conqueror, excluded bastards from the throne. The whole Catholic world—and England was still largely Catholic—believed that the legal heir to the English scepter was Mary

Stuart, great-granddaughter of Henry VII. It was intimated to Elizabeth that if she made her peace with the Church the Pope would wash her free of bastardy and recognize her right to rule. She was not so inclined. Thousands of Englishmen held property that had been expropriated from the Church by Parliament under Henry VIII and Edward VI. These influential possessors, fearing that a continued Catholic restoration might enforce restitution, were prepared to fight for a Protestant queen; and the Catholics of England preferred her to civil war. On January 15, 1559, amid the acclamation of Protestant London, Elizabeth was crowned in Westminster Abbey as "Queen of England, France, and Ireland, Defender of the Faith." For English monarchs, since Edward III, had regularly claimed the throne of France. Nothing had been left undone to provide the Queen with problems.

She was now twenty-five, in all the charm of maturing womanhood. She was moderately tall, with a good figure, fair features, olive complexion, flashing eyes, auburn hair, and beautiful hands which she knew how to display.[3] It seemed impossible that such a lass should cope successfully with the chaos that encompassed her. Hostile creeds divided the land, playing for power and wielding arms. Pauperism was endemic, and vagrancy had survived the terrible penalties laid upon it by Henry VIII. Domestic trade was clogged by a dishonest currency; half a century of false coinage had left the credit of the fisc so low that the government had to pay 14 percent for loans. Mary Tudor, absorbed in religion, had skimped on national defense, the fortresses were neglected, the coasts unprotected, the navy unfit, the army ill paid and ill fed, and its cadres unfilled. England, which under Wolsey had held the balance of power in Europe, was now a political cripple bandied about between Spain and France; French troops were in Scotland, and Ireland was inviting Spain. The Pope was holding over the Queen's head the threat of excommunication and interdict and of invasion by the Catholic states. Invasion definitely loomed in 1559, and fear of assassination was part of Elizabeth's life from day to day. She was saved by the disunion of her enemies, the wisdom of her counselors, and the courage of her soul. The Spanish ambassador was shocked by "the spirit of the woman . . . She is possessed of the Devil, who is dragging her to his place."[4] Europe had not expected to find the spirit of an emperor behind the smiles of a girl.

II. Elizabethan Government

Her penetration proved itself at once in her choice of aides. Like her embattled father—and despite her politic speech at Hatfield—she chose men of untitled birth, for most of the older nobles were Catholic, and some thought themselves fitter than she to wear the crown. As her secretary and principal adviser she named William Cecil, whose genius for prudent policy and assiduous detail became so outstanding a factor in her success that those who did not know her thought him king. His grandfather was a prosperous yeoman become country gentleman; his father was yeoman of the wardrobe to Henry VIII; his mother's dowry raised the family to a comfortable estate. William left Cambridge without a degree, took law at Gray's Inn, sowed his wild oats in London's common fields,[5] entered the House of Commons at twenty-three (1543), and married, as his second wife, Mildred Cooke, whose grim Puritanism helped him toe the Protestant line. He served Protector Somerset, then Somerset's enemy Northumberland. He supported Lady Jane Grey to succeed Edward VI, but switched to Mary Tudor in the nick of time; he became a conforming Catholic at her suggestion, and was appointed by her to welcome Cardinal Pole into England. He was a man of affairs, who did not allow his theological somersaults to disturb his political equilibrium. When Elizabeth made him her secretary she addressed him with her usual sagacity:

> I give you this charge that you shall be of my Privy Council, and content to take pains for me and my realm. This judgment I have of you that you will not be corrupted by any manner of gift, and that you will be faithful to the state; and that without respect of my private will you will give me that counsel which you think best; and if you shall know anything necessary to be declared to me of secrecy, you shall show it to myself only. And assure yourself I will not fail to keep taciturnity therein. And therefore herewith I charge you.[6]

The test of his fidelity and competence is that she kept him as secretary for fourteen years, then as Lord Treasurer for twenty-six more, till his death. He presided over the Council, managed foreign relations, directed public finance and national defense, and guided Elizabeth in the definitive establishment of Protestantism in England. Like Richelieu, he thought the safety and stability of his country required the unifying absolutism of the monarch as against the divisive ambitions of contentious nobles, covetous merchants, and fratricidal faiths. He had some Machiavellian ways, rarely cruel, but relentless against opposition;[7] once he thought of having the Earl of Westmorland assassinated;[8] but that was an impatient moment in a half century of patient tenacity and personal rectitude. He had eyes and spies for everything, but eternal vigilance is the price of power. He was acquisitive and thrifty, but Elizabeth pardoned his wealth for his wisdom and loved the parsimony that accumulated the means for defeating the Armada. Without him she might have been misled by such lighter lights and spendthrift peacocks as Leicester, Hatton, and Essex. Cecil, reported the Spanish ambassador, "has more genius than the rest of the Council put together, and is therefore envied and hated on all sides."[9] Elizabeth sometimes listened to his enemies, and now and then treated him so harshly that he left her presence broken and in tears; but she knew, when out of her tantrums, that he was the steadiest pillar of her reign. In 1571 she made him Lord Burghley, head of the new aristocracy that, in the face of hostile nobles, upheld her throne and made her kingdom great.

Her minor aides deserve a line even in hurried history, for they served her with competence, courage, and scant remuneration, to the exhaustion of their lives. Sir Nicholas Bacon, father of Francis, was Lord Keeper of the Great Seal from the outset of the reign till his death (1579); Sir Francis Knollys was a privy councilor from 1558 and treasurer of the royal household till his end (1596); Sir Nicholas Throckmorton was her skillful ambassador in France, and Thomas Randolph in Scotland, Russia, and Germany. Only next to Cecil in devotion and craft was Sir Francis Walsingham, a Secretary of State from 1573 to his death (1590); a man of sensitive refinement, whom Spenser called "the great Maecenas of his age"; so shocked by repeated plots against the Queen's life that he formed for her protection a web of espionage that stretched from Edinburgh to Constantinople, and caught in its skein the tragic Queen of Scots. Seldom has a ruler had servitors so able, so loyal, and so poorly paid.

For the English government itself was poor. Private fortunes outshone public funds. The revenue in 1600 totaled £500,000,[10] which even now would be a paltry $25,000,000. Elizabeth seldom levied direct taxes, and she took in only £36,000 in customs dues. Ordinarily she relied on income from Crown lands, on grants in aid from the English Church, and on "loans" from the rich, which were practically compulsory but punctually repaid.[11] She honored the debts left by her father, her brother, and her sister, and acquired such a reputation for solvency that she could borrow money at Antwerp at 5 percent, while Philip II of Spain at times could not borrow at all. She was extravagant, however, in her expenditure for dresses and finery, and in gifts of economic privileges to her favorites.

Rarely, and reluctantly, she summoned Parliament to her financial aid, for she did not patiently bear opposition, criticism, or surveillance. She put no stock in theories of popular or parliamentary sovereignty; she believed with Homer and Shakespeare that only one head should rule—and why not hers, in which ran the blood and burned the pride of Henry VIII? She held to the divine right of kings and queens. She imprisoned persons at her own sharp will, without trial or stated cause; and her Privy Council, acting as the Court of Star Chamber to try political offenders, suspended without appeal the rights of habeas corpus and jury trial.[12] She punished M.P.s who obstructed her purposes. She suggested to the local magnates who manipulated elections to Parliament that it would facilitate matters if they chose candidates with no boyish notions about free speech; she wanted pounds without palaver. Her early Parliaments yielded gracefully; her middle Parliaments yielded angrily; her later Parliaments neared revolt.

She got her will because the nation preferred her judicious absolutism to the fury of factions competing for power. No one thought of letting the people rule; politics was—as always—a contest of minorities to determine which should rule the majority. Half of England resented Elizabeth's religious policy, nearly all England resented her celibacy; but by and large the people, grateful for low taxes, flourishing trade, domestic order, and prolonged peace, returned the affection offered them by the Queen. She gave them pageants and "progresses," listened to them without visible boredom, shared in their public games, and in a hundred other ways "fished for men's souls."[13] The Spanish ambassador, while bemoaning her Protestantism, wrote to Philip: "She is much attached to the people, and is confident that they are all on her side, which is indeed true."[14] The attempts that were made on her life strengthened her popularity and power; even the Puritans whom she persecuted prayed for her safety; and the anniversary of her accession became a day of national thanksgiving and festival.

Was she the actual ruler, or only a popular front for the lower nobility of England and the mercantile oligarchy of London? Her aides, though fearing her temper, often corrected her mistakes of policy—but she often corrected theirs. They told her disagreeable truths, gave her their contradictory counsels, and obeyed her decisions; they governed, but she ruled. "She gives her orders," reported the Spanish ambassador, "and has her way as absolutely as her father."[15] Cecil himself seldom knew how she would decide, and he fretted over her frequent rejection of his laborious and meticulous advice. When he urged her not to treat with France, but to rely solely on Protestant support, she pulled him up with some asperity: "Mr. Secretary, I mean to have done with this business; I shall listen to the proposals of the French King. I am not going to be tied any longer to you and your brethren in Christ."[16]

Her statesmanship drove both friends and enemies to tears. She was maddeningly slow and irresolute in determining policy; but in many cases her indecision paid. She knew how to ally herself with time, which dissolves more problems than men solve; her procrastination allowed the complex factors in a situation to settle themselves into focus and clarity. She admired the fabled philosopher who, when importuned for an answer, silently recited the alphabet before replying. She took as her motto *Video et taceo*—"I see and am silent." She discovered that in politics, as in love, he who does not hesitate is lost. If her policy often fluctuated, so did the facts and forces to be weighed. Surrounded by perils and intrigues, she felt her way with forgivable caution, trying now one course, now another, and making no claim to consistency in so fluid a world. Her vacillation stumbled into some serious errors, but it kept England at peace until it was strong enough for war. Inheriting a nation politically in chaos and militarily in decay, her only practicable policy was to keep England's enemies from uniting against it. to encourage the Huguenot revolt against the French monarchy, the Netherlands revolt against Spain, the Protestant revolt against a Scottish Queen too closely bound to France. It was an unscrupulous policy, but Elizabeth believed with Machiavelli that scruples are not becoming in rulers responsible for states. By whatever means her subtle weakness could devise she preserved her country from foreign domination, maintained peace—with some brief intervals—for thirty years, and left England richer than ever before in matter and mind.

As a diplomat she could give the foreign secretaries of the age many a lesson in alert information, resourceful expedients, and incalculable moves. She was the ablest liar of her time. Of the four women—Mary Tudor, Mary Stuart, Catherine de Médicis, and Elizabeth—who illustrated Knox's "monstrous regiment [rule] of women" in the second half of the sixteenth century, Elizabeth was unquestionably supreme in political acumen and diplomatic skill. Cecil thought her "the wisest woman that ever was, for she understood the interest and dispositions of all the princes in her time, and was so perfect in the knowledge of her own realm that no councilor she had could tell her anything she did not know before"[17]—which, of course, requires a grain of salt. She had the advantage of conferring directly with ambassadors in French, Italian, or Latin, and was thereby independent of interpreters and intermediaries. "This woman," said the Spanish ambassador, "is possessed with a hundred thousand devils; yet she pretends to me that she would like to be a nun, live in a cell, and tell her beads from morning till night."[18] Every Continental government condemned and admired her. "If she were not a heretic," said Pope Sixtus V, "she would be worth a whole world."[19]

III. The Amorous Virgin

The secret weapon of her diplomacy was her virginity. This condition, of course, is a recondite detail on which historians must not pretend to certainty; let us be as trustful as Raleigh naming a colony. Cecil, watching Elizabeth's long flirtation with Leicester, had some passing doubts, but two Spanish ambassadors, not loath to dishonor the Queen, concluded to her honor.[20] The gossip of the court, as reported by Ben Jonson to Drummond of Hawthornden, held that "she had a membrane on her which made her incapable of man, though for her delight she tried many. . . . A French surgeon undertook to cut it, yet fear stayed her."[21] "The people," wrote Camden in his *Annales* (1615), "cursed Huic, the Queen's physician, as having dissuaded the Queen from marrying on account of some impediment and defect in her."[22] Yet Parliament, repeatedly begging her to marry, assumed her capacity to bear. Something went wrong, in this regard, with most of Tudor royalty: probably the misfortunes of Catherine of Aragon in childbirth were due to Henry VIII's syphilis; his son Edward died in youth of some ill-described disease; his daughter Mary tried fervently to have a child, only to mistake dropsy for pregnancy; and Elizabeth, though she flirted as long as she could walk, never ventured on marriage. "I have always shrunk from it," she said; and as early as 1559 she declared her intention to remain a virgin.[23] In 1566 she promised Parliament, "I will marry as soon as I can conveniently . . . and I hope to have children."[24] But in that same year, when Cecil told her that Mary Stuart had borne a son, Elizabeth almost wept, and said, "The Queen of Scots is the mother of a fair son, and I am but a barren stock."[25] There for a moment she revealed her lasting grief—that she could not fulfill her womanhood.

The political implications deepened the tragedy. Many of her Catholic subjects believed her sterility a proper punishment for her father's sins and a promise that Catholic Mary Stuart would inherit the crown. But Parliament and the rest of Protestant England dreaded such a prospect and importuned her to find a mate. She tried, but began by losing her heart to a married man. Lord Robert Dudley, tall, handsome, accomplished, courtly, brave, was the son of that Duke of Northumberland who had died on the scaffold for trying to disinherit Mary Tudor and make Jane Grey queen. Dudley was married to Amy Robsart, but was not living with her, and rumor called him an unprincipled philanderer. He was with Elizabeth at Windsor when his wife fell downstairs at Cumnor Hall and died of a broken neck (1560). He and the Queen were suspected, by the Spanish ambassador and others, of having arranged this clumsy annulment; the suspicion was unjust,[26] but it ended for a while Dudley's hopes of becoming consort to Elizabeth. When she thought she was dying (1562), she begged that he might be appointed protector of the realm; she confessed that she had long loved him, but called God to witness that "nothing unseemly" had ever passed between them.[27] Two years later she offered him to the Queen of Scots and made him Earl of Leicester to enhance his charms, but Mary was loath to have her rival's lover in her bed. Elizabeth comforted him with monopolies, and favored him till his death (1588).

Cecil had borne this romance with dignified hostility. For a time he thought of resigning in protest, for his own plan contemplated a marriage that would strengthen England with the friendship of some powerful state. For a quarter of a century a succession of foreign suitors danced about the Queen. "There are twelve ambassadors of us," wrote one of them, "all competing for her Majesty's hand; and the Duke of Holstein is coming next, as a suitor for the King of Denmark. The Duke of Finland, who is here for his brother the King of Sweden, threatens to kill the Emperor's man, and the Queen fears they will cut each other's throat in her presence."[28] She must have felt some satisfaction when Philip II, the greatest potentate in Christendom, offered her his seasoned hand (1559), but she rejected this device for making England a Catholic dependency of Spain. She took more time in answering a proposal from Charles IX of France, for France was meanwhile kept on good behavior. The French ambassador complained that "the world had been made in six days, and she had already spent eighty days and was still undecided"; she artfully replied that the world "had been made by a greater artist than herself."[29] Two years later she allowed English agents to propose her marriage to Charles, Archduke of Austria; but at Leicester's urging she withdrew the plan. When the international situation favored humoring France (1570), the Duke of Alençon (son of Henri II and Catherine de Médicis) was encouraged to think of becoming the sixteen-year-old husband of the thirty-seven-year-old Queen; but the negotiations were wrecked on three obstacles—the Duke's Catholic faith, his tender youth, and his pockmarked nose. Five years softened one of these deterrents, and Alençon, now Duke of Anjou, was considered again; he was invited to London, and for five years more Elizabeth played with him and France. After a final flurry (1581) this gay courtship petered out, and Anjou retired from the field waving as a trophy a garter of the Queen. Meanwhile she had kept him from marrying the Infanta and thereby allying her two enemies, France and Spain. Rarely has a woman derived so much advantage from barrenness, or so much pleasure from virginity.

IV. Elizabeth and Her Court

There was more satisfaction in being courted by virile Elizabethans than in being bedded by a poxy youth, and the courtship could last as long as marriage did not stifle it. Hence Elizabeth enjoyed perennial adulation and savored it insatiably. Lords ruined themselves to entertain her; masques and pageants allegorized her glory; poets smothered her with sonnets and dedications; musicians strummed her praise. A madrigal celebrated her eyes as war-subduing orbs, and her breast as "that fair hill where virtue dwells and sacred skill."[30] Raleigh told her that she walked like Venus, hunted like Diana, rode like Alexander, sang like an angel, and played like Orpheus.[31] She almost believed it. She was as vain as if all the merits of her England were the blessed fruit of her mothering; and to a degree they were. Distrustful of her physical charms, she robed herself in costly dresses, varying them almost every day; at her death she left two thousand. She wore jewelry in her hair, on her arms and wrists and ears and gowns; when a bishop reproved her love of finery she had him warned not to touch on that subject again, lest he reach heaven aforetime.[32]

Her manners could be alarming. She cuffed or fondled courtiers, even foreign emissaries. She tickled the back of Dudley's neck when he knelt to receive his earldom.* She spat as she list—once upon a costly coat. She was usually amiable and easy of access, but she talked volubly, and she could be an unanswerable shrew. She swore like a pirate (which, by proxy, she was); "by God's death" was among her milder oaths. She could be cruel, as in playing cat and mouse with Mary Stuart, or letting Lady Catherine Grey languish and die in the Tower; but she was basically kind and merciful, and she mingled tenderness with her blows. She often lost her temper, but she soon regained control of herself. She roared with laughter when amused, which was often. She loved to dance, and pirouetted till she was sixty-nine. She gamboled and gambled and hunted, and was fond of masques and plays. She kept her spirits up even when her fortunes were low, and in the face of danger she was all courage and intelligence. She was abstemious in food and drink, but covetous of money and jewelry; with relish she confiscated the property of rich rebels; and she managed to get and to hold the crown jewels of Scotland, Burgundy, and Portugal, besides a hoard of gems presented by expectant lords. She was not renowned for gratitude or liberality; sometimes she tried to pay her servants in fair words; but there was a certain patriotism in her parsimony and her pride. When she acceded there was hardly a nation so poor as to do England reverence; when she died England controlled the seas and challenged the intellectual hegemony of Italy or France.

What sort of mind did she have? She had all the learning that a queen could carry gracefully. While ruling England she continued her study of languages; corresponded in French with Mary Stuart, bandied Italian with a Venetian ambassador, and berated a Polish envoy in virile Latin. She translated Sallust and Boethius, and knew enough Greek to read Sophocles and translate a play of Euripides'. She claimed to have read as many books as any prince in Christendom, and it was likely. She studied history almost every day. She composed poetry and music, and played forgivably on the lute and the virginal. But she had sense enough to laugh at her accomplishments, and to distinguish between

---

* Aubrey tells a naughty story. Edward de Vere, "Earle of Oxford, making his low obeisance to Queen Elizabeth, happened to let a Fart, at which he was so abashed and ashamed that he went to Travell, 7 yeares. On his returne the Queen welcomed him home, and sayd, My Lord, I had forgott the Fart."[33]

education and intelligence. When an ambassador complimented her on her languages she remarked that "it was no marvel to teach a woman to talk; it were far harder to teach her to hold her tongue."[34] Her mind was as sharp as her speech, and her wit kept pace with the time. Francis Bacon reported that "she was wont to say of her instructions to great officers that they were like to garments, strait at the first putting on, but did by and by wear loose enough."[35] Her letters and speeches were composed in an English all her own, devious, involved, and affected, but rich in quaint turns, fascinating in eloquence and character.

She excelled in intelligence rather than intellect. Walsingham pronounced her "inapt to embrace any matter of weight";[36] but perhaps he spoke in the bitterness of unrequited devotion. Her skill lay in feminine delicacy and subtlety of perception, not in laborious logic, and sometimes the outcome revealed more wisdom in her feline tentatives than in their reasoning. It was her indefinable spirit that counted, that baffled Europe and enthralled England, that gave spur and color to her country's flowering. She re-established the Reformation, but she represented the Renaissance—the lust to live this earthly life to the full, to enjoy and embellish it every day. She was no exemplar of virtue, but she was a paragon of vitality. Sir John Hayward, whom she sent to the Tower for giving rebellious notions to the younger Essex, forgave her enough to write of her, nine years after she could reward him:

> Now, if ever any person had eyther the gift or the stile to winne the hearts of people, it was this Queene; if ever she did express the same, it was . . . in coupling mildness with majesty as she did, and in stately stouping to the meanest sort. All her facultyes were in motione, and every motione seemed a well-guided actione; her eyes were set upon one, her ears listened to another, her judgment ran upon a third, to a fourth she addressed her speech; her spirit seemed to be everywhere, and yet so intyre in her selfe, as it seemed to bee noe where else. Some she pityed, some she commended, some she thanked, at others she pleasantly and wittingly jested, contemning no person, neglecting no office; and distributing her smiles, lookes, and graces so artificially [artfully] that thereupon the people again redoubled the testimonyes of their joyes.[37]

Her court was her character—loving the things she loved, and raising her flair for music, games, plays, and vivid speech to an ecstasy of poems, madrigals, dramas, and masques, and such prose as England has never known again. In her palaces at Whitehall, Windsor, Greenwich, Richmond, and Hampton Court lords and ladies, knights and ambassadors, entertainers and servitors moved in an exciting alternation of regal ceremony and gallant gaiety. A special Office of the Revels prepared amusements that ranged from "riddles" and backgammon to complex masques and Shakespeare's plays. Ascension Day, Christmas, New Year's, Twelfth Night, Candlemas, and Shrovetide were regularly celebrated with pastimes, athletic contests, jousts, mummings, plays, and masques. The masque was one of many Italian importations into Elizabethan England—a gaudy mixture of pageantry, poetry, music, allegory, buffoonery, and ballet, put together by playwrights and artists, presented at court, or on rich estates, with complex machinery and evolutions, and performed by masked ladies and gentlemen burdened with costly costumes and simple lines. Elizabeth was fond of drama, especially of comedy; who knows how much of Shakespeare would have reached the stage, or posterity, if she and Leicester had not supported the theater through all the attacks of the Puritans?

Not content with her five palaces, Elizabeth sallied out almost every summer on cross-country "progresses" to see and be seen, to keep an eye on her vassal lords, and to enjoy their reluctant homage. Part of the court followed her, delighted with the change and grumbling at the accommodations and the beer. Towns dressed their gentry in velvet and silk to welcome her with speeches and gifts; nobles bankrupted themselves to entertain her; hard-pressed lords prayed that she would not come their way. The Queen rode on horseback or in an open litter, greeting happily the crowds that gathered along the road. The people were thrilled by the sight of their invincible sovereign, and bewitched to fresh loyalty by her gracious compliments and infectious happiness.

The court took on her gaiety, her freedom of manners, her luxury of dress, her love of ceremony, and her ideal of the gentleman. She liked to hear the rustle of finery, and the men around her rivaled the women in molding Oriental stuffs to Italian styles. Pleasure was the usual program, but one had to be ready at any moment for martial exploits beyond the seas. Seductions had to be circumspect, for Elizabeth felt responsible to the parents of her maids of honor for their honor; hence she banished the Earl of Pembroke from the court for making Mary Fitton pregnant.[38] As at any court, intrigue wove many entangling webs; the women competed unscrupulously for the men, the men for the women, and all for the favor of the Queen and the perquisites dependent thereon. Those same gentlemen who exalted in poetry the refinements of love and morality itched in prose for sinecures, took or gave bribes, grasped at monopolies, or shared in piratical spoils; and the avid Queen looked indulgently upon a venality that eked out the inadequate pay of her servitors. Through her grants, or by her permission, Leicester became the richest lord in England; Sir Philip Sidney received vast tracts in America; Raleigh acquired forty thousand acres in Ireland; the second Earl of Essex enjoyed a "corner" on the importation of sweet wines; and Sir Christopher Hatton rose from the Queen's lapdog to Lord Chancellor. Elizabeth was no more sensitive to industrious brains than to handsome legs—for these pillars of society were not yet shrouded in pantaloons. Despite her faults she set a pace and a course to elicit the reserve energies of England's worthies; she raised their courage to high enterprise, their minds to brave thinking, their manners to grace and wit and the fostering of poetry, drama, and art. Around that dazzling court and woman gathered nearly all the genius of England's greatest age.

V. Elizabeth and Religion

But within the court, and through the nation, the bitter battle of the Reformation raged, and created a problem that many thought would baffle and destroy the Queen. She was a Protestant; the country was two-thirds, perhaps three-quarters, Catholic.[39] Most of the magistrates, all of the clergy, were Catholic. The Protestants were confined to the southern ports and industrial towns; they were predominant in London, where their number was swelled by refugees from oppression on the Continent; but in the northern and western counties—almost entirely agricultural—they were a negligible few.[40] The spirit of the Protestants, however, was immeasurably more ardent than the Catholic. In 1559 John Foxe published his *Rerum in ecclesia gestarum . . . commentarii,* describing with passion the sufferings of Protestants under the preceding reign; the volumes were translated (1563) as *Actes and Monuments;* popularly known as *The Book of Martyrs,* they had an arousing influence on English Protestants for over a century. Protestantism in the sixteenth century had the feverish energy of a new idea fighting for the future; Catholicism had the strength of traditional beliefs and ways deeply rooted in the past.

In a spreading minority the religious turmoil had generated skepticism—even, here and there, atheism. The conflict of creeds, their mutual criticism, their bloody intolerance, and the contrast between the professions and the conduct of Christians, had made some matter-of-fact minds doubtful of all theologies. Hear Roger Ascham's *Scholemaster* (1563):

> That Italian that first invented the Italian Proverb against our Englishmen Italianate, meant no more their vanity in living than their lewd opinion in Religion . . . They make more account of Tully's offices [Cicero's *De officiis*] than St. Paul's epistles; of a tale in Boccaccio than a story of the Bible. Then they count as fables the holy mysteries of the Christian Religion. They make Christ and his Gospel only serve civil policy; then neither religion [Protestantism or Catholicism] cometh amiss to them. In time they be promoters of both openly; in place again mockers of both privily . . . For where they dare, in company where they like, they boldly laugh to scorn both Protestant and Papist. They care for no Scripture . . . they mock the Pope; they rail on Luther . . . The heaven they desire is only their personal pleasure and private profit; whereby they plainly declare of whose school . . . they be: that is, Epicures in living, and *atheoi* in doctrine.[41]

Cecil complained (1569) that "deriders of religion, Epicureans, and atheists are everywhere";[42] John Strype declared (1571) that "many were wholly departed from the communion of the church, and came no more to hear divine service";[43] John Lyly (1579) thought "there never were such sects among the heathens . . . such misbelief among infidels, as is now among scholars."[44] Theologians and others wrote books against "atheism"—which, however, could mean belief in God but disbelief in Christ's divinity. In 1579, 1583, and 1589 men were burned for denying the divinity of Christ.[45] Several dramatists—Greene, Kyd, Marlowe—were reputed atheists. The Elizabethan drama, which otherwise so widely pictures life, contains remarkably little about the strife of faiths, but makes a great play of pagan mythology.

In Shakespeare's *Love's Labour's Lost* (IV, iii, 250) are two obscure lines:

> O paradox! black is the badge of hell,
> The hue of dungeons and the school of night.

Many[46] have interpreted the last phrase as referring to the evening assemblies of Walter Raleigh, the astronomer Thomas Harriot, the scholar Lawrence Keymis, probably the poets Marlowe and Chapman, and some others, in Raleigh's country house at Sherborne, for the study of astronomy, geography, chemistry, philosophy, and theology. Harriot, apparently the intellectual leader of the group, "had strange thoughts of the Scriptures," reported the antiquary Anthony à Wood, "and always undervalued the old story of the creation . . . He made a *Philosophical Theology,* wherein he cast off the Old Testament"; he believed in God, but rejected revelation and the divinity of Christ.[47] Robert Parsons, the Jesuit, wrote in 1592 of "Sir Walter Rawleigh's school of Atheisme . . . wherein both Moyses and our Saviour, the olde and Newe Testamentes are jested at, and the schollers taught . . . to spell God backwards."[48] Raleigh was accused of having listened to Marlowe's reading of an essay on "atheism." In March 1594 a government commission sat at Cerne Abbes, Dorset, to investigate rumors of a set of atheists in the vicinity—which included Raleigh's home. The inquiry led to no action now known to us, but charges of atheism were brought against Raleigh during his trial (1603).[49] In the preface to his *History of the World* he made it a point to enlarge upon his belief in God.

Some suspicion of freethinking clings to Elizabeth herself. "No woman," said John Richard Green, "ever lived who was so totally destitute of the sentiment of religion."[50] "Elizabeth," in Froude's judgment, "was without distinct emotional conviction . . . Elizabeth, to whom the Protestant creed was as little true as the Catholic . . . had a latitudinarian contempt for theological dogmatism."[51] She called upon God—with terrible oaths that horrified her ministers—to destroy her if she did not keep her promise to marry Alençon, while in private she jested over his pretensions to her hand.[52] She declared to a Spanish envoy that the difference between the warring Christian creeds was "a mere bagatelle"—whereupon he concluded that she was an atheist.[53]

Nevertheless she took it for granted, like almost all governments before 1789, that some religion, some supernatural source and sanction of morality, was indispensable to social order and the stability of the state. For a time, till she had consolidated her position, she appeared to hesitate, and she played upon the hopes of Catholic potentates that she might be won to their public faith. She liked the Catholic ceremony, the celibacy of the clergy, the drama of the Mass, and she might have made her peace with the Church had not this involved submission to the papacy. She distrusted Catholicism as a foreign power that might lead

Englishmen to put loyalty to the Church above allegiance to the Queen. She had been reared in the Protestantism of her father, which was Catholicism minus the papacy; and this is essentially what she decided to re-establish in England. She hoped that the semi-Catholic liturgy of her Anglican Church would mollify the Catholics of the countryside, while the rejection of the papacy would satisfy the Protestants of the towns; meanwhile state control of education would form the new generation to this Elizabethan settlement, and the disruptive religious strife would be quieted into peace. She made her hesitations in religion, as in marriage, serve her political purposes; she kept potential enemies bemused and divided until she could face them with an accomplished fact.

Many forces urged her to complete the Reformation. Continental reformers wrote to thank her in advance for restoring the new worship, and their letters touched her. Holders of formerly Church property prayed for a Protestant settlement. Cecil urged Elizabeth to make herself the leader of all Protestant Europe. London Protestants indicated their sentiments by beheading a statue of St. Thomas and casting it into the street. Her first Parliament (January 23 to May 8, 1559) was overwhelmingly Protestant. The funds she asked for were voted without reservation or delay, and to raise them a tax was laid upon all persons, ecclesiastical or secular. A new Act of Uniformity (April 28, 1559) made Cranmer's Book of Common Prayer, revised, the law of English liturgy, and forbade all other religious ritual. The Mass was abolished. All Englishmen were required to attend the Sunday service of the Anglican Church or forfeit a shilling for the succor of the poor. A new Act of Supremacy (April 29) declared Elizabeth to be the Supreme Governor of England in all matters, spiritual or temporal. An oath of supremacy acknowledging the religious sovereignty of the Queen was required of all clergymen, lawyers, teachers, university graduates, and magistrates, and all employees of the Church or the Crown. All major ecclesiastical appointments and decisions were to be made by an ecclesiastical Court of High Commission chosen by the government. Any defense of papal authority over England was to be punished by life imprisonment for the first offense, by death for the second (1563). By 1590 all English churches were Protestant.

Elizabeth pretended that she was not persecuting opinion; any man, she said, might think and believe as he pleased, provided he obeyed the laws; all she asked was external conformity for the sake of national unity. Cecil assured her that "that state could never be in safety where there was toleration of two religions"[54]—which did not deter Elizabeth from demanding toleration of French Protestants in Catholic France.[55] She had no objection to peaceful hypocrisy, but freedom of opinion was not to be freedom of speech. Preachers who disagreed with her views on any important subject were silenced or dismissed.[56] The laws against heresy were redefined and enforced; Unitarians and Anabaptists were outlawed;[57] five heretics were burned during the reign—which seemed a modest number in its day.

In 1563 a convocation of theologians defined the new creed. All were agreed on predestination; God of His own free will, before the creation of the world, and without regard to individual human merit or demerit, had chosen some of mankind to be elect and saved, leaving all the rest to be reprobate and damned. They accepted Lutheran justification (salvation) by faith—that is, the elect were saved not by their good works but by belief in the grace of God and the redeeming blood of Christ; however, they interpreted the Eucharist in Calvin's sense as a spiritual, rather than a physical, communion with Christ. By an act of Parliament (1566) the "Thirty-nine Articles" embodying the new theology were made obligatory on all the clergy of England; and they still express the official Anglican creed.

The new ritual too was a compromise. The Mass was abolished, but, to the horror of the Puritans, the clergy were instructed to wear white surplices in reading the service, and copes in administering the Eucharist. Communion was to be received kneeling, in the two forms of bread and wine. The invocation of saints was replaced by annual commemoration of Protestant heroes. Confirmation and ordination were retained as sacred rites, but were not viewed as sacraments instituted by Christ; and confession to a priest was encouraged only in expectation of death. Many of the prayers kept Roman Catholic forms, but took on English dress and became a noble and formative part of the nation's literature. For four hundred years those prayers and hymns, recited by congregation and priest in the spacious splendor of cathedrals or the simple dignity of the parish church, have given English families inspiration, consolation, moral discipline, and mental peace.

VI. Elizabeth and the Catholics

It was now the turn of the Catholics to suffer persecution. Though still in the majority, they were forbidden to hold Catholic services or possess Catholic literature. Religious images in the churches were destroyed by government order, and altars were removed. Six Oxford students were sent to the Tower for resisting the removal of a crucifix from their college chapel.[58] Most Catholics submitted sadly to the new regulations, but a considerable number preferred to pay the fines for nonattendance at the Anglican ritual. The royal Council calculated some fifty thousand such "recusants" in England (1580).[59] Anglican bishops complained to the government that Mass was being said in private homes, that Catholicism was emerging into public worship, and that in some ardent localities it was unsafe to be a Protestant.[60] Elizabeth rebuked Archbishop Parker for laxity (1565), and thereafter the laws were more rigorously enforced. Catholics who had heard Mass in the chapel of the Spanish ambassador were imprisoned; houses in London were searched; strangers found there were ordered to give an account of their religion; magistrates were commanded to punish all persons possessing books of Roman Catholic theology (1567).[61]

We must not judge this legislation in terms of the relative religious toleration earned for us by the philosophers and revolutions of the seventeenth and eighteenth centuries. The faiths were then at war, and were entangled with politics—a field in which toleration has always been limited. All parties and governments in the sixteenth century agreed that theological dissent was a form of political revolt. The religious conflict became explicitly political when Pope Pius V, after what he felt had been a long and patient delay, issued a bull (1570) that not only excommunicated Elizabeth, but absolved her subjects from allegiance to her, and forbade them "to obey her monitions, mandates, and laws." The bull was suppressed in France and Spain, which were then seeking friendship with England, but a copy of it was clandestinely posted on the door of the episcopal residence in London. The culprit was discovered and was put to death. Faced by this declaration of war, the Queen's ministers asked Parliament for stricter anti-Catholic laws. Statutes were passed making it a capital crime to call the Queen a heretic, schismatic, usurper, or tyrant, or to introduce a papal bull into England, or to convert a Protestant to the Roman Church.[62] The Court of High Commission was authorized to examine the opinions of any suspected person and to punish any of his unpunished offenses against any law, including fornication or adultery.[63]

The Catholic monarchs of Europe could not with much face protest against these oppressive measures, which so resembled their own. Most English Catholics continued to submit peaceably, and Elizabeth's government hoped that habit would generate acceptance, and, in time, belief. It was to prevent this that William Allen, an emigré Englishman, founded at Douai, then in the Spanish

Netherlands, a college and seminary to train English Catholics for missionary service in England. He expounded his purpose fervently:

> We make it our first and foremost study . . . to stir up . . . in the minds of Catholics . . . zeal and just indignation against the heretics. This we do by setting before the eyes of the students the exceeding majesty of the ceremonial of the Catholic Church in the place where we live . . . At the same time we recall the mournful contrast that obtains at home: the utter desolation of all things sacred which there exists . . . our friends and kinsfolk, all our dear ones, and countless souls besides, perishing in schism and godlessness; every jail and dungeon filled to overflowing, not with thieves and villains but with Christ's priests and servants, nay, with our parents and kinsmen. There is nothing, then, that we ought not to suffer, rather than to look on at the ills that affect our nation.[64]

The college functioned at Douai till 1578, when the Calvinists captured the town; then at Reims, then again at Douai (1593). The Douay Bible—an English translation of the Latin Vulgate—was produced at Reims and Douai (1582–1610), and reached publication a year before the King James version. Between 1574 and 1585 the college ordained 275 graduates and sent 268 to labor in England. Allen was called to Rome and made a cardinal, but the work went on; 170 additional priests were dispatched to England before Elizabeth's death in 1603. Of the 438 total, ninety-eight suffered the capital penalty.

The leadership of the missionaries passed to a Jesuit, Robert Parsons, a man of enthusiasm and courage, a firebrand of polemics, and a master of English prose. He frankly announced that the bull deposing Elizabeth justified her assassination. Many English Catholics were shocked, but Tolomeo Galli, secretary of state to Pope Gregory XIII, gave the idea his approval.*[65] Parsons urged the Catholic powers to invade England; the Spanish ambassador in England condemned the plan as "criminal folly," and Everard Mercurian, general of the Jesuit order, forbade Parsons to meddle in politics.[67] Undeterred, he decided on

---

* A Catholic historian adds: "If the Secretary of State approved of the killing of Elizabeth, this was in conformity with the principles of law then in force. Gregory, too, with whom the Secretary of State undoubtedly consulted before he sent his letter . . . concurred in this view."[66]

a personal invasion. He disguised himself as an English officer returning from service in the Netherlands; his martial swagger, gold-lace coat, and feathered hat carried him through the frontier officials (1580); he even smoothed the way for another Jesuit, Edmund Campion, to follow him in the guise of a jewel merchant. They were secretly housed in the heart of London.

They visited imprisoned Catholics, and found them leniently treated. Recruiting lay and sacerdotal aides, they began their work of inspiring Catholics to remain faithful to the Church, and reconverting recent "apostates" to the Protestant creed. Secular priests hiding in England, alarmed at the boldness of the missionaries, warned them that they would soon be caught and arrested, and that their detection would make matters worse for the Catholics, and they begged them to return to the Continent. But Parsons and Campion persisted. They moved from town to town, holding secret assemblies, hearing confessions, saying Mass, and giving their benediction to the whispering worshipers who looked upon them as messengers from God. Within a year of their coming they made—it was claimed—twenty thousand converts.[68] They set up a printing press and scattered propaganda; tracts declaring that Elizabeth, having been excommunicated, was no longer the lawful queen of England were found in London streets.[69] A third Jesuit was sent to Edinburgh to urge the Scottish Catholics to invade England from the north. The Earl of Westmorland answered a summons from the Vatican; he brought back from Rome to Flanders a mass of bullion to finance an invasion from the Netherlands; by the summer of 1581, many Catholics believed, the Spanish troops of Alva would cross into England.[70]

Warned by its spies, the English government doubled its efforts to capture the Jesuits. Parsons found his way across the Channel, but Campion was caught (July 1581). He was carried through sympathetic villages and hostile London to the Tower. Elizabeth sent for him and tried to save him. She asked, Did he consider her his lawful sovereign? He replied that he did. But to her next question, Could the Pope lawfully excommunicate her?, he answered that he could not decide an issue on which learned men were divided. She sent him back to the Tower, with instructions that he be kindly treated; but Cecil ordered him to be tortured into naming his fellow conspirators. After two days of agony he yielded a few names, and more arrests were made. Recovering his audacity, Campion challenged Protestant divines to a public debate. By permission of the Council a debate was staged in the chapel of the Tower; courtiers, prisoners, and public were admitted; and the Jesuit stood for hours on weakened legs to plead for the Catholic theology. Neither side convinced the other; but when Campion was brought to trial the charge was not heresy but conspiracy to overthrow the government by internal subversion and external attack. He and fourteen others were convicted, and on December 1, 1581, they were hanged.

Those Catholics proved right who had predicted that the Jesuit mission would exasperate the government into further persecution. Elizabeth issued an appeal to her subjects to judge between her and those who sought her throne or her life. Parliament decreed (1581) that conversion to Catholicism should be punished as high treason; that any priest who said Mass should be fined two hundred marks and be imprisoned for a year; and that those who refused to attend Anglican services should pay twenty pounds a month[71]—enough to bankrupt any but the richest Catholics. Failure to pay the fine incurred arrest and confiscation of property. Soon the prisons were so crowded with Catholics that old castles had to be used as jails.[72] Tension rose on all sides, heightened by the imminent execution of Mary Stuart and the intensified conflict with Spain and Rome. In June 1583 a papal nuncio offered Gregory XIII a detailed plan for the invasion of England by three armies at once from Ireland, France, and Spain. The Pope gave sympathetic consideration to this *disegno per l'impresa d'Inghilterra* and specific measures were prepared;[73] but English spies got wind of them, England made counterpreparations, and the invasion was postponed.

Parliament retaliated with more repressive legislation. All priests ordained since June 1559 and still refusing the oath of supremacy were required to leave the country within forty days or suffer death as treasonous conspirators; and all who harbored them were to be hanged.[74] On the basis of this and other laws, 123 priests and sixty laymen were executed during the reign of Elizabeth, and probably another two hundred died in jail.[75] Some Protestants protested against the severity of this legislation; some were converted to Catholicism; Cecil's grandson William fled to Rome (1585) and pledged obedience to the Pope.[76]

Most English Catholics were opposed to any violent action against the government. One faction among them addressed an appeal to Elizabeth (1585), affirmed their loyalty, and asked for "a merciful consideration of their sufferings." But as if to bear out the government's claim that its measures were justified by war, Cardinal Allen issued (1588) a tract designed to rouse the English Catholics to support the approaching attack on England by Spain. He called the Queen "an incestuous bastard, begotten and born in sin of an infamous courtesan," charged that "with Leicester and divers others she hath abused her body . . . by unspeakable and incredible variety of lust," demanded that the Catholics of England should rise against this "depraved, accursed, excommunicate heretic," and promised a plenary indulgence to all who should aid in deposing the "chief spectacle of sin and abomination in this age."[77] The Catholics of England answered by fighting as bravely as the Protestants against the Spanish Armada.

After that victory the persecution continued as part of the continuing war. Sixty-one priests and forty-nine laymen were hanged between 1588 and 1603; and many of these were cut down from the gibbet and were drawn and quartered—i.e., they were disemboweled and torn limb from trunk—while still alive.[78] In a remarkable address presented to the Queen in the year of her death, thirteen priests petitioned her to be allowed to remain in England. They repudiated all attacks on her right to the throne and denied the authority of the Pope to depose her, but could not in conscience acknowledge anyone but the Pope as head of the Christian Church.[79] The document reached the Queen only a few days before her death, and no result of it is recorded; but unwittingly it outlined the principles on which, two centuries later, the problem would be solved. The Queen died a victor in the greatest struggle of a reign stained with no darker blot than this victory.

VII. Elizabeth and the Puritans

Against an apparently weaker enemy, a handful of Puritans, she did not prevail. They were men who had felt the influence of Calvin; some of them had visited Calvin's Geneva as Marian refugees; many of them had read the Bible in a translation made and annotated by Genevan Calvinists; some had heard or read the blasts of John Knox's trumpet; some may have heard echoes of Wyclif's Lollard "poor priests." Taking the Bible as their infallible guide, they found nothing in it about the episcopal powers and sacerdotal vestments that Elizabeth had transferred from the Roman to the Anglican Church; on the contrary, they found much about presbyters' having no sovereign but Christ. They acknowledged Elizabeth as head of the Church in England, but only to bar the pope; in their hearts they rejected any control of religion by the state, and aspired to control of the state by their religion. Toward 1564 they began to be called Puritans—as a term of abuse—because they demanded the purification of English Protestantism from all forms of faith and worship not found in the New Testament. They took the doctrines of predestination, election, and damnation deeply to heart, and felt that hell could be escaped only by subordinating every aspect of life to religion and morality. As they read the Bible in the solemn Sundays of their homes, the figure of Christ almost disappeared against the background of the Old Testament's jealous and vengeful Jehovah.

The Puritan attack on Elizabeth took form (1569) when the lectures of Thomas Cartwright, professor of theology at Cambridge, stressed the contrast between the presbyter-ian organization of the early Christian Church and the episcopal-ian structure of the Anglican Establishment. Many of the faculty supported Cartwright, but John Whitgift, headmaster of Trinity College, denounced him to the Queen and secured his dismissal from the teaching staff (1570). Cartwright emigrated to Geneva, where, under Théodore de Bèze, he imbibed the full ardor of Calvinist theocracy. Returning to England, he shared with Walter Travers and others in formulating the Puritan conception of the Church. Christ, in their view, had arranged that all ecclesiastical authority should be vested in ministers and lay elders elected by each parish, province, and state. The consistories so formed should determine creed, ritual, and moral code in conformity with Scripture. They should have access to every home, power to enforce at least outward observance of "godly living," and the right to excommunicate recalcitrants and condemn heretics to death. The civil magistrates were to carry out these disciplinary decrees, but the state was to have no spiritual jurisdiction whatever.[80]

The first English parish organized on these principles was set up at Wandsworth in 1572, and similar "presbyteries" sprang up in the eastern and middle counties. By this time the majority of the London Protestants, and of the House of Commons, were Puritans. The artisans of London, powerfully infiltrated by Calvinist refugees from France and the Netherlands, applauded the Puritan attack on episcopacy and ritual. The businessmen of the capital looked upon Puritanism as the bulwark of Protestantism against a Catholicism traditionally unsympathetic to "usury" and the middle classes. Calvin was a bit too strict for them, but he had sanctioned interest and had recognized the virtues of industry and thrift. Even men close to the Queen had found some good in Puritanism; Cecil, Leicester, Walsingham, and Knollys hoped to use it as a foil to Catholicism if Mary Stuart reached the English throne.[81]

But Elizabeth felt that the Puritan movement threatened the whole settlement by which she had planned to ease the religious strife. She thought of

Calvinism as the doctrine of John Knox, whom she had never forgiven for his scorn of women rulers. She despised the Puritan dogmatism even more heartily than the Catholic. She had a lingering fondness for the crucifix and other religious images, and when an iconoclastic fury destroyed paintings, statuary, and stained glass early in her reign,[82] she awarded damages to the victims and forbade such actions in the future.[83] She was not finicky in her own language, but she resented the description which some Puritan had given of the Prayer Book as "culled and picked out of that popish dunghill, the Mass Book," and of the Court of High Commission as a "little stinking ditch."[84] She saw in the popular election of ministers, and in the government of the Church by presbyteries and synods independent of the state, a republican threat to monarchy. Only her monarchical power, she thought, could keep England Protestant; popular suffrage would restore Catholicism.

She encouraged bishops to trouble the troublemakers. Archbishop Parker suppressed their publications, silenced them in the churches, and obstructed their assemblies. Puritan clergymen had organized groups for the public discussion of Scriptural passages; Elizabeth bade Parker put an end to these "prophesyings"; he did. His successor, Edmund Grindal, tried to protect the Puritans; Elizabeth suspended him; and when he died (1583) she advanced to the Canterbury see her new chaplain, John Whitgift, who dedicated himself to the silencing of the Puritans. He demanded of all English clergymen an oath accepting the Thirty-nine Articles, the Prayer Book, and the Queen's religious supremacy; he subpoenaed all objectors before the High Commission Court; and there they were subjected to such detailed and insistent inquiry into their conduct and belief that Cecil compared the procedure to the Spanish Inquisition.[85]

The Puritan rebellion was intensified. A determined minority openly seceded from the Anglican communion, and set up independent congregations that elected their own ministers and acknowledged no episcopal control. In 1581 Robert Browne, a pupil (later an enemy) of Cartwright, and chief voice of these "Independents," "Separatists," or "Congregationalists," crossed over to Holland, and he published there two tracts outlining a democratic constitution for Christianity: Any group of Christians should have the right to organize itself for worship, formulate its own creed on the basis of Scripture, choose its own leaders, and live its religious life free from outside interference, acknowledging no rule but the Bible, no authority but Christ. Two of Browne's followers were arrested in England, were judged in contempt of the Queen's religious sovereignty, and were hanged (1583).

In the campaign for election to the Parliament of 1586 the Puritans waged oratorical war upon any candidate unsympathetic to their cause. One such was branded as a "common gamester and pot companion"; another was "much suspect of popery, cometh very seldom to his church, and is a whoremaster"; those were days of virile speech. When Parliament convened, John Penry presented a petition for reform of the Church, and charged the bishops with responsibility for clerical abuses and popular paganism. Whitgift ordered his arrest, but he was soon released. Antony Cope introduced a bill to abolish the entire episcopal establishment and reorganize English Christianity on the presbyterian plan. Elizabeth ordered Parliament to remove the bill from discussion. Peter Wentworth rose to a question of parliamentary freedom, and four members supported him; Elizabeth had all five lodged in the Tower.

Frustrated in Parliament, Penry and other Puritans took to the press. Eluding Whitgift's severe censorship of publications, they deluged England (1588–89) with a succession of privately printed pamphlets, all signed "Martin Marprelate, Gentleman," and attacking the authority and personal character of the bishops in terms of satirical abuse. Whitgift and the High Commission deployed all the machinery of espionage to find the authors and printers; but the printers moved from town to town, and public sympathy helped them to escape detection until April 1589. Professional writers like John Lyly and Thomas Nash were engaged to answer "Martin" and gave him good competition in scurrility. Finally, as billingsgate ran out, the controversy subsided, and moderate men mourned the degradation of Christianity into an art of vituperation.

Stung by these pamphlets, Elizabeth gave Whitgift a free hand to check the Puritans. The Marprelate printers were found, arrests multiplied, executions followed. Cartwright was sentenced to death, but was pardoned by the Queen. Two leaders of the "Brownian Movement," John Greenwood and Henry Barrow, were hanged in 1593, and soon thereafter John Penry. Parliament decreed (1593) that anyone who questioned the Queen's religious supremacy, or persistently absented himself from Anglican services, or attended "any assemblies, conventicles, or meetings under cover or pretense of any exercise of religion" should be imprisoned and—unless he gave a pledge of future conformity—should leave England and never return, on pain of death.[86]

At this juncture, and amid the turmoil and fury, a modest parson raised the controversy to the level of philosophy, piety, and stately prose. Richard Hooker was one of two clergymen assigned to conduct services in the London Temple; the other was Walter Travers, Cartwright's friend. In the morning sermon Hooker expounded the ecclesiastical polity of Elizabeth; in the afternoon Travers criticized that church government from the Puritan view. Each developed his sermons into a book. As Hooker was writing literature as well as theology, he begged his bishop to transfer him to a quiet rural parsonage. So at Boscombe in Wiltshire he completed the first four books of his great work *Of the Laws of Ecclesiastical Polity* (1594); three years later, at Bishopsbourne, he sent Book V to the press; and there, in 1600, age forty-seven, he died.

His *Laws* astonished England by the calm and even-tempered dignity of its argument and the sonorous majesty of its almost Latin style. Cardinal Allen praised it as the best book that had yet come out of England; Pope Clement VIII lauded its eloquence and learning; Queen Elizabeth read it gratefully as a splendid apology for her religious government; the Puritans were mollified by the gentle clarity of its tone; and posterity received it as a noble attempt to harmonize religion and reason. Hooker astonished his contemporaries by admitting that even a pope could be saved; he shocked the theologians by declaring that "the assurance of what we believe by the Word of God is to us not so certain as that which we perceive by sense";[87] man's reasoning faculty is also a divine gift and revelation.

Hooker based his theory of law on medieval philosophy as formulated by St. Thomas Aquinas, and he anticipated the "social contract" of Hobbes and Locke. After showing the need and boon of social organization, he argued that voluntary participation in a society implies consent to be governed by its laws. But the ultimate source of the laws is the community itself: a king or a parliament may issue laws only as the delegate or representatives of the community. "Law makes the king; the king's grant of any favor contrary to the law is void . . . For peaceable contentment on both sides, the assent of those who are governed seemeth necessary . . . Laws are not which public approbation has not made so."[88] And Hooker added a passage that might have warned Charles I:

The Parliament of England, together with the [ecclesiastical] Convocation annexed thereunto, is that whereupon the very essence of all government within this kingdom doth depend; it is even the body of the whole realm; it consisteth of the king and of all that within the land are subject to him, for they are all there present, either in person, or by such as they voluntarily have derived [delegated] their power unto.[89]

To Hooker religion seemed an integral part of the state, for social order and therefore even material prosperity depend on moral discipline, which collapses without religious inculcation and support. Consequently every state should provide religious training for its people. The Anglican Church might be imperfect, but so would be all institutions made and manned by the children of Adam. "He that goeth about to persuade a multitude that they are not so well off as they ought to be, shall never want attentive and favorable hearers; because they know the manifold defects whereunto every kind of regiment [government] is subject, but the secret lets and difficulties, which in public proceedings are innumerable and inevitable, they have not ordinarily the judgment to consider."[90]

Hooker's logic was too circular to be convincing, his learning too scholastic to meet the issues of his time, his shy spirit too thankful for order to understand the longing for liberty. The Puritans acknowledged his eloquence, but went on their way. Compelled to choose between their country and their faith, many of them emigrated, reversing the movement of Continental Protestants into England. Holland welcomed them, and English congregations rose at Middelburg, Leiden, and Amsterdam. There the exiles and their offspring labored, taught, preached, and wrote, preparing with quiet passion for their triumphs in England and their fulfillment in America.

VIII. Elizabeth and Ireland

Ireland had been conquered by the English in 1169–71, and had been held ever since on the ground that otherwise it would be used by France or Spain as a base for attacks on England. At Elizabeth's accession direct English rule in Ireland was confined to the eastern coast—"the Pale"—around and south of Dublin; the rest of the island was governed by Irish chieftains only nominally acknowledging English sovereignty. The perennial conflict with the English disrupted the tribal administration that had given Ireland chaos and violence, but also poets, scholars, and saints. Most of the land was left to woods and bogs; transport and communication were heroic enterprises, and the native Celtic population of some 800,000 souls lived in a half-lawless misery on the edge of barbarism. The English in the Pale were almost as poor, and they made Elizabeth's problem worse by debauchery, peculation, and crime; they robbed the London government as sedulously as they plundered the Irish peasantry. Throughout the reign English settlers drove Irish proprietors and tenants from "clearances"; the dispossessed fought back with assassinations; and life for conquerors and conquered alike became a persisting fever of force and hate. Cecil himself thought that "the Flemings had not such cause to rebel against the oppression of the Spaniards" as the Irish against English rule.[91]

Elizabeth's Irish policy was based on the conviction that a Catholic Ireland would be a peril to a Protestant England. She ordered a full enforcement of Protestantism throughout the island. Mass was prohibited, the monasteries were closed; public worship ceased outside the narrow Pale. Priests survived in hiding, and administered the sacraments furtively to a few. Morality, deprived of both religion and peace, almost disappeared; murder, theft, adultery, and rape flourished, and men changed wives without grudge or qualm. Irish leaders appealed to the popes and Philip II for protection or aid. Philip feared to invade Ireland, lest the English should invade and help the rebellious Netherlands, but he established centers and colleges for Irish refugees in Spain. Pius IV sent to Ireland an Irish Jesuit, David Wolfe (1560); with the courage and devotion characteristic of his order, Wolfe established clandestine missions, brought in other disguised Jesuits, and restored Catholic piety and hope. The chieftains took heart, and one after another rose in revolt against English rule.

The most powerful of them was Shane (i.e., John) O'Neill of Tyrone. Here was such a man as legend could sing of and Irishmen could fight for. He fiercely defended his title of *the* O'Neill against a usurping brother. He ignored the Commandments and adored the Church. He foiled all English efforts to subdue him, risked his head to visit London and win Elizabeth's alliance and support, and returned in triumph to rule Ulster as well as Tyrone. He fought the rival O'Donnell clan ferociously, was finally defeated by it (1567), and was killed when he took refuge with the MacDonnells, Scottish immigrants whose settlement at Antrim he had formerly attacked.

The history of Ireland after his death was a parade of rebellions, massacres, and lords deputy. Sir Henry Sidney, father of Sir Philip, served Elizabeth faithfully in that ungrateful office for nine years. He joined in defeating O'Neill, hunted Rory O'More to the death, and was recalled (1578) because of the high cost of his victories. In two years as Lord Deputy, Walter Devereux, first Earl of Essex, distinguished himself by a massacre on the island of Rathlin, off the Antrim coast. Thither the rebel MacDonnells had sent for safety their wives and children, their aged and ailing, with a protective guard. Essex dispatched a force to capture the island. The garrison offered to surrender if they might be allowed to sail for Scotland; the offer was refused; they surrendered unconditionally; they and the women and children, the sick and the old, numbering six hundred, were put to the sword (1575).[92]

The great revolt of the reign was that of the Geraldine clan in Munster. After many captivities and escapes, James Fitzmaurice Fitzgerald crossed to the Continent, raised a troop of Spaniards, Italians, Portuguese, Flemings, and English Catholic emigrés, and landed them on the coast of Kerry (1579), only to lose his life in an incidental war with another clan. His cousin Gerald Fitzgerald, fifteenth Earl of Desmond, carried on the revolt, but the neighboring Butler clan, under the Protestant Earl of Ormonde, declared for England. The Catholics of the Pale organized an army and defeated the levies of the new Lord Deputy, Arthur, Lord Grey (1580). Reinforced, Grey beseiged Desmond's main force by land and sea on a promontory in Smerwick Bay. Finding themselves defenseless against Grey's artillery, the six hundred surviving rebels surrendered and begged for mercy; all were slaughtered, women and men, except for officers who could promise substantial ransoms.[93] The war of English against Irish, and of clan against clan, so ravaged Munster that (said an Irish chronicler) "the lowing of a cow, or the voice of a plowman, was not to be heard that year from Dingle to the Rock of Cashel"; and an Englishman wrote (1582) that "there hath died by famine . . . thirty thousand in Munster in less than half a year, besides others that are hanged and killed."[94] For "to kill an Irishman in that province," wrote a great English historian, "was thought no more of than to kill a mad dog."[95] Almost denuded of Irish, Munster was divided into plantations for English settlers (1586)—one of them Edmund Spenser, who there completed *The Faerie Queene*.

The desperate Irish rose again in 1593. Hugh O'Donnell, Lord of Tyrconnel, joined forces with Hugh O'Neill, second Earl of Tyrone. Spain, now at open war with England, promised help. In an interregnum between lords deputy, O'Neill routed an English army at Armagh, captured Blackwater, an

English stronghold in the north (1598), and sent a force to renew the Munster revolt. The English colonists fled, abandoning their plantations. Hope and joy spread in Ireland, and even the English expected that Dublin itself would fall.

It was in this crisis that Elizabeth appointed the youthful Robert Devereux, second Earl of Essex, as her Lord Deputy in Ireland (March 1599). She gave him an army of 17,500 men—the greatest that England had ever sent to the island. She bade him attack O'Neill in Tyrone, make no peace without consulting her, and not return without her permission. Arrived in Dublin, he dallied through the spring, undertook a few skirmishes, let his army waste away with disease, signed an unauthorized truce with O'Neill, and returned to England (September 1599) to explain his failure to the Queen. Quickly replacing him, Charles Blount, Lord Mountjoy, faced with courage and skill a combination of tricky O'Neill, fearless O'Donnell, and a fleet landing at Kinsale with troops and arms from Spain and indulgences from Clement VIII for all who would defend Ireland and the faith. Mountjoy rushed south to meet the Spaniards, and defeated them so decisively that O'Neill submitted; the revolt collapsed, and a general amnesty brought a precarious peace (1603). Meanwhile Elizabeth had died.

Her record in Ireland subtracted from her glory. She underestimated the difficulty of conquering, in an almost roadless country, a people whose love of their land and their faith was their only bond to life and decency. She scolded her deputies for failures that were due in part to her own parsimony; they were unable to pay their troops, who found it more profitable to rob the Irish than to fight them. She vacillated between truce and terror, and never followed one policy to a decision. She founded Trinity College and Dublin University (1591), but she left the people of Ireland as illiterate as before. After the expenditure of £10,000,000, the peace achieved was a desert of desolation over half the lovely isle, and, over all of it, a spirit of unspeakable hatred that only bided its time to kill and devastate again.

IX. Elizabeth and Spain

The Queen was at her best in her management of Spain. She allowed Philip to think she might marry him or his son; and in his hopes of winning England with a wedding ring, he played the game of patience till his friends were alienated and Elizabeth was strong. Pope and Emperor and a hapless Scottish Queen might beg him to invade England, but he was too doubtful of France, too troubled in the Netherlands, to venture upon so incalculable a throw of the political dice. He had no assurance that France would not pounce upon the Spanish Netherlands the moment he became embroiled with England. He was loath to encourage revolution anywhere. He trusted, in his heavy procrastinating way, that Elizabeth would in due time find one or another of the many exits that an ingenious nature has provided from our life; and yet he was in no haste to give the throne of England to a Scottish lass in love with France. For years he held back the Pope from promulgating the excommunication of Elizabeth. He bore in somber silence her treatment of Catholics in England, and her protests against the treatment of English Protestants in Spain. For almost thirty years he kept the peace while English privateers made war upon Spanish colonies and trade.

The nature of man confesses itself in the conduct of states, for these are but ourselves in gross, and behave, for the most part, as men presumably did before morals and laws were laid upon them by religion and force. Conscience follows the policeman, but there were no police for states. On the seas there were no Ten Commandments, and trade existed by permission of piracy. Small pirate craft used the inlets of the British coast as lairs and thence sallied forth to seize what they could; if the victims were Spanish the English could enjoy the religious fervor of plundering a papist. Bold men like John Hawkins and Francis Drake fitted out substantial privateers and took all the oceans for their province. Elizabeth disowned but did not disturb them, for she saw in the privateers the makings of a navy, and in these buccaneers her future admirals. The Huguenot port of La Rochelle became a favorite rendezvous of English, Dutch, and Huguenot vessels, which "preyed on Catholic commerce under whatever flag it sailed,"[96] and, in need, on Protestant commerce too.

From such piracy the buccaneers passed to that lucrative trade in slaves which the Portuguese had opened up a century before. In the Spanish colonies of America the natives were dying out from toil too arduous for their climate and constitutions. A demand arose for a sturdier breed of laborers. Las Casas himself, defender of the natives, suggested to Charles I of Spain that African Negroes, stronger than the Caribbean Indians, should be transported to America, to do the heavy work for the Spaniards there.[97] Charles consented, but Philip II condemned the trade and instructed the Spanish-American governors to prevent the importation of slaves except under license—costly and rare— by the home administration.[98] Aware that some governors were evading these restrictions, Hawkins led three ships to Africa (1562), captured three hundred Negroes, took them to the West Indies, and sold them to Spanish settlers in exchange for sugar, spices, and drugs. Back in England, he induced Lord Pembroke and others to invest in a second venture, and persuaded Elizabeth to put one of her best vessels at his disposal. In 1564 he headed south with four ships, seized four hundred African Negroes, sailed for the West Indies, sold them to Spaniards under threat of his guns if they refused to buy, and returned home to be hailed as a hero and share his spoils with his backers and the Queen, who made 60 percent on her investment.[99] In 1567 she lent him her ship the *Jesus;* with this and four other vessels he sailed to Africa, captured all the Negroes his holds could stow, sold them in Spanish America at £160 a head, and was homeward bound with loot valued at £100,000 when a Spanish fleet caught him off the Mexican coast at San Juan de Ulúa, and destroyed all of his fleet but two small tenders, in which Hawkins, after a thousand perils, returned empty-handed to England (1569).

Among the survivors of that voyage was Hawkins' young kinsman Francis Drake. Educated at Hawkins' expense, Drake became, so to speak, a native of the sea. At twenty-two he commanded a ship on Hawkins' futile expedition; at twenty-three, having lost everything but his reputation for bravery, he vowed vengeance against Spain; at twenty-five he received a privateer's commission from Elizabeth. In 1573, aged twenty-eight, he captured a convoy of silver bullion off the coast of Panama and returned to England rich and revenged. Elizabeth's councilors kept him in hiding for three years while Spain cried out for his death. Then Leicester, Walsingham, and Hatton fitted out for him four small vessels, totaling 375 tons; with these he sailed from Plymouth on November 15, 1577, on what turned out to be the second circumnavigation of the globe. As his fleet issued from the Straits of Magellan into the Pacific, it ran into a heavy storm; the ships were scattered and never reunited; Drake alone, in the *Pelican*, moved up the west coast of the Americas to San Francisco, raiding Spanish vessels on the way. Then he turned boldly westward to the Philippines, sailed through the Moluccas to Java, across the Indian Ocean to Africa, around the Cape of Good Hope, and up the Atlantic to reach Plymouth on September 26, 1580, thirty-four months after leaving it. He brought with him £600,000 of booty, of which £275,000 were handed over to the Queen.[100] England hailed him as the greatest seaman and pirate of the age. Elizabeth dined on his ship and dubbed him knight.

All this time England had been technically at peace with Spain. Philip lodged repeated protests with the Queen; she made excuses, hugged her spoils, and pointed out that Philip also was violating international "law" by sending help to the rebels in Ireland. When the Spanish ambassador threatened war she threatened marriage with Alençon and alliance with France. Philip, busy conquering Portugal, ordered his envoy to keep the peace. As usual, good luck supplemented the vacillating genius of the Queen. What would have happened to her if Catholic France had not been cut in two by civil war, if Catholic Austria and the Emperor had not been harassed by the Turks, if Spain had not been embroiled with Portugal, France, the papacy, and its rebellious subjects in the Netherlands?

For years Elizabeth played fast and loose with the Netherlands, shifting her policy with fluid circumstance, and no charges of irresolution or treachery could make her move in blinders on one course. She had no more liking for Dutch Calvinism than for English Puritanism, and no more liking than Philip for abetting revolution. She recognized the importance, to the English economy, of uninterrupted trade with the Netherlands. She planned to support the revolt of the Netherlands sufficiently to keep them from surrendering to Spain or bequeathing themselves to France. For as long as the revolt continued Spain would stay out of England.

A blessed windfall allowed the Queen to help the rebels at a delectable profit to her treasury. In December 1568 several Spanish vessels, carrying £150,000 to pay Alva's troops in the Netherlands, were driven by English privateers into Channel ports. Elizabeth, who had just heard of Hawkins' disaster at San Juan de Ulúa, recognized a providential opportunity to make up for what England had lost in that defeat. She asked Bishop Jewel whether she had a right to the Spanish treasure; he judged that God, being surely a Protestant, would be pleased to see the papists plundered. Moreover, the Queen learned, the money had been borrowed by Philip from Genoese bankers, and Philip had refused to take title to it until its safe delivery in Antwerp. Elizabeth had the money transferred to her vaults. Philip complained; Alva seized all English nationals and goods that he could lay hands upon in the Netherlands; Elizabeth arrested all Spaniards in England. But the necessities of trade gradually restored normal relations. Alva refused to prod Elizabeth into alliance with the rebels. Philip kept his temper. Elizabeth kept the money.

The uneasy peace dragged on until continued English raids on Spanish shipping, and the appeals of the imprisoned Mary Stuart's friends, involved Philip in a plot to assassinate the Queen.[101] Convinced of his participation, Elizabeth expelled the Spanish ambassador (1584) and gave open aid to the Netherlands. English troops entered Flushing, Brill, Ostend, and Sluys; Leicester was sent to command them; they were defeated by the Spaniards at Zutphen (1586). But now at last the issue was drawn. Both Philip and Elizabeth prepared with all their resources for the war that would decide the mastery of the seas and the religion of England, perhaps of Europe, perhaps of the New World.

Spain had risen to wealth by grace of Columbus and Pope Alexander VI, whose arbitration decrees of 1493 had awarded nearly all of the Americas to his native Spain. With those voyages and bulls the Mediterranean ceased to be the center of the white man's civilization and power, and the Atlantic age began. Of Europe's three great Atlantic nations France was debarred by civil war from the contest for oceanic dominion. England and Spain remained, jutting out like grasping promontories toward the promised land. It appeared impossible to dislodge Spain from her preeminence in America; by 1580 she had hundreds of colonies there, England none; and each year immense riches passed from the mines of Mexico and Peru to Spain. It seemed manifest destiny that Spain should rule all the Western Hemisphere, and make both the Americas in her political and religious image.

Drake was not content with this prospect. For a time the war for the world was between himself and Spain. In 1585, financed by his friends and the Queen, he fitted out thirty vessels and sallied forth against the Spanish Empire. He entered the Estuary of Vigo in northwest Spain, plundered the port of Vigo, disrobed a statue of the Virgin, and carried away the precious metals and costly vestments of the churches. He sailed on to the Canary and Cape Verde islands, pillaged the largest of them, crossed the Atlantic, raided Santo Domingo, took £30,000 as a *douceur* not to destroy the Colombian city of Cartagena, plundered and burned the town of St. Augustine in Florida, and returned to England (1586) only because yellow fever had killed a third of his crew.

This was war without its name. On February 8, 1587, the English government put to death the Scottish Queen. Philip informed Sixtus V that he was now ready to invade England and dethrone Elizabeth. He asked the Pope to contribute 2,000,000 gold crowns; Sixtus offered 600,000, to be paid to Spain only if the invasion actually occurred. Philip bade his best admiral, the Marquis of Santa Cruz, to prepare the largest armada so far known in history. Ships were gathered or built at Lisbon, stores were assembled at Cádiz.

Drake urged Elizabeth to give him a fleet to destroy the Armada before it could take irresistible form. She consented, and on April 2, 1587, with thirty ships, he hurried out from Plymouth before she could change her mind. She did, but too late to reach him. On April 16 he ran his fleet into Cádiz harbor, maneuvered out of range of the batteries on the shore, sank a Spanish man-of-war, raided the transports and storeships, captured their cargoes, set all enemy vessels on fire, and departed unharmed. He anchored off Lisbon and challenged Santa Cruz to come out and fight. The Marquis refused, for his ships were not yet armed. Drake moved north to La Coruña and seized great stores collected there; then to the Azores, where he took a Spanish galleon. With it in tow he returned to England. Even the Spaniards marveled at his audacity and seamanship, and said that "were it not that he was a Lutheran, there was not the like man in the world."[102]

Philip patiently rebuilt his fleet. The Marquis of Santa Cruz died (January 1588); Philip replaced him with the Duke of Medina-Sidonia, a grandee with more pedigree than competence. When finally the Armada was complete, it numbered 130 vessels, averaging 445 tons; half the ships were cargo carriers, half were men-of-war; 8,050 sailors manned them, 19,000 soldiers sailed. Philip and his admirals thought of naval warfare in ancient terms—to grapple and board the enemy and fight man to man; the English plan was to sink the enemy's ships, with their crowded crews, by broadside fire. Philip instructed his fleet not to seek out and attack the English squadrons, but to seize some English beachhead, cross to Flanders, and take on board the 30,000 troops that the Duke of Parma had ready there; so reinforced, the Spanish were to march on London. Meanwhile a letter composed by Cardinal Allen (April 1588) was smuggled into England, bidding the Catholics join the Spanish in deposing their "usurping, heretic, prostitute" Queen.[103] To help restore Catholicism in England, hundreds of monks accompanied the Armada, under the vicar general of the Inquisition.[104] A devout religious spirit moved the Spanish sailors and their masters; they sincerely believed they were on a sacred mission; prostitutes were sent away, profanity subsided, gambling ceased. On the morning when the fleet sailed from Lisbon (May 29, 1588), every man on board received the Eucharist, and all Spain prayed.

The winds favored Elizabeth; the Armada ran into a damaging storm; it took refuge in the harbor of La Coruña, healed its wounds, and set forth again (July 12). England awaited it in a feverish mixture of divided counsels, hurried preparations, and desperate resolve. Now the time had come for Elizabeth to spend the sums that she had saved through thirty years of skimping and deviltry. Her people, Catholic as well as Protestant, came manfully to her rescue; volunteer militia trained in the towns; London merchants financed regiments and, asked to fit out fifteen ships, provided thirty. For ten years now Hawkins had been building men-of-war for the Queen's navy; Drake was now a vice-admiral. Privateers brought their own vessels to the fateful rendezvous. Early in July 1588 the full complement of eighty-two ships, under command of Charles, Lord Howard of Effingham, as Lord High Admiral of England, gathered at Plymouth to greet the advancing foe.

On July 19* the vanguard of the Armada was sighted in the mouth of the Channel. The defending fleet sailed out of Plymouth, and on the twenty-first the action began. The Spaniards waited for the English to come close enough for grappling; instead, the light English vessels—built to low lines and narrow beam—scurried around the heavy Spanish galleons, firing broadsides as they went. The Spanish decks were too high; their guns fired too far above the English vessels, doing only minor damage; the English boats ran beneath the fire, and their maneuverability and speed left the Spaniards helpless and confused. As night fell they fled before the wind, leaving one of their ships to be taken by Drake. Another was blown up, reportedly by a mutinous German gunner, and the wreck fell into English hands. Luckily, both ships contained ammunition, which was soon transferred to the Queen's fleet. On the twenty-fourth more ammunition came, but still the English had only enough for a day's fighting. On the twenty-fifth, near the Isle of Wight, Howard led an attack; his flagship sailed into the center of the Armada, exchanging broadsides with every galleon that it passed; and the superior accuracy of the English fire broke the Spanish morale. "The enemy pursue me," wrote Medina-Sidonia that night to the Duke of Parma; "they fire on me from morn till dark, but they will not grapple . . . There is no remedy, for they are swift and we are slow."[105] He begged Parma to send him ammunition and reinforcements, but Parma's ports were blockaded by Dutch ships.

On the twenty-seventh the Armada anchored in Calais roads. On the twenty-eighth Drake set fire to eight small and dispensable vessels and placed them in the

---

* Old Style, ten days earlier than by the Gregorian calendar, which was adopted by Spain in 1582, but not by England till 1751.

wind to sail amid the Spanish fleet. Fearing them, Medina-Sidonia ordered his ships to put out to sea. On the twenty-ninth Drake attacked them off the French coast at Gravelines, in the main action of the war. The Spaniards fought bravely, but with poor seamanship and gunnery. At noon Howard's squadron came up, and the full English fleet poured such fire into the Armada that many of its ships were disabled and some were sunk; their wooden hulls, though three feet thick, were penetrated by the English shot; thousands of Spaniards were killed; blood could be seen flowing from the decks into the sea. At the close of that day the Armada had lost four thousand men; four thousand more were wounded, and the surviving vessels were with difficulty kept afloat. Seeing that his crews could bear no more, Medina-Sidonia gave orders to withdraw. On the thirtieth the wind carried the broken fleet into the North Sea. The English followed them as far north as the Firth of Forth; then, lacking food and ammunition, they returned to port. They had lost sixty men and not one ship.

For the remnants of the Armada there was no haven nearer than Spain itself. Scotland was hostile, and Irish ports were held by English troops. Desperately the injured ships and starving men made their way around the British Isles. The water was rough and the wind was wild; masts were shattered and sails were torn; day after day some vessel sank or was abandoned, dead men were dropped into the sea. Seventeen ships were wrecked on the rugged Irish shores; at Sligo alone 1,100 drowned Spaniards were washed up on the beach. Some of the crews made landings in Ireland and begged for food and drink; they were refused, and hundreds, too weak to fight, were massacred by the half-savage denizens of the coasts. Of the 130 vessels that had left Spain, 54 returned; of 27,000 men, 10,000, most of them wounded or sick. Philip, learning of the prolonged disaster day by day, shut himself up in his Escorial cell, and none dared speak to him. Sixtus V, pleading that no invasion of England had occurred, sent not one ducat to bankrupt Spain.

Elizabeth was as careful with ducats as the Pope. Wary of peculation in the navy, she demanded account of every shilling spent by navy and army before, during, and after the battle; Howard and Hawkins made up out of their own pockets whatever discrepancies they could not explain.[106] Elizabeth, expecting a long war, had kept the crews and troops on short rations and low pay. Now a violent disease, akin to typhus, ran through the returning men; on some vessels half the crew died or were disabled; and Hawkins wondered what England's fate would have been had the epidemic preceded the enemy.

The naval war continued till Philip's death (1598). Drake took a fleet and fifteen thousand men to help the Portuguese in their revolt against Spain (1589); but the Portuguese hated Protestants more than Spaniards, the English drank themselves drunk on captured wine, and the expedition ended in failure and disgrace. Lord Thomas Howard led a fleet to the Azores to intercept the Spanish *flota* bringing silver and gold to Spain; but Philip's new Armada put Howard's ships to flight—except the *Revenge*, which, caught lagging behind the rest, fought fifteen Spanish ships heroically until overcome (1591). Drake and Hawkins made another sally to the West Indies (1595), but they quarreled and died on the way. In 1596 Elizabeth sent still another fleet to destroy ships in Spanish ports; at Cádiz it found nineteen men-of-war and thirty-six merchantmen; but these escaped to the open sea while Essex plundered the town. This expedition too was a failure, but it demonstrated again the English mastery of the Atlantic.

The defeat of the Armada affected almost everything in modern European civilization. It marked a decisive change in naval tactics; grappling and boarding gave way to cannonading from shipside and deck. The weakening of Spain helped the Dutch to win their independence, advanced Henry IV to the throne of France, and opened North America to English colonies. Protestantism was preserved and strengthened, Catholicism waned in England, and James VI of Scotland ceased to flirt with the popes. Had the Armada been more wisely built and led, Catholicism might have recovered England, the Guises might have prevailed in France, Holland might have succumbed; the great burst of pride and energy that raised up Shakespeare and Bacon as the symbols and fruit of a triumphant England might never have been; and the Elizabethan ecstasy would have had to meet the Spanish Inquisition. So wars determine theology and philosophy, and the ability to kill and destroy is a prerequisite for permission to live and build.

X. Raleigh and Essex: 1588–1601

Though Cecil and Walsingham, Drake and Hawkins had been the immediate instruments of glory and victory, Elizabeth personified triumphant England, and at sixty she was at the top of her fame and power. Her face was a bit wrinkled, her hair was detachable, some teeth were missing and some were black, but in her awesome finery of lacy headdress, flying ruff, padded sleeves, and hoopskirt, all asparkle with encrusted gems, she stood proud and straight and undeniably a queen. Parliament grumbled at her royal ways, but submitted; old councilors offered advice with the timidity of young suitors; and young suitors fluent with adoration surrounded the throne. Leicester and Walsingham paid their debt to nature, Drake and Hawkins would soon be swallowed by the sea they had thought to rule. Cecil—the "Atlas of this commonwealth," Bacon called him[107]—was now old, and he creaked with gout; presently Elizabeth would nurse him in his final illness and feed him his last food with her own hand.[108] She grew sad with these amputations, but she did not let them darken the splendor of her progresses or the vivacity of her court.

New faces shone about her, bringing her some vicarious youth. Christopher Hatton was so handsome that she made him Chancellor (1587). She waited nine years before accepting Burghley's advice to make his sagacious hunchbacked son, Robert Cecil, her Secretary of State. She relished more the fine features and rattling sword of Walter Raleigh, and did not mind his private theological doubts; she had some of her own.

Raleigh was almost the complete Elizabethan man: gentleman, soldier, mariner, adventurer, poet, philosopher, orator, historian, martyr; here was the *uomo universale* of Renaissance dreams, who touched genius at every point, but never let the part become the whole. Born in Devonshire in 1552, entered at Oxford in 1568, he fled from books into life and joined a gallant group of pedigreed volunteers who crossed to France to fight for the Huguenots. Six years in those wars may have taught him some of the unscrupulous violence of action and reckless audacity of speech that molded his later fate. Back in England (1575), he forced himself to study law, but in 1578 he went off again as a volunteer to help the Dutch against Spain. Two years later he was in Ireland as a captain in the army that put down Desmond's rebellion, and he played no hesitant part in the Smerwick massacre. Elizabeth rewarded him with twelve thousand acres in Ireland and favor at her court. Pleased with his figure, his compliments,* and his wit, she listened with less than her customary skepticism to his proposal for English colonies in America; she gave him a charter, and in 1584 he sent out, but did not accompany, the first of several expeditions that tried—and failed—to establish a settlement in Virginia; only the name survived, as a lasting memorial to the Queen's inaccessibility. Elizabeth Throckmorton, a maid

---

* The tale of his coat in the mud beneath her feet is a legend.

of honor, proved more approachable; she accepted Raleigh as her lover, and secretly married him (1593). As no member of the court might marry without the Queen's consent, the ardent couple received an unexpected honeymoon in the Tower. Raleigh earned release—with banishment from the court—by writing to Burghley a letter describing the Queen as an amalgam of all the perfections in history.

He retired to his Sherborne estate, planned voyages and discoveries, played with atheism, and wrote poetry whose every line had a characteristic tang and sting. But two years of quiet exhausted his stability. With the help of Lord Admiral Howard and Robert Cecil, he fitted out five vessels and headed for South America, seeking El Dorado—a fabled land of golden palaces, rivers running gold, and Amazons with undiminished charms. He sailed a hundred miles up the Orinoco, but found no female warriors and no gold. Baffled by rapids and falls, he returned to England empty-handed; but he told how the American natives had marveled at the beauty of the Queen when he showed them her portrait; and soon he was readmitted to the court. His eloquent account *The Discovery of the Large, Rich, and Beautiful Empire of Guiana* reaffirmed his faith that "the sun covereth not so much riches in any part of the world" as the region of the Orinoco. Tirelessly he preached the desirability of getting America's wealth out of Spanish into English hands; and he phrased the doctrine of sea power perfectly: "Whoever commands the sea commands the trade; whoever commands the trade of the world commands the riches of the world, and consequently the world itself."[109]

In 1596 he joined the expedition to Cádiz, fought as vigorously as he wrote, and received a wound in the leg. The Queen now "used him graciously" and made him captain of the guard. In 1597 he commanded part of the fleet that Essex led to the Azores. Separated from the rest by a storm, Raleigh's squadron encountered and defeated the enemy. Essex never forgave him for pre-empting victory.

Robert Devereux, second Earl of Essex, surpassed even Raleigh in fascination. He had Walter's ambition and verve and pride, a little more of his hot temper, a little less of his wit, much more of generosity and *noblesse oblige*. He was a man of action enamored of intellect—victor in jousts and on the athletic field, distinguished for bravery and audacity in war, yet also the helpful and appreciative friend of poets and philosophers. When his mother became Leicester's second wife, Leicester advanced him at court to offset Raleigh's ingratiating charm. The Queen, fifty-three, fell maternally in love with the high-strung, handsome lad of twenty (1587); here was a son to console her childlessness. They talked, rode, heard music, played cards together, and "my Lord," said a gossip, "cometh not to his own lodging till birds sing in the morning."[110] Her aging heart suffered when he secretly married Philip Sidney's widow; but she soon forgave him, and by 1593 he was a member of the Privy Council. However, he was poorly fitted for court life or statesmanship; "he carried his love and hate always on his face," said his servant Cuffe, "and knew not how to hide them."[111] He made enemies of Raleigh, William Cecil, Robert Cecil, finally of the ungrateful Bacon and the reluctant Queen.

Francis Bacon, who was destined to have more influence on European thought than any other Elizabethan, had been born (1561) in the very aura of the court, at York House, official residence of the Lord Keeper of the Great Seal, who was his father, Sir Nicholas; Elizabeth called the boy "the young Lord Keeper." His frail constitution drove him from sports to studies; his agile intellect grasped knowledge hungrily; soon his erudition was among the wonders of those "spacious times." After three years at Cambridge he was sent to France with the English ambassador to let him learn the ways of state. While he was there his father unexpectedly died (1579) before buying an estate that he had intended for Francis, who was a younger son; and the youth, suddenly reduced to meager means, returned to London to study law at Gray's Inn. Being a nephew of William Cecil, he appealed to him for some political place; after four years of waiting, he sent him a whimsical reminder that "the objection of my years will wear away with the length of my suit."[112] Somehow, in that year 1584, he was elected to Parliament, though still but twenty-three. He distinguished himself by favoring more toleration of the Puritans (his mother was one). The Queen ignored his arguments, but he restated them bravely in a privately circulated *Advertisement Touching the Controversies of the Church of England* (1589). He proposed that no man should be molested for his religious faith who promised to defend England against any foreign power—including the papacy—that threatened England's full sovereignty and freedom. Elizabeth and Cecil thought the young philosopher a bit forward; and in truth he was ahead of his times.

Essex relished the keenness of Bacon's mind and invited his advice. The young sage counseled the young noble to seem, if he could not be, modest; to moderate his expenditures; to seek civil rather than military office, since setbacks in politics could be sooner redeemed than defeats in war; and to regard his popularity with the populace as a danger with the Queen.[113] Bacon hoped that Essex would mature into a statesman and give his mentor some opportunity to rise. In 1592 he appealed again to Cecil in famous lines:

> I wax now somewhat ancient; one-and-thirty years is a great deal of sand in the hourglass . . . The meanness of my estate doth somewhat move me . . . I confess that I have as vast contemplative ends as I have moderate civil ends: for I have taken all knowledge to be my province . . . This, whether it be curiosity, or vainglory, or nature . . . is so fixed in my mind as it cannot be removed.[114]

When Essex importuned the Cecils and Elizabeth to give Bacon the vacant office of attorney general, his appeals were in vain; Edward Coke, older and technically more fit, was chosen instead. Essex took the blame handsomely, and gave Bacon an estate at Twickenham with £1,800.[115] Before Bacon could use this he suffered a brief and genteel imprisonment for debt.[116] In 1597 he was appointed to the "Learned Council" of lawyers who advised the Privy Council.[117]

Despite Bacon's advice, Essex joined the war party, and planned to make himself head of the army. His dashing bravery at Cádiz made him too popular for the Council's taste; failure at the Azores and his undiminished pride, extravagance, and sharp tongue alienated the court and irritated the Queen. When she flatly rejected his recommendation of Sir George Carew for office in Ireland, he turned his back on her with a gesture of contempt. Furious, she boxed his ears and cried, "Go to the Devil!" He grasped his sword and shouted at her, "This is an outrage that I will not put up with. I would not have borne it from your father's hands." He rushed in anger from the room, and all the court expected him to be clapped into the Tower (1598).[118] Elizabeth did nothing. On the contrary—or was it to get rid of him?—a few months later she appointed him Lord Deputy for Ireland.

Bacon had cautioned him not to seek that ungrateful task of countering a faith by force; but Essex wanted an army. On March 27, 1599, he left for Dublin amid the acclamations of the populace, the misgivings of his friends, and the satisfaction of his enemies. Six months later, having failed in his mission, he hurried back to England without permission of the Queen, rushed unannounced into her dressing room, and tried to explain his actions in Ireland. She listened to him with patient wrath, and had him committed to the custody of the Lord Keeper at York House until the charges against him could be heard.

The people of London murmured, for they were ignorant of his failure and remembered his victories. The Privy Council ordered a semipublic trial, and commissioned Bacon—as a member of the Learned Council and as a lawyer pledged to defend the Queen—to draw up a statement of the charges. He asked to be excused; they insisted; he consented. The indictment he formulated was moderate; Essex acknowledged its truth and offered humble submission. He was suspended from his offices and was told to remain in his own home till the Queen should be pleased to free him (June 5, 1600). Bacon pleaded for him, and on August 26 Essex was restored to liberty.

Now in his own Essex House, he continued his search for power. One of his intimates was Shakespeare's patron, Henry Wriothesley, Earl of Southampton; him Essex sent to Ireland to propose that Mountjoy, now Lord Deputy there, should return to England with the English army and help Essex take control of the government. Mountjoy refused. Early in 1601 Essex wrote to James VI of Scotland, asking his aid and promising to support him as successor to Elizabeth; James sent him a letter of encouragement. Wild rumors spread through the excited capital: that Robert Cecil was planning to make the Spanish Infanta queen of England; that Essex was to be immured in the Tower; that Raleigh had vowed to kill him. Perhaps to force Essex to show his hand, the younger Cecil induced the Queen to send Essex a message requiring him to attend the Council. His friends warned him that this was a ruse to seize him. One friend, Sir Gilly Merrick, paid the Chamberlain's company to stage, that evening in Southwark, Shakespeare's *Richard II*, showing a sovereign justly deposed.[119]

The next morning (February 7, 1601) some three hundred supporters of Essex, fervent and armed, gathered in the courtyard of his home. When the Lord Keeper and three other dignitaries came to ask the cause of this illegal assembly, the crowd locked them up and swept the hesitant Earl on with them to London and revolution. He had hoped that the people would rise to his cause, but the preachers bade them stay indoors, and they obeyed. The forces of the government were on guard and routed the rebels. Essex was captured and lodged in the Tower.

He was quickly brought to trial on a charge of treason. The Council bade Bacon help Coke in preparing the government's case. His refusal would have ruined his political career; his consent ruined his posthumous reputation. When Coke faltered in presenting the indictment, Bacon rose and stated the matter with convincing, convicting clarity. Essex confessed his guilt and named his accomplices.[120] Five of these were arrested and beheaded. Southampton was sentenced to life imprisonment; James I later released him. Legend told how Essex sent the Queen a ring once given him by her with a promise to come to his aid if he should ever return it in his hour of need. If sent, it did not reach her.[121] On February 25, 1601, aged thirty-five, Essex went gallantly to the fate that was the seal of his character. Raleigh, his enemy, wept when the blow fell. For a year the Tower displayed the severed and decaying head.

XI. The Magic Fades: 1601–3

The sight of that head, or the knowledge that it was staring down upon her night and day, must have shared in the somber mood of Elizabeth's final years. She sat alone for hours in silent, pensive melancholy. She maintained the amusements of her court and made at times a brave pretense of gaiety, but her health was gone and her heart was dead. England had ceased to love her; it felt that she had outlived herself and should make room for younger royalty. The last of her Parliaments rebelled more vigorously than any before against her infringement of parliamentary freedom, her persecution of Puritans, her rising demands for funds, her gifts of trade monopolies to her favorites. To everyone's surprise, the Queen yielded on the last point and promised to end the abuse. All the members of the Commons went to thank her, and they knelt as she gave what proved to be her last address to them, her wistful "Golden Speech" (November 20, 1601):

> There is no jewel, be it of never so rich a price, which I prefer before . . . your love. For I do esteem it more than any treasure . . . And though God has raised us high, yet this I count the glory of my crown, that I have reigned with your loves . . .[122]

She bade them rise and then continued:

> To be a king and wear a crown is a thing more glorious to them that see it than it is pleasant to them that bear it . . . For my own part, were it not for conscience' sake to discharge the duty that God hath

laid upon me, and to maintain His glory, and keep you in safety, in mine own disposition I should be willing to resign the place I hold to any other, and glad to be freed of the glory with the labors; for it is not my desire to live or to reign longer than my life and reign shall be for your good. And though you have had and may have many mightier and wiser princes sitting in this seat, yet you never had, nor shall have, any love you better.[123]

She had postponed as long as she could the question of a successor, for while the Queen of Scots lived, as legal heir to her throne, Elizabeth could not reconcile herself to letting Mary undo the Protestant settlement. Now that Mary was dead, and Mary's son, James VI of Scotland, was heir apparent, it was some comfort to know that, however vacillating and devious, he was Protestant. She knew that Robert Cecil and others of her court were secretly negotiating with James to ease his accession and feather their nests, and were counting the days when she should die.

Rumors moved across Europe that she was dying of cancer. But she was dying of too much life. Her frame could not bear any more the joys and sorrows, the burdens and blows of the relentless years. When her godson, Sir John Harington, tried to amuse her with witty verses, she sent him off, saying, "When thou dost feel creeping time at thy gate, these fooleries will please thee less."[124] In March 1603, having exposed herself too boldly to the winter cold, she caught a fever. Through three weeks it consumed her. She spent them mostly in a chair or reclining on cushions. She would have no doctors, but she asked for music, and some players came. Finally she was persuaded to take to her bed. Archbishop Whitgift expressed a hope for her longer life; she rebuked him. He knelt beside the bed and prayed; when he thought it was enough, he tried to rise, but she bade him continue; and again, when "the old man's knees were weary," she motioned to him to pray some more. He was released only when, late at night, she fell asleep. She never woke. The next day, March 24, John Manningham wrote in his diary: "This morning, about three o'clock, her majesty departed this life, mildly like a lamb, easily like a ripe apple from a tree."[125] So it seemed.

England, which had long awaited her passing, felt the blow nevertheless. Many men realized that a great age had ended, a powerful hand had fallen from the helm, and some, like Shakespeare, feared a chaotic interlude.[120] Bacon thought her such a great queen that if Plutarch were now alive to write lives by parallels, it would trouble him . . . to find for her a parallel among women. This lady was endued with learning in her sex singular, and rare even among masculine princes . . . As for her government . . . this part of the island never had forty-five years of better times; and yet not through the calmness of the season, but through the wisdom of her regiment. For if there be considered, of the one side, the truth of religion established, the constant peace and security; the good administration of justice; the temperate use of the prerogative . . . the flourishing state of learning . . . and if there be considered, on the other side, the differences of religion, the troubles of neighbor countries, the ambition of Spain, and opposition of Rome; and then that she was solitary and of herself: these things I say considered, as I could not have chosen an [other] instance so recent and so proper, so I suppose I could not have chosen one more remarkable or eminent . . . concerning the conjunction of learning in the prince with felicity in the people.[127]

Looking back now in the hindsight of time, we should shade the portrait a little, noting and forgiving the faults of the incomparable Queen. She was no saint or sage, but a woman of temper and passion, lustily in love with life. The "truth of religion" was not quite established, and not all her subjects could, as Shakespeare may have thought, "eat in safety, under their own vines, what they planted, and sing the merry songs of peace."[128] The wisdom of her rule was partly that of her aides. The vacillations of her mind proved often fortunate, perhaps by the chance of change; sometimes they brought such weakness of policy that the internal troubles of her enemies had to help her to survive. But survive she did, and she prospered, by fair means or devious. She freed Scotland from the French and bound it with England; she enabled Henry of Navarre to balance his Mass in Paris with the Edict of Nantes; she found England bankrupt and despised, and left it rich and powerful; and the sinews of learning and literature grew strong in the wealth of her people. She continued the despotism of her father, but moderated it with humanity and charm. Denied husband and child, she mothered England, loved it devotedly, and used herself up in serving it. She was the greatest ruler that England has ever known.

CHAPTER II

MERRIE ENGLAND[1]

1558–1625

I. At Work

What sort of England was it that gave Elizabeth her power and victory, and Shakespeare his language and inspiration? What kind of people were these Elizabethan Englishmen, so recklessly aggressive, so outspoken and exuberant? How did they live and labor, dress and think, love and build and sing?

In 1581 they numbered some five million. Most of them were farmers. Most of these were sharecroppers; some were tenants paying a fixed rent; a rising proportion were freeholding yeomen. Enclosures of common lands continued, as pasturage proved more profitable than tillage. Serfdom was almost gone, but evictions of tenants by enclosures and combinations were generating an unhappy class of laborers who sold their brawn precariously from farm to farm, or from shop to shop in the expanding towns.

Except for the capital, however, the towns were still small. Norwich and Bristol, the largest after London, had little more than twenty thousand souls each. There was a pleasant side to the matter: townsmen were neighborly, and even in London most homes had gardens, or were near to open fields, and could gather the varied flowers that Shakespeare litanied. Houses were heated by burning wood; most industry used charcoal as fuel power; but the price of firewood soared in the sixteenth century, and the rising demand of the towns for coal prompted landowners to explore the deposits of their soil. German operators were imported to improve mining and metallurgy. Elizabeth forbade the use of coal in London, but her imperative proved less categorical than economic need.[2] Textile shops expanded as weavers and fullers fled to England from Alva's oppression in the Netherlands; Huguenots brought from France their artisan and mercantile skills; it was an Englishman, however, the

Reverend William Lee, who invented (1589) the semi-automatic "stocking frame" for knitting. Fishing was the most flourishing industry, for the government encouraged it to inure men to seamanship and provide a reserve for the navy; hence Elizabeth, bowing to the Roman Church, ordered her people to abstain from meat on two days a week and on the traditional fast days of Lent.

The guilds, hamstrung by their medieval regulations, continued to lose markets in this individualistic and innovating age. Clever promoters gathered capital, bought up raw materials, distributed these to shops and families, bought the product, and sold it for all that the traffic would bear. Capitalism in England began in the home, with the work of father, mother, daughter, and son for the entrepreneur; now that "domestic system" took its rise which would prevail until late in the eighteenth century. Nearly every house was a miniature factory, where women wove and spun flax and wool, sewed and embroidered, prepared herb medicines, distilled liquor, and almost succeeded in developing an art of cookery in England.

The Elizabethan state legislated as zealously for the economy as for religion. Aware that municipal restrictions on manufacture and trade were hampering commerce and industry, it replaced communal by national regulation. The famous Statute of Apprentices (1563) established a laborious code of governmental supervision and compulsion that remained the law of England till 1815. Proposing to banish idleness and unemployment, it required every able-bodied youngster to serve as apprentice for seven years, for "until a man grow into twenty-three years, he for the most part, though not always, is wild, without judgment, and not of sufficient experience to govern himself."[3] Every willfully unemployed man under thirty not having an income of forty shillings a year could be forced to take employment as directed by the local authorities. In the countryside all well men under sixty could be compelled to join in harvesting. All workmen were to be hired by yearly contract, at a kind of guaranteed annual wage. The justices of the peace were empowered to fix maximum and minimum remuneration for every employment in their territory; for London laborers the pay was fixed at ninepence a day. Masters unduly dismissing employees were to be fined forty shillings; men unlawfully quitting their jobs were to be jailed; and no employee was to leave his town or parish without permission of his employer and the local magistrate. Hours of work were defined as twelve per day in summer and through daylight in winter. Strikes of any kind were forbidden under penalty of imprisonment or heavy fines.[4]

All in all, the statute had the effect of protecting the employer against the employee, agriculture against industry, and the state against social revolt. A guild of bricklayers at Hull inscribed at the head of its ordinances the consoling proposition that "all men are by nature equal, made all by one Workman of like mire";[5] but nobody believed it, least of all Cecil and Elizabeth; and it was probably Cecil who directed the economic legislation of 1563. Its results for the working classes was to make poverty compulsory. It proposed to readjust wages periodically to the price of basic foods, but the magistrates commissioned to do this belonged to the employing class. Wages rose, but far more slowly than prices; between 1580 and 1640 the price of necessities climbed 100 percent, wages 20 percent.[6] During the century from 1550 to 1650 the conditions of artisans and laborers worsened from day to day.[7] The outskirts of London "filled up with a comparatively poor and often vicious class, dwelling in meanest tenements,"[8] and living in some parts by theft and beggary. At the funeral of the Earl of Shrewsbury (1591) some twenty thousand beggars applied for a dole.[9]

The government attacked these evils with ferocious laws against mendicancy, and a comparatively humane series of Poor Laws (1563–1601) that acknowledged the responsibility of the state for keeping its people from starvation. In every parish a tax was collected to care for the unemployable poor and to put the employable to work in workhouses managed by the state.

The rise of prices proved as stimulating to industry and commerce as it was tragic to the poor. The main causes were the mining of silver in Europe, the importation of precious metals from America, and the debasement of currencies by governments. In the period from 1501 to 1544 the total amount of silver imported or produced in Europe was worth some $150,000,000 in terms of 1957; for the period from 1545 to 1600 it was worth some $900,000,000.[10] Elizabeth struggled nobly against debasement of the English coinage. She accepted the advice of her canny councilor, Sir Thomas Gresham, who warned her (1560), in words that became "Gresham's law," that bad money drives out good—that coins with an honest content of precious metal will be hoarded or sent abroad, while coins without proper content will be used for all other purposes, especially for taxes, the state being "paid in its own coin." Elizabeth and Cecil reformed the currency that her father and brother had debased, and restored the gold or silver content of English coins. Prices rose nevertheless, for the influx or production of silver and gold, and the circulation of currency, outran the production of goods.

Monopolies shared in raising prices. Elizabeth permitted them for the manufacture or sale of iron, oil, vinegar, coal, lead, saltpeter, starch, yarns, skins, leather, glass. She granted these patents partly to encourage capital in importing products and establishing new industries, partly as remuneration for offices and services not otherwise sufficiently paid. When complaints against these monopolies rose to the pitch of parliamentary revolt, Elizabeth agreed to suspend them until their operation had been investigated and approved (1601). Some were maintained.

So hampered, domestic trade developed more slowly than foreign commerce. Except at fairs, no one was allowed to sell goods in any town of which he was not a resident. Such fairs were periodical in many localities, and numbered several hundred a year; the most popular was the Bartholomew Fair, held each August near London, with a circus to draw the people to the merchandise. Goods moved by water rather than by road; the rivers were alive with traffic. Roads were bad but improving, and men could ride a hundred miles on them in a day; the messenger who brought to Edinburgh the news of Elizabeth's death traveled 162 miles on his first day out. Postal service, established in 1517, was for the government only; private mail went by friends, envoys, couriers, or other travelers. Land travel was mostly on horseback. Coaches were introduced about 1564; they remained till 1600 a luxury of the few; but by 1634 they were so numerous that a proclamation forbade their use by private persons because of congestion of traffic.[11] Inns were good, and so were their waitresses, except on demand; but the wayfarer had to watch his purse and conceal his route.[12] You had to be on your toes in Elizabeth's England.

Foreign commerce grew as industry developed. The export of finished products was the preferred way of paying for the import of raw materials and Oriental luxuries. The market was expanding from commune to nation to Europe, even to Asia and America, and the scope and power of national governments grew with the reach and problems of trade. England, like Spain and France, wished to export goods and import gold, for the "mercantilist" theory then prevalent measured a nation's wealth by the precious metals it held. Francis Bacon was apparently the first to speak of a favorable "balance of trade,"[13] by which he meant an excess of exports over imports, and therefore an intake of silver or gold. Cecil declared his aim "by all policies to abridge the use of foreign commodities as be not necessary for us."[14] He knew that silver and gold cannot be eaten or worn, but they were an international currency that could in an emergency buy almost anything, even enemies. Home industries had to be protected in time of peace, lest the nation be dependent on foreign products in time of war. Hence governments discouraged imports by tariffs and encouraged exports with subsidies. "Merchant companies" were formed to sell English products abroad; English "merchant adventurers" developed an export outlet at Hamburg, Anthony Jenkinson led trade missions to Russia (1557) and Persia (1562), another went to India (1583–91), an English Turkey Company was set up in 1581, the Muscovy Company was founded in 1595, and the historic East India Company on December 31, 1600. The stage was prepared for Hastings and Clive. Men in love with the sea or money ventured across oceans to find new trade routes; the science of geography was in part a by-product of their zeal. A fury of shipbuilding was engendered by the quest for markets and colonies; English forests became masts and hulls, Britannia began to rule the waves, and the British Empire was born in fact and phrase.

As commerce spread its sails, financial institutions developed to expedite it. Banks multiplied. In 1553 the Merchant Adventurers organized a joint-stock company for trade with Russia; 240 shares were issued, at £25 each; after each expedition profits were distributed and the invested capital was refunded.[15] The East India Company financed its voyages likewise; and the 87½ percent profit realized on its first venture led to a rush of subscribers—courtiers, judges, clergymen, knights, widows, spinsters, tradesmen—to share in the next enterprise. Men and women loved money as passionately then as now. Interest on loans had been forbidden by Parliament as late as 1552 as "a vice most odious";[16] but the growing strength of business forces in the Commons led to the Usury Bill of 1571, which distinguished interest from usury and legalized a 10 percent return. As stock transactions mounted, bourses were formed for the exchange of ownership in shares or goods, and additional currency was coined to facilitate the sale and purchase of commodities. In 1566 Gresham built the Royal Exchange to cover such mercantile and financial operations. In 1583 it issued the earliest life insurance policy.[17]

The commercial spirit grew as London became one of the thriving marts and centers of the world. The unlit streets were brightened with goods; a traveler to many countries judged the London goldsmiths' establishments as the most sumptuous anywhere.[18] Businessmen were cramped for quarters, and some used the nave of St. Paul's Cathedral as temporary offices, confident that Christ had changed His mind since Calvin; lawyers dealt with clients there, men counted out money on the tombs, and in the courtyard hucksters sold bread and meat, fish and fruit, ale and beer. Pedestrians, peddlers, coaches, and carts swarmed in the narrow and muddy streets. The Thames served as the main thoroughfare, carrying barges, ferries, and pleasure craft; at almost any point a waterman could be found with a boat ready to transfer goods or passengers across the river or upstream or down; hence their lusty cries, "Eastward Ho!" and "Westward Ho!"—which gave titles to Jacobean plays. When its odors abated, the river was a blessing to commerce, recreation, and amours, the setting for stately pageants and rich homes. London Bridge, built in 1209, was the pride of the town and the only road between its north and south sides. The south specialized in taverns, theaters, brothels, and jails. The north was the chief center of business; here the merchant was master, the titled lord entered on sufferance; royalty and nobility lived mostly in palaces outside London. Westminster, where Parliament met, was then a separate city. There too the businessman made himself heard; by 1600 he could frighten the Queen, and a half century later he beheaded the King.

II. In the Schools

The age of Shakespeare was not addicted to education. It had little Latin and less Greek, more of Italian and French. It read books avidly but rapidly, rushing to test them with experience. It went to school to life, and talked back to its teacher with unheard-of insolence.

The language that it used was not that of schools. It was the whole spoken heritage of Celtic, Roman, Saxon, Norman England; it was swollen with the linguistic spoils of France and Italy; it snatched up slang from the London streets,* and dialects from the provinces; and, not content, it made words breed words and let exuberant imagination riot in originative speech. Was there ever a language so vivid, powerful, flexible, and rich? It could not stop to spell consistently; there were, before 1570, no dictionaries to guide orthography, and Shakespeare never decided how to spell his name. Shorthand was used, but did not cool the impatience of bustling business or precipitate poetry.

* In Shakespeare's time *prat* was already popular for "buttocks," and *duds* for "clothes."

All organized education of girls had been ended by Henry VIII's dissolution of the nunneries; but primary education was offered gratis to any boy in reach of a town. Elizabeth opened 100 free grammar schools; James I and Charles I would found 288 more. For lads of pedigree there were already established "public" schools at Winchester, Eton, St. Paul's, and Shrewsbury; now were added Rugby (1567), Harrow (1571), and the Merchant Taylors' School (1561), where Richard Mulcaster left a great pedagogical name. The curriculum was classical plus flogging, and the Anglican religion was compulsory in all schools. At Westminster School classes began at seven and ended at six, with humane interludes for breakfast at eight and a cat nap and short recess in the afternoon. Parents were resolved that the school should fill to the full one of its main functions—to relieve them of their children.

Oxford and Cambridge still monopolized university education. They had fallen, during the turmoil of the Reformation, from their medieval authority and myriad registrations, but they were recovering, and each had some 1,500 students in 1586. At Cambridge Sir Walter Mildmay endowed Emmanuel College (1584), and Frances, Countess of Sussex and aunt of Philip Sidney, founded Sidney Sussex College (1588). At Oxford, Jesus College was set up by governmental and other funds (1571), and Wadham (1610) and Pembroke (1624) were added under James I. Cambridge was thrilled in 1564 by a visit from the Queen. She listened with modest demurrers to a Latin oration in her praise; at Trinity College she replied in Greek to a Greek address; on the streets she bandied Latin with the students; finally she herself made a Latin speech expressing the hope that she might do something for learning. Two years later she visited Oxford, gloried in the lovely halls and fields, and, departing, cried out fervently, "Farewell, my good subjects! farewell, my dear scholars! and may God prosper your studies!"[19] She knew how to be a queen.

Other Englishwomen rivaled her in erudition. The daughters of Sir Anthony Coke were famous for their learning, and Mary Sidney, Countess of Pembroke, made her mansion at Wilton a salon of poets, statesmen, and artists, who found in her a mind capable of appreciating their best. Such women received most of their education from tutors at home. Grammar schools were open to both sexes, but public schools and universities were for men only.

It was a sign of the times when Elizabeth's ablest financier set up in London (1579) Gresham College for law, medicine, geometry, rhetoric, and other studies useful to the business class; he specified that the lectures were to be given in English as well as in Latin, since "merchants and other citizens" would attend.[20] Finally, for the moneyed or titled class, education was completed by travel. Students went to Italy to finish their medical and sexual training or make acquaintance with Italian literature and art, and many learned to like France on the way. Language was then no barrier, for every educated man in Western and Central Europe understood Latin. Nevertheless, when the travelers returned, they brought home some rubbing of Italian and French, and a special fondness for the easy morals of Renaissance Italy.

III. Virtue and Vice

"Every schoolboy" knows Roger Ascham's denunciation of the "Italianate" Englishman (1563):

> I take going thither [to Italy] . . . to be mervelous dangerous . . . Vertue once made that countrie mistress over all the worlde. Vice now maketh that countrie slave to them that before were glad to serve it . . . I know diverse that went out of England, men of innocent life, men of excellent learnyng, who returned out of Italie . . . neither so willing to live orderly, nor yet so liable to speak learnedlie, as they were at home before they went abroad . . . If you think we judge amiss . . . heare what the Italian sayth . . . *Englese Italianato e un diabolo incarnato* . . . I was once in Italie myself, but I thanke God my abode there was but ix days. And yet I saw in that litle tyme, in one Citie, more libertie to sinne, than ever I hard tell of in our noble Citie of London in ix years.[21]

Elizabeth's tutor was not the only one who strummed this tune. "We have robbed Italy of wantonness," wrote Stephen Gosson in *The Schoole of Abuse* (1579); "compare London to Rome, and England to Italy, you shall find the theaters of the one, and the abuses of the other, to be rife among us." Cecil advised his son Robert never to allow his sons to cross the Alps, "for they shall learn nothing there but pride, blasphemy, and atheism."[22] Philip Stubbs, a Puritan, in *The Anatomie of Abuses* (1583), described the Elizabethan English as wicked, vainly luxurious, and proud of their sins. Bishop Jewel, in a sermon before the Queen, lamented that men's morals in London "make a mockery of

God's Holy Gospel, and so become more dissolute, more fleshly, more wanton than ever they were before . . . If our life should give testimony and report to our religion . . . it crieth out . . . "There is no God.'"*[23]

Much of the jeremiads was the exaggeration of moralists fuming against men and women who no longer took to heart the terrors of hell. Probably the bulk of the population was no worse or better than before. But just as the Puritan minority tightened its morals, purses, and lips, so a pagan minority agreed with many Italians that it was better to enjoy life than fuss about death. Possibly Italian wines, popular in England, helped to broaden morals as well as arteries, and more lastingly. From Italy, France, and classical literature may have come a franker sense of beauty, though saddened with a keener consciousness of its brevity. Even the beauty of the youthful male aroused the Elizabethan soul and pen; Marlowe made Mephistopheles praise Faust as fairer than the skies,[24] and Shakespeare's sonnets fluttered between homosexual and heterosexual love. Woman's loveliness was now no mere poetic conceit, but an intoxication that ran through the blood, the literature, and the court, and turned pirates into sonneteers. For at the court women added wit to cosmetics and captured men's minds as well as their hearts. Modesty was an invitation to the chase and doubled beauty's power. Litanies to the Virgin were lost in deprecations of virginity. Romantic love burst into song with all the ardor of denied desire. Women gloried in seeing men fight for them, and gave themselves, in marriage or without, to the victor. It was significant of the decline in the authority of religion that no church sanction or ceremony was now required for the validity of marriage, though the admission was considered an offense to public morals as distinct from law. Most marriages were arranged by the parents after a mutual courtship of properties; then the dizzy goddess of the hour became a disillusioned housekeeper, dedicated to children and chores, and the race survived.

A worse laxity of morals marked public life. Graft, petty or magnificent, ran through the official services; Elizabeth connived at it, as excusing her from

---

* Aubrey tells a tale that gives point to Ascham: "Sir Walter Raleigh, being invited to dinner with some great person . . . His son sat next to his father, and was very demure at least half dinner time. Then said he: 'I, this morning, not having the fear of God before my eyes . . . went to a whore. I was very eager of her . . . and went to enjoy her, but she thrust me from her and vowed I should not, "For your father lay with me but an hour ago."' Sir Walt, being so strangely surprised . . . at so great a table, gives his son a damned blow over the face; his son, as rude as he was, would not strike his father, but strikes over the face of the gentleman that sat next to him, and said, 'Box about, 'twill come to my father anon.'"—*Brief Lives,* 256.

raising salaries.[25] The war treasurer made £16,000 a year besides his pay; by a time-honored swindle the captains kept dead soldiers on the list, pocketed their stipends, and sold the uniforms allotted to them;[26] a soldier was worth more dead than alive. Men in high places took large sums from Philip II to turn English policy to Spanish ends.[27] Admirals practiced piracy and sold slaves. Clergymen sold ecclesiastical emoluments.[28] Apothecaries could be persuaded to concoct poisons, and some doctors to administer them.[29] Tradesmen adulterated goods to the point of international scandal; in 1585 "more false cloth and woolen was made in England than in all Europe besides."[30] Military morals were primitive; unconditional surrender was in many cases rewarded with massacre of soldiers and noncombatants alike. Witches were burned, and Jesuits were taken down from the scaffold to be cut to pieces alive.[31] The milk of human kindness flowed sluggishly in the days of Good Queen Bess.

IV. Justice and the Law

The nature of man, despite so many centuries of religion and government, still resented civilization, and it voiced its protest through a profusion of sins and crimes. Laws and myths and punishments barely stemmed the flood. In the heart of London were four law schools, the Middle Temple, the Inner Temple, Lincoln's Inn, and Gray's Inn, collectively known as the Inns of Court. Law students resided there as other students dwelt in the halls or colleges of Oxford and Cambridge. Only "gentlemen" of blood were admitted; all graduates were sworn to the service of the Crown; their leading or easily led lights became judges in the Queen's courts. Judges and lawyers, in action, wore impressive robes; the majesty of the law was half sartorial.

The courts were by common consent corrupt. One member of Parliament defined a justice of the peace as "an animal who, for half-a-dozen chickens, would dispense with a dozen laws";[32] Francis Bacon required higher inducements. "Plate sin with gold," said Shakespeare's saddened Lear, "and the strong lance of justice hurtless breaks."[33] As judges were removed at the Queen's pleasure, they weighed it in their judgments, and royal favorites accepted bribes to induce her interference with decisions of the courts.[34] Jury trial was maintained except for treason, but the juries were often intimidated by the judges or other officers of the Crown.[35] Treason was loosely defined to include all actions endangering the life or majesty of the sovereign; such cases could be summoned before the Star Chamber—the Privy Council in its judicial capacity; there the defendant was denied jury trial, counsel, and habeas corpus, he was subject to exhausting interrogation or torture, and he was usually condemned to imprisonment or death.

Criminal law relied on deterrents rather than surveillance or detection; laws being weak, punishments were severe. Death was the statutory penalty for any of two hundred offenses, including blackmail, cutting down young trees, and stealing more than a shilling; in an average Elizabethan year eight hundred persons were hanged in Merrie England for crime.[36] Minor crimes were punished by the pillory, the stool, whipping at the cart's tail, burning a hole in the ears or the tongue, cutting out the tongue, or cutting off an ear or a hand.[37] When John Stubbs, a Puritan lawyer, wrote a pamphlet condemning Elizabeth's proposed marriage to Alençon as a surrender to Catholicism, his right hand was cut off by order of a magistrate. Holding up the bleeding stump, and raising his hat with his left hand, Stubbs cried, "Long live the Queen!"[38] Philip Sidney sent Elizabeth a protest against the barbarity, and Cecil, ashamed, gave Stubbs a government sinecure. Torture was illegal, but the Star Chamber used it. We perceive that despite the profound and powerful literature of the age, its general level of civilization had not yet reached that of Petrarch's Italy or Avignon, much less that of Augustus' Rome.

V. In the Home

English life began by risking infantile mortality, which was high. Sir Thomas Browne was a leading physician, yet six of his ten children died in childhood.[39] Then there were epidemics, like the "sweating sickness" of 1550 and the plague visitations of 1563, 1592–94, and 1603. Tenure of life must have been low; one calculation places it at eight and a half years.[40] Men matured and grew old faster than today. Those who survived were the hardy, and their adventures with death toughened them for stratagems and spoils.

Sanitation was improving. Soap was graduating from a luxury to a necessity. About 1596 Sir John Harington invented a flush toilet. Private bathrooms were few; most families used a wooden tub placed before an open fire. Many towns had public baths, and Bath and Buxton provided fashionable bathing establishments for the upper classes. "Hot houses" offered sweat baths and facilities for meals and assignations. Only the well-to-do had their own domestic water supply; most families had to fetch water from public conduits opening at ornamental spouts.

Houses in villages and towns were built of plaster and brick, under roofs thatched with straw; Anne Hathaway's cottage near Stratford-on-Avon is a well-restored example. In the cities dwellings usually adjoined each other, used more brick and stone, and had tiled roofs; mullioned bay windows and overhanging upper stories make them attractive to unfamiliar eyes. Interiors were decorated with carvings and pilasters; fire-places gave the main room or "great hall" dignity and warmth; and ceilings—of timber or plaster—might be cut into symmetrical or fanciful designs. Chimneys took off the smoke that had formerly sought exit through a hole in the ceiling, and stoves were helping the hearth. Glass windows were now common, but night lighting was still by torch or candle power. Floors were covered with rushes and herbs, sweet-smelling when fresh, but soon malodorous and sheltering insects; carpets were forty-five years in the future. Walls were adorned with tapestries, which, under Charles I, would give way to paintings. Most people sat on benches or stools; a chair with a back was a luxury reserved for an honored guest or the master or mistress of the house; hence to "take the chair" came to mean to preside. Otherwise the furniture was strong and admirable: buffets, cabinets, tables, chests, four-posters were cut and mortised in walnut or oak to last for centuries; some beds, with thick mattresses of feather, embroidered coverings, and silk canopies, cost a thousand pounds and were the proudest heirloom of the home. Around or behind the house, in nearly all classes, a garden provided trees, shrubs, shade, and such flowers as women used to grace their homes and hair, and Shakespeare to scent his verse—primrose, hyacinth, honeysuckle, larkspur, sweet William, marigold, Cupid's-flower, love-lies-bleeding, love-in-a-mist, lily of the valley, roses white or red, Lancaster or York. "God Almighty first planted a garden," said Bacon, "without which buildings and palaces are but gross handiworks."[41]

Ornamentation of the person was often more costly than decoration of the home. No age surpassed Elizabethan England in splendor of dress. "Costly thy habit as thy purse can buy," advised Polonius. In moneyed ranks all the fashions of France, Italy, and Spain were merged to redeem the human figure from the depredations of appetite and time. Portia laughed at young Falconbridge—"I think he bought his doublet in Italy, his round hose in France, his bonnet in Germany, and his behavior everywhere."[42] Elizabeth set an example and a vogue of finery, so that in her reign fashions changed repeatedly as common imitation blurred class distinction. "The fashion," mourns a character in *Much Ado about Nothing,* "wears out more apparel than the man."[43] Sumptuary laws tried to end this sartorial chorea; so a statute of 1574, to heal "the wasting and undoing of a great number of young gentlemen" who were wearing their acres on their backs, decreed that none but the royal family, dukes, marquesses, and earls should wear purple, silk, cloth of gold, or sable furs; none but barons and their betters should sport furs, crimson or scarlet velvets, imported woolens, gold or silver or pearl embroidery.[44] Such laws were soon evaded, for the ambitious bourgeoisie denounced them as not only invidious but restraining trade, and in 1604 they were repealed.

Hats were of any shape or color, of velvet, wool, silk or fine hair. Outside the home and the court men wore them nearly always, even in church, doffing them ceremoniously on meeting a lady, but at once covering again. Men wore their hair as long as the women, and grew fancy beards. Around the neck both sexes wore a ruff, a collar of linen and cambric built upon a frame of pasteboard and wire, and stiffened into broad sharp pleats by "a certain liquid matter which they call starch,"[45] which was then making its debut in England. Catherine de Médicis had introduced this noose into France (1533) as a small frill, but fashion expanded it into a pillory reaching to the ears.

Clothing made women a temporarily impenetrable mystery. Half their day must have been taken up with taking on and taking off; "a ship is sooner rigged than a woman."[46] Even hair could be put off or on, for Elizabeth gave the example of wearing a wig, dyed to resemble the golden curls of her youth. False hair was common; poor women, said Shakespeare, sold their locks "by the weight."[47] Instead of hats most women preferred a tiny cap or a transparent net, which let their hair display its allure. Cosmetics colored the face and penciled the eyebrows; ears were pierced for pendants or rings; jewelry sparkled everywhere. The female ruff was as in men, but the bosom was sometimes bare to a point.[48] Elizabeth, narrow-chested and long-bellied, set a fashion of prolonging the bodice or jacket triangularly to a sharp apex below the corseted waist. The skirt was spread out from the hips by a "farthingale" or hoop. Gowns of delicate material and elaborate design covered the legs. Silk stockings were introduced by the Queen. Skirts trailed, sleeves bulged, gloves were embroidered and perfumed. In summer a lady could speak with a jeweled fan, and utter thoughts too kind for words.

But life in the home was seldom in full dress. Breakfast at seven, dinner at eleven or twelve, supper at five or six redeemed the day. The main meal was near noon and plentiful. "The English," said a Frenchman, "stuff their sacks."[49] Fingers still served in place of forks, which came into their present use in the reign of James I. Silver plate adorned prosperous homes; the hoarding of it was already a hedge against inflation. The lower middle classes had vessels of pewter; the poor got along with dishes of wood and spoons of horn. Meat, fish, and bread were the staple foods, and nearly everybody who could afford it suffered from gout. Dairy products were popular only in the countryside, for means of refrigeration were still scant in the towns. Vegetables were widely used only by the poor, who grew them in their garden plots. Potatoes, introduced from America by Raleigh's expeditions, were a garden product, not yet a crop in the fields. Puddings were an English specialty, relished beyond dessert. Sweets were as favored as now; hence Elizabeth's black teeth.

These hearty meals required liquid lubricants—ale, cider, beer, and wine. Tea and coffee were not yet Anglicized. Whiskey* came into general use throughout Europe in the sixteenth and seventeenth centuries, being distilled from grain in the north, from wine in the south. Drunkenness was a protest against the damp climate; the phrase "drunk as a lord" suggests that this remedy rose in favor along the social scale. Tobacco was brought into England by Sir John Hawkins (1565), by Drake, and by Sir Ralph Lane; Raleigh made smoking of it fashionable at court, and took a puff or two before he went to the scaffold. In Elizabeth's time it was too costly for its use to be widespread; at social gatherings a pipe might be passed around to let each guest get his quota. In 1604 King James sent forth a mighty *Counterblast to Tobacco,* lamenting its introduction into England and warning against "a certain venomous quality" in it.

> Is it not both great vanity and uncleanness that at the table, a place of respect, of cleanliness, of modesty, men should not be ashamed to sit tossing of Tobacco pipes, and puffing the smoke one to another, making the filthy smoke and stink thereof to exhale athwart the dishes and infect the air? . . . The public use whereof, at all times and in all places, hath now so far prevailed as divers men . . . have been at least forced to take it also, without desire . . . ashamed to seem singular . . . Moreover, which is a great iniquity . . . the husband shall not be ashamed to reduce thereby his delicate, wholesome, and clean

---

* From Gaelic *uisque-beatha,* "water of life," *eau-de-vie.*

complexioned wife to that extremity, that either she must also corrupt her sweet breath therewith, or else resolute to live in a perpetual
stinking torment . . . A custom loathesome to the eye, hateful to the
nose, harmful to the brain, dangerous to the lungs, and, in the black
stinking fume thereof, nearest resembling the horrible Stygian smoke
of the pit that is bottomless.[50]

Despite this and heavy taxes, there were seven thousand tobacco shops in
London. Lighting and puffing did not take the place of conversation. Both sexes
spoke freely of matters now confined to smoking rooms, street corners, and scientists; and women vied with men in oaths that verged on blasphemy. In the Elizabethan drama whores rub elbows with heroes, and *doubles-entendres* sprinkle
high tragedy. Manners were ceremonious rather than polite; words often graduated into blows. Manners, like morals, came from Italy and France, and also
manuals of courtesy that strove to make gentlemen of aristocrats and ladies of
queens. Modes of salutation were effusive, often osculatory. Homes were more
cheerful with light and jollity than before under medieval terror or afterward
under Puritan gloom. Festivals were frequent; any excuse served for a procession
or parade; weddings, lyings-in, even funerals, gave occasion for festivities, at least
for meals. Games of all sorts were played in homes and fields and on the Thames.
Shakespeare mentions billiards, and Florio speaks of cricket. Blue laws and blue
Sundays were laughed at; if the Queen set the merry pace, why should not her
people keep step with her? Nearly everybody danced, including, said Burton,
"old men and women that have more toes than teeth." And all England sang.

VI. English Music: 1558–1649

No one who knows only post-Puritan England can feel the joyous role of music
in Elizabethan days. From the home, the school, the church, the street, the
stage, the Thames, rose sacred or profane song—masses, motets, madrigals,
ballads, and delicate little lyrics of love such as those that found a setting in
Elizabethan plays. Music was a main course in education; at Westminster
School it received two hours a week; Oxford had a chair of music (1627). Every
gentleman was expected to read music and play some instrument. In Thomas
Morley's *Plaine and Easie Introduction to Practicall Musicke* (1597) an imaginary untutored Englishman confesses this shame:

Supper being ended, and musicke bookes, according to the custome, being brought to the table, the mistresse of the house presented me with a part, earnestly requesting me to sing; but when, after many excuses, I protested unfeignedly that I could not, everyone began to wonder, some whispering to others, demanding how I was brought up.[51]

Barbershops provided instruments for waiting customers to play.

Elizabethan music was predominantly secular. Some composers, like Tallis, Byrd, and Bull, remained Catholic despite the laws and wrote for the Roman ritual, but such compositions were not publicly performed. Many Puritans objected to church music as diverting piety; Elizabeth and the bishops saved church music in England, as Palestrina and the Council of Trent rescued it in Italy. The Queen supported with her wonted determination the chapelmasters who organized large choirs and formal music for the royal chapel and the cathedrals. The Book of Common Prayer became a magnificent libretto for English composers, and the Anglican services almost rivaled the Continental Catholic in polyphonic splendor and dignity. Even the Puritans, following Calvin's lead, approved psalm singing by the congregations; Elizabeth laughed at these "Geneva jigs," but they matured into some noble hymns.

Since the Queen was a profanely secular spirit and loved to be courted, it was fitting that the musical glory of her reign should be the madrigal—love in counterpoint, a part song unaccompanied by instruments. Italian madrigals reached England in 1553 and set the key. Morley tried his hand at the form, expounded it in his graceful dialogue, and invited imitation. A madrigal for five voices, by John Wilbye, suggests the themes of these "ayres":

> Alas, what a wretched life this is, what a death,
> Where the tyrant love commandeth!
> My flowering days are in their prime declining,
> All my proud hope quite fallen, and life entwining;
> My joys each after other in haste are flying
>   And leave me dying
>   For her that scorns my crying;
> Oh, she from here departs, my Love restraining,
> For whom, all heartless, alas, I die complaining.[52]

William Byrd was the Shakespeare of Elizabethan music, famous for masses and madrigals, for vocal and instrumental compositions alike. His contemporaries honored him as *homo memorabilis;* Morley said he was "never without reverence to be named among the musicians."[53] Almost as highly rated and versatile were Orlando Gibbons and John Bull, royalchapel organists. These and Byrd joined (1611) in producing the initial book of keyboard music in England, *Parthenia, or The Maydenhead of the first musicke that ever was printed for the Virginalls.* Meanwhile the English sustained their reputation for composing solo songs of a wholesome freshness redolent of the English countryside. John Dowland, renowned as a virtuoso of the lute, won praise for his *Songes or Ayres,* and Thomas Campion gave him close rivalry. Who does not know Campion's "Cherry Ripe"?[54]

Musicians were organized in a strong union, disturbed under Charles I by internal strife.[55] Instruments were nearly as various as today: lute, harp, organ, virginal or spinet, clavichord or harpsichord, flute, recorder (our flageolet), hautboy, cornet, trombone, trumpet, drums, and many forms of viol, which was now giving place to the violin. The lute was favored for virtuoso performance and to accompany songs; the virginal, modest mother of the piano, was popular with young women, at least before marriage. Instrumental music was intended chiefly for the virginal, the viol, and the lute. A kind of chamber music was composed for an ensemble or "consort" of viols varying in size and range. Campion, in a masque for James I's Queen Anne, used an orchestra of lutes, harpsichords, cornets, and nine viols (1605). Much instrumental music by Byrd, Morley, Dowland, and others has come down to us. It is largely based on dance forms, follows Italian models, and excels in a delicate and tender beauty rather than in vigor or range. Fugue and counterpoint are developed, but no thematic variation, no ingenuity in modulation, no resolved discords or chromatic harmonies. And yet when our nerves are frayed with the pounding stimuli of modern life, we find something cleansing and healing in Elizabethan music; no bombast, no rasping dissonances, no thundering finales, only the voice of an English youth or girl singing plaintively or merrily the timeless canticles of impeded love.

VII. English Art: 1558–1649

The Elizabethan was a minor age in art. Metalworkers turned out some lovely silverware, like the Mostyn salt cellar, and majestic grilles like that in St. George's Chapel at Windsor. The making of Venetian glass was domiciled in England about 1560; vessels of such glass were by many valued above corresponding pieces in silver or gold. Sculpture and pottery were undistinguished. Nicholas Hilliard developed a school of miniature painting, and Elizabeth granted him a monopoly in so reproducing her features. Portrait painters were importees: Federigo Zuccaro from Italy, Marcus Gheeraerts and his son of the same name from the Netherlands. The son has left us an imposing portrait of William Cecil in resplendent, voluminous robes as a Knight of the Garter.[56] Otherwise there was no great painting in England between Holbein and Vandyck.

Only architecture was a major art in the England of Elizabeth and James, and it was almost entirely secular. While Europe was fighting the battle of the faiths, art, like conduct, neglected religion. In medieval centuries, when the profoundest poetry and art had their roots in the sky, architecture dedicated itself to church building, and made homes a form of life imprisonment. In Tudor England religion departed from life into politics; the wealth of the Church passed into lay hands and was transformed into civic structures and lordly palaces. Style changed accordingly. In 1563 John Shute returned from Italy and France bursting with Vitruvius, Palladio, and Serlio; soon he published *The First and Chief Grounds of Architecture,* lauding the classic styles; so the Italian scorn of Gothic entered England, and Gothic verticals fought for air amid the encompassing horizontals of the Renaissance.

In civic architecture the age could boast some handsome achievements: the gate of honor of Caius College and the quadrangle of Clare College at Cambridge, the Bodleian Library at Oxford, the Royal Exchange in London, and the Middle Temple. As lawyers, since Wolsey, had replaced bishops in the administration of England, it was fitting that the civic masterpiece of Elizabethan Renaissance architecture should be the great hall of a law school, finished in the Middle Temple in 1572. No woodwork in England was finer than the oak screen at the inner end of that hall. It was demolished by bombs in the Second World War.

When Elizabethan magnates could afford it they built palaces rivaling the châteaux of the Loire. Sir John Thynne raised Longleat House; Elizabeth, Countess of Shrewsbury, had her Hardwick Hall; Thomas, Earl of Suffolk, built Audley End at a cost of £190,000, "mainly procured from Spanish bribes";[57] Sir Edward Phillips reared Montacute House in chaste Renaissance style; and Sir Francis Willoughby erected Wollaton Hall. William Cecil poured part of his gleanings into an immense château near Stamford; and his son Robert spent almost as much on Hatfield House, whose long gallery is one of the grandest interiors in all the architecture of the age. Such long galleries, on an upper floor, replaced in Elizabethan palaces the timbered great hall of the manor house. Magnificent chimney pieces, massive furniture in walnut or oak, majestic stairways, carved balustrades, and timbered ceilings gave these palatial chambers a warmth and dignity missing in the more brilliant rooms of the French châteaux. So far as we know, the designers of these palaces were the first to receive the title of architect. The epitaph of Robert Smythson, creator of Wollaton Hall, called him "architector," i.e., master builder; now at last the great profession found its modern name.

Now, too, English art became personal, and a man stamped his work with his character and his will. Born in Smithfield in 1573, Inigo Jones showed in youth such a flair for design that an earl sent him to Italy (1600) to study Renaissance architecture. Back in England (1605), he prepared the scenery of many masques for James I and his Danish Queen. He visited Italy again (1612–14) and returned an enthusiast for the classic architectural principles that he had studied in the English translation (1567?) of Vitruvius, and which he found illustrated in the buildings of Palladio, Peruzzi, Sanmicheli, and Sansovino in Venice and Vicenza. He rejected the anomalous mixtures of German, Flemish, French, and Italian forms that had predominated in Elizabethan architecture; he proposed a pure classic style, in which the Doric, Ionic, and Corinthian orders would be kept apart or combined in a congenial sequence and unity.

In 1615 he was put in charge of all royal construction as surveyor general of the works. When the banqueting hall in the palace of Whitehall was burned down (1619), Jones was commissioned to build a new hall for the King. He planned an immense congeries of structures—all in all, 1,152 feet by 874—which, if completed, would have given the British ruler a vaster home than the Louvre, the Tuileries, the Escorial, or Versailles. But James preferred drinking for the day to building for centuries; he confined his outlay to the new banqueting hall, which, deprived of its intended setting, presented an unprepossessing façade of classical and Renaissance lines. When Archbishop Laud asked James to repair the old Cathedral of St. Paul the architect committed the crime of encasing the Gothic nave in a Renaissance exterior. Fortunately this structure was destroyed in the Great Fire of 1666. Jones's Palladian fronts gradually replaced the Tudor style, and it dominated England till the middle of the eighteenth century.

Jones not only served as chief architect for Charles I, but learned to love that luckless gentleman so visibly that when the Civil War broke out he buried his savings in the Lambeth marshes and fled to Hampshire (1643). Cromwell's soldiers captured him there, but gave him his life for £1,045.[58] During this absence from London he designed a country house in Wiltshire for the Earl of Pembroke. The façade was simple Renaissance, but the interior was a model of grandeur and elegance; the "double-cube" hall, sixty by thirty by thirty feet, has been judged the most beautiful room in England.[59] As royal armies consumed aristocratic wealth, Jones lost patronage as well as popularity; he retired into obscurity and died in poverty (1651). Art slept while war remade the government of England.

VIII. Elizabethan Man

How can we understand the Elizabethan Englishman from the supposedly staid and silent Briton of our youth? Can it be that national character is a function of place and time and change? Puritanism and Methodism intervened between the two ages and types; centuries of Eton, Harrow, and Rugby; and reckless conquerors quiet down when they sit supreme.

All in all, the Elizabethan Englishman was a scion of the Renaissance. In Germany the Reformation overwhelmed the Renaissance; in France the Renaissance rejected the Reformation; in England the two movements merged. Under Elizabeth the Reformation triumphed; *in* Elizabeth, the Renaissance. There were some stolid—not speechless—Puritans there, but they did not set the key. The dominant man of the age was a charge of energy released from old dogmas and inhibitions and not yet bound to new; boundless in ambition, longing to develop his capacities, unshackled in humor, sensitive to literature if it breathed life, given to violence of action and speech, but struggling, amid his bombast, vices, and cruelties, to be a gentleman. His ideal hovered between the amiable courtesies of Castiglione's *Courtier* and the ruthless immoralism of Machiavelli's *Prince*. He admired Sidney, but he aspired to be Drake.

Meanwhile philosophy made its way through the cracks of crumbling faith, and the best minds of the age were the most disturbed. There were orthodox and conservative souls, timid and gentle souls, amid this undammed flux; there were good men like Roger Ascham, desperately preaching the virtues that had served the past. But their students were in a venturesome mood. Hear Gabriel Harvey on Cambridge:

The Gospel taught, not learned; Christian Key cold; nothing good but by imputation, the ceremonial law, in word abrogated; the judicial in effect disannulled; the moral indeed abandoned . . . All inquisitive after news, new books, new fashions, new laws . . . some after new heavens, and hells too . . . Every day fresh span new opinions: heresy in divinity, in philosophy, in humanity, in manners . . . The Devil not so hated as the pope.[60]

Copernicus had upset the world and sent the earth whirling dizzily through space. Giordano Bruno came to Oxford in 1583 and talked of the new astronomy and infinite worlds, the sun dying of its own heat, the planets decaying into atomic mist. Poets like John Donne felt the earth slipping beneath their feet.

In 1595 Florio began to publish his translation of Montaigne; after that nothing was certain, and doubt was the air men breathed; as Marlowe is Machiavelli, so Shakespeare is Montaigne. While wise men doubted, young men schemed. If heaven seemed lost in a philosophic cloud, youth could resolve to suck this life dry and sample all truth however lethal, all beauty however fleeting, all power however poisonous. So Marlowe conceived his Faust and Tamburlaine.

It was this plowing up of old ideas, this liberation of the mind for the impassioned utterance of new hopes and dreams, that made Elizabethan England memorable. What would we have cared for its political rivalries, its religious disputes, its martial triumphs, its thirst for gold, if its literature, confined to these passing things, had not voiced the longings, hesitations, and resolves of thoughtful souls in every age? All the influences of that exciting time came to the Elizabethan ecstasy: the voyages of conquest and discovery that expanded the globe, the market, and the mind; the wealth of the middle classes enlarging the scope and goals of enterprise; the revelation of pagan literature and art; the upheaval of the Reformation; the rejection of papal influence in England; the theological debates that unwittingly led men from dogma to reason; education and the widening audience for books and plays; the long and profitable peace, and then the arousing challenge and exhilarating victory over Spain; the great crescendo of confidence in human power and thought: all these were the stimuli that prodded England into greatness, these the germs that made her big with Shakespeare. Now, after almost two silent centuries since Chaucer, she burst into a passion of prose and poetry, drama and philosophy, and spoke out bravely to the world.

CHAPTER III

ON THE SLOPES OF PARNASSUS

1558–1603

I. Books

They were a swelling legion. "One of the great diseases of this age," wrote Barnaby Rich in 1600, "is the multitude of books that doth so overcharge the world that it is not able to digest the abundance of idle matter that is every day hatched and brought into the world." "Already," wrote Robert Burton (1628), "we shall have a vast chaos and confusion of books; we are oppressed with them, our eyes ache with reading, our fingers with turning."[1] Both these plaintiffs wrote books.

The aristocracy, having learned to read, rewarded with material patronage authors who had softened them with dedications. Cecil, Leicester, Sidney, Raleigh, Essex, Southampton, the earls and the Countess of Pembroke were good patrons, who established between English nobles and authors a relation that continued even after Johnson lectured Chesterfield. Publishers paid authors some forty shillings for a pamphlet, some five pounds for a book.[2] A few authors managed to live by their pens; the desperate profession of "man of letters" now took form in England. Private libraries were numerous among the well-to-do, but public libraries were rare. On the way home from Cádiz in 1596 Essex stopped at Faro, in Portugal, and appropriated the library of Bishop Jerome Osorius; he gave it to Sir Thomas Bodley, who included it in the Bodleian Library that he bequeathed to Oxford (1598).

The publishers themselves led a harried existence, subject to state law and public whim. There were 250 of them in Elizabeth's England, for publishing and bookselling were still one trade. Most of them did their own printing;

71

the separation of printer and publisher began toward the end of this reign. Publishers, printers, and booksellers united (1557) in a Stationers' Company; registry of a publication with this guild constituted copyright, which, however, protected not the author but only the publisher. Normally the company would register only such publications as had obtained a legal license to be printed. It was a felony to write, print, sell, or possess any material injurious to the reputation of the Queen or the government, to publish or import heretical books or papal bulls or briefs, or to possess a book that upheld the supremacy of the popes over the English Church.[3] There were several executions for violation of these decrees. The Stationers' Company was empowered to search all printing establishments, to burn all unlicensed publications, and to imprison their publishers.[4] Elizabethan censorship was more severe than any before the Reformation, but literature flourished; as in eighteenth-century France, wits were sharpened by the peril of print.

Scholars were few; it was an age of creation rather than criticism, and the humanistic current had run dry in those hot theological years. Most historians were still chroniclers, dividing their narratives by years; Richard Knolles, however, surprised Burghley with the comparative excellence of his *General History of the Turks* (1603). Raphael Holinshed's *Chronicles* (1577) gave him an unearned increment of fame by supplying Shakespeare with stories of the English kings. John Stow's *Chronicles of England* (1580) was dressed up with "some colors of wisdom, invitements to virtue, and loathing of naughty facts,"[5] but its scholarship was lamentable, and its prose had a powerful *virtus dormitiva*. His *Survey of London* (1598) was more scholarly, but brought him no more bread; in old age he had to be given a license to beg.[6] William Camden, in good Latin, recorded the geography, scenery, and antiquities of England in *Britannia* (1582); and his *Rerum Anglicarum et hibernicarum annales regnante Elizabetha* (1615–27) based its story on conscientious study of original documents. Camden glorified the great Queen indiscriminately, lauded Spenser, ignored Shakespeare, and praised Roger Ascham, but mourned that so fine a scholar had died poor through love of dicing and cockfighting.[7]

Ascham, secretary to "Bloody Mary" and tutor to Elizabeth, left at his death (1568) the most famous of English treatises on education, *The Scholemaster*

(1570), primarily on the teaching of Latin, but containing, in strong, simple English, a plea for the replacement of Etonian severity with Christian kindness in education. He told how, at a dinner with men high in Elizabeth's government, the conversation had turned on education through flogging; how Cecil had favored gentler methods; and how Sir Richard Sackville had privately confessed to Ascham that "a fond [foolish] schoolmaster . . . drave me, with fear of beating, from all love of learning."[8]

The major and most fruitful function of the scholars was to impregnate the English mind with foreign thought. In the second half of the sixteenth century a wave of translations swept over the land from Greece, Rome, Italy, and France. Homer had to wait till 1611 for George Chapman, and the lack of English versions of Greek plays probably shared in giving the Elizabethan drama a "romantic" rather than a "classical" form. But there were translations of Theocritus' idyls, Musaeus' *Hero and Leander,* Epictetus' *Enchiridion*, Aristotle's *Ethics* and *Politics,* Xenophon's *Cyropaedia* and *Oeconomicus,* the speeches of Demosthenes and Isocrates, the histories of Herodotus, Polybius, Diodorus Siculus, Josephus, and Appian, the novels of Heliodorus and Longus, and Sir Thomas North's racy translation (1579) of Amyot's French translation of Plutarch's *Lives.* From the Latin came Virgil, Horace, Ovid, Martial, Lucan, the plays of Plautus, Terence, and Seneca, the histories of Livy, Sallust, Tacitus, and Suetonius. From Italy came Petrarch's sonnets, Boccaccio's *Filocopo* and *Fiammetta* (but no *Decameron* till 1620), the histories of Guicciardini and Machiavelli, the *Orlandos* of Boiardo and Ariosto, Castiglione's *Libro del cortegiano*, the *Gerusalemme liberata* and *Aminta* of Tasso, Guarini's *Pastor fido*, and many fabulous *novelle* by Bandello and others, gathered into such collections as William Painter's *Palace of Pleasure* (1566). Machiavelli's *Il Principe* was not done into English till 1640, but its substance was familiar to the Elizabethans; Gabriel Harvey reported that at Cambridge "Duns Scotus and Thomas Aquinas, with the whole rabblement of Schoolmen . . . were expelled the University," and were replaced with Machiavelli and Jean Bodin.[9] From Spain came one of the longest romances, *Amadis de Gaula*; one of the first picaresque novels, *Lazarillo de Tormes;* one of the classic pastorals, the *Diana* of Montemayor. The best spoils from France were the poems of the Pléiade, and the essays of Montaigne, nobly Englished by John Florio (1603).

The influence of these translations upon Elizabethan literature was immense. Classical allusions began—and for two centuries continued—to encumber English poetry and prose. French was known to most memorable Elizabethan authors, so that translations were not indispensable. Italy fascinated England; English pastorals looked back to Sannazaro, Tasso, and Guarini, English sonnets to Petrarch, English fiction to Boccaccio and the *novelle*; these last gave plots to Marlowe, Shakespeare, Webster, Massinger, and Ford, and Italian locales to many Elizabethan plays. Italy, which had rejected the Reformation, had gone beyond it to break down the old theology, even the Christian ethic. While Elizabethan religion debated Catholicism and Protestantism, Elizabethan literature, ignoring that conflict, returned to the spirit and verve of the Renaissance. Italy, struck down for a time by a change in trade routes, handed the torch of the Rebirth to Spain, France, and England.

II. The War of the Wits

In this Elizabethan exuberance both poetry and prose poured down in a turbulent flood. We know the names of two hundred Elizabethan poets. But until Spenser introduced his *Faerie Queene* (1590), it was prose that caught the ear of Elizabethan England.

John Lyly did it first with his fanciful *Euphues, or the Anatomy of Wit*—i.e., of intelligence—in 1579. Lyly proposed to show how a fine mind and character can be formed through education, experience, travel, and wise counsel. Euphues (Good Speech) is a young Athenian whose adventures provide the scaffolding for wordy discourses on education, manners, friendship, love, atheism. What made the book the best seller of its time was its style—a flux of antitheses, alliterations, similes, puns, balanced clauses, classical allusions, and conceits that took the court of Elizabeth by storm and held the fashion for a generation. For example:

> This young gallant, of more wit than wealth, and yet of more wealth than wisdom, seeing himself inferior to none in pleasant conceits, thought himself superior to all in honest conditions, insomuch that he deemed himself so apt to all things that he gave himself almost to nothing.[10]

Whether Lyly caught this disease from the Italian Marini or the Spaniard Guevara or the *rhetoriker* of Flanders is in dispute. In any case Lyly welcomed the virus and transmitted it to a host of Elizabethans; it spoiled Shakespeare's early comedies, tinged Bacon's *Essays*, and gave a word to the language.

It was a word-conscious age. Gabriel Harvey, a Cambridge tutor, exerted all his influence to turn English poetry from accent and rhyme to classic meters based on syllabic quantities. At his urging, Sidney and Spenser formed in London a literary club, the Areopagus, which strove for a time to force Elizabethan vitality into Virgilian forms. Thomas Nash parodied Harvey's "hopping" hexameters and laughed them literally out of court. When Harvey added insult to pedantry by condemning the morals of Nash's friend Greene, he became the prime target in a pamphlet war that brought into England all the resources of Renaissance vituperation.

Robert Greene's life summarized a thousand literary Bohemian careers from Villon to Verlaine. He was a fellow student at Cambridge with Harvey, Nash, and Marlowe; there he spent his time among "wags as lewd as" himself, with whom he "consumed the flower of his youth."

> I was drowned in pride; whoredom was my daily exercise, and gluttony with drunkenness was my only delight. . . . I was so far from calling upon God that I seldom thought on God, but took much delight in swearing and blaspheming the name of God. . . . If I may have my desire while I live, I am satisfied; let me shift after death as I may. . . . I feared the judges of the bench no more than I dread the judgments of God.[11]

He traveled in Italy and Spain, and there, he tells us, he "saw and practiced such villainy as is abominable to declare." Returning, he became a familiar figure in London taverns, with his red hair, pointed beard, silk stockings, and personal bodyguard. He married and wrote tenderly of marital fidelity and bliss; then he forsook his wife for a mistress, upon whom he spent his wife's fortune. From his firsthand knowledge he described the arts of the underworld in *A Notable Discovery* [uncovering] *of Cozenage* (1591) and warned rural visitors to London against the wiles of swindlers, cardsharpers, pickpockets, panders, and prostitutes; whereupon the underworld tried to kill him. It surprises us that in a life so assiduously devoted to vice he found time to write, with journalistic haste and verve, a dozen novels (in *Euphuestic* style), thirty-five pamphlets, and many successful plays. As his vigor and income declined, he saw some sense in virtue, and repented as eloquently as he had sinned. In 1591 he published a *Farewell to Folly*. In 1592 he composed two tracts of some moment. One, *A Quip for an Upstart Courtier*, attacked Gabriel Harvey. In the other, *Greene's Groatsworth of Wit Bought with a Million of Repentance,* he attacked Shakespeare and called upon his fellow lechers—apparently Marlowe, Peele, and Nash—to quit their sinning and join him in piety and remorse. On September 2, 1592, he sent to his forsaken wife an appeal to reimburse with ten pounds a shoemaker without whose charity "I had perished in the streets."[12] The next day, in the house of this shoemaker, he died—according to Harvey, from "a surfeit of pickled herring and Rhenish wine." His landlady, forgiving his debts for his verse, crowned his head with a laurel wreath and paid for his funeral.[13]

Of all the Elizabethan pamphleteers, Greene's friend Tom Nash had the sharpest tongue and the widest audience. Son of a curate and tired of decency, Nash graduated from Cambridge into London's Bohemia, buttered his bread with his pen, and learned to write "as fast as [his] hand could trot." He established the picaresque novel in England with *The Unfortunate Traveller, or The Life of Jack Wilton* (1594). When Greene died, and Harvey assailed both Greene and Nash in *Four Letters*, Nash retaliated with a series of pamphlets culminating in *Have with You to Saffron Walden*—Harvey's birthplace—in 1596.

> Readers, be merry, for in me there shall want nothing I can do to make you merry . . . It shall cost me a fall, but I will get him hooted out of the University . . . ere I give him over. What will you give me when I bring him upon the stage in one of the principalest colleges in Cambridge?[14]

Harvey survived this experience, outlived the Bohemians, and died at eighty-five in 1630. Nash completed his friend Marlowe's play *Dido,* collaborated with Ben Jonson in *The Isle of Dogs* (1597), was indicted for sedition, and subsided into a cautious obscurity. At the age of thirty-four (1601) he crowned a fast life with an early death.

III. Philip Sidney: 1554–85

Far from this maddened crowd, Sidney rode serenely to an even earlier end. Facing us still in the National Portrait Gallery of London, he seems too delicate for a man: slender of face, with auburn hair, and "not a morsel too much of health," said Languet;[15] "extremely beautiful," said Aubrey,[16] "not masculine enough, yet . . . of great courage." Some grumblers thought him a bit pompous[17] and felt that he carried perfection to excess; only his heroic end won him pardon for his virtues.

But who would not be proud to have had for his mother Lady Mary Dudley, daughter of that Duke of Northumberland who had ruled England under Edward VI; and to have had for his father Sir Henry Sidney, Lord President of Wales and thrice Lord Deputy of Ireland; and to have received his Christian name from King Philip II of Spain as his godfather? Part of his fleeting life was lived in spacious Penshurst Place, whose oakbeam ceilings, picture walls, and crystal chandelier are among the fairest relics of that time. At the age of nine he was appointed lay rector to a church benefice, which brought him sixty pounds a year. At ten he entered Shrewsbury School, which was not too far from Ludlow Castle, his father's residence as Lord President of Wales. To the boy of eleven Sir Henry wrote loving words of wisdom.[18]

Philip learned these lessons well and became a favorite with his uncle Leicester and his father's friend William Cecil. After three years at Oxford he was sent to Paris as a minor member of an English mission. He was received at the court of Charles IX and witnessed the Massacre of St. Bartholomew. He traveled leisurely in France, the Netherlands, Germany, Bohemia, Poland, Hungary, Austria, and Italy. At Frankfurt he began a lifelong friendship with Hubert Languet, one of the intellectual leaders of the Huguenots; at Venice he had his portrait painted by Paolo Veronese; at Padua he imbibed the traditions of the Petrarchan sonnet. Back in England, he was welcomed at court and for almost two years danced attendance on the Queen, but he forfeited her favor for a time by opposing her prospective marriage with the Duke of Alençon. He had all the knightly qualities—pride of bearing, skill and bravery in tournament, courtesy in court, honor in all dealings, and eloquence in love. He studied Castiglione's *Courtier* and tried to model his conduct on that gentle philosopher's ideal of a gentleman, and others modeled themselves on Sidney. Spenser called him "the President of Noblesse and of Chivalry."

It was a mark of the times that the aristocracy, which had once scorned literacy, now wrote poetry and suffered poets to come to them. Sidney, though not rich, became the most active literary patron of his generation. He helped Camden, Hakluyt, Nash, Harvey, Donne, Daniel, Jonson, and, above all, Spenser, who thanked him as "the hope of all learned men and the patron of my young muse."[19] It was quite out of order that Stephen Gosson should dedicate to Sidney his *Schoole of Abuse* (1579), whose title page described it as "a pleasant invective against poets, pipers, players, jesters, and such like caterpillars of the commonwealth." Sidney took up the gauntlet and wrote the first of the Elizabethan classics—*The Defence of Poesy.*

Taking a lead from Aristotle and Italian critics, he defined poetry as "an art of imitation . . . representing, counterfeiting, or figuring forth . . . a speaking picture" designed "to teach and delight."[20] Placing morals far above art, he justified art as teaching morality by pictured examples:

> The philosopher . . . and the historian . . . would win the goal, the one by precept, the other by example; but both, not having both, do both halt. For the philosopher, setting down with thorny arguments the bare rule [of morals], is so hard of utterance, and so misty to be conceived, that one that hath no other guide but him shall wade in him till he be old, before he shall find sufficient cause to be honest. For his knowledge standeth so upon the abstract and the general that happy is that man that may understand him . . . On the other side the historian, wanting the precept, is tied, not to what should be but to what is . . . that his example draweth no necessary consequence, and therefore a less fruitful doctrine.
>
> Now doth the peerless poet perform both, for whatsoever the philosopher said should be done, he gives a perfect picture of it by some one by whom he supposeth it was done, so as he completeth the general notion with the particular example. A perfect picture, I say, for he yieldeth to the powers of the mind an image of that whereof the philosopher bestoweth but a wordish description, which doth neither strike, pierce, nor possess the sight of the soul so much as that other doth.[21]

Poetry, therefore, in Sidney's view, includes all imaginative literature—drama, verse, and imaginative prose. "It is not rhyming and versifying that maketh poetry. One may be a poet without versifying, a versifier without poetry."

He added example to precept. In the same year 1580 that produced the *Defence*, he began to write *The Countess of Pembroke's Arcadia*. This Countess, his sister, was one of the best-flattered ladies of the century. Born in 1561 and therefore seven years younger than Philip, she received all the education she could stand, including Latin, Greek, and Hebrew, but her charm survived. She became a member of Elizabeth's household and accompanied the Queen on the royal progresses. Her uncle Leicester advanced part of the dowry that enabled her to marry Henry, Earl of Pembroke. "She was very salacious," according to Aubrey, and took some lovers to supplement her husband; but this did not deter Philip from adoring her and writing the *Arcadia* at her request.

Following the example of Sannazaro's *Arcadia* (1504), Sidney imagined, at length and ease, a world of brave princes, exquisite princesses, knightly combats, mystifying disguises, and fascinating scenery. "The loveliness of Urania is the greatest thing the world can show, but the least that may be praised in her";[22] and Palladius had "a piercing wit quite devoid of ostentation, high erected thoughts seated in a heart of courtesy, an eloquence as sweet in the uttering as slow to be uttering, a behavior so noble as gave majesty to adversity";[23] clearly Sidney had read *Euphues*. The story is an amorous maze: Pyrocles disguises himself as a woman to be near the fair Philoclea; she frustrates him by loving him as a sister; her father falls in love with him, thinking him a woman; her mother falls in love with him, perceiving him to be a man; however, everything ends according to the Ten Commandments. Sidney did not take the tale very seriously; he never corrected the sheets he had dashed off for his sister; on his deathbed he ordered them burned. They were preserved, edited, and published (1590), and were for a decade the most admired work in Elizabethan prose.

While writing this romance and the *Defence*, and amid his life as diplomat and soldier, Sidney composed a sonnet sequence that paved the way for Shakespeare's. For this he needed some unsuccessful love. He found it in Penelope Devereux, daughter of the first Earl of Essex; she welcomed his sighs and rhymes as lawful game, but married Baron Rich (1581); Sidney continued to address sonnets to her, even after his own marriage to Frances Walsingham. Few Elizabethans were shocked by this poetic license; no one expected a man to write sonnets to his own wife, whose generosity stilled the muse. The sequence was published (1591) after Sidney's death under the title of *Astrophel and Stella*—star lover and star. It followed the style of Petrarch, whose Laura had strangely anticipated the eyes, hair, brow, cheeks, skin, and lips of Penelope. Sidney was quite aware that his passion was a poetic mechanism; he himself had written: "If I were a mistress, [sonneteers] would never persuade me they were in love."[24] Once accepted as fair play, these sonnets are England's best before Shakespeare's. Even the moon is sick with love:

> With how sad steps, O Moon, thou clim'st the skies,
>   How silently, and with how mean a face!
> What, may it be that even in heavenly place
> That busy Archer his sharp arrows tries?
> Sure, if that long-with-love-acquainted eyes
>   Can judge of love, thou feel'st a lover's case,
>   I read it in thy looks, thy languish'd grace
> To me, that feel the like, thy state descries.
> Then, even of fellowship, O Moon, tell me,
>   Is constant love deemed there but want of wit?
> Are beauties there as proud as here they be?
>   Do they above love to be loved, and yet
> Those lovers scorn whom that love doth possess?
>   Do they call virtue there ungratefulness?[25]

In 1585 Sidney was sent by Elizabeth to aid the Netherland rebels against Spain. Though not yet thirty-one, he was made governor of Flushing. He displeased the pinching Queen by asking for more supplies and better wages for his soldiers, who were being paid in debased currency.[26] He led his men to the capture of Axel (July 6, 1586) and fought in the front of the action. But in the battle of Zutphen (September 22) he was too brave. His horse having been killed in a charge, Sidney leaped upon another and fought his way into the enemy's ranks. A musket ball entered his thigh. His horse, out of control, fled back to Leicester's camp.* Thence Sidney was taken to a private home in Arn-

---

* A story not sufficiently verified relates that when a bottle of water was offered to the wounded Sidney, he handed it to a dying soldier nearby, saying, "Thy need is greater than mine." (Fulke Greville, *Life of the Renowned Sir Philip Sidney*.)[27]

hem. For twenty-five days he suffered under incompetent surgeons. Gangrene set in, and on October 17 the "wonder of our age" (so Spenser mourned him) welcomed death. "I would not change my joy," he said on that last day, "for the empire of the world."[28] When his corpse was brought to London it received such a funeral as England would not see again before Nelson's death.

IV. Edmund Spenser: 1552–99

"Sidney is dead," wrote Spenser, "dead is my friend, dead is the world's delight."[29] It was Sidney who had given Spenser the courage to be a poet. Edmund had begun unpropitiously as the son of a journeyman clothmaker, too distantly related to the aristocratic Spensers to allow the boy to be noticed. Charitable funds sent him to the Merchant Taylors' School, then to Pembroke Hall in Cambridge, where he worked for his board. By seventeen he was writing—even publishing—poetry. Harvey tried to guide him into classic molds and themes; Spenser tried humbly to please him, but soon rebelled against the bonds that uncongenial meters placed upon his muse. In 1579 he showed Harvey the first portion of *The Faerie Queene*; Harvey had no fancy for its medieval allegorical content, no appreciation for its fine metrical form. He advised the poet to abandon the project. Spenser continued it.

It was the gruff and bellicose Harvey who secured for Spenser a place in the service of the Earl of Leicester. There the poet met Sidney, loved him, dedicated to him *The Shepherd's Calendar* (1579). The form echoed Theocritus, but followed the plan of popular almanacs, allotting the tasks of shepherds according to the season of the year. The theme was the unrequited love of the shepherd Colin Clout for the cruel Rosalind. It is not recommended reading, but Sidney's praise won Spenser some acclaim. To butter his bread, the poet accepted the post of secretary to Arthur, Lord Grey, the new Lord Deputy of Ireland (1579); accompanied him to war, and saw and approved Grey's slaughter of the surrendering Irish and Spaniards at Smerwick. After seven years of clerical service to the English government in Ireland he was granted, from the confiscated property of Irish rebels, the Castle of Kilcolman, on the road between Mallow and Limerick, and three thousand acres.

There Spenser settled down to gentleman farming and genteel poetry. He commemorated Sidney's death in an eloquent but lengthy elegy, *Astrophel* (1586). Then he polished and elongated *The Faerie Queene*. Warm with enthusiasm, he crossed to England in 1589, was presented by Raleigh to the Queen, and dedicated the first three "books" to her "to live with the eternity of her fame." To ensure a wide reception he prefaced the poem with laudatory verses addressed to the Countess of Pembroke, Lady Carew, Sir Christopher Hatton, Raleigh, Burghley, Walsingham, Lords Hunsdon, Buckhurst, Grey, and Howard of Effingham, and the earls of Essex, Northumberland, Oxford, Ormonde, and Cumberland. Burghley, feuding with Leicester, called Spenser an idle rhymer, but many hailed him as the greatest poet since Chaucer. The Queen relaxed enough to award him a pension of fifty pounds a year, which Burghley, as Lord Treasurer, delayed in paying. Spenser had hoped for something more substantial. Disappointed, he returned to his Irish castle and continued his idealistic epic amid barbarism, hatred, and fear.

He had planned the poem to be in twelve books; he published three in 1590 and three more in 1596, and proceeded no further; even so *The Faerie Queene* is twice the length of *The Iliad,* thrice that of *Paradise Lost.* Each book was offered as an allegory—of holiness, temperance, chastity, friendship, justice, courtesy; the whole was intended "to fashion a gentleman or noble person in virtuous and gentle discipline"[30] by giving him formative instances; all this accorded with Sidney's conception of poetry as morality conveyed by imagined examples. So dedicated to decency, Spenser could allow himself only a few voluptuous passages; he glances once at a "snowy breast bare to ready spoil,"[31] but goes *ne plus ultra.* Through six cantos he sings the high note of chivalric love as unselfish service to fair women.

To us, who have forgotten chivalry and are bored by knights and confused by allegories, *The Faerie Queene* is at first quaintly delightful, at length unbearable. Its political allusions, which contemporaries enjoyed or resented, are lost upon us; the theological battles that it adumbrates are the subsiding tremors of our infancy; its narratives are at best melodious echoes of Virgil, Ariosto, and Tasso. No poem in the world's literature surpasses *The Faerie Queene* in artificial conceits, awkward inversions, pretentious archaisms and neologisms, and romantic grandiosities unleavened with Ariosto's smile. And yet Keats and Shelley loved Spenser and made him "the Poets' poet." Why? Was it because, here and there, some sensuous beauty of form redeemed a medieval absurdity, some splendor of description adorned an unreality? The new nine-line Spenserian stanza was a difficult medium, and Spenser often startles us with its rounded perfection and flowing ease; but how many times he spoils its reason for a rhyme!

He interrupted the *Queene* to write some briefer poems that perhaps justify his fame. His *Amoretti,* "little loves" in sonnet form (1594), may have been Petrarchan fantasies, or may have reflected his year-long courtship of Elizabeth Boyle. He married her in 1594 and sang his wedding joy in his finest poem, *Epithalamium.* He shares her charms with us unselfishly:

> Tell me, ye merchants' daughters, did ye see
> So fayre a creature in your towne before,
> So sweet, so lovely, so mild as she,
> Adornd with beautyes grace and vertues store,
> Her goodly eyes like saphyres shining bright,
> Her forehead yvory white,
> Her cheekes like apples which the sun hath rudded,
> Her lips like cherryes charming men to byte,
> Her breast like to a bowl of cream uncrudded,
> Her paps like lyllies budded,
> Her snowie necke lyke a marble toure,
> And all her body like a palace fayre . . .

When the wedding and feasting are over he bids his guests depart without delay:

> Now cease, ye damsels, your delights forepast;
> Enough is it that all the day was yours;
> Now day is doen, and night is nighing fast.
> Now bring the bryde into the brydall bowres . . .
> And in her bed her lay;
> Lay her in lilies and in violets,
> And silken curteins over her display,
> And odoured sheets, and Arras coverlets . . .
> But let the night be calme and quietsome,
> Without tempestuous storms or sad afray,
> Lyke as when Jove with fayre Alcmena lay . . .
> And let the mayds and yongmen cease to sing;
> Ne let the woods them answer, nor their echo ring.

Was ever maid brought to fulfillment more melodiously?

Spenser sustained this flight in *Four Hymns* (1596) honoring earthly love, earthly beauty, heavenly love, and heavenly beauty. Following Plato, Ficino, and Castiglione, and leading to Keats's *Endymion*, he cried *peccavi* over his "many lewd layes," and bade his soul pierce through physical loveliness to find and feel the divine beauty that hides in divers degrees in all earthly things.

Living on a volcano of Irish misery, Spenser's life was every day near death. Just before the volcano of resentment erupted again, he wrote in fine prose (for only a poet can write good prose) his *View of the Present State of Ireland,* advocating a better deployment of English funds and forces for the thorough subjugation of the island. In October 1598 the dispossessed Irish of Munster rose in wild revolt, drove out English settlers, and burned down the Castle of Kilcolman. Spenser and his wife barely escaped with their lives and fled to England. Three months later, all funds and passion spent, the poet died (1599). The young Earl of Essex, destined soon to follow him, paid for the funeral; nobles and poets walked in the procession, and threw flowers and elegies into the Westminster Abbey grave.

A craze for sonnets now ran through England, rivaling the drama's fury—nearly all excellent in form, stereotyped in theme and phrase, nearly all addressed to virgins or patrons and bemoaning their strait-laced or tight-fisted frugality. Beauty is urged to let itself be reaped before it rots on the stalk; sometimes an original note intrudes, and the lover promises the lady a child as reward for expeditious conjugation. Every poet seeks and finds a Laura—Daniel's Delia, Lodge's Phillis, Constable's Diana, Fulke Greville's Caelia. Most famous of these sonneteers was Samuel Daniel; however, Ben Jonson, who was more tough than "rare," called him "an honest man, but no poet."[32] Michael Drayton's Pegasus roamed through all forms of poetry with his feet of prose, but one of his sonnets struck a fresh note, stinging the lass out of her stinginess by bidding her farewell—"Since there's no help, come, let us kiss and part!"

All in all, outside the drama, Elizabethan literature was still a generation behind the French. The prose was vigorous, flexible, often involved, verbose, and fanciful, but sometimes moving with a royal dignity or a stately rhythm; it produced no Rabelais or Montaigne. The poetry echoed foreign models timidly, except for the *Epithalamium* and *The Faerie Queene.* Spenser never found an audience on the Continent, but neither did Ronsard in England; poetry makes of language and feeling a music that cannot be heard across the frontiers of speech. Ballads noticed and reached the people more intimately than the poetry of the palace and the court; they were posted on house and tavern walls, and were sung and sold in the streets; "Lord Randall" still moves us with its dirge.[33] Perhaps it was this popular poetry, and not the pretty artifices of the sonneteers, that prepared the Elizabethans to appreciate Shakespeare.

V. The Stage

How, then, did English literature, so negligible in the long drought between Chaucer and Spenser, rise to Shakespeare? Because of wealth growing and spreading; because of a long and fruitful peace, a stimulating and triumphant war; because of foreign literature and travel broadening the English mind. Plautus and Terence were teaching England the art of comedy, Seneca the technique of tragedy; Italian actors played in England (1577f.); a thousand experiments were made; between 1592 and 1642 England saw 435 comedies performed. Farces and interludes developed into comedies; mysteries and moralities gave way to secular tragic dramas as the once sacred myths lost their hold on belief. In 1553 Nicholas Udall produced in *Ralph Roister Doister* the first English comedy in classic form. In 1561 the lawyers of the Inner Temple staged there *Gorboduc,* the first English tragedy in classic form.

For a time that form, descended from Rome, seemed destined to mold the Elizabethan drama. University scholars like Harvey, lawyer-poets like George Gascoyne, men of classical learning like Sidney, pleaded for the observance of the three "unities" in a play: that there should be only one *action* or plot, and that this should occur in one *place*, and represent no longer *time* than a day. These unities, so far as we know, were first formulated by Lodovico Castelvetro (1570) in a commentary on Aristotle's *Poetics*. Aristotle himself requires only unity of action; he recommends that the action should fall "within a single revolution of the sun"; and he adds what might be called unity of mood—that comedy, as "a representation of inferior people," should not be mingled with tragedy, as "a representation of heroic action."[34] Sidney's *Defence of Poesy* took the doctrine of the dramatic unities from Castelvetro and applied it with rigor and yet good humor to Elizabethan plays, in whose highhanded geography

you shall have Asia of the one side, and Africa of the other, and so
many other under kingdoms, that the player, when he comes in, must
ever begin with telling where he is. . . . Now of time they are much
more liberal; for ordinary it is, that two young princes fall in love;
after many traverses she is got with child; delivered of a fair boy;
he . . . groweth a man, falleth in love, and is ready to get another
child; and all this in two hours' space.[35]

France followed the classic rules and produced Racine; England rejected
them, gave its tragic drama romantic freedom and naturalistic scope, and
produced Shakespeare. The ideal of the French Renaissance was order, reason, proportion, propriety; the ideal of Renaissance England was liberty, will,
humor, life. The Elizabethan audience, composed of lordlings, middlings,
and groundlings, had to have a rich and varied diet; it demanded action, not
lengthy reports of hidden actions; it had a belly for laughter and did not mind
gravediggers bandying philosophies with a prince; it had an untamed imagination that could leap from place to place and cross a continent at the bidding of
a sign or the hint of a line. The Elizabethan drama expressed the Elizabethan
English, not the Periclean Greeks or the Bourbon French; hence it became the
national art, while arts that followed alien models took no English root.

The English drama had to fight another battle before it could proceed to
Marlowe and Shakespeare. The nascent Puritan movement rejected the Elizabethan stage as a home of paganism, obscenity, and profanity; it denounced
the presence of women and prostitutes in the audience, and the propinquity of
brothels to the theaters. In 1577 John Northbrooke published a furious diatribe
against "dicing, dancing, plays, and interludes," writing:

I am persuaded that Satan hath not a more speedy way and fitter
school to work and teach his desire, to bring men and women into
his snare of concupiscence and filthy lusts of wicked whoredom, than
those plays and theaters are; and therefore it is necessary that those
places and players should be forbidden and dissolved, and put down
by authority, as the brothels and stews are.[36]

Stephen Gosson's *Schoole of Abuse* was relatively moderate, and acknowledged some plays and actors to be "without rebuke"; but when Lodge replied

to him Gosson abandoned all distinctions, and in *Players Confuted in Five Actions* he described plays as "the food of iniquity, riot, and adultery," and actors as "masters of vice, teachers of wantonness."[37] Critics saw in the comedies demoralizing pictures of vice and rascality, and in tragedies stimulating examples of murder, treachery, and rebellion.[38] In the earlier years of Elizabeth's reign, Sunday was the usual day for plays; trumpets announced them just as church bells called the people to afternoon prayer, and clergymen were dismayed to find their congregations skipping services to crowd the theater. "Will not a filthy play, with the blast of a trumpet," asked a preacher, "sooner call thither a thousand than an hour's tolling of a bell bring to a sermon a hundred?"[39] And North-brooke proceeded: "If you will learn . . . to deceive your husbands, or husbands their wives, how to play the harlot . . . how to flatter, lie . . . murder . . . blaspheme, sing filthy songs . . . shall you not learn, at such interludes, to practice them?"[40]

The dramatists replied with pamphlets, and by making fun of Puritans in the plays, as of Malvolio in *Twelfth Night*. "Dost thou think, because thou art virtuous," asks Sir Toby Belch of the clown in that play, "there shall be no more cakes and ale?" And the clown replies, "Yes, by Saint Anne, and ginger shall be hot i' the mouth, too!"[41] The playwrights, even Shakespeare, continued to salt their tales with violence, rage, incest, adultery, and prostitution; one scene in Shakespeare's *Pericles* shows a room in a brothel, whose general manager complains that his personnel "with continual action are even as good as rotten."[42]

The city authorities of London—some of them Puritans—thought the Puritans had the better of the argument. In 1574 the Common Council forbade the performance of plays except after censorship and licensing; hence Shakespeare's line about "art made tongue-tied by authority."[43] Fortunately, Elizabeth and her Privy Council enjoyed the drama; several lords had companies of players, and under this royal protection and a lax censorship six troupes were licensed to produce plays in the city.

Before 1576 theatrical performances had taken place chiefly on temporary platforms in the courtyards of inns, but in that year James Burbage built the first permanent theater in England. It was called simply The Theatre. To escape the jurisdiction of the London magistrates, it was located just outside the City proper, in the suburb of Shoreditch. Soon other theaters rose: the Curtain (1577?), the Blackfriars (1596), the Fortune (1599). In this last year Richard and Cuthbert Burbage demolished their father's Theatre and raised the famous Globe in Southwark, just across the Thames. It was octagonal in outer form but probably circular within; hence Shakespeare could call it "this wooden O."[44] All the London theaters were of wood before 1623. Most of them were large amphitheaters, seating some two thousand spectators in several tiers of encircling galleries, and allowing another thousand to stand in the "yard" around the stage; these latter were the "groundlings," whom Hamlet rebuked for their "dumb-shows and noise."[45] In 1599 the price of standing room was one penny, of a seat in the galleries two or three pence; a little more bought a seat on the stage. This was a spacious platform projecting from one wall into the center of the yard. At its rear was a "tiring," or attiring, room, where the actors donned their costumes and the "stage-keeper" managed the properties. These included tombs, skulls, box trees, rosebushes, caskets, curtains, caldrons, ladders, weapons, implements, phials of blood, and some severed heads. Machines could let gods and goddesses down from heaven or raise ghosts or witches up through the floor; "rain" could be produced at the pull of a string, and "double girts" could hang the sun in the sky.[46] These properties had to make up for the absence of scenery; the open and uncurtained stage forbade any rapid change of the setting. In recompense the action transpired in the very midst of the audience, which could almost feel itself a part of the event.

The audience was no minor portion of the spectacle. Caterers sold tobacco, apples, nuts, and pamphlets to the spectators; in later days, if we may believe the Puritan William Prynne, the women were offered pipes.[47] Women came to the plays in considerable number, not deterred by pulpit warnings that such mingling was an invitation to seduction. Sometimes—the class war interrupting the drama—the groundlings threw the leavings of their collations at the dandies on the stage. To understand an Elizabethan play we must remember that audience: the sentiment that welcomed a love story, the hearty humor that wanted clowns with kings, the swagger that relished rhetoric, the rough vitality that enjoyed scenes of violence—and the nearness of the three-sided stage, inviting soliloquies and asides.

Actors abounded. Strolling players might be seen in almost any town on festival days, performing in the village square, the tavern courtyard, a barn or a palace, and at wakes. There were in Shakespeare's day no actresses; female parts were played by boys, and sometimes an Elizabethan audience could see a boy representing a woman disguised as a boy or a man. In the aristocratic public schools the students presented dramas as part of their training. Companies of such boy actors competed with adult troupes by giving performances in private theaters for public and paying audiences. Shakespeare complained of this competition,[48] and after 1626 it ceased.

To avoid being classed as vagrants, the adult actors were organized in companies under the patronage and protection of opulent nobles—Leicester, Sussex, Warwick, Oxford, Essex. The Lord Admiral had a company; so did the Lord Chamberlain. The actors were paid by their patrons only for performances in the baronial halls; for the rest they lived precariously on the earnings of their shares in their company. Shares were unevenly divided; the manager took a third, and the leading actors received the lion's share of the rest. Richard Burbage, the most famous of these "stars," left property bringing £300 a year; his rival, Edward Alleyn, founded and endowed Dulwich College, London. The celebrities of the stage were rewarded also with public idolatry and a succession of mistresses. In his diary for March 1602, John Manningham tells a famous story:

> Once upon a time, when Burbage played *Richard III,* there was a citizen gone so far in liking with him that before she went from the play she appointed him to come that night unto her by the name of Richard III. Shakespeare, overhearing their conclusion, went before, was entertained and at his game before Burbage came. Then, message being brought that Richard III was at the door, Shakespeare caused return to be made that William the Conqueror was before Richard III.[49]

VI. Christopher Marlowe: 1564–93

The dramatists did not fare so well as the actors. They sold their plays outright to one of the theatrical companies for some four to eight pounds; they retained no rights to the manuscript, and usually the company prevented publication of the text lest it be used by a rival troupe. Sometimes a stenographer would record a play while it was being acted, and a printer would publish from this report a pirated and garbled edition, which brought the author nothing but hypertension. Such editions did not always bear the author's name; hence some plays, like *Arden of Faversham* (1592), have survived centuries of anonymity.

After 1590 the English stage was alive with plays of some moment, though only a few exceeded a day's run. John Lyly graced his comedies with charming lyrics; the fairy enchantments of his *Endymion* prepared for *A Midsummer Night's Dream.* Robert Greene's *Friar Bacon and Friar Bungay* (1589?), dealing with the marvels of magic, may have exchanged ideas with Marlowe's *Doctor Faustus* (1588? 1592?). Thomas Kyd's *Spanish Tragedy* (1589?) told a bloody tale of homicide, leaving hardly anyone alive at the end; its success inspired the Elizabethan playwrights to rival the generals and the doctors in shedding blood. Here, as in *Hamlet,* we have a ghost demanding revenge, and a play within a play.

Christopher Marlowe was christened just two months before Shakespeare. Son of a Canterbury shoemaker, he might have missed a university education had not Archbishop Parker given him a scholarship. During his college years he was engaged as a spy by Sir Francis Walsingham to check on plots against the Queen. His study of the classics unsettled his theology, and his acquaintance with Machiavelli's ideas gave his skepticism a cynical turn. Moving to London after receiving his M.A. (1587), he shared a room with Thomas Kyd, and joined the freethinking circle of Raleigh and Harriot. Richard Barnes, a government agent, reported to the Queen (June 3, 1593) that Marlowe had declared that "the first beginning of religion was only to keep men in awe . . . that Christ was a bastard . . . that if there be any good religion, then it is in the Papists, because the service of God is performed with more ceremonies . . . that all Protestants are hypocritical asses . . . that all the New Testament is filthily written." Furthermore, said Barnes, "this Marlowe . . . almost in any company he cometh, persuadeth men to atheism, willing them not to be afraid of bugbears and hobgoblins, and utterly scorning both God and His ministers."[50] For good measure Barnes (who was hanged in 1594 for a "degrading" offense) added that Marlowe defended homosexuality.[51] Robert Greene, in his dying appeal to his friends to reform, described Marlowe as given to blasphemy and atheism.[52] And Thomas Kyd, arrested on May 12, 1593, stated (under torture) that Marlowe was "irreligious, intemperate, and of cruel heart," accustomed to "jest at the divine Scriptures" and "gibe at prayers."[53]

Long before these reports were made to the government, Marlowe had written and staged powerful dramas hinting at his unbelief. Apparently *Tamburlaine the Great* was composed in college; it was produced in the year of his graduation, and its exaltation of knowledge, beauty, and power reveal the Faustian temper of the poet.

> Our souls, whose faculties can comprehend
> The wondrous architecture of the world,
> And measure every wandering planet's course,
> Still climbing after knowledge infinite,
> And always moving as the restless spheres,
> Will us to wear ourselves, and never rest
> Until we reach the ripest fruit of all.[54]

The two plays about Timur are crude with immaturity. The characterization is too simplified—each person is one quality; so Tamburlaine is pride of power, and the pride is rather the conceit of a collegian swollen with undigested novelties than the calm self-confidence of a victorious sovereign. The story runs on rivers of blood, obstructed with improbabilities. The style inclines to bombast. What, then, made this play the greatest success, so far, of the Elizabethan stage? Presumably its violence, bloodshed, and bombast, but also, we may believe, its heresies and its eloquence. Here were thoughts more boldly ranging, images more deeply felt, phrases more aptly turned, than the Elizabethan stage had yet heard; here were scores of those "mighty lines" that Jonson was to praise, and passages of such melodious beauty that Swinburne thought them supreme in their kind.

Quickened with acclaim, Marlowe wrote with all the intensity of his spirit his greatest play, *The Tragical History of Doctor Faustus* (1588?). Medieval ethics, perhaps recognizing that "the joy of understanding is a sad joy,"[55] and that "in much wisdom is much grief,"[56] had branded the unchecked lust for knowledge as a great sin; yet medieval aspirations had braved this prohibition, even to calling upon magic and Satan for the secrets and powers of nature. Marlowe represents Faustus as a learned and famous physician of Wittenberg who frets at the limits of his knowledge, and dreams of magic means that will make him omnipotent:

> All things that move between the quiet poles
> Shall be at my command . . .
> Shall I make spirits fetch me what I please,
> Resolve me of all ambiguities,
> Perform what desperate enterprise I will?
> I'll have them fly to India for gold,

> Ransack the oceans for orient pearl,
> And search all corners of the new-found world
> For pleasant fruits and princely delicates;
> I'll have them read me strange philosophy,
> And tell the secrets of all foreign kings.[57]

At his call Mephistophilis appears and offers him twenty-four years of lim-itless pleasure and power if he will sell his soul to Lucifer. Faustus agrees, and signs the contract with blood from his cut arm. His first requisition is the fairest maid in Germany to come to be his wife, "for I am wanton and lasciv-ious"; but Mephistophilis dissuades him from marriage and suggests instead a succession of courtesans. Faustus calls for Helen of Troy; she comes, and he swells into ecstasy.

> Was this the face that launch'd a thousand ships,
> And burnt the topless towers of Ilium?
> Sweet Helen, make me immortal with a kiss. . . .
> O, thou art fairer than the evening air
> Clad in the beauty of a thousand stars . . .

The final scene is rendered with great power: the despairing appeal to God for mercy, for at least a term to damnation—"Let Faustus live in hell a thou-sand years, a hundred thousand, and at last be sav'd!"—and the disappearance of Faustus, on the stroke of midnight, in a fury of clashing, blinding clouds. The chorus sings his epitaph—and Marlowe's:

> Cut is the branch that might have grown full straight,
> And burnéd is Apollo's laurel-bough.

In these plays Marlowe might have purged his own passions for knowledge, beauty, and power; the catharsis, or cleansing effect, that Aristotle ascribed to tragic drama could better purge the author than the audience. In *The Jew of Malta* (1589?) the will to power takes the intermediate form of greed for wealth, and defends itself in the Prologue spoken by "Machiavel":

Admired I am of those that hate me most.
Though some speak openly [publicly] against my books,
Yet they will read me, and thereby attain
To Peter's chair; and when they cast me off,
Are poison'd by my climbing followers.
I count religion but a childish toy,
And hold there is no sin but ignorance.

Barabas the moneylender is again one quality personified, greed raised to hatred of all who hinder his gains, an unpleasant caricature redeemed by majestic vices.

I learn'd in Florence how to kiss my hand,
Heave up my shoulders when they call me dog,
And duck as low as any barefoot friar,
Hoping to see them starve upon a stall.[58]

Contemplating his jewels, he thrills at their "infinite riches in a little room."[59] When his daughter recovers his lost money bags he cries out, in a confusion of affections anticipating Shylock, "O my girl, my gold, my fortune, my felicity!"[60] There is a power, almost a fury, in this play, a sting of epithet and force of phrase, that lead Marlowe now and then to the very verge of Shakespeare.

He came still closer in *Edward II* (1592). The young King, just crowned, sends for his "Greek friend" Gaveston, and lavishes kisses, offices, and wealth upon him; the neglected nobles rise and depose Edward, who, driven to philosophy, calls to his remaining comrades:

Come, Spencer, come, Baldock, come sit down by me;
Make trial now of that philosophy
That in our famous nurseries of arts
Thou suck'dst from Plato and from Aristotle.

From this well-constructed drama, this poetry of sensitivity, imagination, and power, these characters distinctly and consistently drawn, this King so mingled of pederasty and pride and yet forgivable in his young simplicity and grace, it was but a step to Shakespeare's *Richard II,* which followed it by a year.

What would this twenty-seven-year-old dramatist have accomplished had he matured? At that age Shakespeare was writing trifles like *Love's Labour's Lost, Two Gentlemen of Verona,* and *A Comedy of Errors.* In *The Jew of Malta* Marlowe was learning to make every scene advance an orderly plot; in *Edward II* he was learning to conceive character as more than a single quality personified. In a year or two he might have purged his plays of bombast and melodrama; he might have risen to a broader philosophy, a greater sympathy with the myths and foibles of mankind. His distorting defect was lack of humor; there is no genial laughter in his plays, and the incidental comedy does not, as in Shakespeare, serve its proper function in tragedy—to ease the hearer's tension before lifting him to greater tragic intensities. He could appreciate the physical beauty of women, but not their tenderness, solicitude, and grace; there is no vivid female character in his plays, not even in the unfinished *Dido, Queen of Carthage.*

What remains is the poetry. Sometimes the orator overcame the poet, and declamation shouted "a great and thundering speech."[61] But in many a scene the lucid verse flows with such vivid imagery or melody of speech that one could mistake the lines for some Shakespearean stream of fantasy. In Marlowe blank verse proved itself as the English drama's proper vehicle, sometimes monotonous, but usually varied in its rhythm, and achieving a seemingly natural continuity.

His own "tragical history" was now suddenly closed. On May 30, 1593, three government spies, Ingram Frizer, Nicholas Skeres, and Robert Poley, joined the poet—perhaps himself still a spy—at dinner in a house or tavern in Deptford, a few miles from London. According to the report of William Danby, coroner, Frizer and Marlowe "uttered one to the other divers malicious words for the reason that they could not . . . agree about the payment" for the meal. Marlowe snatched a dagger from Frizer's belt and struck him with it, inflicting some superficial cuts. Frizer seized Marlowe's hand, turned the weapon upon him, and "gave the said Christopher then and there a mortal wound over his right eye, of the depth of two inches . . . of which the aforesaid Christopher Morley then and there instantly died"; the blade had reached the brain. Frizer, arrested, pleaded self-defense, and he was released after a month. Marlowe was buried on June 1, in a grave now unknown.[62] He was twenty-nine years old.

He left, besides the *Dido,* two fragments of high excellence. *Hero and Leander* is a romantic version, in heroic couplets, of the story Musaeus had told, in the fifth century, of the youth who swam the Hellespont to keep a tryst. "The

Passionate Shepherd to His Love" is one of the great Elizabethan lyrics. Shakespeare made handsome acknowledgments to Marlowe by putting snatches of that poem into the mouth of Sir Hugh Evans in *The Merry Wives of Windsor* (III, i), and by a tender reference in *As You Like It* (III, v):

> Dead Shepherd, now I find thy saw of might,
> "Who ever loved that loved not at first sight?"

—which is line 76 of *Hero and Leander.*

Marlowe's achievement was immense in its brief moment. He made blank verse a flexible and powerful speech. He saved the Elizabethan stage from the classicists and the Puritans. He gave their definite forms to the drama of ideas and that of English history. He left his mark on Shakespeare in *The Merchant of Venice,* in *Richard II,* in love poetry, and in a tendency to magniloquent rhetoric. Through Marlowe, Kyd, Lodge, Greene, and Peele the way had been opened; the form, structure, style, and material of the Elizabethan drama had been prepared. Shakespeare was not a miracle, he was a fulfillment.

CHAPTER IV

WILLIAM SHAKESPEARE

1564–1616

I. Youth: 1564–85

Let us, for the adequacy of this record, summarize what half the world knows about Shakespeare. Now that devout scholarship has rummaged among his relics for three centuries, it is remarkable how much we do know—far more than enough to set aside, as not meriting debate, all doubts about his authorship of nearly all the plays ascribed to his name.

However, we are not sure about his name. Elizabeth allowed more freedom of spelling than of religion; the same document might use different spellings of the same word, and a man might sign his name variously according to his haste or mood. So contemporaries wrote Marlowe as Marlo, Marlin, Marley, Morley; and Shakespeare's six surviving signatures appear to read Willm Shaksp, William Shakespē, Wm Shakspē, William Shakspere, Willm Shakspere, and William Shakspeare; the now prevalent spelling has no warrant in his autographs. The last three signatures are all on the same will.

His mother was Mary Arden, of an old Warwickshire family. She brought to John Shakespeare, son of her father's tenant, a goodly dowry in cash and land, and gave him eight children, of whom William was the third. John became a prosperous businessman in Stratford on Avon, bought two houses, served his town as ale taster, constable, alderman, and bailiff, and contributed liberally to the poor. After 1572 his fortunes fell; he was sued for thirty pounds, he failed to answer, and an order was issued for his arrest. In 1580, for reasons unknown, he was required by the court to give security against a breach of the peace. In 1592 he was listed as "not coming monthly to church according to her Majesty's laws"; some have concluded from this that he was a "recusant" Catholic, others that he was a Puritan, others that he dared not face his creditors.

William later restored his father's finances, and when the father died (1601) two houses in Henley Street remained in the Shakespeare name.

The Stratford parish church registered William's baptism on April 26, 1564. Nicholas Rowe, his first biographer, recorded in 1709 the Stratford tradition, now generally credited, that the father "bred him . . . for some time at a free school . . . But the narrowness of his circumstances, and the want of his assistance at home, forced his father to withdraw him from thence."[1] Ben Jonson, in the elegy prefixed to the First Folio edition of the plays, addressed his dead rival, "Thou hadst small Latin and less Greek." Apparently the Greek dramatists remained Greek to Shakespeare, but he learned enough Latin to clutter his lesser plays with Latin odds and ends and bilingual puns. If he had learned more he might have become another scholar, laborious and unknown. London was to be his school.

Another tradition, recorded by Richard Davies about 1681, described young William as "much given to all unluckiness in stealing venison and rabbits, particularly from Sir [Thomas] Lucy, who had him oft whipped and sometimes imprisoned."[2] On November 27, 1582, when said miscreant was eighteen, he and Anne Hathaway, then about twenty-five, obtained a marriage license. Circumstances indicate that Anne's friends compelled Shakespeare to marry her.[3] In May 1583, six months after the marriage, a daughter was born to them, whom they named Susanna. Later Anne presented the poet with twins, who were christened Hamnet and Judith on February 2, 1585. Probably toward the end of that year Shakespeare left his wife and children. We have no record of him between 1585 and 1592, when we find him an actor in London.

II. Development: 1592–95

The first reference to him there is uncomplimentary. On September 3, 1592, Robert Greene issued from his deathbed a warning to his friends that they were being displaced in the London theater by "an upstart Crow, beautified with our feathers, that with his *Tygers hart wrapt in a Players hyde* [parody of a line from *3 Henry VI*] supposes he is as well able to bombast out a blanke verse as the best of you; and being an absolute *Johannes fac totum,* is in his own conceit the only Shake-scene in a countrey."[4] This morsel was prepared for the press as part of *Greene's Groatsworth of Wit* by Henry Chettle, who in a later epistle offered an apology to *one* of the two persons (probably Marlowe and Shakespeare) who had been attacked by Greene:

With neither of them that take offence was I acquainted, and with one of them I care not if I never be. [As to] the other . . . I am sorry . . . because myself have seen his demeanour no less civil than he was excellent in the quality [calling] he professes. Besides, divers of worship have reported his uprightness of dealing, which argues his honesty, and his facetious [agreeable] grace in writing, that approves his art.[5]

There seems no doubt that Greene's attack and Chettle's apology referred to Shakespeare. By 1592, then, the former poacher of Stratford had become an actor and playwright in the capital. Dowdall (1693) and Rowe (1709) related that he "was received into the playhouse as a servitor" in "a very mean rank,"[6] which is probable. But he fretted with ambition, "desiring this man's art and that man's scope," with "not a thought but turned on dignity."[7] Soon he was acting minor parts, making himself "a motley to the view";[8] then he played the kindly Adam in *As You Like It* and the Ghost in *Hamlet.* Probably he rose to higher roles, for his name headed the list of actors in Jonson's *Every Man in His Humour* (1598), and in Jonson's *Sejanus* (1604) he and Richard Burbage were specified as the "principal tragedians."[9] By the end of 1594 he was a shareholder in the Chamberlain's company of players. It was not as a dramatist, but as an actor and shareholder in a theatrical company, that Shakespeare made his fortune.

However, by 1591 he was writing plays. He seems to have begun as a play doctor, editing, touching up, and adapting manuscripts for his company. From such work he passed to collaboration; the three parts of *Henry VI* (1592) appear to have been such a composite production. Thereafter he wrote plays at the rate of almost two per year—thirty-six or thirty-eight in all. Several early ones, *A Comedy of Errors* (1592), *Two Gentlemen of Verona* (1594), and *Love's Labour's Lost* (1594) are lighthearted trifles, frothy with now tiresome badinage; it is instructive to see that Shakespeare had to grow into greatness by hard work. But the growth was rapid. Taking a hint from Marlowe's *Edward II,* he found in English history many a dramatic theme. *Richard II* (1595) equaled the earlier play; *Richard III* (1592) had already surpassed it. In some measure he fell into the fault of making a whole man out of one quality—the hunchback King out of treacherous and murderous ambition; but he lifted the play now and then out of Marlowe's reach by depth of analysis, intensity of feeling, and flashes of brilliant phrase; soon "A horse! A horse! My kingdom for a horse!" was a London cliché.

Then, in *Titus Andronicus* (1593), genius flagged; imitation took the lead and presented a repulsive dance of death. Titus kills his son, and others kill his son-in-law, on the stage; a bride, raped behind the scenes, comes on the boards with her hands cut off, her tongue cut out, her mouth bubbling blood; a traitor chops off Titus' hand before the groundlings' avid eyes; the severed heads of two of Titus' sons are displayed; a nurse is killed on stage. Reverent critics have labored to burden collaborators with part or all of the responsibility for this slaughter, on the mistaken theory that Shakespeare could not write nonsense. He wrote reams of it.

It was at about this point in his development that he composed his narrative poems and his sonnets. Perhaps the plague that caused the closing of all London theaters between 1592 and 1594 left him with penurious leisure, and he thought it advisable to cast a hopeful line to some patron of poetry. In 1593 he dedicated *Venus and Adonis* to Henry Wriothesley, third Earl of Southampton. Lodge had adapted the tale from Ovid's *Metamorphoses;* Shakespeare adapted it from Lodge. The Earl was young, handsome, and addicted to venery; perhaps the poem was spiced to his taste. Much of it seems jejune to jaded years; but in this proliferated seduction there are passages of sensuous beauty (e.g., lines 679–708) such as England had rarely read before. Encouraged by public applause and a gift from Southampton, Shakespeare issued in 1594 *The Ravyshement of Lucrece,* where the seduction was accomplished with a greater economy of verse. This was the last of his voluntary publications.

About 1593 he began to write, but kept from the press, the sonnets that first established his pre-eminence among the poets of his time. Technically the most nearly perfect of Shakespeare's works, they borrow heavily from the Petrarchan treasury of sonnet themes—the transitory beauty of the beloved, her cruel hesitations and inconstancy, the dreary crawl of unused time, the jealousies and the panting thirst of the lover, and the poet's boast that in his rhymes the lady's loveliness and fame would shine forever. Even some phrases and epithets are appropriated from Constable, Daniel, Watson, and other sonneteers, who themselves were links in a chain of pilferings. No one has succeeded in arranging the sonnets in any consistent narrative order; they were the casual labor of scattered days. We must not take too seriously their hazy plot—the love of the poet for a young man, his passion for a "dark lady" of the court, her rejection of him and acceptance of his friend, the winning of that friend by a rival poet, and Shakespeare's despairing dalliance with thoughts of death. It is possible that Shakespeare, acting before the court, cast looks of distant longing at the Queen's ladies in waiting, so intoxicatingly perfumed and gowned; it is unlikely that he ever spoke to them or followed the scent to the prey. One such lady, Mary Fitton, became the mistress of the Earl of Pembroke. She appears to have been blond, but this may have been merely a passing dye. However, she was unmarried, whereas Shakespeare's lady broke her "bed-vow" in loving the poet and his "boy."[10]

In 1609 Thomas Thorpe published the sonnets, apparently without Shakespeare's consent. As the author supplied no dedication, Thorpe provided one, to the puzzlement of centuries: "To the onlie begetter of these ensuing sonnets Mr. W. H. all happinesse and that eternitie promised by our ever-living poet, wisheth the well-wishing adventurer in setting forth." The signature, "T. T.," presumably meant Thomas Thorpe, but who was "W. H."? The initials might mean William Herbert, third Earl of Pembroke, who had seduced Mary Fitton and was destined, with his brother Philip, to receive the dedication of the posthumous First Folio as "the greatest Maecenas, to learned men, of any peer of his time or since." Herbert was only thirteen when the sonnets began (1593), but their composition extended to 1598, by which time Pembroke was ripe for love and patronage. The poet speaks ardently of his "love" for the "boy"; "love" was then often used for friendship; but Sonnet 20 calls the lad "the master-mistress of my passion" and ends with an erotic play on words; and Sonnet 128 (apparently addressed to the "lovely boy" of 126) talks of amorous ecstasy. Some Elizabethan poets were literary pederasts, capable of winding themselves up to rapturous love for any man of means.

The important point about the sonnets is not their story but their beauty. Many of them (e.g., 29, 30, 33, 55, 64, 66, 71, 97, 106, 117) are rich in lines whose depth of thought, warmth of feeling, glow of imagery, or grace of phrase has made them ring for centuries through the English-speaking world.

III. Mastery: 1595–1608

But the artifices and restraint of the sonnet clipped the wings of fancy, and Shakespeare must have rejoiced in the fluent freedom of blank verse when, still young and ardent, he let himself go in one of the great love poems of all time. The story of Romeo and Juliet came to England from the *novelle* of Masuccio and Bandello; Arthur Brooke rephrased it in narrative verse (1562);

and Shakespeare, following Brooke and perhaps an earlier play on the subject, staged his *Romeo and Juliet* about 1595. The style is cloyed with conceits that may have clung to his pen from his sonneteering, the metaphors run wild, Romeo is weakly drawn beside the effervescent Mercutio, and the denouement is a concatenation of absurdities. But who that remembers youth, or has a dream left in his soul, can hear that honeyed music of romance without jettisoning all canons of credibility and rising breathless at the poet's bidding into this world of precipitate ardor, trembling solicitude, and melodious death?

Almost yearly now Shakespeare won a dramatic victory. On June 7, 1594, Elizabeth's Jewish physician, Rodrigo López, was executed on the charge of having accepted a bribe to poison the Queen. The evidence was inconclusive, and Elizabeth long hesitated to sign the death warrant; but the London populace took his guilt for granted, and anti-Semitism ran hot in the pubs.[11] Possibly Shakespeare was moved or commissioned to tap this mood by writing *The Merchant of Venice* (1596?). He shared in some measure the feelings of his audience;* he allowed Shylock to be represented as a comic character in slovenly dress and with a vast artificial nose; he rivaled Marlowe in bringing out the moneylender's hatred and greed; but he gave Shylock some lovable qualities that must have made the injudicious grieve, and he put into his mouth so bold a statement of the case for the Jews that competent critics still debate whether Shylock is pictured as more sinned against than sinning.[12] Here, above all, Shakespeare showed his skill in weaving into one harmonious tapestry divers threads of story coming from the Orient and Italy; and he made the converted Jessica the recipient of such moonstruck poetry as only a spirit of supreme sensitivity could have conceived.

For five years Shakespeare gave himself chiefly to comedy; perhaps he had learned that our harassed species reserves its richest rewards for those who can distract it with laughter or imagination. *A Midsummer Night's Dream* is powerful nonsense, only redeemed by Mendelssohn; *All's Well That Ends Well* is not salvaged by Helena; *Much Ado about Nothing* lives up to its title; *Twelfth Night* is bearable only because Viola makes a very handsome boy; and *The Taming of the Shrew* is boisterously incredible; shrews are never tamed. All these plays were potboilers, sops to the groundlings, ways of keeping the herd in the pit and the wolf from the door.

---

* Cf. *Two Gentlemen of Verona,* V, ii, 3,6; *Merry Wives of Windsor,* II, i.

But with the two parts of *Henry IV* (1597–98) the great magician rose again to mastery, and mingled clowns and princes—Falstaff and Pistol, Hotspur and Prince Hal—with a success that would have given Sidney pause. London relished this serving of royal history garnished with rogues and tarts. Shakespeare carried on with *Henry V* (1599), at once moving and amusing his audience with dying Falstaff's "babbling o' green fields," rousing it with the fanfare of Agincourt, and delighting it with the bilingual courtship of Princess Kate by the invincible King. If we may believe Rowe, the Queen was not content to let Falstaff rest; she bade his creator revive him and show him in love;[13] and John Dennis (1702), relating the same story, adds that Elizabeth desired the miracle to be accomplished in two weeks. If all this be true, *The Merry Wives of Windsor* was an astonishing tour de farce; for though the play is noisy with slapstick and punctured with puns, it has Falstaff at the height of his verve, until he is cast into the river in a hamper of wash. The Queen, we are told, was pleased.

It is startling to find a dramatist capable of producing in one season (1599–1600?) such nugatory nonsense as this and then so ethereal an idyl as *As You Like It.* Perhaps because it took a lead from Lodge's novel *Rosalynde* (1590), the play has a music of refinement in it—still hobbled with arid badinage, but tender and delicate in feeling, gay and elegant in speech. What pretty friendship is here between Celia and Rosalind—and Orlando carving Rosalind's name into the bark of trees, "hanging odes upon hawthorns and elegies on brambles"; what a Fortunatus' fund of eloquence spilling immortal phrases on every page—and songs that have been welcome on a million lips: "Under the greenwood tree," "Blow, blow, thou winter wind," "It was a lover and his lass." The whole outpour is such delectable foolery and sentiment as cannot be matched in any literature.

But amid this cornucopia of sweets Monsieur Melancholy Jaques mingles some bitter fruit, announcing that life's "wide and universal theatre presents more woeful pageants than do the scene we play" upon the boards, that nothing is certain except death, usually after a toothless, eyeless, tasteless old age.

> And so, from hour to hour we ripe and ripe,
> And then from hour to hour we rot and rot,
> And thereby hangs a tale.[14]

So the Swan of Avon warned us that *As You Like It* was the swan song of his gaiety, and that thereafter, till further notice, he proposed to flay the surface of life and show us its bloody reality. Now he would open his vein of tragedy and mingle gall with his ambrosia.

In 1579 Sir Thomas North's Plutarch exposed a treasure trove of drama. Shakespeare took three of the *Lives* and molded them into *The Tragedy of Julius Caesar* (1599?). He found North's translation so spirited that he appropriated several passages word for word, merely measuring the prose into blank verse; however, the speech of Antony over Caesar's corpse was the poet's own invention, a masterpiece of oratory and subtlety, and the sole defense he allows to Caesar. His admiration for Southampton, Pembroke, and the young Essex may have moved him to see the assassination from the standpoint of endangered and conspiring aristocrats; so Brutus becomes the center of the play. We, who have Mommsen's details as to the odorous corruption of the "democracy" that Caesar overthrew, are more inclined to sympathize with Caesar, and are taken aback to find the title character dead at the outset of Act III. The past is helpless in the hands of the present, which repeatedly remolds it to the hour's whim.

In writing *Hamlet* (1600?), as in *Julius Caesar,* Shakespeare had the aid and challenge of an earlier play on the theme; a *Hamlet* had been performed in London only six years before. We do not know how much he took from that lost tragedy, or from François de Belleforest's *Histoires tragiques* (1576), or from the *Historia Danica* (1514) of the Danish historian Saxo Grammaticus; nor can we say if Shakespeare read *Of the Diseases of Melancholy,* the recent English translation of a French medical work by Du Laurens. Doubting stoically every attempt to turn the plays into autobiography, we are yet warranted in asking whether some personal grief—in addition to the sobering of time—entered into the pessimism that cried out in *Hamlet* and grew bitterer in succeeding plays. It might have been a second disillusionment with love. Was it the first arrest of Essex (June 5, 1600), or the collapse of Essex' revolt, the arrest of Essex and Southampton, the execution of Essex (February 25, 1601)? Presumably these events moved the sensitive poet who had so warmly praised Essex in the prologue to the last act of *Henry V* and, in the dedication to *Lucrece,* had pledged himself to Southampton forever. In any case, Shakespeare's greatest plays were written during or after these calamities. They are subtler in plot, deeper in thought, more magnificent in language than their predecessors, but also they voice against life the bitterest reproaches in all literature. Hamlet's vacillating will, and almost his "noble and most sovereign reason," are disordered by discovering the reality and the nearness of evil, and by feeding on the venom of revenge till he himself sinks to feelingless cruelty, and sends Ophelia not to a nunnery but to madness and death. In the end the slaughter is general. Only Horatio survives, too simple to be mad.

Meanwhile Elizabeth too had found the final balm, and James VI of Scotland became James I of England. Soon after his accession he confirmed and extended the privileges of Shakespeare's company, which became "the King's Men." Shakespeare's plays were regularly performed before the King and met with ample royal encouragement. The three seasons between 1604 and 1607 brought the poet to the fullness of his genius and his bitterness. *Othello* (1604?) is as powerful as it is incredible. The audience was moved to pity by the devotion and the death of Desdemona and fascinated by the intelligent malignancy of Iago; but in picturing such unmixed and unmotived evil in a man Shakespeare fell into Marlowe's fault of monolithic characters, and even Othello, despite his union of generalship and stupidity, lacks that rich admixture of elements which makes Hamlet and Lear, Brutus and Antony human.

Macbeth (1605?) is a still more macabre contemplation of unmitigated evil. Shakespeare could cite Holinshed for the stark facts, but he made the story darker with his passionate disillusionment. The mood reached its nadir, the art its apogee, in *King Lear* (1606?). The tale had been elaborated by Geoffrey of Monmouth, carried down by Holinshed, and lately staged by a now unknown dramatist in *The True Chronicle of King Lear* (1605); plots were common property. The earlier play had followed Holinshed in giving Lear a happy ending, through reunion with Cordelia and restoration to the throne; Shakespeare is apparently guilty of the King's madness and dethroned death, and he added the bloody blinding of Gloucester on the stage. Bitterness is the organ tone of the play. Lear bids fornication thrive and adultery increase, "for I lack soldiers";[15] all virtue, in his darkened view, is a front for lechery, all government is bribery, all history is humanity preying upon itself. He goes mad perceiving the profundity and the apparent victory of evil, and he sheds all faith in a sustaining Providence.

Antony and Cleopatra (1607?) reaches lesser heights and depths. There is something nobler in Antony's defeat than in Lear's rage, something more believable and bearable in the Roman's infatuation with the Egyptian Queen than in the Briton's unlikely cruelty to a daughter absurdly frank; and Cleopatra, cowardly in battle, is magnificent in suicide. Here too Shakespeare had previous plays to work on, and again he bettered them, renewing and brightening the oft-told tale with subtler analyses of character and the unwearied magic and sparkle of his speech.

In *Timon of Athens* (1608?) the pessimism is sardonic and unrelieved. Lear aims his shafts at women, but feels some tardy pity for mankind; the hero of *Coriolanus* (1608?) despises the people as the fickle, sycophantic, brainless spawn of carelessness; but Timon denounces all, high or low, and curses civilization itself as having demoralized mankind. Plutarch in his life of Antony had mentioned Timon as a famous misanthrope; Lucian had put him in a dialogue; and an English play had been written about him some eight years before Shakespeare, with an unknown collaborator, took up the theme. Timon is an Athenian millionaire, surrounded by receptive flattering friends. When he loses his money and sees his friends vanish overnight, he kicks the dust of civilization from his feet and retires—a Jaques in dour earnest—to a forest solitude, where, he hopes, he "shall find the unkindest beasts more kinder than mankind."[16] He wishes Alcibiades were a dog, "that I might love thee something."[17] He lives on roots, digs, finds gold. Friends appear again; he drives them off with lashing scorn; but when prostitutes come he gives them gold, on condition that they will infect as many men as possible with venereal disease:

> Consumptions sow
> In hollow bones of man; strike their sharp shins,
> And mar men's spurring [marriages]. Crack the
>   lawyer's voice,
> That he may never more false title plead,
> And sound his quillets [quibbles] shrilly; hoar
>   the flamen [priest],
> That scolds against the quality of flesh,
> And not believes himself; down with the nose,
> Down with it flat; take the bridge quite away . . .
> And let the unscarr'd braggarts of the war
> Derive some pain from you: plague all;
> That your activity may defeat and quell
> The source of all erection.—There's more gold;
> Do you damn others, and let this damn you . . .[18]

In an ecstasy of hatred he bids nature cease to breed men, and hopes that vicious beasts may multiply to wipe out the human race. The excesses of this misanthropy make it seem unreal; we cannot believe that Shakespeare felt this ridiculous superiority to sinful men, this cowardly incapacity to stomach life. Such a *reductio ad nauseam* suggests that the disease was purging itself, and that Shakespeare would soon smile again.

IV. Artistry

How did a man of so little education come to write plays of such varied erudition? But it was not really erudition. In no field except psychology was it extensive or accurate. Shakespeare knew the Bible only so far as his boyhood studies might have opened it to him; his Biblical references are incidental and ordinary. His classical learning was casual, careless, and apparently confined to translations. He knew most of the pagan deities, even the lesser or looser ones, but this knowledge could have been from the English version of Ovid's *Metamorphoses*. He made little errors that Bacon, for example, could never have made: called Theseus a duke, had Hector of the eleventh century B.C. refer to Aristotle of the third,[19] and let a character in *Coriolanus*[20] (fifth century B.C.) quote Cato (of the first).

He had little French and less Italian. He had some knowledge of geography, and gave his plays exotic locales from Scotland to Ephesus; but he gave Bohemia a seacoast,* and he sent Valentine by sea from Verona to Milan,[23] and Prospero from Milan in an ocean-going vessel.[24] He took much of his Roman history from Plutarch, of his English history from Holinshed and from earlier plays. He made historical *faux-pas* unimportant to a dramatist: put a clock in Caesar's Rome, billiards in Cleopatra's Egypt. He wrote *King John* without mentioning Magna Charta, and *Henry VIII* without bothering about the Reformation; again we see the past changing with each present. In outline the English historical plays are correct from our current view; in detail they are untrustworthy; in standpoint they are colored by patriotism—Joan of Arc, in Shakespeare, is merely a wanton witch. Nevertheless many Englishmen, like

---

* Ben Jonson pounced upon this in his talks with Drummond at Hawthornden.[21] Shakespeare took it from a novel by Robert Greene—a university graduate. Under Ottokar II (r. 1253–78) Bohemia extended her rule to the Adriatic shores.[22]

Marlborough, confessed that most of their knowledge of English history came from Shakespeare's plays.

Like other Elizabethan dramatists, Shakespeare used many legal terms, sometimes improperly; he could have gleaned them in the Inns of Court—the law schools in which three of his plays were staged—or in the several lawsuits engaged in by his father or himself. He is rich in musical terms and was evidently sensitive to music—"Is it not strange that sheeps' guts should hale souls out of men's bodies?"[25] He lovingly remembers the flowers of England, strings them on a rosary in *The Winter's Tale,* and decks Ophelia with them in her delirium; he alludes to 180 different plants. He was acquainted with the sports of the field and the points of a horse. But he had little interest in science, which was soon to fascinate Bacon. Like Bacon, he retained the Ptolemaic astronomy.[26] At times (Sonnet 15) he seems to accept astrology, and he speaks of Romeo and Juliet as "star-crossed lovers";[27] but Edmund in *Lear* and Cassius in *Julius Caesar* vigorously reject it: "The fault, dear Brutus, is not in our stars, but in ourselves, that we are underlings."[28]

All in all, the evidence indicates that Shakespeare had the incidental learning of a man of affairs too busy with acting, managing, and living to sink his head into books. He knew the more startling of Machiavelli's ideas, he referred to Rabelais, he borrowed from Montaigne; but it is unlikely that he read their works. Gonzalo's description of an ideal commonwealth[29] is taken from Montaigne's essay "On Cannibals"; and Caliban, in the same play, may be Shakespeare's satire on Montaigne's idealization of the American Indians. Whether the skepticism of Hamlet owed anything to Montaigne's genial doubts is an unsolved problem; the play was published in 1602, a year before the printing of Florio's translation, but Shakespeare knew Florio and may have seen the manuscript. Montaigne's subtle criticism of traditional ideas may have helped to deepen Shakespeare, but there is nothing in the Frenchman that corresponds to Hamlet's soliloquy, or to the bitter indictment of life in *Lear, Coriolanus, Timon,* and *Macbeth.* Shakespeare is Shakespeare—pilfering plots, passages, phrases, lines anywhere, and yet the most original, distinctive, creative writer of all time.

The originality is in the language, the style, the imagination, the dramatic technique, the humor, the characters, and the philosophy. The language is the richest in all literature: fifteen thousand words, including the technical terms of heraldry, music, sports, and the professions, the dialects of the shires, the argot of the pavement, and a thousand hurried or lazy inventions—*occulted, unkenneled, fumitory, burnet, spurring* . . . He relished words and explored the nooks and crannies of the language; he loved words in general and poured them forth in frolicsome abandon; if he names a flower he must go on to name a dozen—the words themselves are fragrant. He makes simple characters mouth polysyllabic circumlocutions. He plays jolly havoc with the grammar: turns nouns, adjectives, even adverbs into verbs, and verbs, adjectives, even pronouns into nouns; gives a plural verb to a singular subject or a singular verb to a plural subject; but there were as yet no grammars of English usage, no rules. Shakespeare wrote in haste, and had no leisure to repent.

The marvelous style, "manneristic and baroque,"[30] has the faults of its lawless wealth: phrases fancifully artificial or involved, farfetched images, word plays tiresomely elaborate; puns amid tragedy, metaphors falling over one another in contradictory confusion, repetitions innumerable, sententious platitudes, and, now and then, hilarious, nonsensical bombast filling the unlikeliest mouths. Doubtless a classical training would have chastened the style, silenced the *doubles-entendres;* but then consider what we should have lost. Perhaps he was thinking of himself when he made Ferdinand describe Adriano as a man

> That hath a mint of phrases in his brain;
> One whom the music of his own vain tongue
> Doth ravish like enchanting harmony . . .
> But, I protest, I love to hear him lie . . .[31]

From this mint issued an almost universal currency of phrases: the winter of our discontent;[32] piping time of peace;[33] wish father to the thought;[34] tell the truth and shame the devil;[35] sits the wind in that corner?;[36] uneasy lies the head that wears a crown;[37] paint the lily;[38] one touch of nature makes the whole world kin;[39] what fools these mortals be!;[40] the Devil can quote Scripture to his purpose;[41] midsummer madness;[42] the course of true love never did run smooth;[43] wear my heart upon my sleeve;[44] every inch a king;[45] to the manner born;[46] brevity is the soul of wit[47] . . . but this is a hint to stop. And of metaphors another thousand, of which one may serve—"to see the sails conceive and grow big-bellied with the wanton wind."[48] And entire passages now almost as familiar as the phrases: Ophelia's disordered herbal of flowers, Antony over dead Caesar, Cleopatra dying, Lorenzo on the music of the spheres. And a whole repertoire of songs: "Who is Silvia?,"[49] "Hark, hark! the lark at heaven's gate sings,"[50] "Take, O take those lips away."[51] Probably Shakespeare's audience came for his plumage as well as for his tale.

"The lunatic, the lover, and the poet are of imagination all compact";[52] Shakespeare was two of these and may have touched the third. He creates a world with every play, and, not content, he fills imagined empires, woods, and heaths with childlike magic, scurrying fairies, awesome witches and ghosts. His imagination makes his style, which thinks in images, turns all ideas into pictures, all abstractions into things felt or seen. Who but Shakespeare (and Petrarch) would have made Romeo, exiled from Verona, fume with envy that its cats and dogs might gaze on Juliet and he be disallowed? Who else (but Blake) would have made the banished Duke, in *As You Like It,* regret that he must live by hunting beasts so often more beautiful than man? Little wonder that a spirit so keen in every sense should have reacted passionately against the ugliness, greed, cruelty, lust, pain, and grief that seemed at times to dominate the panorama of the world.

His originality is least in dramatic technique. As a man of the theater he knew the tricks of his trade. He began his plays with scenes or words calculated to jolt the attention of his nut-cracking, card-playing, ale-swilling, woman-ogling audience. He took full advantage of the abundant "properties" and machinery of the Elizabethan stage. He studied his fellow actors and created parts suitable to their physical and mental peculiarities. He used all the jugglery of disguises and recognitions, all the shifts of scenery and the complications of a play within a play. But in his craftsmanship he shows some scars of haste. Sometimes the plot within the plot tears the tale in two; what has Gloucester's tragedy to do with Lear's? Almost all the stories turn on improbable coincidences, concealed identities, highly opportune revelations; we may be reasonably asked to make believe, in drama as in opera, for the sake of the story or the song, but an artist should reduce to a minimum the "baseless fabric" of his dream. Less important are the inconsistencies of time or character;[53] presumably Shakespeare, thinking of rapid production, not of careful publication, judged that these flaws would pass unnoticed by an excited audience. Classical norms and modern taste alike condemn the violence that often dyes Shakespeare's stage; this was another concession to the pit, and an effort to meet the competition of the slaughterhouse school of Elizabethan-Jacobean dramatists.

As he developed, Shakespeare redeemed the violence with humor and learned the difficult art of intensifying tragedy with comic relief. The early comedies are wit and humor unrelieved, the early historical plays are stodgy for lack of humor; in *Henry IV* tragedy and comedy alternate but are not well integrated; in *Hamlet* the integration is achieved. Sometimes the humor seems too broad; Sophocles and Racine would have turned up their classical noses at the jokes about human flatulence[54] or equine micturition.[55] An erotic quip now and then is more to the modern taste. Generally, Shakespeare's humor is good-natured, not the savage misanthropy of Swift; he felt that the world was better for a clown or two; he suffered fools patiently, and emulated God in seeing little difference between them and world-explaining philosophers.

His greatest clown rivals Hamlet as Shakespeare's supreme achievement in the creation of character—which is the supreme test of a dramatist. Richard II and Richard III, Hotspur and Wolsey, Gaunt and Gloucester, Brutus and Antony rise out of the limbo of history into a second life. Not in Greek drama, not even in Balzac, are imagined persons so endowed with consistent character and vital force. Most real are those creations that only seem contradictory because of their complexity—Lear cruel and then tender, Hamlet thoughtful and impetuous, hesitant and brave. Sometimes the characters are too simple—Richard III merely villainy, Timon merely cynicism, Iago merely hate. Some of the women in Shakespeare seem plucked from the same mold—Beatrice and Rosalind, Cordelia and Desdemona, Miranda and Hermione—and lose reality, and then at times a few words make them live; so Ophelia, told by Hamlet that he had never loved her, answers without recrimination, but with sad and moving simplicity, "I was the more deceived." Observation, feeling, empathy, astonishing receptivity of senses, penetrating perception, alert selection of significant and characteristic detail, tenacious remembering, come together to people this living city of dead or imagined souls. Play after play these personae grow in reality, complexity, and depth, until, in *Hamlet* and *Lear,* the poet matures into a philosopher and his dramas become the glowing vehicles of thought.

V. Philosophy

"Hast any philosophy in thee, shepherd?"[56] So Touchstone asks Corin, and we ask Shakespeare. One of his confessed rivals gave a negative answer to the question;[57] and we may accept that judgment as Bernard Shaw meant it—that there is no metaphysics in Shakespeare, no view as to the ultimate nature of reality, no theory of God. Shakespeare was too wise to think that a creature could analyze his creator, or that even *his* mind, poised on a moment of flesh, could comprehend the whole. "There are more things in heaven and earth, Horatio, than are dreamt of in your philosophy."[58] If he made a guess he kept it to himself, and perhaps thereby proved himself a philosopher. He speaks with no reverence of professed philosophers, and doubts that any of them ever bore the toothache patiently.[59] He laughs at logic and prefers imagination's light; he does not offer to solve the mysteries of life or mind, but he feels and visions them with an intensity that shames or deepens our hypotheses. He stands aside and watches the dogmatists destroy one another or disintegrate in the catalysis of time. He hides himself in his characters and is hard to find; we must beware of attributing an opinion to him unless it is expressed with some emphasis by at least two of his creations.

He is at first sight more of a psychologist than a philosopher; but again not as a theorist but, rather, as a mental photographer, catching the secret thoughts and symptomatic actions that reveal the nature of a man. However, he is no surface realist; things do not happen, people do not speak, in life as in his plays; but in the sum we feel that through these improbabilities and extravagances we are nearing the core of human instinct and thought. Shakespeare knows as well as Schopenhauer that "reason panders will";[60] he is quite Freudian in putting erotic ditties into the virgin mouth of the starved and crazed Ophelia; and he reaches beyond Freud to Dostoevski in studying Macbeth and his "worser" half.

If we interpret philosophy not as metaphysics but as any large perspective of human affairs, as a generalized view not only of the cosmos and the mind but as well of morals, politics, history, and faith, Shakespeare is a philosopher, profounder than Bacon, as Montaigne is deeper than Descartes; it is not form that makes philosophy. He recognizes the relativity of morals: "There's nothing good or bad but thinking makes it so,"[61] and "our virtues lie in the interpretation of the time."[62] He feels the puzzle of determinism: some men are bad by heredity, "wherein they are not guilty, since nature [character] cannot choose his origin."[63] He knows the Thrasymachus theory of morals: Richard III holds that "conscience is but a word that cowards use, devised at first to keep the strong in awe; our strong arms be our conscience, swords our law";[64] Richard II judges that "they well deserve to have, that know the strong'st and surest way to get";[65] but both these Nietzscheans are brought to a sorry fate. Shakespeare notes, too, the feudal-aristocratic ethic of honor and gives it many a noble phrase, but he deprecates, as in Hotspur, its bent toward pride and violence, "defect of manners, want of [self-]government."[66] In the end his own ethic is one of Aristotelian measure and Stoic control. Measure and reason are the theme of Ulysses' speech reproving Ajax and Achilles.[67] Reason alone, however, is not enough; a stoic fiber must strengthen it:

> Men must endure
> Their going hence even as their coming hither:
> Ripeness is all . . .[68]

Death is forgivable if it comes after we have fulfilled ourselves. Shakespeare welcomes Epicurus, too, and admits no inherent contradiction between pleasure and wisdom. He snaps at the Puritans, and makes the maid Maria tell Malvolio, "Go shake your ears"[69]—i.e., "You're an ass." He is as lenient as a pope to sins of the flesh, and puts into the mad Lear's mouth a hilarious paean to copulation.[70]

His political philosophy is conservative. He knew the sufferings of the poor and made Lear voice them feelingly. A fisherman in *Pericles* (1609?) notes that fishes live in the sea

> as men do a-land,—the great ones eat up the little ones. I can compare our rich misers to nothing so fitly as to a whale; a' plays and tumbles, driving the poor fry before him, and at last devours them all at a mouthful: such whales have I heard on o' the land, who never leave gaping till they've swallowed the whole parish, church, steeple, bells, and all.[71]

Gonzalo, in *The Tempest,* dreams of an anarchistic communism where "all things in common nature should produce," and there should be no laws, no magistrates, no labor, and no war;[72] but Shakespeare smiles this utopia away as made impossible by the nature of man; under every constitution the whales will eat the fish.

What was Shakespeare's religion? Here especially the search for his philosophy is difficult. He expresses through his characters almost every faith, and with such tolerance as must have made the Puritans think him an infidel. He quotes the Bible often and reverently, and lets Hamlet, supposedly skeptical, talk believingly of God, prayer, heaven, and hell.[73] Shakespeare and his children were baptized according to Anglican rites.[74] Some of his lines are vigorously Protestant. King John speaks of papal pardons as "juggling witchcraft," and quite anticipates Henry VIII:

> . . . no Italian priest
> Shall tithe or toll in our dominions;
> But as we, under heaven, are supreme head,
> So, under Him, that great supremacy,
> Where we do reign, we will alone uphold . . .
> So tell the Pope, all reverence set apart
> To him and his usurpt authority.[75]

Though, of course, John goes to Canossa in the end. A later play, *Henry VIII,* only partly by Shakespeare, gives very favorable pictures of Henry and Cranmer and ends with a eulogy of Elizabeth—all chief architects of the Reformation in England. There are some pro-Catholic touches, as in the sympathetic portrayal of Catherine of Aragon and Friar Lawrence;[76] but the latter character had come to Shakespeare as formed in the *novelle* of Italian Catholics.

Some faith in God survives throughout the tragedies. Lear in his bitterness thinks that

> As flies to wanton boys are we to the gods,—
> They kill us for their sport.[77]

But: "The gods are just," answers the good Edgar, "and of our pleasant vices make instruments to plague us";[78] and Hamlet affirms his faith in "a divinity that doth shape our ends, rough-hew them how we will."[79] Despite this struggling faith in a Providence that deals with us justly there is, in Shakespeare's greatest plays, a spreading cloud of unbelief in life itself. Jaques sees in all the "seven ages" of man nothing but slow riping and fast rotting. We hear the same refrain in *King John*:

> Life is as tedious as a twice-told tale
> Vexing the dull ear of a drowsy man;[80]

and in Hamlet's scorn of the world:

Fie on't! O, fie! 'tis an unweeded garden,
That grows to seed; things rank and gross in nature
Possess it merely;[81]

and in Macbeth's

Out, out, brief candle!
Life's but a walking shadow; a poor player
That struts and frets his hour upon the stage,
And then is heard no more: it is a tale
Told by an idiot, full of sound and fury,
Signifying nothing.[82]

Does any sense of immortality soften this pessimism? Lorenzo, after describing to Jessica the music of the spheres, adds that "such harmony is in immortal souls."[83] Claudio, in *Measure for Measure*, visions an afterlife, but in somber terms of Dante's Inferno or Pluto's Hades:

Ah, but to die, and go we know not where;
To lie in cold obstruction, and to rot;
This sensible warm motion to become
A kneaded clod; and the delighted spirit
To bathe in fiery floods, or to reside
In thrilling region of thick-ribbed ice;
To be imprison'd in the viewless winds,
And blown with restless violence round about
The pendent world . . . 'tis too horrible![84]

Hamlet speaks casually of the soul as immortal,[85] but his soliloquy affirms no faith; and his dying words in the older version of the play, "Heaven receive my soul," were changed by Shakespeare to read, "The rest is silence."

We cannot say with confidence how much of this pessimism came from the demands of tragic drama and how much voiced Shakespeare's mood; but its repetition and emphasis suggest that it expressed the darker moments of his philosophy. The sole mitigation of it in these culminating plays is a hesitant recognition that amid the evils of this world there are blessings and delights, amid the villains many heroes and some saints—for every Iago a Desdemona, for every Goneril a Cordelia, for every Edmund an Edgar or a Kent; even in Hamlet a fresh wind blows from Horatio's faithfulness and Ophelia's wistful tenderness. After the tired actor and playwright leaves the chaos and crowded loneliness of London for the green fields and parental consolations of his Stratford home he will recapture the strong man's love of life.

VI. Reconciliation

However, he had no obvious reason to complain of London. It had given him success, acclaim, and fortune. There are over two hundred references to him, almost all favorable, in the surviving literature of his time. In 1598 Francis Meres's *Palladis Tamia: Wits Treasury* listed Sidney, Spenser, Daniel, Drayton, Warner, Shakespeare, Marlowe, and Chapman, in that order, as England's leading authors, and ranked Shakespeare first among the dramatists.[86] In that same year Richard Barnfield, a rival poet, declared that Shakespeare's work (of which the best was yet to come) had already placed his name in "Fame's immortal Book."[87] He was popular even with his competitors. Drayton and Jonson and Burbage were among his closest friends; and though Jonson criticized his inflated style, his careless facility in composition, and his outrageous neglect of classic rules, it was Jonson who, in the First Folio, rated Shakespeare above all other dramatists ancient or modern and judged him to be "not of an age, but for all time." In the papers that Jonson left at his death he wrote, "I loved the man . . . this side idolatry."[88]

Tradition joins Jonson with Shakespeare in the meetings of literary men at the Mermaid Tavern in Bread Street. Francis Beaumont, who knew them both, exclaimed:

> What things have we seen
> Done at the Mermaid!—heard words that have been
> So nimble and so full of subtle flame
> As if that everyone from whence they came
> Had meant to put his whole wit in a jest,
> And had resolved to live a fool the rest
> Of his dull life.[89]

And Thomas Fuller's *Worthies of England* (1662) reported:

> Many were the wit combats betwixt Shakespeare and Ben Jonson, which two I behold like a Spanish great galleon and an English man-of-war. Master Jonson (like the former) was built far higher in learning, solid but slow in his performances. Shakespeare . . . lesser in bulk but lighter in sailing, could turn with all tides, tack about, and take advantage of all winds by the quickness of his wit and invention.[90]

Aubrey, about 1680, continued the easily credible tradition of Shakespeare's "very ready and pleasant smooth wit," and added that he "was a handsome, well-shaped man, very good company."[91] The only extant likenesses of him are the bust placed over his tomb in the Stratford church and the engraving prefixed to the First Folio; they agree well enough, showing a man half bald, with mustache and (in the bust) beard, sharp nose, and meditative eyes, but giving no sign of the flame that burns in the plays. Perhaps the plays mislead us about his character; they suggest a man of high-strung energy and passion fluctuating between the summits of thought and poetry and the depths of melancholy and despair; while his contemporaries describe him as civil and honest, slow to take offense, "of an open and free nature,"[92] enjoying life, careless of posterity, and showing a vein of practicality unbecoming a poet. Whether by thrift or gift, he was already rich enough in 1598 to join in financing the Globe theater; and in 1608 he and six others built the Blackfriars. His shares in these enterprises, added to his earnings as actor and playwright, gave him a substantial income—diversely estimated between £200[93] and £600[94] a year. The latter figure seems better able to explain his purchases of Stratford realty.

"He was wont," says Aubrey, "to go to his native country once a year."[95] Sometimes he stopped on the way at Oxford, where a John Davenant kept an inn; Sir William Davenant (poet laureate in 1637) liked to suggest that he was the unpremeditated result of Shakespeare's dalliance there.[96] In 1597 the dramatist, for sixty pounds, bought New Place, the second-largest house in Stratford, but he continued to live in London. His father died in 1601, leaving him two houses in Henley Street, Stratford. A year later, for £320, he bought near the town 127 acres of land, which he probably leased to tenant farmers. In 1605 he bought for £440 a share in the prospective ecclesiastical tithes of Stratford and three other communities. While he was writing his greatest plays in London he was known in Stratford chiefly as a successful businessman, frequently engaged in litigation about his properties and investments.

His son Hamnet had died in 1596. In 1607 his daughter Susanna married John Hall, a prominent Stratford physician, and a year later she made the poet a grandfather. He had now new ties to draw him homeward. About 1610 he retired from London and the stage and moved into New Place. Apparently it was there that he composed *Cymbeline* (1609?), *The Winter's Tale* (1610?), and *The Tempest* (1611?). Two of these are of minor rank, but *The Tempest* shows Shakespeare still master of his powers. Here is Miranda, who at the outset reveals her nature when, seeing a shipwreck from the shore, she cries out, "Oh, I have suffered with those that I saw suffer!"[97] Here is Caliban, Shakespeare's answer to Rousseau. Here is Prospero, the kindly magician, surrendering the wand of his art and bidding his airy world a fond goodbye. There is an echo of the poet's melancholy in the undiminished eloquence of Prospero's lines:

> Our revels now are ended. These our actors,
> As I foretold you, were all spirits, and
> Are melted into air, into thin air:
> And, like the baseless fabric of this vision,
> The cloud-capp'd towers, the gorgeous palaces,
> The solemn temples, the great globe itself,
> Yea, all which it inherit, shall dissolve,
> And, like this insubstantial pageant faded,
> Leave not a rack behind. We are such stuff
> As dreams are made on; and our little life
> Is rounded with a sleep.[98]

But this is not now the dominant mood; on the contrary, the play is Shakespeare relaxing, talking of brooks and flowers, singing songs like "Full fathom five" and "Where the bee sucks, there suck I." And, despite all cautious demurrers, it is the aging poet who speaks through Prospero's farewell:

> . . . graves at my command
> Have waked their sleepers, oped, and let 'em forth
> By my so potent art. But this rough magic
> I here abjure . . . I'll break my staff,

Bury it certain fathoms in the earth,
And deeper than did ever plummet sound
I'll drown my book.[99]

And perhaps it is Shakespeare again, rejoiced by his daughters and his grand-child, who cries out, through Miranda:

O wonder!
How many goodly natures are there here!
How beauteous mankind is! O brave new world
That hath such people in it![100]

On February 10, 1616, Judith married Thomas Quiney. On March 25 Shakespeare made his will. He left his property to Susanna, £300 to Judith, small bequests to fellow actors, and his "second-best bed" to his estranged wife. Perhaps he had arranged with Susanna to take care of her mother. Anne Hathaway survived him by seven years. In April, according to John Ward, vicar (1662–81) of Stratford Church, "Shakespeare, Drayton, and Ben Jonson had a merry party, and it seems drank too hard, for Shakespeare died of a fever there contracted."*[101] Death came on April 23, 1616. The body was buried under the chancel of the Stratford church. Nearby on the floor, graved on a stone bearing no name, is an epitaph which local tradition ascribes to Shakespeare's hand:

GOOD FRIEND, FOR JESUS SAKE FORBEARE
TO DIGG THE DUST ENCLOASED HEARE.
BLESE BE YE MAN YT [THAT] SPARES THES STONES,
AND CURST BE HE YT MOVES MY BONES.

VII. Post-Mortem

He had, so far as we know, taken no steps to have his plays published; the sixteen that severally appeared in his lifetime were printed, apparently, without his co-operation, usually in quarto form, and in various degrees of textual

* "There is no reason to reject this report."—Sir E. K. Chambers, *William Shakespeare*, I, 89.

corruption. Stirred by these piracies, two of his former associates, John Heming and Henry Condell, issued in 1623 the First Folio, containing in one tall volume of some nine hundred double-column pages the authoritative text of thirty-six of the plays. "We have but . . . done an office to the dead," said the foreword, ". . . without ambition either of self-profit or fame; only to keep the memory of so worthy a friend . . . alive as was our Shakespeare." The volume could then be bought for a pound; each of the approximately two hundred extant copies is now valued at £17,000, more highly than any book except Gutenberg's Bible.

Shakespeare's reputation fluctuated curiously in time. Milton (1630) praised "sweetest Shakespeare, Fancy's child," but during the Puritan interval, when the theaters were closed (1642–60), the fame of the bard faded. It revived with the Restoration. Sir John Suckling, in his portrait by Vandyck (in the Frick Gallery, New York), holds the First Folio open at *Hamlet*. Dryden, the oracle of the later seventeenth century, commended Shakespeare as having, "of all modern, and perhaps ancient, poets . . . the largest and most comprehensive soul . . . always great when some great occasion is presented to him," but "many times flat, insipid, his comic art degenerating into clenches, his serious swelling into bombast."[102] John Evelyn noted in his diary (1661) that "the old plays disgust this refined age, since his Majesty's being so long abroad"—i.e., since Charles II and the returning royalists had brought to England the dramatic norms of France; soon afterward the Restoration theater produced the bawdiest dramas in modern literature. Shakespeare's plays were still performed, but usually in "adaptation" by Dryden, Otway, or other models of Restoration taste.

The eighteenth century restored the plays to Shakespeare. Nicholas Rowe published (1709) the first critical edition and the first biography; Pope and Johnson issued editions and commentaries; Betterton, Garrick, Kemble, and Mrs. Siddons made Shakespeare popular on the stage as never before; and Thomas Bowdler made his own name a verb by publishing (1818) an expurgated version omitting parts "which cannot with propriety be read aloud in a family." In the early nineteenth century the romantic movement took Shakespeare to its heart, and the superlatives of Coleridge, Hazlitt, De Quincey, and Lamb transformed him into a tribal god.

France demurred. By 1700 its literary standards had been formed by Ronsard, Malherbe, and Boileau in the Latin tradition of order, logical form, polite taste, and rational control; it had adopted, in Racine, the classical rules of drama; it was disturbed by Shakespeare's windy word play, his bubbling torrent of phrases, his emotional storms, his coarse clowns, his mingling of comedy with tragedy. Voltaire, returning from England in 1729, brought with him some appreciation of Shakespeare and "first showed the French a few pearls which I found in his enormous dunghill";[103] but when someone ranked the Englishman above Racine, Voltaire rose to the defense of France by calling Shakespeare "an amiable barbarian."[104] His *Philosophical Dictionary* (1765) made some amends: "In this same man there are passages which exalt the imagination and penetrate the heart. . . . He reaches sublimity without having searched for it."[105] Mme. de Staël (1804), Guizot (1821), and Villemain (1827) helped France to bear with Shakespeare. Finally the translation of the plays into good French prose by Victor Hugo's son François won Shakespeare the respect of France, though never the devout admiration there accorded to Racine.

The bard had a better press in Germany, where no native playwright contested the prize. It was Germany's first great dramatist, Gotthold Lessing, who in 1759 informed his countrymen that Shakespeare was superior to all other poets, ancient or modern; and Herder supported him. August von Schlegel, Ludwig Tieck, and other leaders of the Romantic school raised the Shakespearean banner, and Goethe contributed an enthusiastic discussion of *Hamlet* in *Wilhelm Meister* (1796).[106] Shakespeare became popular on the German stage; and for a time German scholarship snatched the lead from England in the clarification of Shakespeare's life and plays.

For those brought up in the aura of Shakespeare an objective estimate or comparison is impossible. Only one who knows the language, the religion, the art, the customs, and the philosophy of the Periclean Greeks will feel the unequaled dignity of the Dionysian tragic drama, the stark simplicity and inexorable logic of its structure, its proud self-restraint in word and deed, the moving commentary of its choral chants, the high enterprise of seeing man in the perspective of his cosmic place and destiny. Only one who knows the French language and character, and the background of the *grand siècle*, can feel, in the plays of Corneille and Racine, not merely the majesty and music of their verse, but as well the heroic effort of reason to overspread emotion and impulse, the stoic adherence to difficult classic norms, the concentration of the drama into a few tense hours summarizing and deciding lives. Only one who knows English in its Elizabethan fullness, who can ride with gusto the Elizabethan winds of rhetoric, lyric, and vituperation, who puts no bounds to the theater's mirroring of nature and release of imagination, can bring to Shakespeare's plays their merited acceptance with open arms and heart; but such a man will tremble with delight at the splendor of their speech, and he will be moved to the depths of his spirit to follow and fathom their thought. These are the three epochal gifts of the world's drama, and we must, despite our limitations, welcome them all to our deepening, thanking our heritage for Greek wisdom, French beauty, and Elizabethan life.

(But, of course, Shakespeare is supreme.)

CHAPTER V

MARY QUEEN OF SCOTS

1542–87

I. The Fairy Queen

Within the interlocking dramas of the Scottish Reformation and Elizabethan politics the tragedy of Mary Stuart moved with all the fascination of beauty, passionate love, religious and political conflict, murder, revolution, and heroic death. Her ancestry almost assured a violent end. She was the daughter of the Stuart James V of Scotland and of Mary of Guise, Lorraine, and France; she was the granddaughter of Margaret Tudor, who was the daughter of Henry VII of England; she was therefore niece, loosely called cousin, of "Bloody Mary" and Elizabeth; by common consent she was the legitimate heir to the English crown if Elizabeth should die without issue; and for those who—like all Catholics (and, at one time, Henry VIII)—considered Elizabeth a bastard and therefore ineligible to rule, Mary Stuart, and not Elizabeth Tudor, should have succeeded to the throne of England in 1558. To make tragedy certain, Mary, on becoming Queen of France (1559), allowed her followers and her state papers to call her Queen of England. It had long been a vain pretense of French kings to be also kings of England, and of English kings to be also kings of France; but in this case the pretense came close to a generally acknowledged claim. Elizabeth could not be sure of her crown as long as Mary lived. Only common sense could have saved the situation, and sovereigns rarely stoop so low.

Mary was offered kingdoms within a year of her birth. Within a week of her birth her father's death made her Queen of Scots. Henry VIII, hoping to unite Scotland as an appanage to England, proposed that the infant be betrothed to his son Edward, be sent to England, and be there brought up, presumably as a Protestant, to be Edward's Queen. Her Catholic mother accepted, instead, the offer of Henry II of France (1548) to give her in marriage to his son the

Dauphin. To guard her against being kidnapped into England, Mary, aged six, was hurried off to France. She remained there thirteen years, was educated with the royal children, and became completely French in spirit, being already half French in blood. As she matured into youth she developed all the charms of young womanhood in beauty of features and form, sprightliness of mind, and merry grace of ways and speech. She sang sweetly, played the lute well, talked Latin, and wrote poetry that poets affected to praise. Courtiers throbbed to "the snow of her pure face" (Brantôme),[1] "the gold of her curled and plaited hair" (Ronsard),[2] the slender elegance of her hands, the fullness of her bust; and even the grave and sober L'Hôpital thought that such loveliness must be the vesture of a god.[3] She became the most attractive and accomplished figure at the most polished court in Europe. When, aged sixteen, she married the Dauphin (April 24, 1558), and still more when, aged seventeen, she became through his accession Queen of France, all the hopes of a fanciful dream seemed to have come true.

But Francis II died (December 5, 1560) after two years of rule. Mary, a widow at eighteen, thought of retiring to an estate in Touraine, for she loved France. But meanwhile Scotland had gone Protestant; it was in danger of being lost to France as an ally. The French government held it to be Mary's duty to go to Edinburgh and lead her native land back to the French alliance and the Catholic faith. Unwillingly, Mary reconciled herself to leaving the comforts and brilliance of French civilization for life in a Scotland which she could barely remember, and which she pictured as a land of barbarism and cold. She wrote to the leading Scottish nobles, affirming her fidelity to Scotland; she did not tell them that in her marriage contract she had deeded Scotland to the kings of France if she died without issue. The nobles, Protestant as well as Catholic, were charmed; the Scottish Parliament invited her to come and possess her throne. She asked Elizabeth for a safe-conduct through England; it was refused. On August 14, 1561, Mary sailed from Calais, bidding France a tearful farewell, and gazing at the receding coast till nothing remained but the sea.

Five days later she disembarked at Leith, the port of Edinburgh, and discovered Scotland.

II. Scotland, 1560–61

It was a nation of ancient roots and rooted ways: bound by the rough high-lands of the north to a feudal regime of almost independent nobles organizing and exploiting a half-primitive culture of hunting, herding, and tenant tillage; favored in the south by lovely lowlands fertile with rain but darkened by long winters and crippling cold; a people struggling to create a moral and civilized order out of illiteracy, illegitimacy, corruption, lawlessness, and violence; riddled with superstition, and sending witches to the stake; seeking in a tense religious faith some hope of a less arduous life. To offset the divisive power of the barons, the kings had supported the Catholic clergy, and had dowered these with wealth leading to venality, lethargy, and concubines.[4] The nobles itched for the riches of the Church; they debased the clergy by filling ecclesiastical offices with their worldly sons; they declared for the Reformation and made the Scottish Parlia-ment, which they controlled, the master alike of Church and state.

External danger was the strongest incentive to internal unity. England felt unsafe in an island shared with her by untamed Scots; time and again she sought, by diplomacy, marriage, or war, to bring Scotland under English rule. Fearful of absorption, Scotland allied herself with a France traditionally hostile to England. Cecil advised Elizabeth to support the Protestant nobles against their Catholic Queen; so Scotland would be divided and would cease to be a peril to England or a support to France. Moreover, the Protestant leaders, if successful, might reject Mary, enthrone a Protestant noble, and make all Scot-land Protestant; privately Cecil dreamed of uniting such a Scotland to England by persuading Elizabeth to marry such a king.[5] When France sent a force into Scotland to suppress the Protestants, Elizabeth dispatched an army to protect them and drive out the French. Beaten in the field, the French representatives in Scotland signed at Edinburgh (July 6, 1560) a fateful treaty requiring not only that the French should leave Scotland but that Mary should cease to claim the throne of England. On the advice of her husband, Francis II, Mary refused to ratify the treaty. Elizabeth took note.

The religious situation was equally confused. The Scottish "Reformation Par-liament" of 1560 officially abolished Catholicism, and established Calvinist Prot-estantism, as the religion of the state; but these acts did not receive from Mary the royal ratification then required to make parliamentary decrees the law of the land. Catholic priests still held most of the Scottish benefices; half the nobles were "papists," and John Hamilton, of royal blood, still came to Parliament as the Catholic primate of Scotland. In Edinburgh, however, and in St. Andrews, Perth, Stirling, and Aberdeen, a large proportion of the middle classes had been won to Calvinism by devoted preachers under the lead of John Knox.

In the year before Mary's coming Knox and his aides drew up a Book of Discipline defining their doctrine and purposes. Religion was to mean Protestantism; "the godly" were to mean Calvinists alone; "idolatry" was to include "the Mass, invocation of saints, adoration of images, and the keeping . . . of the same," and "the obstinate maintainers and teachers of such abominations ought not to escape the punishment of the civil magistrate." All doctrine "repugnant to" the Gospel was to "be utterly suppressed as damnable to man's salvation."[6] Ministers were to be elected by the congregations, were to establish schools open to all godly children, and were to have control of the Scottish universities—St. Andrews, Glasgow, and Aberdeen. The wealth of the Catholic Church and the continued ecclesiastical tithes were to be devoted to the needs of the ministers, the education of the people, and the relief of the poor. The new Kirk, and not the secular state, was to legislate on morals and prescribe penalties for offenses—drunkenness, gluttony, profanity, extravagance of dress, oppression of the poor, obscenity, fornication, and adultery. All who resisted the new doctrine or persistently absented themselves from its services were to be turned over to the secular arm, with the Kirk's recommendation that they be put to death.[7]

However, the lords who dominated Parliament refused to accept the Book of Discipline (January 1561). They had no relish for a powerful and independent Kirk, and they had their own plans for using the wealth of the superseded Church. The Book remained the goal and guide of the Kirk's development.

Defeated in his attempt to establish a theocracy—a government by priests claiming to speak for God—Knox labored with massive tenacity to organize the new ministry, to find funds for its support, and to spread it throughout Scotland in the face of a still functioning Catholic clergy. The dogmatic force of his preaching and the enthusiasm of his congregation made him a power in Edinburgh and in the state. The Catholic Queen would have to reckon with him before she could consolidate her rule.

III. Mary and Knox: 1561–65

She had arranged to arrive in Scotland a fortnight before she was expected, for she had feared some opposition to her landing. But word of her arrival at Leith spread through the capital, and soon the streets were crowded with people. They were surprised to find that their Queen was a pretty and vivacious girl not yet nineteen years old; most of them cheered her as she rode gracefully on her palfrey to Holyrood Palace; and there the lords, Protestant and Catholic, welcomed her, proud that Scotland had so charming a ruler, who might someday, in person or through a son, bring England under a Scottish sovereign.

The two portraits[8] that have come down to us support her reputation as one of the most beautiful women of her time. We cannot tell how far the now nameless painters idealized her, but in both cases we see the finely molded features, the lovely hands, the luxuriant chestnut hair that entranced barons and biographers. Yet those pictures hardly reveal to us the real attractiveness of the young Queen—her buoyant spirit, her "laughing mouth," her nimble-witted speech, her fresh enthusiasm, her capacity for kindness and friendliness, her longing for affection, her reckless admiration of strong men. It was her tragedy that she wished to be a woman as well as a queen—to feel all the warmth of romance without abating the privileges of rule. She thought of herself in terms of chivalric tales—of proud yet gentle beauties, at once chaste and sensuous, capable of ardent longing and sensitive suffering, of tender pity, incorruptible loyalty, and a courage rising as danger rose. She was an expert horsewoman, leaped fences and ditches rashly, and could bear the hardship of campaigns without weariness or complaint. But she was neither physically nor mentally fit to be a queen. She was frail in all but nervous vigor, she was subject to fainting fits that looked like epilepsy, and some undiagnosed ailment often hampered her with pain.[9] She had not the masculine intelligence of Elizabeth. She was often clever, but rarely wise; repeatedly she let passion ruin diplomacy. At times she showed remarkable self-control, patience, and tact, and then again she would let go with hot temper and sharp tongue. She was cursed with beauty, unblessed with brains; and her character was her fate.

She tried hard to meet the manifold dangers of her situation, poised between grasping lords, hostile preachers and a decadent Catholic clergy that did no honor to her trusting faith. She chose as leaders of her Privy Council two Protestants: her bastard half-brother Lord James Stuart, later Earl of Murray (or

Moray), aged twenty-six, and William Maitland of Lethington, thirty-six, who had more intellect than his character could handle, and who shifted from side to side in compromises till his death. The goal of Lethington's diplomacy was admirable—the union of England and Scotland as the only alternative to a consuming hostility. In May of 1562 Mary sent him to England to arrange an interview between herself and Elizabeth; Elizabeth consented, but her Council demurred, fearing that even the most indirect admission of Mary's claim to the succession would encourage Catholic attempts to assassinate Elizabeth. The two queens corresponded with diplomatic affection, while each sought to play cat to the other's mouse.

Mary's first three years of rule were a success in everything but religion. Though she could never reconcile herself to the climate or the culture of Scotland, she sought, with dances, masques, and charm, to make Holyrood Palace a little Paris in a subarctic zone, and most of the lords thawed under the sun of her gaiety; Knox growled that they were bewitched. She allowed Murray and Lethington to administer the kingdom, which they did reasonably well. For a time even the religious problem seemed to be solved by her concessions. When papal agents urged her to restore Catholicism as the official religion of the land she replied that this was at present impossible; Elizabeth would forcibly intervene. To appease the Scottish Protestants she issued (August 26, 1561) a proclamation forbidding the Catholics to attempt changes in the established religion, but she asked to be allowed to practice her own worship privately and to have Mass said for her in the royal chapel.[10] On Sunday, August 24, Mass was there celebrated. A few Protestants gathered outside and demanded that "the idolatrous priest should die";[11] but Murray barred their entry into the chapel, while his aides led the priest to safety. On the following Sunday Knox denounced the lords for permitting the Mass, and told his congregation that to him one Mass was more offense than ten thousand armed foes.[12]

The Queen sent for him and strove to win his tolerance. On September 4, in her palace, the two faiths met in a historic interview, whose details are known to us only from Knox's report.[13] She reproached him for having stirred up rebellion against the duly constituted authority of her mother, and for having written his "blast" against "the monstrous regiment of women"—which had denounced all female sovereigns. He answered that "if to rebuke idolatry be to raise subjects against their princes, then cannot I be excused, for it has pleased God . . . to make me one (amongst many) to disclose unto this realm the vanity of the papistical religions, and the deceit, pride, and tyranny of that Roman Antichrist," the Pope. As for the blast, "Madam, that book was written most especially against that wicked Jezebel of England," Mary Tudor. Knox's report continues:

"Think ye (quod she) that subjects may resist their princes?"

"If (he [Knox] replied) their princes exceed their bounds . . . it is no doubt they may be resisted, even by power."

. . . The Queen stood as it were amazed . . . At length she said:

"Well, then, I perceive that my subjects shall obey you, and not me."

"God forbid (answered he) that ever I take upon me to command any to obey me, or yet to let subjects at liberty to do what pleaseth them. But my travail is that both princes and subjects obey God . . . And this subjection, Madam, unto God and unto His troubled Church, is the greatest dignity that flesh can get upon this earth."

"Yea (quod she), but ye are not the Kirk that I will nourish. I will defend the Kirk of Rome, for I think it is the true Kirk of God."

"Your will (quod he), Madam, is no reason; neither doth your thought make that Roman harlot to be the true and immaculate spouse of Jesus Christ. And wonder not, Madam, that I call Rome a harlot, for that Church is altogether polluted with all kind of spiritual fornication . . ."

"My conscience (said she) is not so."

If this conversation is faithfully reported, it was a dramatic confrontation of monarchy with theocratic democracy, of Catholicism with Calvinism. If we may believe Knox, the Queen took his reproofs without retaliation, merely saying, "Ye are oure sain [overmuch sore] for me"; she went off to dinner, and Knox to his ministry. Lethington wished "Mr. Knox would deal more gently with her, being a young princess unpersuaded."[14]

His followers did not feel that he had been too hard with her. When she appeared in public some called her idolater, and children informed her that hearing Mass was a sin. The Edinburgh magistrates issued a decree of banishment for "monks, friars, priests, nuns, adulterers, and all sic filthy persons."[15] Mary deposed the magistrates and ordered new elections. At Stirling the priests who tried to minister to her were driven off with bloody heads, "while she wept helplessly."[16] The General Assembly of the Kirk demanded that she should be forbidden to hear Mass anywhere, but the lords of the Council refused to comply. In December 1561 a hot dispute arose between the Council and the Kirk over the distribution of ecclesiastical revenues: the Protestant ministers were allotted a sixth, the Queen a sixth, the Catholic clergy (still in the great majority) two thirds. Knox summarized the matter by saying that two parts were given to the Devil and the third was divided between the Devil and God.[17] The ministers received, on an average, one hundred marks ($3,333?) per year.[18]

Throughout the ensuing year the clergy of the Kirk continued to denounce the Queen. They were scandalized by the masques and revels, the singing, dancing, and flirting, that went on at Mary's court. She diminished her amusements in deference to the protests, but the ministers felt that she had yet far to go, for she still heard Mass. "John Knox," wrote a contemporary, "thundereth out of the pulpit, so that I fear nothing so much as that one day he will mar all. He ruleth the roost, and of him all men stand in fear."[19] Here again the Reformation came to grips with the Renaissance.

On December 15, 1562, Mary summoned Knox. Before Murray, Lethington, and others she accused him of teaching his followers to hate her. He answered, he says, that "princes . . . are more exercised in fiddling and flinging than in reading or hearing of God's most blessed word; and fiddlers and flatterers . . . are more precious in their eyes than men of wisdom and gravity, who, by wholesome admonition, might beat down in them some part of that vanity and pride whereunto all are born, but in princes take deep root and strength by wicked education." According to Knox, the Queen replied (with unwonted meekness), "If ye hear anything of myself that mislikes you, come to myself and tell me, and I shall hear you"; and he answered, "I am called, Madam, to a public function within the Kirk of God, and was appointed by God to rebuke the sins and vices of all. I am not appointed to come to every man in particular to show him his offense, for that labor were infinite. If your Grace please to frequent the public sermons, then doubt I not but that ye shall fully understand both what I like and mislike."[20]

She let him go in peace, but the war of faiths went on. At Easter of 1563 several Catholic priests who had violated the law by saying Mass were seized by local agents and were threatened with death for idolatry.[21] Some were jailed, some escaped and hid in the woods. Mary sent for Knox once more and interceded for the imprisoned priests; he replied that if she would enforce the law he would guarantee Protestant docility; otherwise he thought the papists deserved a lesson. "I promise to do as you require," she said, and for a moment they were friends. At her order the Archbishop of St. Andrews and forty-seven other priests were tried for saying Mass and were sentenced to prison. The ministers rejoiced, but a week later (May 26, 1563), when Mary and her ladies attended Parliament in their best raiment and some of the people cried "God bless that sweet face!" the ministers denounced "the targetting [tasseling] of their tails," and Knox wrote, "Such stinking pride of women . . . was never seen before in Scotland."[22]

Shortly thereafter he heard that Lethington was trying to arrange a marriage between Mary and Don Carlos, son of Philip II. Feeling that such a marriage would be fatal to Scottish Protestantism, Knox spoke his mind on the subject in a sermon preached to the nobles attending Parliament:

> And now, my Lords, to put an end to all, I hear of the Queen's marriage . . . This, my Lords, will I say: Whensoever the nobility of Scotland professing to Lord Jesus consents that an infidel (and all papists are infidels) shall be head to your sovereign, ye do so far as in ye lieth to banish Christ Jesus from this realm.[23]

The Queen lost her temper. She summoned him and asked (he reports). "What have ye to do with my marriage? Or what are ye in this commonwealth?" He made a famous reply: "A subject born within the same, madam. And albeit I neither be earl, lord, nor baron within it, yet has God made me (how abject that ever I be in your eyes) a profitable member within the same."[24] Mary broke into tears and bade him leave her.

His boldness reached its peak in October (1563). A crowd again gathered about the royal chapel to protest against the Mass that was about to be said there. Andrew Armstrong and Patrick Cranstoun entered the chapel and frightened the priest into retiring. The Queen, who had not been present, ordered the trial of the two Calvinists for invading her premises. On October 8 Knox sent out a letter bidding all "my brethren, of all estates [classes], that have preferred the truth," to attend the trial. The Queen's Council judged this call to be treason, and cited Knox to stand trial before her. He came (December 21, 1563), but so great a crowd of his supporters gathered in the courtyard and on the stairs and "even to the chamber door where the Queen and her Council sat," and he defended himself so skillfully, that the Council acquitted him, and the Queen said, "Mr. Knox, you may return to your home for this night." "I pray God," he replied, "to purge your heart from papistry."[25]

On Palm Sunday, 1564, the indomitable prophet, aged fifty-nine, married his second wife, Margaret Stuart, aged seventeen, a distant relative of the Queen. A year later the Queen too married a second time.

IV. The Queen in Love: 1565–68

Whom could she marry without a diplomatic mess? A Spaniard? But France and England would protest, and Protestant Scots would rage. A Frenchman? But England would oppose, even to war, any renewal of the Scottish-French alliance. An Austrian—the Archduke Charles? But Knox from the pulpit already thundered against union with a Catholic "infidel," and Elizabeth let Mary know that marriage with a Hapsburg—old foes of the Tudors—would be construed as a hostile act.

In a moment of passion Mary cut the diplomatic knot. Matthew Stuart, Earl of Lennox, who held himself to be the next in line to Mary for the Scottish throne, had lost his estates by supporting Henry VIII against Scotland, and had fled to England to elude the Scots' revenge; now (October 1564) he thought it timely to return. Soon thereafter came his nineteen-year-old son Henry Stuart, Lord Darnley, who through his mother was (like Mary) descended from Henry VII of England. Mary was charmed by the beardless youth; she admired his skill at tennis and on the lute; she forgave his vanity as the due of his good looks, and rushed into love before she could discern his lack of mind. On July 29, 1565, over the protests of Elizabeth and half her own Council, Mary made the lad her husband and named him king. Murray retired from the Council and joined the enemies of the headstrong Queen.

She enjoyed a few months of troubled happiness. Her need for love had mounted in her four years of widowhood; it was pleasant to be desired! She gave her love unstintedly, and without stint she lavished gifts upon her mate. "All dignities that she can indue him with," reported Elizabeth's ambassador, Thomas Randolph, "are already given and granted. No man pleases her that contenteth not him. . . . She hath given over unto him her whole will."[26] Good fortune turned the boy's head; he became dictatorial and insolent, and he demanded joint powers of rule with the Queen. Meanwhile he caroused, drank heavily, alienated the Council, had fits of jealousy, and suspected Mary of adultery with David Rizzio.

Who was Rizzio? An Italian musician, he had come to Scotland in 1561, aged twenty-eight, in the train of the ambassador from Savoy. Mary, fond of music, attached him to her service as organizer of musical fetes. She enjoyed his wit, his quick intelligence, his varied Continental culture. As he knew French and Latin well and wrote a fine Italian hand, she used him also as secretary. Soon she let him draft as well as write her foreign correspondence; he became an adviser, a power; he shared in directing policy; he ate with the Queen; sometimes he sat closeted with her far into the night. The Scottish nobles, seeing themselves superseded, and suspecting Rizzio of serving the Catholic cause, plotted to destroy him.

At first Darnley himself had been captivated by the clever Italian. They had played together, slept together. But as Rizzio's functions and honors grew, and Darnley's foolishness reduced him to political impotence, the affection of the King for the servant-become-minister descended the gamut of feeling to hatred. When Mary became pregnant Darnley thought she was bearing Rizzio's child. Randolph believed it; and, a generation later, Henri Quatre quipped that James I of England *must* be "the modern Solomon," since his father was the harpist David.[27] Having warmed his courage with whiskey, Darnley joined with the Earl of Morton, Baron Ruthven, and other nobles in a plot to murder Rizzio. They signed a "band" pledging themselves to uphold Protestantism in Scotland and to give Darnley the "crown matrimonial"—full rights as Scotland's king—and the right of succession should Mary die. Darnley promised to protect the signers from the consequences "of whatever crime," and to restore Murray and other banished lords.[28]

On March 6, 1566, Randolph revealed the plot to Cecil.[29] On March 9 it was carried out. Darnley entered the boudoir where Mary, Rizzio, and Lady Argyll were at supper; he grasped and held the Queen; Morton, Ruthven, and others rushed in, dragged Rizzio from the room over Mary's helpless protests, and stabbed him to death on the stairs—fifty-six wounds for good measure and sure. Someone rang the town tocsin; a crowd of armed citizens marched on the palace, proposing to cut Mary "to collops,"[30] but Darnley persuaded them to disperse. All that night and the next day Mary remained in Holyrood Palace, a prisoner of the assassins. Meanwhile she played upon Darnley's terror and love, and he helped and accompanied her when, on the following night, she escaped and fled to Dunbar. There, vowing revenge, she issued an appeal to all loyal supporters to come to her defense. Perhaps to divide her enemies, she recalled Murray to her Council.

The most effective of those who offered her protection was James Hepburn, fourth Earl of Bothwell. A strange and fateful character: not handsome, but strong of body, passions, and will; an adventurer on land and sea, skilled with sword and rapier; cowing men with his cool audacity, alluring women with his talk, his recklessness, and his reputation for seducing them; but also a man of superior education, a lover of and author of books in an age when many a noble Scot could not write his name. At first the Queen had disliked him, for he had spoken ill of her; but that is one way of winning a woman's interest. Then, seeing his martial qualities, she had appointed him Lieutenant of the Border; hearing of his familiarity with ships, she had made him Lord Admiral; learning of his desire for Lady Jane Gordon's hand, she promoted their marriage.

Now, fearing the assassins of Rizzio and suspecting her husband's complicity, she turned to Bothwell for protection and advice. She did not take to him precipitately, but his masculine qualities of courage, vigor, and confidence were those that her feminine nature had longed for and had not found in Francis II or Darnley. She noted how respect for his sword and his troops drove the conspirators into hiding or submission; soon she felt secure enough to return to Holyrood. Though Knox had approved the murder of Rizzio, Mary quieted the ministers for a while by making better provision for their maintenance. The common Scots, never in love with the lords, sympathized with her, and for a few months more she enjoyed a general popularity. "I never saw the Queen so much beloved, esteemed, and honored," wrote the French ambassador, "or so great harmony among her subjects."[31] Nevertheless, as she approached her confinement she was obsessed with the thought that she would be murdered or deposed in her helplessness.[32] When she safely gave birth to a boy (June 19, 1566), all Scotland rejoiced, as if foreseeing that this lad would be king of both Scotland and England. Mary was in apogee.

But she was miserable with Darnley. He resented her renewed trust in Murray and her rising admiration for Bothwell. There was talk that Bothwell would kidnap the royal infant and rule in its name.[33] Darnley accused the nobles of killing Rizzio and claimed innocence; in revenge they sent to the Queen proof of his participation.[34] Argyll, Lethington, and Bothwell proposed to the Queen that she should divorce him; she objected that this might endanger the succession. Lethington replied that they would find some means of freeing her from Darnley without prejudice to her son. She did not approve; she offered rather to retire from Scotland to let Darnley rule; and she ended the interview with a caution: "I will that ye do nothing whereby any spot may be laid to my honor or conscience; and therefore, I pray you, let the matter be as it is, abiding till God of His goodness put remedy thereto."[35] Several times now she talked of suicide.[36]

In or about October 1566, Argyll, Sir James Balfour, Bothwell, and perhaps Lethington signed a pact to get rid of Darnley. The Earl of Lennox got wind of the plot and warned his son; Darnley, who had been living apart from Mary, joined his father in Glasgow (December 1566). There he fell ill, apparently from smallpox, though rumors of poison rose. Meanwhile Mary's developing intimacy with Bothwell put her under suspicion of adultery; Knox openly called her a whore.[37] She seems to have approached Archbishop Hamilton about arranging a divorce of Bothwell from his wife. She offered to visit Darnley; he sent her an insulting reply; she went to him nevertheless (January 22, 1567), asserted her fidelity, and reawakened his love. She begged him to return to Edinburgh, where, she promised, she would nurse him back to health and happiness.

Here the "Casket Letters" enter upon the scene, and the rest of the story hinges in part on their authenticity, which is still in dispute after four hundred years. They were allegedly found in a silver casket which was presented by Mary to Bothwell and was taken from a servant of Bothwell on June 20, 1567, by agents of the nobles who were then seeking to dethrone the Queen. The casket was opened on the following day by Morton, Lethington, and other members of the Privy Council. As exhibited soon thereafter to the Scottish Parliament, and later to the English commission that tried Mary in 1568, the contents were eight letters and some fragmentary poems, all in French, undated and unaddressed but allegedly from Mary to Bothwell. The lords of the Council swore to the Scottish Parliament that the letters were genuine and had not been tampered with; Mary claimed that they had been forged. Her son apparently considered them authentic, for he destroyed them;[38] only copies remain. Continental rulers, shown copies, acted as if believing them genuine.[39] Elizabeth at first questioned, then hesitantly accepted, their authenticity. Our first impulse on reading them is to doubt that a woman meditating the murder of her husband would so carelessly and extensively express her intentions in letters entrusted to carriers who might be intercepted or corrupted; it appears improbable that letters so incriminating to Bothwell should have been preserved by him; and it is equally improbable that anyone in Scotland, even the clever Lethington (who is especially suspected), could have forged any substantial part of these letters in the single day between the capture of the casket and the display of the letters to the Council or the Parliament. The most incriminating letter—the second—is strangely long, taking up ten pages in print; if it was forged it is a most remarkable forgery, for its emotional content seems as true to Mary's nature as its writing is like her hand. It shows Mary as a pitying, hesitating, and ashamed accomplice in the murder of Darnley.*

The ailing, fearful, trusting King allowed himself to be carried across Scotland in a litter and placed in the old parsonage of Kirk o' Field on the outskirts of Edinburgh. Mary explained that she could not at once take him to Holyrood, lest he infect their child. For two weeks he lay there. Mary visited him daily and nursed him so sedulously that his strength returned, and he wrote to his father (February 7, 1567), ". . . my good health is the . . . sooner come through the good treatment of . . . the Queen, which I assure you hath all this while, and yet doth, use herself like a natural and loving wife. I hope yet that God will lighten our hearts with joy that have so long been afflicted with trouble."[41] Why she should have nursed him back through tedious weeks if she knew that he was to be killed is part of the mystery of Mary Stuart. On the evening of February 9 she left him to attend the wedding of one of her maids at Holyrood. That night an explosion occurred in the Kirk o' Field house, and in the morning Darnley was found dead in the garden.

Mary at first behaved like an innocent woman. She mourned and lamented and vowed vengeance; she had her room draped in black and curtained from the light, and she remained there in darkness and solitude. She ordered a judicial inquiry, and proclaimed a reward in money and land for information leading to the capture of the criminals. When placards appeared on city walls charging Bothwell with the murder, some implicating the Queen, a proclamation called upon the accusers to come forth with their evidence and promised the informers protection and rewards. The author(s) of the placards refused to

---

* Critical opinion inclines to describe the letters as mostly genuine, with some interpolations. Lord Acton, informed, Catholic, and honest, thought four of the letters genuine, the second forged.[40] Their text can be read in Andrew Lang's *Mystery of Mary Stuart*, 391–414.

appear, but the Earl of Lennox urged the Queen to bring Bothwell to trial at once. Bothwell seconded their demand. On April 12 he stood trial; Lennox, either lacking proofs or fearing Bothwell's soldiers in the capital, remained in Glasgow; Bothwell was acquitted, and the Parliament officially declared him innocent. On April 19 he persuaded Argyll, Huntly, Morton, and a dozen other nobles to sign "Ainslee's band," attesting their faith in his innocence, pledging themselves to defend him, and approving his marriage with Mary. She now favored Bothwell publicly and added to the many costly presents that she had already given him.

On April 23 she visited her son at Stirling; she was fated never to see him again. On her way back to Edinburgh she and Lethington were waylaid by Bothwell and his soldiers and were carried by force to Dunbar (April 24). Lethington protested; Bothwell threatened to kill him. Mary saved him and he was released; thereafter he joined the enemies of the Queen. At Dunbar negotiations were resumed for Bothwell's divorce. On May 3 he and Mary returned to Edinburgh; she declared herself free from constraint; on May 7 he was granted a divorce, and on the fifteenth, her Catholic confessor having refused to marry them, they were married according to the Protestant rite by the once Catholic Bishop of Orkney. Catholic Europe, formerly devoted to Mary, now turned against her as a lost soul. The Catholic clergy of Scotland stood aloof from her; the Protestant ministry called for her deposition; the populace was hostile; a sympathetic few attributed her reckless infatuation to a love potion given her by Bothwell.

On June 10 an armed band surrounded Borthwick Castle, where Mary and Bothwell were staying. They escaped, Mary dressed as a man. At Dunbar Bothwell gathered a thousand men, and with them he and Mary sought to force their way back to Edinburgh. They were opposed at Carberry Hill (June 15) by an equal force bearing a banner painted with figures of Darnley dead and the child James VI. Bothwell offered to settle the issue by single combat; Mary refused to allow him; she agreed to surrender if Bothwell were permitted to escape; later she claimed that the rebel leaders had promised loyalty to her if she joined them peacefully.[42] Bothwell fled to the coast and made his way to Denmark; there, after ten years of imprisonment by the Danish King, he died at the age of forty-two (1578).

Mary accompanied her captors to Edinburgh amid cries of soldiers and populace: "Burn the whore! Burn her!" "Kill her!" "Drown her!"[43] She was placed under guard in the provost's house; under her window, where she appeared disheveled and half clad, the crowd continued to threaten her with the coarsest epithets. On June 17, over her wild protests, she was removed to a remote and more secure imprisonment on an island in Loch Leven, a lake some thirty miles north of the capital. There, according to her secretary Claude Nau, she gave birth prematurely to twins.[44] She sent an appeal to the French government; it refused to interfere. Elizabeth instructed her envoy to promise Mary protection and to threaten the nobles with dire punishment if they should harm the Queen. Knox called for Mary's execution, and predicted that God would scourge Scotland with a great plague if Mary should be spared.[45] On June 20 the lords secured the Casket Letters. She appealed to the Parliament for a hearing; it refused, on the ground that the letters sufficiently disposed of her case. On July 24 she signed her abdication, and Murray was made regent for her son.

For almost eleven months she remained a captive in Lochleven Castle. Gradually the rigor of her confinement was relaxed; she ate with the family of William Douglas, lord of the castle; his younger brother George fell in love with her and helped her to escape (March 25, 1568). She was captured, but on May 2 she tried again and succeeded. Protected by young Douglas, she reached the mainland, where she was met by a party of Catholics. They rode through the night to the Firth of Forth, crossed it, and found refuge in the home of the Hamiltons. In five days six thousand men gathered there, sworn to set her again on the throne. But Murray called the Protestants of Scotland to arms; at Langside, near Glasgow, the two forces met (May 13); Mary's ill-disciplined army was overwhelmed. She took flight once more and rode wildly through three nights to Dundrennan Abbey on Solway Firth. Now she returned to its donor the diamond that Elizabeth had once given "her dearest sister," and she added a message: "I send back to its Queen this jewel, the token of her promised friendship and assistance."[46] On May 16, 1568, she crossed Solway Firth in an open fishing boat, entered England, and left her fate to her rival.

V. Expiation: 1568–87

From Carlisle she dispatched another message to Elizabeth, asking for an interview in which she might explain her behavior. Elizabeth, on principle averse to supporting rebellion against a legitimate sovereign, was inclined to invite her, but her Council confused her with cautions. If Mary were allowed to proceed to France, the French government would be tempted to send an army to Scotland to restore her and make Scotland again a Catholic ally of France and a thorn in England's rear; Mary's claim to the throne of England would then be supported by French arms as well as by English Catholics. If Mary remained free in England she would always be a possible source and center of Catholic revolt, and England was at heart still predominantly Catholic. If England should force the Scottish nobles to re-enthrone their Queen, their lives would be endangered and England would lose her Protestant allies in Scotland. Cecil would probably have agreed with Hallam that the forcible detention of the Queen of Scots violated all law, "natural, public, and municipal,"[47] but he felt that his overriding responsibility was to protect England.

As one function of diplomacy is to dress realism in morality, Mary was told that before her request for an interview with Elizabeth could be granted she must clear herself of various charges before a trial commission. Mary replied that she was a queen and could not be judged by lay commissioners, especially of another nation, and she demanded freedom to return to Scotland or go to France. She asked to meet Morton and Lethington in Elizabeth's presence, and promised to prove them guilty of Darnley's death. The English Council ordered her removed from Carlisle (as too near the border) to Bolton Castle, near York (July 13, 1568). Mary submitted to loose imprisonment there on Elizabeth's promise, "Put yourself in my hands without reserve; I will listen to nothing which shall be said against you; your honor shall be safe, and you shall be restored to your throne."[48] So mollified, Mary consented to appoint representatives to an examining commission. She tried to please Elizabeth by pretending to accept the Anglican faith and creed, but she assured Philip of Spain that she would never abandon the Catholic cause.[49] From that time onward Mary and Elizabeth ran an equal race in duplicity, the one excusing herself as a betrayed and royal prisoner, the other as an endangered queen.

The trial commission met at York October 4, 1568. Mary was represented by seven men, chiefly John Leslie, Catholic Bishop of Ross, and the Catholic Lord Herries of the western marches of Scotland; Elizabeth had appointed three Protestants: the Duke of Norfolk, the Earl of Sussex, and Sir Ralph Sadler. Before them appeared Murray, Morton, and Lethington, who privately showed the Englishmen the Casket Letters. If, they said, Mary would recognize Murray as regent and agree to reside in England on a large pension from Scotland, the letters would not be made public. Norfolk, who dreamed of marrying Mary and thereby becoming King of England on Elizabeth's death, refused, and Sussex wrote to Elizabeth that Mary seemed likely to prove her case.[50]

Elizabeth ordered the trial transferred to Westminster. There Murray laid the Casket Letters before her Council. Opinion remained divided as to the authenticity of the documents; but Elizabeth ruled that she could not receive Mary until the authenticity had been disproved. Mary asked to be shown the letters, either originals or copies; the commissioners refused, and Mary never saw either copies or originals.[51] The commission disbanded without announcing a decision (January 11, 1569); Murray was received by Elizabeth and then returned to Scotland with the letters; Mary, angry and defiant, was removed to stricter custody at Tutbury on the Trent. Foreign governments protested; Elizabeth replied that if they saw the evidence that had been presented to the commission they would consider her treatment of Mary rather lenient than severe.[52] The Spanish ambassador advised Philip to invade England and promised the collaboration of Catholic north England. Philip was skeptical of such aid, and Alva warned him that Elizabeth might order Mary's death at the first sign of invasion or revolt.

Revolt came. On November 14, 1569, the earls of Northumberland and Westmorland led a rebel army of 5,700 men into Durham, overthrew the Anglican Communion board, burned the Book of Common Prayer, restored the Catholic altar, and heard Mass. They planned a dash into Tutbury to release Mary, but Elizabeth balked them by transferring Mary to Coventry (November 23, 1569). The Earl of Sussex, with an army largely composed of Catholics, rapidly suppressed the rebellion. Elizabeth ordered all captured insurgents and their conniving servants to be hanged, and "the bodies were not to be removed, but remain till they fell to pieces where they hung."[53] Some six hundred men were so disposed of, and their property was confiscated by the Crown. Northumberland and Westmorland escaped to Scotland. In February 1570 Leonard Dacres led another uprising of Catholics; he too was defeated and fled across the border.

In January 1570 Knox wrote to Cecil advising him to order Mary's death at once, for "if ye strike not at the root, the branches that appear to be broken will bud again."[54] He had now finished his *History of the Reformation of Religioun within the Realme of Scotland*—a book making no pretense to impartiality, a narrative inaccurate but vivid and vital, a style quaint and idiomatic, sharp with the tongue of a preacher who called a whore a whore. A bitter man but a great man, building his dream to power more complete than Calvin's, hating heartily, fighting bravely, consuming to the last flicker the incredible energy of a tenacious will. By 1572 he had worn himself out. He could no longer walk unsupported, but he had himself aided every Sunday to his pulpit at St. Giles's. On November 9, 1572, he preached for the last time, and the entire congregation escorted him to his home. He died on November 24, aged sixty-seven, almost as poor as he had been born; he "had not made merchandise of the Word of God." He left posterity to judge him. "What I have been to my country, albeit this unthankful age will not know, yet the ages to come will be compelled to bear witness to the truth."[55] Few men have had so decisive an influence upon the beliefs of a people; few of his time equaled him in encouragement given to education, fanaticism, and self-government. He and Mary divided the soul of Scotland between them: he was the Reformation, she was the Renaissance. She lost because she did not know, like Elizabeth, how to marry them.

Mary, like some restless tiger caged, tried every corner and possibility of escape. In March 1571 Roberto di Ridolfi, a Florentine banker active in London, made himself an intermediary between Mary, the Spanish ambassador, the Bishop of Ross, Alva, Philip, and Pope Pius V. He proposed that Alva should send Spanish troops into England from the Netherlands, that a Catholic force should simultaneously invade England from Scotland, that Elizabeth should be dethroned, that Mary should be made Queen of England and Scotland, and that Norfolk should marry her. Norfolk was told of the plan, did not clearly approve of it, did not reveal it. Mary tentatively consented.[56] The Pope gave Ridolfi money for the enterprise and promised to recommend it to Philip;[57] Philip made his own approval conditional on Alva's; Alva ridiculed the project as visionary, and nothing came of it but tragedy for Mary's friends. Letters of Ridolfi and Norfolk were found on arrested servants of Mary and the Duke; Norfolk, Ross, and several Catholic nobles were imprisoned; Norfolk was tried for treason and convicted. Elizabeth hesitated to sign the death warrant of so prominent a noble, but Cecil, the English Parliament, and the Anglican hierarchy called for the execution of both Norfolk and Mary. Elizabeth compromised by sending Norfolk to the block (June 2, 1572). When news reached England of the Massacre of St. Bartholomew (August 22), there were revived cries for the death of Mary,[58] but Elizabeth still refused.

Only by remembering that Mary's captivity lasted almost nineteen years can we understand her desperation and her sense of bitter wrong. Her place of imprisonment was repeatedly changed, lest the sympathy felt for her in the neighborhood and among her custodians should beget or abet new plots. The conditions of her confinement were humane. She was permitted to receive her French pension of £1,200 a year; the English government gave her a substantial sum for food, medical treatment, servants, and entertainment; she was allowed to attend Mass and other Catholic services. She tried to pass the long hours with embroidery, reading, gardening, and play with her pet spaniels. As her hope of freedom faded, she lost interest in caring for herself; she took less exercise and became flaccid and fat. She suffered from rheumatism; sometimes her legs were so swollen that she could not walk. By 1577, when she was only thirty-five, her hair had turned white, and thereafter she covered it with a wig.

In June 1583 she offered, if released, to withdraw all claim to the English crown, never more to communicate with conspirators, to live anywhere in England according to Elizabeth's choice, never to go more than ten miles from that residence, and to submit to surveillance by neighboring gentlemen. Elizabeth was advised not to trust her.

Mary resumed her schemes for escape. By a variety of desperate devices she managed to correspond secretly with the French and Spanish ambassadors and governments, with her adherents in Scotland, and with representatives of the Pope. Letters were smuggled in and out, in the washing, in books, in sticks, in wigs, in the lining of shoes. But the spies of Cecil and Walsingham uncovered every plot in time. Even among the students and priests at the Jesuit college in Reims Walsingham had an agent who kept him informed.

The romantic aura of the captive Queen touched the sympathy of many young Englishmen, and aroused the ardor of Catholic youths. In 1583 Francis Throckmorton, Catholic nephew of Elizabeth's late ambassador to France, organized another plot to release her. He was soon detected; tortured into confession, he moaned, "I have disclosed the secrets of her who was the dearest to me in all the world."[59] He died under the executioner's ax at the age of thirty.

A year later William Parry, a spy in Cecil's service, induced a papal nuncio in Paris to forward to Gregory XIII a request for a plenary indulgence on the ground that he was entering upon a dangerous attempt to free Mary Stuart and bring England back to the Catholic Church. The papal secretary of state replied (January 30, 1584) that the Pope had seen Parry's petition, rejoiced at his resolve, was sending him the desired indulgence, and would reward his efforts.[60] Parry took this reply to Cecil. Another English spy, Edmund Neville, accused Parry of urging him to assassinate Elizabeth. Parry was arrested, confessed, was hanged, and, still alive, was cut down and dismembered.[61]

Angered by a long succession of conspiracies, and frightened by the assassination of William of Orange, Elizabeth's Council drew up (October 1584) a "Bond of Association" pledging the signers never to accept, as successor to their Queen, any person in whose behalf Elizabeth's life had been attempted, and to prosecute to the death any person involved in such an enterprise. The bond was signed by the Council, by most members of Parliament, and by prominent men throughout England. A year later Parliament gave it the sanction of law.

It did not deter further plots. In 1586 John Ballard, a Roman Catholic priest, induced Anthony Babington, a rich young Catholic, to organize a conspiracy for the assassination of Elizabeth, the invasion of England by armies from Spain, France, and the Low Countries, and the enthronement of Mary. Babington wrote to Mary about the plot, told her that six Catholic nobles had agreed to "get rid of the usurper of the throne," and asked her approval of the plan. In a letter of July 17, 1586, Mary accepted Babington's proposals, gave no explicit consent to the assassination of Elizabeth, but promised rewards for the success of the undertaking.[62] The messenger to whom her secretary entrusted this reply was a secret agent of Walsingham; he had the letter copied and sent the copy to Walsingham and the letter itself to Babington. On August 14 Babington and Ballard were arrested; soon three hundred prominent Catholics were jailed; the two leaders confessed, and Mary's secretary was induced to acknowledge the authenticity of Mary's letter.[63] Thirteen of the conspirators were executed. Bonfires were lighted throughout London, bells rang, and children sang psalms, in thanksgiving for the preservation of Elizabeth's life. All Protestant England cried out for Mary's death.

Mary's rooms were searched and all her papers were seized. On October 6 she was transferred to Fotheringay Castle. There she was tried by a commission of forty-three nobles. She was not allowed a defender, but she defended herself resolutely. She admitted complicity in the Babington plot, but denied having sanctioned assassination. She protested that, as a person unjustly and illegally imprisoned for nineteen years, she had a right to free herself by whatever means. She was unanimously condemned, and Parliament asked Elizabeth to order her death. Henry III of France made a polite plea for mercy, but Elizabeth thought that such a plea came with poor grace from a government that had massacred thousands of Protestants without trial. Most of Scotland now defended its Queen, but her son made only a halfhearted intercession, for he suspected that, because of his Protestantism, she had disowned him in her will. His agent in London suggested to Walsingham that James VI, though anxious that his mother should not be beheaded, might be reconciled to much if the English Parliament would confirm his title to succeed Elizabeth, and if Elizabeth would increase the pension she had been sending him. The very canny Scot dallied so greedily that the citizens of Edinburgh hooted him in the streets.[64] Nothing remained between Mary and death but Elizabeth's hesitation.

The harassed Queen allowed almost three months to drag by before she made up her mind, and then she did not. She was capable of generosity and mercy, but she was tired of living every day in fear of assassination by the adherents of a woman who had claimed her throne. She considered the danger of invasion from France, Spain, and Scotland in protest against the execution of a queen; and she calculated the possibility that she herself might suffer a natural or violent death in time to let Mary and Catholicism inherit England. Cecil urged her to sign the death warrant and promised to take full responsibility for the results. She thought to avoid decision by intimating that Sir Amias Paulet, Mary's keeper, could clear up the confusion by ordering Mary's execution on a merely verbal understanding that the Queen or her Council desired it; but Paulet refused to act without a written order from Elizabeth. Finally she signed the warrant; her secretary, William Davison, delivered it to the Council, which at once dispatched it to Paulet before Elizabeth could change her mind.

Mary, who during this long delay had begun to hope, met the news at first with unbelief, then with courage. She wrote a touching letter to Elizabeth, asking her to "permit my poor desolated servants . . . to carry away my corpse, to bury it in holy ground, with the other queens of France." On the morning of her execution, we are told, she wrote a little Latin poem having all the grace and fervor of a medieval hymn:

> *O Domine Deus! speravi in te.*
> *O care mi Jesu! nunc libera me.*
> *In dura catena, in misera poena, desidero te;*
> *Languendo, gemendo, et genu flectendo,*
> *Adoro, imploro, ut liberes me.*[*65]

---

* O Lord God! I have hoped in Thee.
O my dear Jesus! now free me.
In cruel chains, in bitter pain, I desire Thee.
Longing, moaning, and bending the knee,
I adore. I implore, that you set me free.

She asked to be allowed to confess to her Catholic chaplain; she was refused. Her jailers offered her an Anglican dean instead; she rejected him. She robed herself royally to meet death, arranged her false hair carefully, and covered her face with a white veil. A golden crucifix hung from her neck, an ivory crucifix was in her hand. She inquired why her attendant women were forbidden to be present at her execution; she was told that they might make a disturbance; she promised that they would not, and she was allowed to take two of them and four men. Some three hundred English gentlemen were admitted to the scene in the great hall of Fotheringay Castle (February 8, 1587). Two masked executioners asked and received her forgiveness. When her women began to cry she checked them, saying, "I promised for you." She knelt and prayed, then laid her head upon the block. The wig fell from her severed head and disclosed her white hair. She was forty-four years old.

———————————————

Pardon is the word for all. Pardon for Mary, who labored bravely to be a just as well as a joyful queen; we cannot believe that she who tended her husband so long and brought him back to health had consented to his murder; we can forgive the young woman who gave up everything for a love however foolish; we must pity the desolate woman who came to England for refuge and found, instead, nineteen years of imprisonment; and we can understand her wild attempts to regain her liberty. But we can also forgive the great Queen, whose councilors insisted on Mary's confinement as vital to England's security, who saw her life and policy continually threatened by plots to free and enthrone her rival, and who prolonged that cruel captivity only because she could not bring herself to end it with a warrant for Mary's execution. They were both noble women: one noble and hastily emotional, the other noble and hesitantly wise. Fitly they lie near each other in Westminster Abbey, reconciled in death and peace.

CHAPTER VI

JAMES VI AND I

1567–1625

I. James VI of Scotland: 1567–1603

James VI was crowned King of Scotland (July 29, 1567) at the age of thirteen months, while his mother lay captive at Lochleven. He was eight months old when his presumptive father, Darnley, was killed, ten months old when he saw his mother for the last time; she could never be anything more to him than a name and an imagination blurred with contumely and far-off tragedy. He was brought up by self-seeking lords and by teachers hostile to his mother. He received ample education in the humanities, too much in theology and too little in morals, and he became the most learned hard drinker in Europe.

Four regents in succession ruled Scotland in his name—Murray, Lennox, Mar, Morton; all but one died by violence. Rival noble bands fought for the King's person as the aegis of power. In 1582 some Protestant lords, supported by the Kirk, confined him in Ruthven Castle for fear that he might submit to the influence of his Catholic relative Esmé Stuart. Released, he promised to defend Protestantism, signed an alliance with Protestant England, and, aged seventeen, undertook to be actual king (1583).

He was unique among sovereigns. His manners were rough, his gait ungainly, his voice loud, his conversation a cross of coarseness with pedantry. One not too kindly to him judged that "in languages, sciences, and affairs of state he has more learning than any man in Scotland."[1] But the same observer added, "He is prodigiously conceited"; perhaps this trait was a life preserver in a sea of troubles, as well as the warped perspective of one who could never recall when he had not been king. He must have had some saving intelligence to keep his crown on his head in Scotland and wear a greater one in England to a natural death. He was a bit unsteady about sex; he married the Danish Catholic Princess Anne, but he had little taste for women, and indulged his friendliness with favorites to the point of giving gossip a lead.

He had to weave his way craftily amid the furious dogmatisms of his time. The Guises in France, Philip in Spain, the Pope in Rome, pleaded with him to bring Scotland back to the Catholic Church, but the Scottish Kirk watched his every word lest he deviate from the Calvinist line. He burned no bridges behind him. He corresponded politely with Catholic powers and was inclined to soften the laws against Catholic worship; he secretly released a captured Jesuit and connived at another's escape.[2] But Catholic plots angered him, England's victorious Protestantism impressed him; he cast in his lot with the Kirk.

It was no comfortable bedfellow. By 1583 its ministers formed the great majority of the Scottish clergy. Poor in income and in secular learning, they were rich in devotion and courage. They labored to restore neglected churches, they organized schools, administered charity, defended the peasants against the lords, and preached long sermons which their congregations absorbed in place of printed material. In the kirk sessions, the provincial synods, and the General Assembly the new clergy now enjoyed a power rivaling that which the Catholic hierarchy had wielded before them. Claiming divine inspiration and therefore infallibility in faith and morals, they assumed over public and private conduct a control much more rigorous than under the lax guardians of the older creed. In many towns they levied fines on Scots who failed to attend kirk services. They prescribed public penitence, sometimes physical penalties, for detected sins.[3] Alarmed by the prevalence of fornication and adultery, they commissioned the elders to watch with especial severity over sexual deviations, and to report these to the sessions and the synods of the Kirk. Shocked by the license of the English stage, they sought to prohibit theatrical performances in Scotland; and failing in this, they forbade their people to attend them. Like their predecessors, they made heresy a capital crime. They pursued witches with burning zeal and voted firewood for the pyres.[4] They persuaded the Parliament to decree the death penalty for any priest who thrice said Mass; this edict, however, was not enforced. On hearing of the Massacre of St. Bartholomew, the Kirk called for a massacre of Catholics in Scotland, but the state neglected to co-operate.[5]

Except for the ministerial claim to inspiration and infallibility, the Kirk was one of the most democratic institutions of its time. The parish parson was chosen by the elders, subject to the approval of the congregation, and the laity shared in the sessions, the synods, and the General Assembly. These democratic tentatives irritated the aristocratic Parliament and the anointed King. Arguing—perhaps believing—that he ruled by divine right, James complained that "some fiery-spirited men in the ministry got such a guiding of the people . . . that, finding the gust [taste] of government sweet, they began to fancy a democratic form . . . I was calumniated in their sermons not for any vice in me but because I was king, which they thought the highest evil."[6] The medieval struggle between Church and state was resumed.

Now it took the form of an attack by the ministers on the bishops. These, a Catholic legacy to the Kirk, were formally chosen by the ministers, but were actually nominated, and often forced upon the clergy, by the Regent or the King, and they handed over a large part of their ecclesiastical revenues to the state. The ministers saw no warrant in Scripture for episcopacy, and resolved to run it out of Scotland as incompatible with the popular organization of the Kirk.

Their leader, Andrew Melville, was a fiery Scot equipped by nature to inherit the mantle of John Knox. After a university education at St. Andrews, he continued his studies in Paris and then imbibed the Calvinist gospel from Bèze in Geneva. Returning to Scotland (1574), he was at once appointed, at the age of twenty-nine, principal of Glasgow University, and he ably reorganized its curriculum and discipline. In 1578 he shared in compiling the Second Book of Discipline, which denounced episcopacy in the name of ministerial equality. He argued for the definite separation of spheres between Church and state, and this influenced their separation in the United States; but he claimed the right of the ministers to teach the civil magistrates how to exercise their powers "according to the word."[7] James, however, wanted to be an absolute ruler like Henry VIII or Elizabeth; he believed in bishops as necessary in ecclesiastical administration, and as convenient intermediaries between Church and state.

In 1580 the General Assembly of the Kirk "damned" the office of bishops as a "folly of men's invention"; all bishops were commanded, under penalty of excommunication, to cease their functions, and to apply to the Assembly for admission as simple ministers. The government rejected the Second Book of Discipline and held that no excommunication should be valid unless ratified by the state. In 1581 Lennox, then regent, nominated Robert Montgomerie to be Archbishop of Glasgow. The Glasgow ministry refused to elect him; he insisted on officiating nevertheless; the General Assembly, led by Melville, excommunicated him (1582); Montgomerie yielded and withdrew. Melville, accused of sedition, rejected a civil, demanded an ecclesiastical, trial; condemned for contempt of court, he fled to England (1584). James persuaded the Parliament to declare treasonable any refusal to submit to secular jurisdiction, any meddling of ministers in affairs of state, any resistance to the episcopate, any convocations unlicensed by the King. Many ministers, rather than accept these decrees, followed Melville into exile. James, savoring his sovereignty, indulged himself in a reign of terror: ministers were punished because they prayed for their exiled brethren; two men were put to death for communicating with them; two others were executed on a charge of conspiracy.

The clergy and their congregations resisted with Scottish tenacity. Pamphlets of undiscovered origin blackened the King, ballads sang the shame of his tyranny, even women wrote diatribes committing him to hell. His bishops received less and less money, transmitted ever less to the state; James found himself starved of coin—the very sinews of his will. Year by year he weakened, until the Parliament of 1592, with his dour consent, voted a charter of liberty to the Kirk, restoring to it all its powers of jurisdiction and discipline, and abolishing the episcopate. The exiles returned.

Melville, bolder than ever, called James to his face "God's silly vassal," and gave the theocratic gospel to him in 1596 as firmly as Gregory VII to Emperor Henry IV five hundred years before (1077): "There are two kings and two kingdoms in Scotland: there is Christ Jesus and His Kingdom the Kirk, whose subject King James VI is . . . not a king, nor a head, nor a lord, but a member."[8] David Black, minister at St. Andrews, told his congregation (1596) that all kings were children of the Devil, Elizabeth was an atheist, and James was Satan himself.[9] The English ambassador protested. The Privy Council summoned Black to trial. He refused to appear, saying that an offense in the pulpit was subject only to a court of the Kirk, and that, besides, he had received his message from God. James ordered him tried in absentia. A committee of ministers came to the King; he yielded nothing; on the contrary, he demanded that acts of the ecclesiastical Assembly, as of Parliament, must be subject to his ratification. The ministers proclaimed a general fast, and declared ominously that, whatever happened, "they were free of his Majesty's blood."[10]

A riotous crowd gathered about the building where James was staying (December 17, 1596). He fled to Holyrood Palace, and next morning removed with all his court from Edinburgh. He declared to its people, by a herald, that it was not fit to be a capital, and that he would never return except to execute judgment on rebels;

and he ordered all clergy and nonresidents to leave the city. The rioters, having no one to kill, dispersed. The merchants bemoaned the loss of court trade; the citizens wondered whether the dispute was worth economic martyrdom; James returned in angry triumph (January 1, 1597). The General Assembly, meeting at Perth, offered the Kirk's submission; it agreed that no ministers were to be appointed in the chief cities without the consent of the King and the congregation; that ministers were not to preach about acts of Parliament or the Privy Council, and that no man was to be personally attacked from the pulpit. The ministers were allowed to re-enter the capital (1597), but the episcopate was restored. A sullen truce settled down upon the ancient war between Church and state.

Two figures stand out in the Scottish literature of this period: the King himself and the most famous of his teachers. George Buchanan had an astonishing career. Born in Stirlingshire in 1506, he studied in Paris, served as a soldier in France and Scotland, caught scholastic and political fire from the lectures of John Major, returned for love and learning to Paris, came back to Scotland a satirical heretic, was imprisoned by Cardinal Beaton, escaped to Bordeaux, taught Latin there, wrote poems and dramas in remarkably good Latin, saw his pupil Montaigne act in one of these plays, headed a college in Coimbra, was imprisoned by the Spanish Inquisition for making fun of friars, went back to Scotland, to France, to Scotland, tutored Mary Queen of Scots (1562), was made moderator of the General Assembly (1567), pronounced the Casket Letters authentic, was accused of forging part of them,[11] condemned Mary without mercy in his *Detectio Mariae Reginae* (1571), tutored her son over her protests, and gave up the ghost in 1582. His *Rerum Scoticarum historia* (1579) labored to free his country's history from "English ties and Scottish vanity." His treatise *De iure regni apud Scotos* (1579) boldly reaffirmed, in the face of his soon-to-be-autocratic pupil, the medieval doctrine that the sole source of political power, under God, is the people; that every society rests on an implicit social contract of mutual obligations and restraints between the governed and the governors; that the will of the majority may rightly rule the whole; that the king is subject to the laws passed by the representatives of the people; and that a tyrant may justly be resisted, deposed, or killed.[12] Here was the social-contract myth a century before Hobbes, two centuries before Rousseau. The book was condemned by the Scottish Parliament and burned by the University of Oxford, but it had a powerful influence. Samuel Johnson thought that Buchanan was the only man of genius that Scotland had produced.[13] Hume modestly gave this plume to Napier; Carlyle, being Knox *redivivus*, offered it to Knox; and James VI had his own views on the matter.

The King was as proud of his books as of his regalia. In 1616 he published, in a huge folio, *The Works of the Most High and Mighty Prince James,* which he dedicated to Jesus Christ. He wrote poems, advice to poets, a translation of the Psalms, a study of the Apocalypse, a treatise on demons, and, in the *annus mirabilis* 1598, two royal octavos in defense of absolute monarchy. One, the *Basilikon Doron* (1598), or *Kingly Gift,* was a book of advice to his son Henry on the art and the duties of sovereignty; it emphasized the ruling of the Kirk as "no small part of the king's office." The other volume, *The True Law of Free Monarchies,* expounded absolutism with considerable eloquence: kings were chosen by God, since all important events were dictated by His Providence; their divine appointment and anointment constituted a mystery as holy and ineffable as any sacrament; therefore their rule had every right to be absolute, and resistance to it was a folly, a crime, and a sin bound to cause more harm than any tyranny. What to Elizabeth had been a useful myth became to James a passionate principle, born of being born of a queen. His son Charles inherited the doctrine and paid the penalty.

England, however, did not in 1598 foresee 1649. After James had pledged himself to Protestantism, the leaders of Elizabeth's Privy Council recognized him as heir, through Mary, to the English crown. Four days after Elizabeth's death James began (April 5, 1603) a festive progress from Edinburgh to London; he stopped leisurely en route to be feted by the English nobility; on May 6 he reached a London which was all decked out to welcome him—crowds genuflecting before him, lords kissing his hands. After a millennium of useless strife the two nations (not till 1707 the two parliaments) were united under one king. So fruitful had been Elizabeth's barren womb.

II. James I of England: 1603–14

What sort of a man had he become in thirty-seven years? Of middle stature, weak legs, slightly swollen paunch, padded doublet and breeches to impede assassins' knives; brown hair, ruddy cheeks, knobby nose, a look of suspicion and sadness in the blue eyes, as if the god were conscious of his clay. A little lazy, resting on Elizabeth's oars. Profane in his language, coarse in his amusements; stammering and absolute, wagging too loosely his burry tongue. Vain and generous, timorous and deceitful because often endangered and deceived; ready to take and give offense, to grant and sue for pardon. When John Gib denied having lost some precious documents, James lost his temper, kicked him; then, having found the papers, he knelt down before his humiliated aide and would not rise till Gib had forgiven him. Tolerant amid intolerance, sometimes hard, usually kind and affectionate, suspecting his son Henry as too popular, loving his son Charles to foolishness; unblemished in his relations with women, but given to fondling handsome young men. Superstitious and learned, silly and shrewd, taking demons and witches seriously but favoring Bacon and Jonson; jealous of scholars and enamored of books. One of his first acts as King of England was to empower Oxford and Cambridge to send representatives to Parliament. When he saw the Bodleian Library he cried out, "If I were not a king, I would be a university man; and if it were so that I must be a prisoner, if I might have my wish, I would desire to have no other prison than that Library, and to be chained together with so many good authors and dead masters."[14] All in all, a man a bit off balance and key, but at bottom good-natured, good-humored, ridiculed by the clever, but forgiven by his people because, till near his melancholy end, he gave them security and peace.

He was so unfriendly to water that he resented having to use it for washing. He drank to excess and allowed some court festivities to end in a general and bisexual intoxication. Extravagance in dress and entertainment prevailed at his court even beyond Elizabethan precedent. Masques had been favored by Elizabeth; but now, when Ben Jonson wrote the lines and Inigo Jones designed the costumes and scenery, and the roles were played by gorgeous lords and ladies swathed in the revenues of the kingdom, the fabulous, fantastic art reached its apogee. The court became gayer than ever, and more corrupt. "I do think," says a lady in one of Jonson's plays, "if nobody should love me but my poor husband, I should e'en hang myself."[15] Courtiers accepted substantial "gifts" to use their influence in getting charters, patents, monopolies, or offices for applicants; Baron Montagu paid £20,000 for appointment as Lord Treasurer;[16] one tender soul, we are told on not the best authority, grew sick and died when he learned how much his friends had paid to have him made recorder.[17]

James took all such matters in his stride, and did not trouble himself too laboriously with government. He left administration to a Privy Council of six

Englishmen and six Scots, headed by Robert Cecil, whom he made Earl of Salisbury in 1605. Cecil had every advantage of heredity except health. He was crippled with a humped back and made a lamentable appearance to the world; but he had all his father's acumen in the selection and ordering of men, and a silent tenacity and crafty courtesy that outwitted domestic rivals and foreign courts. When "my little beagle" died (1612), James fell under the sway of handsome young Robert Carr, made him Earl of Somerset, and allowed him to supersede, in policy and administration, such older and far more accomplished men as Francis Bacon and Edward Coke.

Coke was the embodiment and the watchdog of the law. He rose to fame by his tenacious prosecution of Essex in 1600, Raleigh in 1603, the Gunpowder Plotters in 1605. In 1610 he issued a historic opinion:

> It appears in our books that in many cases the common law will control [override] acts of Parliament, and sometimes adjudge them to be utterly void. For when an act of Parliament is against common right and reason . . . or impossible to be performed, the common law will control it and adjudge such an act to be void.[18]

Parliament may not have relished this, but James made Coke chief justice of the King's Bench (1613), and a member of the Privy Council. From being the King's man he became the King's gadfly, condemning inquisitions into private opinions, upholding parliamentary freedom of speech, and puncturing the royal absolutism with sharp reminders that kings are the servants of the law. In 1616 Bacon, his rival, brought charges of malfeasance against him. Coke was dismissed, but he was returned to Parliament; continuing to lead the resistance to the King, he was sent to the Tower (1621), but was soon released. He died impenitent (1634), obstinately faithful to the letter and rigor of the law, and leaving behind him four volumes of *Institutes* that still stand as a pillar and monument of English jurisprudence.*

---

* Aubrey informs us that Coke's second wife, the widow of Sir William Hatton, "was with child when he married her. Laying his hand on her belly (when he came to bed), and finding a child to stir, 'What,' said he, 'flesh in the pot?' 'Yea,' quoth she, 'or else I would not have married a cook.'"[19]—for so his name was pronounced. We might add that she had already refused Bacon.

Meanwhile James had been carrying on with Parliament the debate that in his son's reign would eventuate in civil war and regicide. He did not merely assume all the powers that Henry VIII and Elizabeth had wielded over their cowed or grumbling legislators; he formulated his claims as divine imperatives. To the Parliament of 1609 he announced:

> The state of monarchy is the supremest thing upon earth. For kings are not only God's lieutenants on earth, and sit upon God's throne, but even by God Himself are called gods. . . . Kings are justly called gods, for that they exercise a manner or resemblance of divine power on earth; for if you will consider the attributes of God, you shall see how they agree in the person of a king. God hath power to create or destroy, make or unmake at His pleasure, to give life or send death, to judge all and be judged nor accountable to none . . . And the like power have kings; they make and unmake their subjects, they have power of raising and casting down, of life and death; judges over all their subjects and in all causes, and yet accountable to none but God only. They have power to . . . make of their subjects like men at the chess—a pawn to take a bishop or a knight—and to cry up or down any of their subjects, as they do their money.[20]

This was quite a step backward, for medieval political theory had regularly made the king a delegate of the sovereign people; only the popes had professed to be the viceroys of God. To put the best philosophical front on this claim we must assume that the popes, as the final heads of authority in the Middle Ages, had believed the individualistic impulses of men to be so powerful that social order could be maintained only by inculcating in the people a traditional reverence for ecclesiastical authority, and for the popes as the voice and vicars of God. The weakening or destruction of papal authority by the Reformation had left the political powers primarily or ultimately responsible for social order; and they too judged that a purely human authority would be too challengeable to restrain effectively, or economically, the antisocial proclivities of men. Hence the doctrine of the divine right of kings grew side by side with the development of nationalism and the reduction of papal power. The Lutheran princes of Germany, having assumed the spiritual powers of the old Church in their realms, felt justified in transferring to themselves the divine aura which almost all rulers before 1789 considered indispensable to moral authority and social peace. James made the mistake of expressing this assumption too clearly, and in the most extreme form.

Parliament might have yielded (with private smiles) some theoretical acceptance of this royal absolutism if, as in Elizabeth's heyday, its members had been great landowners largely indebted to the Tudors for their title deeds. But the House of Commons now included among its 467 members many representatives of the rising mercantile classes—who could not stomach a limitless royal power over their money—and many Puritans who repudiated the claim of the King to rule their religion. The House defined its rights in bold disregard of James's divinity. It declared itself the sole judge in contested elections to its membership. It demanded freedom of speech and security from arrest during its sessions; without these, it argued, Parliament would be meaningless. It proposed to legislate on matters religious, and denied the authority of the king to decide such issues without parliamentary consent; the Anglican bishops, however, claimed for their Convocation the right to rule in ecclesiastical affairs, subject only to the approval of the king. The Speaker of the Commons informed James that the king could not institute any law, but could only ratify or reject the laws that Parliament had passed. "Our privileges and liberties," declared the Commons (June 1604), "are our rights and due inheritance, no less than our very lands and goods . . . They cannot be withheld from us . . . but with apparent wrong to the whole state of the realm."[21]

So the lines were drawn for that historic struggle between the "prerogative" of the king and the "privilege" of Parliament—which, after a hundred victories and defeats, would create the democracy of England.

III. The Gunpowder Plot: 1605

Above the economic and political strife, but deeply rooted in it, the religious warfare raged. Half the pamphlets that bruised the air were blasts of Puritans against Anglican bishops and ritual, of Anglicans against Puritan rigor and intransigence, or of both against Catholic plots to restore England to papal obedience. James underrated the intensity of these hatreds. He dreamed of an *entente demi-cordiale* between Puritans and Anglicans, and for that purpose called their leaders to a conference at Hampton Court (January 14, 1604). He presided like another Constantine, and astonished both parties by his theological learning and his debating skill, but he insisted on "one doctrine and one discipline, one religion in substance and ceremony,"[22] and declared episcopacy indispensable. The Bishop of London thought the King divinely inspired, "the like of whom had not been seen since the time of Christ";[23] but the Puritans complained that James had acted like a partisan rather than a judge; and nothing came of the conference except the unexpectedly historic decision to make a new translation of the Bible. The Convocation of 1604 issued canons requiring conformity of all clergymen to Anglican worship; those refusing to comply were dismissed, and several were imprisoned; many resigned; some migrated to Holland or America.

James disgraced himself by having two Unitarians burned for doubting the divinity of Christ despite the proofs which he offered them (1612), but he distinguished himself by never thereafter allowing an execution for religious dissent; these were the last men to die for heresy in England. Slowly, as secular rule improved, the idea that religious toleration was compatible with public morals and national unity was making headway against the almost universal conviction that social order required a faith and a Church which were unchallengeable. In 1614 Leonard Busher's *Religious Peace* argued that religious persecution intensified dissent, compelled hypocrisy, and injured trade; and he reminded James that "Jews, Christians, and Turks are tolerated in Constantinople and yet are peaceable."[24] However, Busher thought that persons whose religion was "tainted with treason"—probably meaning such Catholics as put the pope above the king—should be forbidden to hold assemblies or to live within ten miles of London.

For the most part James was a tolerant dogmatist. He offended the Puritans by permitting—encouraging—Sunday sports, provided one had first attended Anglican services. He was inclined to relax the laws against Catholics. Over the heads of Robert Cecil and the Council he suspended the recusancy laws; he allowed priests to enter the country and say Mass in private homes. He dreamed, in his loose and philosophic way, of reconciling Catholic and Protestant Christendom.[25] But when Catholics multiplied in this sunshine and the Puritans denounced his lenience, he allowed the Elizabethan anti-Catholic laws to be renewed, extended, and enforced (1604). To send anyone abroad to a Catholic college or seminary was made punishable by a fine of one hundred pounds. All Catholic missionaries were banished, all Catholic teaching prohibited. Persons neglecting Anglican services were fined twenty pounds per month; any default in paying such fines involved forfeiture of property, real and personal; all the cattle on the delinquent's lands, all his furniture and wearing apparel, were to be seized for the Crown.[26]

Some half-crazed Catholics thought there was now no remedy but assassination. Robert Catesby had seen his father suffer imprisonment for recusancy under Elizabeth; he had joined in Essex' rebellion against the Queen; it was he who now conceived the Gunpowder Plot to blow up Westminster Palace while the King, the royal family, the Lords, and the Commons were assembled there for the opening of Parliament. He brought into the conspiracy Thomas Winter, Thomas Percy, John Wright, and Guy Fawkes. The five men swore one another to secrecy and sealed their oaths by taking the Sacrament from a Jesuit missionary, John Gerard. They engaged a house adjacent to the palace; sixteen hours a day they labored to dig a tunnel from one cellar to the other; they succeeded and placed thirty casks of gunpowder directly under the meeting chamber of the House of Lords. Repeated postponements of Parliament kept the project in precarious abeyance; through a year and a half the conspirators had to feed the fires of their wrath. At times they doubted the morality of an enterprise in which many innocent persons would perish with those whom the Catholics thought mercilessly guilty. To reassure them, Catesby asked Henry Garnett, provincial of the Jesuits in England, whether in war it was permissible to share in actions that would bring death to innocent noncombatants; Garnett answered that divines of all faiths agreed in the affirmative, but warned Catesby that any plot against the lives of governmental officials would only bring greater suffering to English Catholics. The provincial conveyed his suspicions to the Pope and the general of the Jesuits; they bade him keep aloof from all political intrigues and discourage all attempts against the state.[27] To another Jesuit, Oswald Greenway, Catesby in confession revealed the plot, which now included measures for a general rising of Catholics in England. Greenway reported the plot to Garnett. The two Jesuits hesitated between betraying the conspirators to the government and remaining silent; they chose to keep silent, but to do all in their power to dissuade the conspirators.

Catesby sought to quiet the qualms of his associates by arranging that on the morning of the appointed day friendly members of Parliament should receive urgent messages to call them away from Westminster. A minor figure in the plot warned his friend Lord Monteagle several days before the session was to begin. Mounteagle laid the matter before Cecil, who told the King.

Their agents entered the cellars, found Fawkes there and the explosives in due place. Fawkes was arrested (November 4, 1605); he confessed his intentions to blow up Parliament the next day, but, despite extreme torture, refused to name his accomplices. These, however, revealed themselves by taking up arms and attempting flight. They were pursued and gave battle; Catesby, Percy, and Wright were mortally wounded, and several subalterns were hunted and secured. When the prisoners were tried they freely acknowledged the conspiracy, but no threat or torment could induce them to implicate the Jesuit priests. Fawkes and three others were drawn on hurdles from the Tower to Parliament House and were there executed (January 27, 1606). England still celebrates November 5 as Guy Fawkes Day, with bonfires and fireworks and the carrying of "guys," or effigies, through the streets.

Gerard and Greenway escaped to the Continent, but Garnett was captured, and with him another Jesuit, Oldcorne. In the Tower these two found means of what they supposed to be secret conversation, but spies reported their words. Separately accused of these conferences, Garnett denied them, Oldcorne admitted them; Garnett confessed that he had lied. Breaking down, he conceded that he had had knowledge of the plot; but as this had come to him from Greenway, and Greenway had received it under the seal of confession, he had not felt free to reveal it; however, he had done all in his power to discourage it. He was pronounced guilty, not of the plot but of concealing it. For six weeks the King delayed signing the death warrant. Garnett, falsely informed that Greenway was in the Tower, sent him a letter; it was intercepted; asked if he had communicated with Greenway, he denied it; confronted with the letter, he argued that equivocation was permitted to a person to save his life. On May 3, 1606, he was hanged, drawn, and quartered.[28]

Parliament felt justified in intensifying the statutes against Catholics (1606). They were barred from the practice of medicine or law, and from serving as executors or guardians; they were forbidden to travel more than five miles from their houses; and a new oath was demanded of them which not only denied the power of the popes to depose secular rulers, but branded the assertion of that power as impious, heretical, and damnable.[29] Pope Paul V forbade the taking of this oath; a majority of English Catholics obeyed him; a large minority accepted it. In 1606 six priests were executed for refusing it and for saying Mass; between 1607 and 1618 sixteen more were put to death.[30] The prisons held several hundred priests, several thousand Catholic laymen. Despite these terrors, Jesuits continued to enter England; there were at least 68 there in 1615, 284 in 1623.[31] Some Jesuits found their way into Scotland; one of them, John Ogilvie, was put to death there in 1615, after having his legs crushed in torture by "the boots," and being kept awake for eight consecutive days and nights by the insertion of pins into his flesh.[32] All the sins of the old Church were visited upon her by the new certainties and powers.

IV. The Jacobean Stage

The English ecstasy continued in literature as well as in religion. To the age of James I belong the better half of Shakespeare's plays, much of Chapman, most of Jonson, Webster, Middleton, Dekker, Marston, some of Massinger, all of Beaumont and Fletcher; in poetry Donne, in prose Burton and, noblest of all, the King James version of the Bible: these are glories enough for any reign. The King had a taste for drama; in one Christmas season fourteen plays were acted at his court. The Globe theater was burned to the ground in 1613 by the firing of two cannons in a production of *Henry VIII,* but it was soon rebuilt, and by 1631 there were seventeen theaters in or near London.

George Chapman was five years older than Shakespeare and outlived him by eighteen, spanning three reigns (1559–1634). He took his time maturing; by 1598 he had successfully completed Marlowe's *Hero and Leander,* and had published seven books of *The Iliad;* but his translation of Homer was not finished till 1615, and his best plays came between 1607 and 1613. He opened a new field to English drama by taking a theme from recent French history in his *Bussy d'Ambois* (1607?)—five acts of blusterous oratory rarely redeemed with magic of phrase, but rising to corrosive power in a page where Bussy and his enemy exchange ironic compliments as indigestible as truth. Chapman never recovered from his education; his much Greek and more Latin sat stiflingly upon his muse, and to read his plays is now a labor of lore, hardly of love. Nor do we thrill as Keats did "on first looking into Chapman's Homer." There is a sturdy vigor in these heptameters that here and there lifts them above Pope's generally better version, but the music of poetry dies in translation; the leaping hexameters of the original carry us on with swifter melody than the measured, fettered feet of rhyming verse. No long English poem in rhyme has escaped the somnolence of a barcarolle. Chapman changed to "heroic couplets"—ten-syllable lines in rhyming pairs—for his rendering of *The Odyssey*, with similar lulling power. King James must have slept, under these massive blankets, beyond Homer's casual nods, for he neglected to pay the three hundred pounds which the late Prince Henry had promised Chapman when the translation should be complete; but the Earl of Somerset rescued the aging poet from poverty.

Shall we tarry with Thomas Heywood, Thomas Middleton, Thomas Dekker, Cyril Tourneur, and John Marston, or beg them to let us off with a humble salute to their flickering fame? John Fletcher cannot be so scrimped, for in his heyday (1612–25) England honored him, in the drama, only next to Shakespeare and Jonson. Son to a Bishop of London, nephew or cousin to three poets of a sort, he was nursed on verse and reared with rhyme; and to all this heritage he added the privilege of collaborating with Shakespeare on *Henry VIII* and *The Two Noble Kinsmen*, with Massinger on *The Spanish Curate*, and, with most success, with Francis Beaumont.

"Frank" was also to the manner born, being the son of a prominent judge, and brother to a minor poet who eased by a year the way for Frank's entrance into the world. Failing to graduate from Oxford or the Inner Temple, Beaumont tried his hand at voluptuous poetry, and joined with Fletcher in writing plays. The two handsome bachelors shared bed and board, goods and clothes, mistresses and themes; "they had one wench between them," says Aubrey, and "a wonderful consimility of phansey."[33] For ten years they collaborated in producing such plays as *Philaster, or Love Lies a-Bleeding, The Maid's Tragedy, The Knight of the Burning Pestle.* The dialogue is vigorous but windy, the plots artfully tangled but artificially resolved, the thought seldom reaching to philosophy; nevertheless, toward the end of the century (Dryden assures us) these dramas were twice as popular on the stage as Shakespeare's.[34]

Beaumont died at thirty, in the year of Shakespeare's death. Thereafter Fletcher wrote, alone or with others, a long series of plays successful and forgotten; some of his comedies of involved and boisterous intrigue stemmed from Spanish models, and in turn, with their accent on adultery, led to the Restoration drama. Then, tiring of these bloody or bawdy scenes, he issued (1608) a pastoral play, *The Faithful Shepherdess,* as nonsensical as *A Midsummer Night's Dream,* and sometimes rivaling it in poetry. Clorin, her shepherd lover dead, retires to a rustic bower by his grave, and vows to stay there intact till her death:

Hail, holy earth, whose cold arms do embrace
The truest man that ever fed his flocks
By the fat plains of fruitful Thessaly!
Thus I salute thy grave; thus do I pay
My early vows and tribute of mine eyes
To thy still-lovéd ashes; thus I free
Myself from all ensuing heats and fires
Of love; all sports, delights, and jolly games,
That shepherds hold full dear, thus put I off:
Now no more shall these smooth brows be begirt
With youthful coronals, and lead the dance;
No more the company of fresh fair maids
And wanton shepherds be to me delightful,
Nor the shrill pleasing sound of merry pipes
Under some shady dell, when the cool wind
Plays on the leaves: all be far away,
Since thou art far away, by whose dear side
How often have I sat crowned with fresh flowers
For summer's queen, whilst every shepherd's boy
Puts on his lusty green, with gaudy hook,
And hanging scrip of finest cordevan.
But thou art gone, and these are gone with thee,
And all are dead but thy dear memory;
That shall outlive thee, and shall ever spring,
Whilst there are pipes or jolly shepherds sing.

The idyl had one performance and disappeared from the stage. What chance had such a paean to chastity in an age still simmering with the Elizabethan fire?

The most powerful and disagreeable of the Jacobean dramatists is John Webster. We know almost nothing of his life, and it is just as well. We gather his mood from the preface to his best play, *The White Devil* (1611), where he calls the audience "ignorant asses," and deposes that "the breath that comes from the incapable multitude is able to poison . . . the most sententious [profound] tragedy." The story is that of Vittoria Accoramboni, whose sins and trial (1581–85) had stirred Italy in Webster's childhood. Vittoria feels that her husband's income does no justice to her beauty. She accepts the attentions of the moneyed Duke of Brachiano, and suggests that he dispose of her husband and his own wife. He attends to the matter at once, with the aid of Vittoria's pander brother Flamineo, who provides for these crimes the most cynical obbligato in all English literature. She is arrested on suspicion, but defends herself with such audacity and skill as scares a lawyer out of his Latin and a cardinal out of his hat. She is kidnaped from justice by Brachiano; they are pursued; finally pursuers and pursued, the just and the unjust, are slaughtered in a dramatic holocaust that left Webster's blood lust sated for a year. The plot is well managed, the characters are consistently drawn, the language is often virile or vile, the crucial scenes are powerful, the poetry rises at times to Shakespeare's eloquence. But to a taste made squeamish by civilization the play is deformed by the forced and gutter coarseness of Flamineo, by the hot curses that pour even from pretty mouths ("Oh, could I kill you forty times a day, and use 't four years together, 'twere too little!"),[35] by the pervasive obscenity, the word *whore* on every second page, the endless double meanings that would have made even Shakespeare blush.

Webster returned to the shambles in *The Duchess of Malfi* (1613). Ferdinand, Duke of Calabria, forbids his young widowed sister, the Duchess of Amalfi, to marry again, for if she dies mateless he will inherit her fortune. She mourns her enforced chastity:

> The birds that live i' the field
> On the wild benefit of nature, live
> Happier than we, for they may choose their mates,
> And carol their sweet pleasures to the spring.[36]

Excited by lust and prohibition, she lures her steward, Antonio, into a secret marriage and a precipitate bed. Ferdinand has her killed. In the final act someone is slain almost every minute; doctors are ready with poisons, ruffians with daggers; no one has the patience to wait for a legal execution. The worst villain of the piece—who kills the Duchess, steals her property, takes a mistress and then murders her—is a cardinal; Webster was no papist. Here, too, are *doubles-entendres* of quite urological candor, a resolve to exhaust the vocabulary of execration, and a wild, indiscriminate condemnation of human life. Only in the remote corners of this dark canvas do we find nobility, fidelity, or tenderness. Ferdinand forgets himself and is soft for a line as he looks upon his sister, still beautiful in death:

> Cover her face! Mine eyes dazzle, she died young . . .[37]

But he soon recalls himself to barbarism.

Let us hope to find something sweeter than all this in the man who could write "Drink to me only with thine eyes."

V. Ben Jonson: 1573?–1637

He was a posthumous product, being born in Westminster a month after his father's death. He was christened Benjamin Johnson; he dropped the *h* to distinguish himself, but the printers continued to use it, over his dead body, till 1840; it still appears in the plaque on Westminster Abbey's walls. The mother, having had a minister for her first husband, took a bricklayer for her second. The family was poor; Ben had to scrape for an education; only the kindness of a discerning friend financed his entry into Westminster School. There he had the luck to come under the influence of its "under-master," the historian and antiquarian William Camden. He took to the classics with less than normal animosity, made intimates of Cicero, Seneca, Livy, Tacitus, Quintilian, and later claimed, apparently with justice, to know "more in Greek and Latin than all the poets of England."[38] Only his excitable "humour" and the rough-and-tumble of the London world kept his learning from ruining his art.

After graduating from Westminster, he attended Cambridge, "where," says his earliest biographer, "he continued but a few weeks for want of further maintenance."[39] His stepfather needed him as apprentice brick-layer, and we picture Ben sweating and fretting for seven years as he laid bricks and meditated poetry. Then suddenly he was off to the wars, caught in the draft, or rushing to them as livelier than bricks. He served in the Netherlands, fought a duel with an enemy soldier, killed and despoiled him, and came home to tell expanding tales. He married, begot many children, buried three or more of them, quarreled with his wife, left her for five years, rejoined her, and lived with her incompatibly till her death. Clio herself knows not how he buttered the family's bread.

The mystery deepens when we learn that he became an actor (1597). But he was bursting with bright ideas and happy lines, and merely reciting other men's thoughts could not long contain him. He rejoiced when Tom Nash invited him to collaborate on *The Isle of Dogs*, and doubtless he contributed his share to the "very seditious and slanderous matter" that the Privy Council found in the play. The Council ordered the performance stopped, the theater closed, the authors arrested. Nash, an old hand at such scrapes, lost himself in Yarmouth; Jonson found himself in jail. As the custom of the prison required him to pay for his food, his lodging, and his shackles, he borrowed four pounds from Philip Henslowe, and, released, joined Henslowe's (and Shakespeare's) theatrical company (1597).

A year later he wrote his first important comedy, *Every Man in His Humour*, and saw Shakespeare act in it at the Globe. Perhaps the great dramatist did not relish the prologue, which proposed, despite current example, to follow the classic unities of action, time, and place, and not

> To make a child, now swaddled, to proceed
> Man, and then shoot up, in one beard and weed,
> Past threescore years . . . You will be pleased to see
> One such today as other plays should be,
> Where neither chorus wafts you o'er the seas,
> Nor creaking throne comes down, the boys to please . . .
> But deeds and language such as men do use,
> And persons such as comedy should choose
> When she would show an image of the times,
> And sport with human follies, not with crimes.

So Jonson turned his back upon the aristocratic badinage of Shakespeare's early comedies, and upon the miraculous geography and chronology of the "romantic" drama; he brought the slums of London to the stage, and concealed his erudition in a remarkable reproduction of lower-class dialects and ways. The characters are caricatures rather than complex philosophical creations, but they live; they are as worthless as in Webster, but they are human; they are mentally unkempt, but they are not murderers.

The Latins had used *umor* to mean "moisture" or "a fluid"; the Hippocratic medical tradition had used *humor* to designate four fluids of the body—blood, phlegm, black bile, and yellow bile; according to the predominance of one or another of these in a person, he was said to be of a sanguine, phlegmatic, melancholic, or choleric "humour," or temperament. Jonson defined his own interpretation of the term:

As when some one peculiar quality
Doth so possess a man that it doth draw
All his affects [feelings], his spirits, and his powers,
In their confluctions, all to run one way—
That may be truly said to be a humour.[40]

The word came to life in the hilarious portrayal of Captain Bobadil, a direct descendant of Plautus' *miles gloriosus*, but reeking with his own peculiar "humour" and unconscious humor—always brave except in peril, bursting to fight except when challenged, a master of the sheathed sword.

The play was well received, and Ben could sow his wild oats less niggardly. He was now bouncy with confidence, proud as a poet, talking to lords without servility, standing his ground stubbornly, absorbing life hurriedly at every chance and pore, relishing forthrightness and rough humor, seducing women now and then, but finally (he told Drummond) preferring "the wantonness of a wife to the coyness of a mistress."[41] He left off acting and lived rashly by his pen. For a time he prospered by writing masques for the court; the light fantastic lines he wrote fitted well the scenes that Jones designed. But Ben, hot-tempered, quarreled widely. In the year of his first success he fell out with Gabriel Spencer, an actor, dueled with him, killed him, and was jailed for murder (1598). To make matters worse for himself, he was converted to Catholicism in prison. Nevertheless he received a fair trial, and he was allowed to plead "benefit of clergy" because he read the Latin psalter "like a clerk"; he was released, but only after having the letter *T* stamped with a hot iron on his thumb so that he might be readily identified as a second offender if he killed again; all the rest of his life he was a branded felon.

After a year of liberty he was returned to jail for debt. Henslowe again bailed him out, and in 1600 Jonson wooed solvency by writing *Every Man out of His Humour*. He weighted the comedy with classical tags; added to the dramatis personae three characters who served as a commenting chorus; rained invectives upon Puritans who had "religion in their garments, and their hair cut shorter than their eyebrows"; and brandished his lore at playwrights who were wrecking the Aristotelian unities. Instead of impossible romances about incredible lords, he proposed to show London mercilessly to itself, to

oppose a mirror
As large as is the stage whereon we act,

Where they shall see the time's deformity
Anatomized in every nerve and sinew
With constant courage, and contempt of fear.[42]

The play made more enemies than royalties, and it is not recommended read-ing today. Dissatisfied with the noisy audience at the Globe, Jonson wrote his next comedy, *Cynthia's Revels* (1601), for a company of boy actors and a smaller, choicer audience at the Blackfriars theater. Dekker and Marston felt themselves satirized in the play; in 1602 the Chamberlain's company, angered by the com-petition of the Blackfriars' boys, produced Dekker's *Satiromastix* (i.e., the satirist flogged), which pilloried Jonson as a puny, pockmarked, conceited pedant, mur-derer, and bricklayer. The quarrel ended in an exchange of eulogies, and for a time fortune smiled. A prospering lawyer took Ben into his home, and the Earl of Pembroke sent the poet twenty pounds "to buy books."[43] So fortified, he tried his hand at tragedy. He took as his subject Sejanus, the evil favorite of Tiberius. He based his narrative carefully upon Tacitus, Suetonius, Dio Cassius, and Juvenal; he achieved a scholarly masterpiece, some moving scenes (e.g., V, x) and stately lines; but the audience resented the long speeches, the tedious moralism of life-less characters; the play was soon withdrawn. Jonson printed the text and in the margin gave his classical sources, with notes in Latin. Lord Aubigny, impressed, gave the sorrowing author asylum for five years.

He returned to the arena in 1605 with his greatest play. *Volpone, or The Fox* attacked with burning satire the money lust that raged in London. As usual with comedies—from Plautus to *The Admirable Crichton*—a clever servant is the brains of the plot. Mosca (Italian for fly) brings to his miser master, Vol-pone, who pretends to be seriously ill, a succession of legacy hunters—Voltore (vulture), Corbaccio (crow), Corvino (raven)—who leave substantial presents in the hope of being named Volpone's heir. The "fox" accepts each gift with grasping reluctance, even to borrowing Corbaccio's wife for a night. Mosca finally deceives Volpone into making the servant sole legatee. But Bonario (good nature) exposes the trick, and the Venetian Senate sends nearly all the cast to jail. The play at last brought the Globe audience to Jonson's feet.

He moved hurriedly from success to adversity. He collaborated with Marston and Chapman on *Eastward Ho!* (1605); the government arrested the authors on the ground that the comedy insulted the Scots; the prisoners were threatened with circumcision of their noses and ears, but they were released intact, and such dignitaries as Camden and Selden joined in the banquet given by the liberated triumvirate. Then, on November 7, 1605, Ben was summoned to the Privy Council as a Catholic who might know something about the Gunpowder Plot. Though he had dined with a chief conspirator, Catesby, a month before, he escaped implication; but on January 9, 1606, he was hailed to court as a delinquent recusant. Since he was too poor to be profitably fined, the charge was not pressed. In 1610 he returned to the Anglican fold, and "with such enthusiasm that he drank all the wine in the cup when he attended" Communion.[44]

In that year he staged his most famous play. *The Alchemist* satirized not merely alchemy, which was a flagging quest, but half a dozen impostures that harried London with quackery. Sir Epicure Mammon is sure that he has found the secret of alchemy:

> This night I'll change
> All that is metal in my house to gold,
> And, early in the morning, will I send
> To all the plumbers and the pewterers,
> And buy their tin and lead up, and to Lothbury
> For all the copper . . . I'll purchase Devonshire and Cornwall,
> And make them perfect Indies . . . For I do mean
> To have a list of wives and concubines
> Equal with Solomon, who had the stone
> Alike with me; and I will make me a back,
> With the elixir, that shall be as tough
> As Hercules, to encounter fifty a night
>   . . . And my flatterers
> Shall be the pure and gravest of divines
> That I can get for money . . .
> My meat shall all come in in Indian shells,
> Dishes of agate set in gold, and studded
> With emeralds, sapphires, hyacinths, and rubies;
> The tongues of carps, dormice, and camel's heels . . .
> Old mushrooms, and the swelling unctuous paps
> Of a fat pregnant sow, newly cut off . . .
> For which I'll say unto my cook, "There's gold;
> Go forth, and be a knight."[45]

Sir Epicure is a rare morsel, but the others of the cast are dregs, and their talk is sticky with scatological filth; it is a pity to see scholarly Ben so erudite in scum and in the argot of the slums. The Puritans forgivably attacked such plays. Jonson retaliated by caricaturing them in *Bartholomew Fair* (1614).

He produced many more comedies, full of life and lees; *non ragionam di lor.* At times he rebelled against his own coarse realism, and in *The Sad Shepherd* he let his imagination roam quite recklessly.

> Her treading would not bend a blade of grass
> Or shake the downy blowball from his stalk,
> But like the soft west wind she shot along,
> And where she went the flowers took thickest root,
> As she had sowed them with her odorous foot.[46]

But he left the play unfinished, and, for the rest, confined his romanticism to pretty lyrics scattered in his comedies like jewels set in dross. So, in *The Devil Is an Ass* (1616), suddenly he sings:

> Have you seen but a bright lily grow
>   Before rude hands have touched it?
> Ha' you marked but the fall o' the snow
>   Before the soil hath smutched it?
> Ha' you felt the wool of beaver,
>   Or swan's down ever?
> Or have smelt o' the bud o' the briar,
>   Or the nard in the fire?
> Or have tasted the bag of the bee?
>   O so white! O so soft! O so sweet is she!

Still finer, of course, is the song "To Celia," which he pilfered from the Greek of Philostratus and transformed, with perfect scholarship and skill, into "Drink to me only with thine eyes."

After Shakespeare's death Jonson was the acknowledged head of the poetic guild. He became the uncrowned poet laureate of England—not officially so named, but most often recognized by the government, and receiving from it a pension of one hundred marks a year. The many friends who gathered round him at the Mermaid Tavern saw his rough good nature behind his bad temper and sharp tongue; they fed on his juicy speech and let him play the lead almost as presidentially as his namesake of the next century. Ben was now as corpulent as Samuel would be, and no handsomer; he mourned his "mountain belly" and "rocky face" pocked with scurvy; he could hardly visit a friend without breaking a chair. In 1624 he moved his dais to the Devil Tavern in Fleet Street; there the Apollo Club, which he had founded, met regularly to feast on victuals, wine, and wit; and Jonson, at one end of the room, had a raised seat, with a handrail that guided his magnitude into the throne. Tradition called his followers the Tribe of Ben, and numbered among them James Shirley, Thomas Carew, and Robert Herrick, who called him "Saint Ben."[47]

He needed a saintly and uncongenial patience to bear with the poverty and sickness of his disintegrating years. He reckoned that all his plays had brought him less than two hundred pounds. He spent in haste and starved at leisure; he had none of the financial sense that had made Shakespeare an expert in realty. Charles I continued his pension, but when Parliament stinted the royal funds the pension was not always paid. Charles, however, sent him one hundred pounds in 1629, and the dean and the chapter of Westminster Abbey voted five pounds for "Mr. Benjamin Johnson in his sickness and want."[48] His last plays failed, his fame waned, his friends disappeared, his wife and children were dead. By 1629 he lived alone, bedridden with paralysis, with only one old woman to take care of him. He lingered in pain and penury for eight years more. He was buried in Westminster Abbey, and John Young carved, upon the stone that faced the grave, a famous epitaph:

O RARE BEN JOHNSON

Only the first two words remain, but every educated Englishman can fill out the rest.

VI. John Donne: 1573–1631

At the Hampton Court Conference a Puritan delegate proposed a new translation of the Bible. The Bishop of London objected that existing versions were good enough; King James overruled him and ordered "special pains taken for a uniform translation, which should be done by the best learned in both universities, then reviewed by the bishops, presented to the Privy Council, lastly ratified by royal authority, to be read in the whole Church, and no other."[49] Sir Henry Savile and forty-six other scholars undertook the task, leaning on earlier translations by Wyclif and Tyndale, and completed it in seven years (1604–11). This "Authorized Version" became official in 1611 and began its immense influence on English life, literature, and speech. A thousand pithy phrases passed from it into the language. The adoration of the Bible, already so strong in Protestant lands, took on fresh fervor in England, raising the Puritans, then the Quakers, then the Methodists, to a knowledge and worship of the text equaled only by Moslem devotion to the Koran. The influence of the translation on English literary style was completely beneficent: it broke up the long and fanciful involutions of Elizabethan prose into sentences short and strong and clear and natural; it replaced foreign terms and constructions with racy Anglo-Saxon words and English idioms. It made a thousand mistakes in scholarship, but it transformed the noble Hebrew and the common Greek of the Testaments into the finest monument of English prose.

Two other works of distinguished prose honored the reign: Sir Walter Raleigh's *History of the World* (of which more later), and Robert Burton's *Anatomy of Melancholy* (1621)*—the massive matrix in which the vicar of St. Thomas' at Oxford set his garnered fragments of theological, astrological, classical, and philosophical lore. The dons at first thought him "very merry and facete," but later in life he became so melancholy that nothing could make him happy but the ribaldry of the bargemen on the Thames.[50] To relieve his "black bile" Burton "devoured authors" supplied to him by the Bodleian Library. With these, and his manuscript, and astrology, and priestly ministrations, he passed his gloomy days and starry nights. He calculated his own horoscope, and predicted therefrom the day of his death with such accuracy that Oxford lads suspected him of having hanged himself to prove his prescience.[51]

He is very much alive in his book. Setting out to examine and prescribe for hypochondria, he finds digression more pleasant than his plan. With eccentric humor Rabelaisian only in its pathless wandering, he discusses everything as casually as Montaigne, peppering his pages with Latin and Greek, and genially beckoning his reader on and on to nowhere. He disclaims originality; he feels

* Some undistinguished prose acquired historical distinction: the newssheets that fluttered about Jacobean London graduated in 1622 into the first English newspaper, *The Weekly Newes*.

that all authorship is pilfering: "We can say nothing but what has been said; the composition and method is ours only."[52] He confesses that he knows the world only through books, and through the news that filters into Oxford:

> I hear new news every day, and those ordinary rumors of war, plagues, fires, inundations, thefts, murders, massacres, meteors, comets, spectrums, prodigies, apparitions, of towns taken, cities besieged in France, Germany, Turkey, Persia, Poland, etc., daily musters and preparations, and such like, which these tempestuous times afford, battles fought, so many men slain . . . shipwrecks, piracies, and sea fights; peace, leagues, stratagems, and fresh alarms. A vast confusion of vows, wishes, actions, edicts, petitions, lawsuits, pleas, laws, proclamations . . . opinions, schisms, heresies . . . weddings, masquings, mummeries, entertainments, jubilees . . . burials[53]—

and he feels (like Thoreau) that if he reads the news of one day he may take it for granted the rest of the year, merely changing names and dates. He doubts that man progresses, yet "I will make an Utopia of mine own . . . in which I will freely domineer," and he describes it in fanciful detail; actually, however, he prefers browsing at peace in his study or on the banks of the Thames to going forth to reform mankind. Meanwhile all the authors in the world bring sweetmeats to his feast. He gets clogged with quotations, becomes dismal again, and after 114 fat pages he resolves to come to grips with the causes of melancholy, which are sin, concupiscence, intemperance, demons, witches, stars, constipation, venereal excess . . . and its symptoms, which include "wind rumbling in the guts . . . sour belchings . . . troublesome dreams."[54] Having completed two hundred digressions, he prescribes cures for melancholy: prayer, diet, medicine, laxatives, diuretics, fresh air, exercise, games, shows, music, merry company, wine, sleep, blood-letting, baths; and then he digresses again, so that every page is a disappointment and a delight—if time would stop.

Now, in poetry, the sonneteers subside and the "metaphysical poets" come: Richard Crashaw, Abraham Cowley, John Donne, George Herbert—who phrased with gentle grace the peace and piety of an Anglican parsonage. Samuel Johnson called them metaphysical only partly because they inclined to philosophy, theology, and argument, chiefly because they adopted—from Lyly or Góngora or the Pléiade—a style of linguistic novelties and conceits, verbal wit and involutions, classical excerpts and labored obscurities. All of which did not prevent Donne from becoming the finest poet of the age.

Like Jonson and Chapman, he overspread three reigns. Under Elizabeth he wrote of love, under James of piety, under Charles of death. Brought up a Catholic, educated by Jesuits, Oxford, and Cambridge, he knew the sting of persecution and the brooding of concealment. His brother Henry was arrested for harboring a proscribed priest, and died in jail. Sometimes John fed his melancholy on the mystical writings of St. Teresa and Luis de Granada. But by 1592 his proud young intellect had rejected the marvels of his faith, and the third decade of his life revolved around martial adventures, erotic pursuits, and skeptical philosophy.

For a time he dedicated his muse to candid promiscuity. In Elegy XVII he celebrated "Love's sweetest part, Variety"—

> How happy were our sires in ancient time,
> Who held plurality of love no crime![55]

In Elegy XVIII he swam "the Hellespont between the Sestos and Abydos of her breasts." In Elegy XIX, "To His Mistress Going to Bed," he undressed her poetically and bade her "licence my roving hands." He mixed entomology with love and argued that since a flea, by biting both, had mingled his blood with hers, they were now married in blood and might sport in sinless ecstasy.[56] Then, surfeited with surfaces, he found fault ungenerously with generous women, forgot their dated charms, and saw only the tricks they had learned in a heart-less world; he flayed his Julia with a raging litany of execrations, and counseled his reader to choose a homely mate, since "love built on beauty soon as beauty dies."[57] Now, singing antistrophe to Villon, he drew up a poetic testament in which each stanza struck a blow at "love."

He shipped with Essex in 1596, helped raid Cádiz, and shipped with him again in 1597 to the Azores and Spain. Back in England, he found a good berth as secretary to Sir Thomas Egerton, Lord Keeper of the Great Seal; but he ran away with the Lord Keeper's niece, married her (1600), and set himself to support her with poetry. Children came as easily as rhymes; often he could not feed or clothe them; his wife's health broke down; he wrote a defense of suicide.

At last relenting, Egerton sent the family an allowance (1608), and in 1610 Sir
Robert Drury gave them an apartment in his mansion in Drury Lane. A year
later Sir Robert lost his only daughter, and Donne published anonymously, as
an elegy for her, his first major poem, "An Anatomy of the World." He enlarged
the death of Elizabeth Drury into the decay of man and the universe:

> So did the world from the first hour decay . . .
> And new philosophy calls all in doubt.
> The element of fire is quite put out;
> The sun is lost, and th' earth, and no man's wit
> Can well direct him where to look for it.
> And freely men confess that this world's spent,
> When in the Planets and the Firmament
> They seek so many new, then see that this
> Is crumbled out again . . .
> 'Tis all in pieces, all coherence gone,
> All just supply, and all relation.[58]

He mourned to see "how lame and cripple" this earth is, once the scene of
divine redemption, now, in the new astronomy, a mere "suburb" of the world.
In one mood he had exalted the "sacred hunger of science"; in another he wondered whether science would destroy mankind:

> With new diseases on ourselves we war,
> And with new Physic a worse Engine far.[59]

And so he turned to religion. His repeated illnesses, the ominous death of
friend after friend, led him to the fear of God. Though his reason still questioned theology, he had learned to distrust reason too as but another faith, and
he decided that the old creed should be accepted without further argument,
if only to bring peace of mind and security of bread. In 1615 he became an
Anglican priest; and now he not only preached sermons in somber and stirring
prose, but composed some of the most moving religious poetry in the English
language. In 1616 he was made chaplain to James I; in 1621 he became dean
of St. Paul's. He had never published the erotic lyrics of his youth, but he had

allowed copies to circulate in manuscript; now he "repenteth highly," Ben Jonson reported, "and seeketh to destroy all his poems."[60] He wrote, instead, "Holy Sonnets" and, whistling in the dark, challenged death:

> Death, be not proud, though some have called thee
> Mighty and dreadful, for thou art not so;
> For those whom thou thinks't thou dost overthrow
> Die not, poor Death, nor yet canst thou kill me . . .
> Our short sleep past, we wake eternally,
> And death shall be no more; Death, *thou* shalt die.[61]

In 1623, recovering from a serious illness, he wrote in his diary some famous lines: "Any man's death diminishes me, because I am involved in mankind; and therefore never send to know for whom the bell tolls; it tolls for thee."[62] On the first Friday in Lent, 1631, he rose from a sickbed to preach what men were soon to call his own funeral sermon; his aides had tried to dissuade him, seeing how (said his devoted friend Izaak Walton) "his sickness had left him but so much flesh as did only cover his bones."[63] Having delivered his sermon, eloquent in the confidence of resurrection, and "being full of joy that God had enabled him to perform this desired duty, he hastened to his house; out of which he never moved till . . . he was carried by devout men to his grave."[64] He died in the arms of his mother, who had borne patiently with his sins and lovingly with his sermons, March 31, 1631.

It was a full, tense life, running the gamut of lust and love, of doubt and decay, and ending in the warm comfort of old faith. We of today, who sleep so readily over Spenser, find ourselves startled on almost every page by this strangely fanciful realist and modern medieval soul. His verse is rough, but he wished it so; he rejected the affected graces of Elizabethan speech, and relished unworn words and arresting prosody; he liked harsh discords that could be resolved into unwonted harmonies. There was nothing trite in his verse, once he had graduated from the stews; and this man, who had polished obscenity like another Catullus, grew to such delicacy and depth of feeling and thought, such originality of phrase and sentiment, as no other poet could match, in that amazing age, but Shakespeare himself.

VII. James Sows the Whirlwind: 1615–25

Love and diplomacy are treacherous bedfellows. In 1615 King James fell in love, in his kindly ambidextrous way, with handsome, dashing, rich George Villiers, twenty-three. He made him Earl, then Marquis, then Duke of Buckingham and, after 1616, allowed him to direct the policies of the state. Buckingham's wife, Lady Katherine Manners, outwardly conforming to the Anglican rite, was at heart a Roman Catholic, and may have inclined him to friendship with Spain.

James himself was a man of peace, and did not allow theology or piracy to keep him embroiled with the Continent. Soon after his accession he ended the long war that England had waged with Spain. When Frederick, Prince of the Palatinate and husband to James's beloved daughter Elizabeth, lost his principality at the outset of the Thirty Years' War, James played with the hope that the Hapsburg King of Spain, properly appeased, would influence the Hapsburg Emperor, Ferdinand II, to let Frederick regain his throne. To the disgust of his people, James proposed to Philip IV the marriage of Philip's sister, The Infanta Maria, with Prince Charles.

Raleigh came to his bloody end as a sacrifice to this Spanish policy. He had privately opposed James's succession, and bitterly opposed James's supporter Essex. Soon after reaching London James dismissed him from all governmental posts. With characteristic passion and rashness, Raleigh allowed himself to be implicated in several attempts to unseat the King.[65] He was sent to the Tower, protested his innocence, and attempted suicide. He was tried, was convicted on dubious evidence, and was condemned to die, December 13, 1603, with all the tortures of a traitor. On December 9 he wrote to his wife a letter[66] warm with such tenderness and piety as he had seldom shown to the world. James rejected the pleas of the Queen and Prince Henry to forgive him, but permitted the prisoner to live on for fifteen years more, always keeping the death penalty over his head. Raleigh's wife was allowed to come and dwell with him in a little house that he built within the Tower precincts. He was supplied with books by his friends; he made experiments in chemistry, composed some excellent poems, and wrote his *History of the World*. As published in 1614, it began with a pious preface involved and verbose, revealing a mind harassed and distraught. The narrative opened with Nineveh, passed on through Egypt, Judea, Persia,

Chaldea, Greece, and Carthage, and ended with Imperial Rome. Raleigh was not anxious to reach recent times, for "whosoever, in writing a modern history, shall follow truth too near the heels, it may haply strike out his teeth."[67] His style improved as he went on, attained a noble splendor in describing the battle of Salamis, and came to a climax in the concluding apostrophe to "eloquent, just, and mighty Death."[68]

But he was not reconciled to defeat. In 1616, having raised £1,500, he bribed the Duke of Buckingham to intercede for him with the King.[69] He promised that, if released, he would sail to South America, find what he alleged to be the rich gold deposits of Guiana, and bring back royal spoils for the thirsty treasury. James freed him provisionally, and agreed to let him and his partners keep four fifths of any treasure he might capture from "heathen and savage people"; but the canny ruler held the death sentence still in force as an inducement to good behavior. The Count of Gondomar, the Spanish ambassador, pointed out that there were Spanish settlements in Guiana and hoped they would not be disturbed. James, anxious for peace and marriage with Spain, forbade Raleigh, on pain of immediate execution of his death sentence, to interfere with Christian communities anywhere, particularly the Spanish.[70] Raleigh consented in writing to these restrictions.[71] Gondomar still protesting, James vowed that if Raleigh violated his instructions the death penalty would be enforced.[72]

With the aid of his friends Raleigh equipped fourteen ships, and with these he sailed (March 17, 1617) to the mouth of the Orinoco. A Spanish settlement, Santo Tomás, barred the way up the river to the supposed—quite legendary—mines. Raleigh's men (he himself staying on board) landed, attacked and burned the village, and killed its governor. Then, discouraged by further Spanish resistance, the depleted force abandoned the gold quest and returned empty-handed to the ships. Raleigh was disheartened to learn that his son had been slain in the assault. He reproved his second in command, who thereupon committed suicide. His men lost confidence in him; vessel after vessel deserted his fleet. Returning to England and finding that the King was in a rage against him, he negotiated for escape to France; he was arrested; he tried again to escape and got as far as Greenwich; there a French agent betrayed him. He was captured and sent to the Tower, and the King, pressed by Gondomar, ordered the death sentence carried out.

Tired at last of life and welcoming the boon of a sudden death, Raleigh walked to his execution (October 29, 1618) with a calm dignity that made him the hero of a people that hated Spain. "Let us dispatch," he asked the sheriffs. "At this hour mine ague comes upon me; I would not have mine enemies to think I quaked from fear." He tested with his thumb the edge of the ax. "This," he said, "is a fair sharp medicine to cure me of all diseases and miseries."[73] His loyal widow claimed the corpse and had it buried in a church. "The Lords," she wrote, "have given me his dead body, though they denied me his life. God hold me in my wits."[74]

Raleigh's expedition was one of many that took James's subjects hopefully to America. Peasants hungry for land of their own, adventurers seeking fortunes in trade or spoils, criminals fleeing the cruelty of the law, Puritans resolved to plant the flag of their faith on virgin soil—these and others bore the risks and the tedium of the sea to make new Englands everywhere. Virginia was settled in 1606–7, Bermuda in 1609, Newfoundland in 1610. "Separatist" clergymen refusing to accept the Prayer Book and the ritual of the Anglican Church fled to Holland with their followers (1608). From Delft (July 1620), Southampton, and Plymouth (September) these "Pilgrims" took sail across the Atlantic; after three months of ordeal, they set foot on Plymouth Rock (December 21).

In Asia the English East India Company, confined to £30,000 and seventeen ships, tried in vain to capture trading ports and routes from the Dutch East India Company, sailing sixty ships and sinewed with £540,000. But in 1615 the mission of Sir Thomas Roe resulted in the establishment of trade depots at Ahmadabad, Surat, Agra, and elsewhere in India; and Fort St. George was built and armed to protect them (1640). The first steps had been taken toward the British Empire in India.

Despite all temptations of mercantile interests, parliamentary prodding, and popular chauvinism, James for sixteen years kept to his policy of peace. The House of Commons begged him to enter the Thirty Years' War on the side of the endangered Protestants of Bohemia and Germany. It pleaded with him to marry his sole surviving son not to a Spanish but to a Protestant princess. It condemned James's relaxation of the anti-Catholic laws, urged him to order all Catholic children to be separated from their parents and brought up as Protestants, and warned him that toleration would lead to the growth of a Catholic Church frankly pledged to intolerance.[75]

In 1621 the divergence of views between Parliament and King almost rehearsed the conflict (1642) between the Long Parliament and Charles I. The Commons denounced the extravagance of the court and the persisting monopolies in restraint of trade; it fined and banished monopolists, rejecting their plea that a nascent industry had to be protected from competition. When James rebuked it for meddling in executive business, it issued (December 18) a historic "Great Protestation," which again affirmed that "the liberties, franchises, privileges, and jurisdictions of Parliament are the ancient and undoubted birthright and inheritance of the subjects of England," and added that "the arduous and urgent affairs concerning the king, state, and defense of the realm . . . are proper subjects and matter of council and debate in Parliament."[76] James angrily tore from the journal of the Commons the page containing this protestation; he dissolved the Parliament (February 8, 1622), ordered the imprisonment of four parliamentary leaders, Southampton, Selden, Coke, and Pym, and defiantly proceeded with Buckingham's plea for a marital alliance with Spain.

The reckless minister now urged the King to let him take Prince Charles to Madrid to show him off, to see the Infanta, and to conclude the match. James consented reluctantly, for he feared that Philip would send Charles back to England the laughingstock of Europe.

Arrived in Madrid (March 1623), Prince and Duke found the lovely Infanta unapproachable, and the Spanish populace as furious at the thought of her marrying a Protestant as the English were at the idea of Charles bringing home a Catholic. Philip and his minister Olivares gave the visitors every courtesy; Lope de Vega wrote a play for the welcoming festivities; Velázquez painted a portrait of Charles; and Buckingham wooed the Spanish beauties almost to the point of honor. But it was made an indispensable condition of the marriage that English Catholics should receive religious freedom. Charles at once, James at last, agreed; the marriage treaty was signed; but when James further required Philip to promise the use of Spanish arms, if needed, to restore the Palatinate to Frederick, Philip refused to commit himself, and James ordered his son and his favorite home. We see the human side of a king in his letter to Charles (June 14, 1623): "I now repent me sore that ever I suffered you to go away. I care [neither] for match nor nothing, so I may once have you in my arms again. God grant it! God grant it! God grant it!"[77] The Infanta, in bidding Charles farewell, made him promise that he would have a care for the Catholics of England.[78] The returning Prince was hailed by England as a hero because he brought no bride. He brought a set of Titians instead.

And now Buckingham, angry at having made a fool of himself in Spain (as Olivares had assured him), turned to France for a marital alliance, and secured for Charles the youngest daughter of Henry IV—that Henrietta Maria whose Catholic faith was to be one of many thorns in the side of coming Parliaments. Then the rash young minister regained popularity with the House of Commons by importuning James—failing in health and in mind—to declare war against Spain. Reassembled in February 1624, Parliament followed policies formed in part by mercantile interests eager to capture Spanish booty, colonies or markets, and in part by a resolve to deflect Spain from lending aid to the Catholic Emperor against the Protestants of Germany. The people, having called James a coward for loving peace, now called him a tyrant for conscripting men to military service. The regiments raised, the funds voted, were inadequate, and James had the bitterness of concluding a peaceful reign with a futile war.

His ailments crowded upon him in these final years. He had poisoned his organs with Gargantuan and indiscriminate food and drink; now he suffered from catarrh, arthritis, gout, stone, jaundice, diarrhea, and hemorrhoids; he had himself bled every day until the least royal of his troubles made this superfluous.[79] He refused medicine, received the sacraments of the Church of England, and died (March 27, 1625) murmuring the last consolations of his faith.

Despite his vanity and coarseness, he was a better king than some who excelled him in vigor, courage, and enterprise. His absolutism was mainly a theory, tempered with a timidity that often yielded to a powerful Parliament. His pretensions to theology did not impede a will to tolerance far more generous than that of his predecessors. His brave love of peace gave England prosperity, and checked the venal bellicosity of his Parliament and the vicarious ardor of his people. His flatterers had called him the British Solomon because of his worldly wisdom, and Sully, failing to embroil him in Continental strife, termed him "the wisest fool in Christendom." But he was neither philosopher nor fool. He was only a scholar miscast as a ruler, a man of peace in an age mad with mythology and war. Better the King James Bible than a conqueror's crown.

CHAPTER VII

THE SUMMONS TO REASON

1558–1649

I. Superstition

Are people poor because they are ignorant, or ignorant because they are poor? It is a question that divides political philosophers between conservatives stressing heredity (inborn inequalities of mental capacity) and reformers relying on environment (the power of education and opportunity). In societies knowledge grows, and superstition wanes, with the increase and distribution of wealth. And yet even in a widely prosperous country—and especially among the harassed poor and the idle rich—thought has to live in a jungle of superstitions: astrology, numerology, palmistry, portents, the evil eye, witches, goblins, ghosts, demons, incantations, exorcisms, dream interpretations, oracles, miracles, quackery, and occult qualities, curative or injurious, in minerals, plants, and animals. Consider, then, the intellectual miasma poisoning the roots and wilting the flowers of science in a people whose wealth is scant or centered in a few. To the poor in body and mind superstition is a treasured element in the poetry of life, gilding dull days with exciting marvels, and redeeming misery with magic powers and mystic hopes.

Sir Thomas Browne, in 1646, required 652 pages to list and briefly treat the superstitions current in his day.[1] Nearly all these occultisms flourished among the Britons under Elizabeth and the early Stuarts. In 1597 King James VI published an authoritative *Demonologie*, which is one of the horrors of literature. He ascribed to witches the power to haunt houses, to make men and women love or hate, to transfer disease from one person to another, to kill by roasting a wax effigy, and to raise devastating storms; and he advocated the death penalty for all witches and magicians, and even for their customers.[2] When a tempest nearly wrecked him on his return from Denmark with his bride, he caused four suspects to be tortured into confessing that they had plotted to destroy him by magic means; and one of them, John Fain, after the most barbarous torments, was burned to death (1590).[3]

In this matter the Kirk agreed with the King, and lay magistrates lenient to witches were threatened with excommunication.[4] Between 1560 and 1600 some eight thousand women were burned as witches in a Scotland having hardly a million souls.[5] In England the belief in witchcraft was almost universal; learned physicians like William Harvey and Sir Thomas Browne shared it; the hardheaded Elizabeth allowed her laws of 1562 to make witchcraft a capital crime; eighty-one women were executed for it in her reign.[6] James moderated his fanaticism after passing from VI to I; he insisted on fair trials of the accused, exposed false confessions and accusations, and saved the lives of five women charged by a hysterical boy.[7] The hunt nearly ceased after Charles I, but it was resumed, and reached its height, under the rule of the Long Parliament, when in two years (1645–47) two hundred "witches" were consumed.[8]

One voice, amid the fury, appealed to reason. Reginald Scot, an Englishman despite his name, published at London in 1584 *The Discoverie of Witchcraft*, second only to Johann Wier's *De praestigiis daemonum* (Basel, 1564) in the dangerous attempt to moderate the sadistic superstition. Scot described the "witches" as poor old women who could harm no one; even if Satan did work through them they were rather to be pitied than to be burned; and to ascribe miracles to these crones was an insult to the miracles of Christ. He exposed the awful tortures that made witchcraft confessions worthless, the lax irregularity and injustice of trial procedure, the incredibilities gulped down by judges and inquisitors. The book had no effect.

In this atmosphere science tried to grow.

II. Science

Nevertheless, the expansion of commerce and industry were compelling the development of science. The Platonic and artistic strains in the Renaissance hardly harmonized with the swelling economy; the demand grew for a mental procedure that would deal with facts and quantities as well as with theories and ideas; the Aristotelian empiricism revived, shorn of its Alexandrian and medieval masks. The emphasis of Italian humanism on the glories of ancient literature and art made way for a less ethereal stress on current practical needs. Men had to count and calculate, measure and design, with competitive accuracy and speed; they needed tools of observation and recording; demands arose which were met by the invention of logarithms, analytical geometry, calculus, machines, the microscope, the telescope, statistical methods, navigational guides, and astronomical instruments. Throughout Western Europe lives were henceforth dedicated to meeting these needs.

In 1614 John Napier in Scotland and in 1620 Joost Bürgi in Switzerland independently proposed a system of logarithms (i.e., a logic of numbers) by which products, quotients, and roots could be quickly calculated from the tabulated relation of the given numbers as powers of a fixed number used as a base. Henry Briggs (1616) modified the method for common computation by proposing 10 as a base, and published tables giving the logarithms of all numbers from one to 20,000. Now two numbers could be multiplied by finding, in such tables, the number whose "log" was the sum of the logs of the numbers to be multiplied; and *a* could be divided by *b* by finding the number whose log was the log of *b* subtracted from the log of *a*. William Oughtred (1622) and Edmund Gunter (1624) constructed slide rules by which the results of logarithmic calculations could be read in a few seconds. These inventions halved the time given to arithmetical work by mathematicians, astronomers, statisticians, navigators, and engineers, and in effect lengthened their lives.[9] Kepler, who used the new method in computing planetary motions, addressed an enthusiastic panegyric to the Laird of Merchiston (1620), not knowing that Napier was then three years dead. Napier himself had made a little miscalculation, having figured that the world would come to an end between 1688 and 1700.[10]

Mathematicians and astronomers were still closely allied, for the reckoning of celestial motions, the charting of the calendar, and the guidance of navigation required complex manipulations of astronomic measurements. As a mathematician, Thomas Harriot established the standard form of modern algebra, introduced the signs for root, "greater than" and "less than," replaced clumsy capitals with small letters to indicate numbers, and hit upon the beneficent trick of placing all the quantities in an equation on one side and zero on the other. As an astronomer, he discovered the spots on the sun, and his observations of Jupiter's satellites were made independently of Galileo's. George

Chapman, himself a monster of learning, thought Harriot's knowledge to be "incomparable and bottomless."[11]

Astronomy was still dripping with astrology. "Horary" astrology decided whether the stars favored the enterprise of the hour; "judicial" astrology foretold affairs in general, usually with judicious ambiguity; "natural" astrology disclosed the destiny of an individual from his horoscope—an examination of the position of the stars at the moment of his birth; all these are found in Shakespeare (though not proving his belief), and in our time. The moon, in astrological theory, produced tides, tears, madmen, and thieves (cf. Shakespeare, *I Henry IV*, I, ii, 15), and each sign of the zodiac controlled the character and fate of specific organs in the human anatomy (*Twelfth Night*, I, iii, 146–51). John Dee symbolized the time by mingling astrology, magic, mathematics, and geography: he engaged in crystal gazing, wrote a *Treatise of the Rosie Crucean Secrets,* was charged with practicing sorcery against Queen Mary Tudor (1555), drew up geographical and hydrographical charts for Elizabeth, proposed a northwest passage to China, invented the phrase "the British Empire," lectured on Euclid before large audiences in Paris, defended the Copernican theory, advocated the adoption of the Gregorian calendar (170 years before England resigned itself to such a papistical contraption), and died at eighty-one; here was a full life! His pupil, Thomas Digges, promoted the acceptance of the Copernican hypothesis in England, and anticipated Bruno's notion of an infinite universe.[12] Thomas and his father, Leonard Digges, used "perspective glasses" which were probably forerunners of the telescope; and William Gascoigne invented (c. 1639) the micrometer, which enabled observers to adjust a telescope with unprecedented accuracy. Jeremiah Horrocks, a poor Lancashire curate who died at twenty-four, ascribed an elliptical orbit to the moon, and predicted—and observed (1639) for the first recorded time—the transit of Venus across the sun. His speculations on the forces moving the planets helped Newton to the theory of universal gravitation.

Meanwhile the study of terrestrial magnetism was also preparing for Newton. In 1544 Georg Hartmann, a German clergyman, and in 1576 Robert Norman, an English compass maker, independently discovered the tendency of the magnetic needle, when freely suspended at its center of gravity, to "dip" from a horizontal position to one at an angle to the earth's surface. Norman's book, *The Newe Attractive* (1581), suggested that the "joynt Respective" to which the needle dipped lay within the earth.[13]

This fascinating lead was followed by William Gilbert, physician to Elizabeth. After seventeen years of research and experiment—financed by his inherited fortune, and sometimes watched by the Queen—he set forth his results in the first great book of English science, *De magnete . . . et de magno magnete tellure* (1600)—*On the Magnet . . . and the Great Magnet the Earth.* He laid a pivoted compass needle successively at different points upon a globular lodestone, he marked with lines on the globe the directions in which the needle successively set, he prolonged each line to form a great circle around the stone, and he found that all these circles crossed at two diametrically opposite points on the globe; these were the magnetic poles, which, in the case of the earth, Gilbert mistakenly identified with the geographical poles. He described the earth as an enormous magnet, explained thereby the behavior of the magnetic needle, and showed that any iron bar left for a long time in a north-and-south position would become magnetized. A magnet placed at either pole of the globular lodestone took a position vertical to the globe; placed at any point midway between the poles (such points constituting the magnetic equator), the magnet lay horizontal. Gilbert concluded that the dip of the needle would be greater the nearer it was placed to the geographical poles of the earth; and though this was not quite correct, it was approximately confirmed by Henry Hudson in his exploration of the Arctic in 1608. From his own observations Gilbert drew up directions for calculating latitude from the degree of the magnetic dip. He suggested that "from about a magnetic body the virtue magnetical is poured out on every side"; he ascribed the rotation of the earth to the influence of this magnetic field. Passing on to the study of electricity—wherein little had been done since antiquity—he proved that many other substances besides amber could, when rubbed, generate frictional electricity; and from the Greek for *amber* he formed the word *electric* to denote a power to deflect a magnetic needle. He believed that all heavenly bodies are endowed with magnetism; Kepler was to use this idea to explain the motion of the planets. Most of Gilbert's work was an admirable example of experimental procedure, and its effects on science and industry were immeasurable.

The advance of science appeared more dramatically in the efforts of adventurous or acquisitive spirits to explore the "great magnet" for geographical or commercial purposes. In 1576 Sir Humphrey Gilbert (no kin to William) published a suggestive *Discourse . . . for a New Passage to Cataia*—i.e., "Cathay," or China—proposing a northwest sailing through or around Canada. Sir Martin Frobisher, in that year, set out with three small vessels to find such a route. One of his ships foundered, another deserted; he went ahead in the tiny twenty-five-ton *Gabriel*; he reached Baffin Land, but the Eskimos fought him, and he returned to England for more men and supplies. His later voyages were diverted from geography by a vain hunt for gold. Gilbert took up the quest for a northwest passage, but was drowned in the attempt (1583). Four years later John Davys pushed through the strait now named for him; then he fought the Armada, went off to the South Seas with Thomas Cavendish, discovered the Falkland Islands, and was killed by Japanese pirates near Singapore (1605). Cavendish explored southern South America, accomplished the third circum-navigation of the globe, and died at sea (1592). Henry Hudson navigated the Hudson River (1609), and, in another voyage, reached Hudson Bay; but his crew, maddened with hardships and longing for home, mutinied and set him adrift, with eight others, in a small open boat (1611); they were never heard of again. William Baffin explored the bay and the island that bear his name, ventured as far north as 77° 45'—a latitude not reached again for 236 years—and had the further distinction of first finding longitude by observation of the moon. Richard Hakluyt saw in such ships and hearts of oak an epic of courage and terror surpassing any *Iliad*, and he gathered their narratives into successive volumes, the best-known of which are those published as *The Principal Naviga-tions, Voyages, and Discoveries of the English Nation* (1589, 1598–1600); Samuel Purchas expanded the record in *Hakluytus Posthumus, or Purchas his Pilgrimes* (1625). So, by the greed for gold or trade, and the zest for far-off peril and scenes, geography unwittingly grew.

The best work of this age in physics, chemistry, and biology was done on the Continent; in England, however, Sir Kenelm Digby discovered the neces-sity of oxygen to plant life, and Robert Fludd, mystic and medico, advocated vaccination 150 years before Jenner. Medical prescriptions continued to rely on their repulsiveness for their effect; the official London pharmacopoeia of 1618 recommended bile, blood, claws, cockscomb, fur, sweat, saliva, scorpions, snakeskin, wood lice, and spider web as medicaments; and bloodletting was a first resort.[14] Nevertheless this period boasts of Thomas Parr ("old Parr"), who was presented to Charles I in 1635 as still in good health at the alleged age of 152. Parr did not profess to know his exact age, but his parish authorities dated his birth in 1483; he claimed to have joined the army in 1500, and he recalled in detail the dissolution of the monasteries by Henry VIII (1536). "You have lived longer than other men," said Charles I. "What have you done more than they?" Parr replied that he had fertilized a wench when he was over a hundred years old and had done public penance for it. He had subsisted almost entirely on potatoes, greens, coarse bread, and buttermilk, with rarely a taste of meat. For a while he became a lion in London parlors and pubs, and he was so handsomely feasted that he died within a year of meeting the King. Sir William Harvey performed a post-mortem on him, found him free of arteriosclerosis, and diagnosed his death as due to change of air and food.[15]

It was Harvey who provided the scientific climax of the age by explaining the circulation of the blood—"the most momentous event in medical history since Galen's time."[16] Born at Folkstone in 1578, he studied at Cambridge, then at Padua under Fabrizio d'Acquapendente. Returning, he settled down to medical practice in London, and became personal physician to James I and Charles I. Through patient years he carried on experiments and dissections on animals and cadavers, and particularly studied the flow and the course of blood in wounds. He came to his main theory in 1615,[17] but belatedly published it at Frankfurt in 1628 as a modest *Exercitatio anatomica de motu cordis et sanguinis in animalibus*—the first and greatest classic in English medicine.

The steps to his discovery illustrate the internationalism of science. For over a thousand years the functions of heart and blood had been interpreted as by Galen in the second century A.D. Galen had supposed that blood flowed to the tissues from the liver as well as the heart; that air passed from the lungs to the heart; that the arteries and veins carried twin streams of blood, which were propelled and received by the heart in tides of ebb and flow; and that blood passed from the right to the left side of the heart through pores in the septum between the ventricles. Leonardo da Vinci (c. 1506) questioned the view that air passed from lungs to heart; Vesalius (1543) denied the existence of pores in the septum, and his masterly sketches of arteries and veins revealed their terminals as so minute and neighborly as almost to suggest passage and circulation; Fabrizio showed that valves in the veins made it impossible for venous blood to flow from the heart. The Galenic theory faded away. In 1553 Michael Servetus, and in 1558 Realdo Colombo, discovered the *pulmonary* circulation of the blood—its passage from the right chamber of the heart through the pulmonary artery to and through the lungs, its purification there by aeration, and its return via the pulmonary vein to the left chamber of the heart. Andrea Cesalpino (c. 1571) tentatively—as we shall see—anticipated the full theory of circulation. Harvey's work turned the theory into a demonstrated fact.

While Francis Bacon, his patient, was extolling induction, Harvey proceeded to his illuminating conclusion by a striking combination of deduction and induction. Estimating the amount of blood pressed out of the heart by each systole, or contraction, to be one half a fluid ounce, he calculated that in half an hour the heart would pour into the arteries over 500 fluid ounces—a larger quantity than the entire body contained. Where did all this blood come from? It seemed impossible that so great a quantity should be produced, hour after hour, from the digestion of food. Harvey concluded that the blood pumped out of the heart was returned to it, and that there was no other apparent avenue for this but the veins. By simple experiments and observations—as by pressing a finger upon some superficial vein—it was readily shown that venous blood flowed away from the tissues and toward the heart.

> When I surveyed my mass of evidence, whether derived from vivisections and my previous reflections on them, or from the ventricles of the heart and the vessels that enter into and issue from them . . . and frequently and seriously bethought me . . . what might be the quantity of blood which was transmitted . . . and not finding it possible that this could be supplied by the juices of the ingested aliment without the veins on the one hand becoming drained, and the arteries on the other getting ruptured through the excessive charge of blood, unless the blood should somehow find its way from the arteries into the veins, and so return to the right side of the heart; when, I say, I surveyed all this evidence, I began to think whether there might not be *a motion as it were in a circle* . . . And now I may be allowed to give my view of the circulation of the blood.[18]

He had long hesitated to publish his conclusions, knowing the conservatism of the medical profession of his time. He predicted that no one over forty years of age would accept his theory.[19] "I have heard him say," reported Aubrey, "that after his book of the *Circulation of the Blood* came out, he fell mightily in his practice, and 'twas believed by the vulgar that he was crack-brained."[20] Not until Malpighi in 1660 demonstrated the existence of capillaries conveying blood from the arteries to the veins did the learned world concede the circulation to be a fact. The new view illuminated almost every field of physiology, and affected the old problem of the interrelation between body and mind. Said Harvey:

Every affection of the mind that is attended with either pain or pleasure, hope or fear, is the cause of an agitation whose influence extends
to the heart . . . In almost every affection [emotion] . . . the counte-
nance changes, and the blood appears to course hither and thither.
In anger the eyes are fiery and the pupils contracted; in modesty the
cheeks are suffused with blushes . . . in lust how quickly is the member distended with blood![21]

Harvey continued to serve Charles I almost to the latter's bitter end. He
accompanied Charles when revolution drove the King from London, was with
him at the battle of Edgehill, and narrowly escaped death.[22] Meanwhile the
rebels sacked his London house and destroyed his manuscripts and anatomical
collections. Perhaps he had made a variety of enemies by his sharp temper and
views. He rated man as "but a great mischievous baboon," says Aubrey, and
thought that "we Europeans knew not how to order or govern our Woemen,"
and that "the Turks were the only people who used them wisely."[23] Still vigorous at seventy-three, he published a treatise on embryology, *Exercitationes de
generatione animalium* (1651). Rejecting the prevalent belief in the spontaneous
generation of minute organisms out of decaying flesh, Harvey held that "all
animals, even those that produce their young alive, including man himself, are
evolved out of an egg"; and he coined the phrase *Omne animal ex ovo*—"Every
animal comes from an agg." He died six years later of paralysis, bequeathing
most of his fortune of twenty thousand pounds to the Royal College of Physicians, and ten pounds to Thomas Hobbes "as a token of his love."

III. The Rise and Fall of Francis Bacon: 1561–1621

We come now to the greatest and proudest intellect of the age. We have already
noted his birth and lineage, his education in letters, diplomacy, and law, his unexpected poverty, his unheard pleas for office, his futile cautioning and reluctant
prosecution of his beneficent, guilty friend. Learning and ambition so consumed
him that he had no lust left for women; he had, however, a liking for young
men.[24] Finally, at forty-five (1606), he married Alice Barnham, who brought him
£220 a year. But he gave no "hostages to fortune"—he had no children.

On the accession of James I, Bacon, in a letter of adulation profuse in
the manner of the time, suggested himself to the King as fit and due for a

governmental post. Son of a Lord Keeper of the Great Seal, nephew or cousin to the Cecils, he felt that his long wait for office reflected some hostility on the part of the commanding ministers; and perhaps his impatient opportunism was an effect as well as a cause of his tardy admission to place. He had already served in Parliament for nineteen years, usually defending the government, and winning repute for wide learning, constructive thought, and clear and striking speech. Periodically he sent to the King "memories" eloquent with prudent advice: how to improve mutual understanding and co-operation between Commons and Lords, to unite the parliaments of England and Scotland, to end persecution for religious diversity, to pacify Ireland by conciliating its Catholics, to give greater freedom to Catholics in England without opening the door to papal claims, and to find a compromise between Anglicans and Puritans. "To carry out this program," in the judgment of the historian who has most thoroughly studied the politics of this period, "would have been to avert the evils of the next half-century."[25] James put the proposals aside as impracticable in the current state of opinion, and contented himself with including Bacon in the three hundred knighthoods that he distributed in 1603. Sir Francis still cooled his heels.

Nevertheless his skill as a lawyer slowly raised him to affluence. By 1607 he estimated his wealth at £24,155.[26] On his luxurious estate at Gorhambury, manned with select and expensive servants and alert secretaries like Thomas Hobbes, he could enjoy the beauty and comfort that he loved wisely but too well. He nursed his health by gardening, and built amid his gardens a costly retreat for his scholastic privacy. He wrote like a philosopher and lived like a prince. He saw no reason why reason should be penniless, or why Solomon should not be king.

He did not fall far short. In 1607 James, valuing him at last, made him solicitor general; in 1613, attorney general; in 1616, a member of the Privy Council; in 1617, Lord Keeper of the Great Seal; in 1618, Chancellor. New dignities were added to grace his powers: in 1618 he was created first Baron Verulam; in January 1621, Viscount St. Albans. When James went to Scotland he left his Chancellor to rule England. Bacon "gave audience in great state to ambassadors." and lived in such splendor at Gorhambury that it "seemed as if the court was there, and not in Whitehall or St. James."[27]

All was won save honor. In the pursuit of place Bacon had repeatedly sacrificed principle. As attorney general he used his influence to secure judicial verdicts desired by the King.[28] As Keeper of the Seal he defended and protected the most oppressive monopolies, apparently to keep the good will of Buckingham. As judge he accepted substantial presents from persons suing in his court. All this was in the loose custom of the age: public officials were poorly paid, and they recompensed themselves with "gifts" from those whom they aided; James confessed, "If I were . . . to punish those who take bribes, I should soon not have a single subject left"; and James himself took bribes.[29]

The Parliament that assembled in January 1621 was in angry revolt against the King. It hated Bacon as James's best advocate, who had ruled that monopolies were legal. If it could not yet depose the King it could impeach his minister. In February it named a committee to inquire into the courts of justice. In March the committee reported that it had found many irregularities, especially in the conduct of the Lord Chancellor. Twenty-three specific cases of corruption were charged against him. He appealed to the King to save him, predicting that "those who now strike at the Chancellor will soon strike at the Crown."[30] James advised him to acknowledge the charge and so set an example deterrent to further venality in office. On April 22 Bacon sent in his confession to the House of Lords. He admitted taking gifts from litigants, as other judges did; he denied that his decisions had been thereby influenced—in several cases he had ruled against the giver. The Lords condemned him "to pay a fine of £40,000; to be imprisoned in the Tower during the King's pleasure; to be forever incapable to holding any public office . . . in the Commonwealth; never to sit in Parliament nor come within the verge of the Court." He was taken to the Tower on May 31, but was released within four days by order of the King, who also remitted the ruinous fine. The chastened Chancellor retired to Gorhambury and tried to live more simply. In cipher, on a paper left by Bacon at his death, his first biographer, Rawley, found the famous statement, "I was the justest judge that was in England these fifty years. But it was the justest censure in Parliament that was these 200 years."[31]

The effects of the impeachment were good. It lessened corruption in office, especially in the courts; and it set a precedent for the responsibility of the King's ministers to Parliament. It turned Francis Bacon back from politics, where he had been a liberal in views and a reactionary in practice, to his alternative pursuit of science and philosophy, where he would "ring the bell that called the wits together," and would proclaim, in majestic prose, the revolt and program of reason.

IV. The Great Renewal

Philosophy had long been his refuge from affairs, if not his secret love and happiest aptitude. He had already, in 1603–5, published a noble work, *The Proficience and Advancement of Learning*, but that seemed to him rather a prospectus than a performance. In 1609 he had written to the Bishop of Ely, "If God give me leave to write a just and perfect volume of philosophy . . .";[32] and in 1610 to Casaubon, "To bring about the better ordering of man's life . . . by the help of sound and true contemplations—this is the thing I aim at."[33]

During those harassed years of office he had conceived—with a rash assumption of abundant days—a magisterial plan for the renovation of science and philosophy. Seven months before his fall he announced the plan in a Latin work addressed to all Europe, boldly entitled *Instauratio Magna (The Great Renewal)*. The title page itself was a challenge: it showed a vessel passing full sail through the Pillars of Hercules into the Atlantic; and where a medieval motto had set between those pillars the warning *"Ne plus ultra"* ([Go] no farther beyond), Bacon wrote, *"Multi pertransibunt, et augebitur scientia"* (Many will pass through, and knowledge will be increased). The proud proemium added, "Francis of Verulam reasoned thus with himself, and judged it to be for the interest of the present and future generations that they should be made acquainted with his thoughts."[34]

Finding that "in what is now done in the matter of science there is only a whirling round about, and perpetual agitation, ending where it begins," he concluded that

> there was but one course left . . . to try the whole thing anew upon a better plan, and to commence a total reconstruction of sciences, [practical] arts, and all human knowledge, raised upon the proper foundation; . . . Moreover, because he knew not how long it might be before these things would occur to any one else . . . he resolved to publish at once so much as he had been able to complete . . . that in case of his death there might remain some outline and project of that which he had conceived . . . All other ambition seemed poor in his eyes compared with the work which he had in hand.[35]

He dedicated the entire project to James I, with apologies for "having sto-
len from your affairs so much time as was required for this work," but hoping
that the result would "go to the memory of your name and the honor of your
age"—and it did. James was a man of considerable learning and good will; if
he could be persuaded to finance the plan, what progress might not be made?
As Roger Bacon, far back in 1268, had sent to Pope Clement IV his *Opus
majus* seeking aid for a proposed expansion of knowledge, so now his namesake
appealed to his sovereign to undertake, as a "royal work," the organization of
scientific research and the philosophical unification of the results for the material and moral benefit of mankind. He reminded James of the "philosopher
kings"—Nerva, Trajan, Hadrian, Antoninus Pius, and Marcus Aurelius—who
had given good government to the Roman Empire for a century (A.D. 96–180).
Was it because of his need and hope for state funds that he had consistently and
ruinously supported the King?

A further preface asked the reader to look upon current science as porous
with error and shamefully stagnant, for

> the greatest wits in each successive age have been forced out of their
> own course; men of capacity and intellect above the vulgar had been
> fain, for reputation's sake, to bow to the judgment of the time and
> the multitude; and thus, if any contemplations of a higher order took
> light anywhere, they were presently blown out by the winds of vulgar
> opinions.[36]

And to pacify the theologians, who were powerful with the people or the King,
he cautioned his readers to "confine the sense" of his undertaking "within the
limits of duty in respect of things divine." He disclaimed any intention to deal
with religious beliefs or affairs; "the business in hand . . . is not an opinion to
be held, but a work to be done . . . I am laboring to lay the foundation not of
any sect or doctrine, but of human utility and power."[37] He urged others to
come forward and join him in the work, and trusted that successive generations
would carry it on.

In an imperial prospectus, *Distributio operis*, he offered a plan of the
enterprise. First, he would attempt a new classification of existing or desirable sciences, and would allot to them their problems and fields of research;
this he accomplished in *The Advancement of Learning*, which he translated and

expanded in *De augmentis scientiarum* (1623) to reach a Continental audience. Second, he would examine the shortcomings of contemporary logic, and seek a "more perfect use of human reason" than that which Aristotle had formulated in his logical treatises collectively known as the *Organon*; this Bacon did in his *Novum Organum* (1620). Third, he would begin a "natural history" of the "phenomena of the universe"—astronomy, physics, biology. Fourth, he would exhibit, in a "Ladder of the Intellect" (*Scala intellectus*), examples of scientific inquiry according to his new method. Fifth, as "Forerunners" (*Prodromi*), he would describe "such things as I myself have discovered." And sixth, he would begin to expound that philosophy which, from sciences so pursued, would be developed and certified. "The completion, however, of this last part is . . . both above my strength and beyond my hope." To us who now flounder and gasp in the ocean of knowledge and specialties, Bacon's program seems majestically vain; but knowledge was not then so immense and minute; and the brilliance of the parts performed forgives the presumption of the whole. When he told Cecil, "I have taken all knowledge to be my province," he did not mean that he could embrace all sciences in detail, but only that he purposed to survey the sciences "as from a rock," with a view to their co-ordination and encouragement. William Harvey said of Bacon that he "wrote philosophy like a lord chancellor";[38] yes, and planned it like an imperial general.

We feel the range and sharpness of Bacon's mind as we follow him in *The Advancement of Learning*. He offers his ideas with unwonted modesty, as "not much better than that noise . . . which musicians make while they are tuning their instruments";[39] but he strikes here nearly all his characteristic notes. He calls for the multiplication and support of colleges, libraries, laboratories, biological gardens, museums of science and industry; for the better payment of teachers and researchers; for ampler funds to finance scientific experiments; for better intercommunication, co-operation, and division of labor among the universities of Europe.[40] He does not lose his perspective in the worship of science; he defends a general and liberal education, including literature and philosophy, as promoting a wise judgment of ends to accompany the scientific improvement of means.[41] He tries to classify the sciences in a logical order, to determine their fields and bounds, and to direct each to major problems awaiting inquiry and solution. Many of his demands have been met by the sciences—for better clinical records, for the prolongation of life by preventive medicine, for the careful examination of "psychical phenomena," and for the development of social psychology. He even anticipated our contemporary stud-ies in the technique of success.[42]

The second and boldest part of the Great Renewal was an attempt to for-mulate a new method of science. Aristotle had recognized, and occasionally preached, induction, but the predominant mode of his logic was deduction, and its ideal was the syllogism. Bacon felt that the old *Organon* had kept sci-ence stagnant by its stress on theoretical thought rather than practical observa-tion. His *Novum Organum* proposed a new organ and system of thought—the inductive study of nature itself through experience and experiment. Though this book too was left incomplete, it is, with all its imperfections, the most brilliant production in English philosophy, the first clear call for an Age of Reason. It was written in Latin, but in such lucid, pithy sentences that half of it radiates epigrams. The very first lines compacted a philosophy, announcing the inductive revolution, foreshadowing the Industrial Revolution, and giving the empirical key to Hobbes and Locke and Mill and Spencer.

> Man, being the servant and interpreter of Nature, can do and under-stand so much, and so much only, as he had observed, in fact or in thought, of the course of Nature; beyond this he neither knows any-thing nor can do anything . . . Human knowledge and human power meet in one; for where the course is not known, the effect cannot be produced. Nature, to be commanded, must be obeyed.*

And as Descartes seventeen years later, in the *Discourse on Method*, would propose to begin philosophy by doubting everything, so Bacon here demands an "expurgation of the intellect" as the first step in the Renewal. "Human knowl-edge as we have it is a mere medley and ill-digested mass, made up of much credulity and much accident, and also of the childish notions which are at first imbibed."[44] Therefore we must, at the start, clear our minds, so far as we can, of all preconceptions, prejudices, assumptions, and theories; we must turn away even from Plato and Aristotle; we must sweep out of our thought the "idols," or time-honored illusions and fallacies, born of our personal idiosyncrasies of

---

* The famous phrase "Knowledge is power" does not occur, in that form, in Bacon's extant works; but in a fragment of his *Meditationes sacrae* he writes, ". . . *ipsa scientia protestas est*"—knowledge itself is power.[43] The idea, of course, runs all through Bacon's writings.

judgment or the traditional beliefs and dogmas of our group; we must banish all logical tricks of wishful thinking, all verbal absurdities of obscure thought. We must put behind us all those majestic deductive systems of philosophy which proposed to draw a thousand eternal verities out of a few axioms and principles. There is no magic hat in science; everything taken from the hat in works must first be put into it by observation or experiment. And not by mere casual observation, nor by "simple enumeration" of data, but by "experience . . . sought for, experiment." Thereupon Bacon, so often belittled as ignoring the true method of science, proceeds to describe the actual method of modern science:

> The true method of experience first lights the candle [by hypothesis], and then by means of the candle shows the way, commencing as it does with experience duly ordered . . . and from it educing axioms ["first fruits," provisional conclusions], and from established axioms again new experiments . . . Experiment itself shall judge.[45]

However, Bacon was wary of hypotheses; they were too often suggested by tradition, prejudice, or desire—i.e., again by "idols"; he distrusted any procedure in which hypothesis, consciously or not, would select from experience confirmatory data and gloss over, or be blind to, contrary evidence. To avoid this pitfall, he proposed a laborious induction by accumulation of all facts pertinent to a problem, their analysis, comparison, classification, and correlation, and, "by a due process of exclusion and rejection," the progressive elimination of one hypothesis after another, until the "form" or underlying law and essence of a phenomenon should be revealed.[46] Knowledge of the "form" would give increasing control of the event, and science would gradually remake the environment and possibly man himself.

For this, Bacon felt, is the ultimate aim—that the method of science shall be applied to the rigorous analysis and resolute remolding of human character. He urges a study of the instincts and emotions, which bear the same relation to the mind as winds to the sea.[47] But here especially the fault lies not merely in the seeking of knowledge but in its transmission. Man could be remade by an enlightened education, if we were willing to draw first-rate minds into pedagogy by giving them adequate remuneration and honor.[48] Bacon admires the Jesuits as educators and wishes they were "on our side."[49] He condemns compendiums, approves college dramatics, and pleads for more science in the curriculum. Science and education so conceived would be (as in *The New Atlantis*) not the tool and handmaid, but the guide and goal, of government. And the confident Chancellor concludes, "I stake all on the victory of art over Nature in the race."

V. A Statesman's Philosophy

Here, we feel, is a powerful mind—a man, one in a century, at home equally in philosophy and politics. It would be interesting to know what this philosopher thought in politics, and what this politician thought in philosophy.

Not that he had any system in philosophy, or left any orderly exposition of his thought, except in logic. The trend of his ideas is clear, but their form is that of a man who had to rush repeatedly out of the calm of philosophy to try a case in law, to fight an opposition in Parliament, or to counsel an unteachable King. We must gather his views from incidental remarks and literary fragments, including his *Essays* (1597, 1612, 1625). With the vanity inherent in authorship, Bacon wrote, in dedicating these to Buckingham, "I do conceive . . . [the] volume may last as long as books last." In his letters his style is labored and involved, so that his wife confessed, "I do not understand his enigmatical folded writing";[50] in the *Essays* he concealed still intenser labor, disciplined his pen to clarity, and achieved such compact force of expression that very few pages in English prose can match them for significant matter pressed with luminous similes into perfect form. It is as if Tacitus had taken to philosophy, and had condescended to be clear.

Bacon's wisdom is worldly. He leaves metaphysics to the mystical or the rash; even his vaulting ambition rarely leaped from the fragment to the whole. Sometimes, however, he seems to plunge into a determinist materialism: "In nature nothing really exists besides individual bodies performing pure individual acts according to a fixed law";[51] and "inquiries into nature have the best result when they begin with physics and end in mathematics";[52] but "nature" here may mean only the external world. He preferred the skeptical pre-Socratic philosophers to Plato and Aristotle, and he praised the materialistic Democritus.[53] But then he accepts a sharp distinction between body and soul,[54] and anticipates Bergson's chiding of the intellect as a "constitutional materialist": "The human understanding is infected by the sight of what takes place in the mechanical arts . . . and so imagines that something similar goes on in the universal nature of things."[55] He rejects in advance the mechanistic biology of Descartes.

With careful ambivalence he "seasons" his philosophy "with religion as with salt."[56] "I had rather believe all the fables in the [Golden] Legend, and the Talmud, and the Alcoran, than that this universal frame is without a mind."[57] He puts atheism in its place in a famous passage twice repeated.[58] His analysis of the causes of atheism illuminates the theme of this volume:

> The causes of atheism are divisions in religion, if they be many; for any one main division addeth zeal to both sides, but many divisions introduce atheism. Another is scandal of priests. And lastly, learned times, specially with peace and prosperity; for troubles and adversities do more bow men's minds to religion.[59]

He lays it down as a rule that "all knowledge is to be limited by religion."[60] According to his chaplain, Rawley, he "repaired frequently, when his health would permit him, to the services of the church . . . and died in the true faith established in the Church of England."[61] Nevertheless, like his great predecessor William of Ockham, he availed himself of the distinction between theological and philosophical truth: faith might hold to beliefs for which science and philosophy could find no evidence, but philosophy should depend only on reason, and science should seek purely secular explanations in terms of physical cause and effect.[62]

Despite his zest for knowledge, Bacon subordinates it to morality; there would be no gain to humanity if the extension of knowledge brought no gain in benevolence. "Of all virtues and dignities of the mind, goodness is the greatest."[63] However, his usual enthusiasm subsides when he speaks of the Christian virtues. Virtue should be practiced in moderation, for the wicked may take advantage of the indiscreetly good.[64] A little dissimulation is necessary to success, if not to civilization. Love is a madness, and marriage is a noose. "He that hath wife and children hath given hostages to fortune; for they are impediments to great enterprises . . . The best works, and of the greatest merit for the public, have proceeded from the unmarried or childless men." Like Elizabeth and Hildebrand, Bacon approved of clerical celibacy. "A single life doth well with churchmen, for charity will hardly water the ground when it must first fill a pool."[65] (Note his flair for metaphor and Anglo-Saxon brevity.) Friendship is better than love, and married men make unsteady friends. Bacon talks of love and marriage in the strain of a man who has sacrificed the tender emotions to ambition, and who could rule a kingdom better than his home.

His political philosophy faced conditions rather than theories. He had the courage to say a good word for Machiavelli, and candidly accepted the principle that states are not bound by the moral code taught to their citizens. He felt, like Nietzsche, that a good war halloweth any cause. "Neither is the opinion of some of the Schoolmen to be received, that a war cannot be justly made but upon a precedent injury or provocation . . . A just fear of an imminent danger, though there be no blow given, is a lawful cause of war." In any event, "a just and honorable war is the true exercise" to keep a nation in trim.[66] "For empire and greatness it is of most importance that a nation profess arms as their principal honor, study, and occupation." A powerful navy is a guarantee of neighborly respect; "to be master of the sea is the very epitome of monarchy."[67] "In the youth of a state arms do flourish; in the middle age of a state, learning; and then both of them together for a time; in the declining age of a state, mercantile acts and merchants."[68] Townsmen make poor warriors, peasants better, yeomen best. Hence Bacon, like More, condemned enclosures, as reducing the proportion of landowners in the population. He deprecated the concentration of wealth as a chief cause of sedition and revolt. Of these

> the first remedy or prevention is to remove by all means possible that material cause . . . which is want and poverty. . . . To which purpose serveth the opening and well-balancing of trade; the cherishing of manufactures; the banishing of idleness; the repression of waste and excess by sumptuary laws; the improvement and husbanding of the soil; the regulating of prices of things vendible; the moderation of taxes . . . Above all things good policy is to be used that the treasures and monies in a state be not gathered into a few hands . . . Money is like muck, not good except it be spread.[69]

Bacon distrusted Parliament as composed of uneducated and intolerant landowners and merchants or their agents; he thought James I by comparison informed and humane; even the King's theoretical absolutism seemed benevolent as the alternative to greedy factions and violent creeds. Like his contemporary Richelieu, he considered the centralization of authority in the king, and the royal subordination of the great landlords, a necessary step in the evolution of orderly government; and like Voltaire, he thought it easier to educate one man than a multitude. His own great wealth did not disturb him, and James proved obdurately wedded to extravagance, taxes, and peace.

Bacon had smiled at "the philosophers" who "make imaginary laws for imaginary commonwealths; their discourses are as the stars, which give little light because they are so high." But in his tired age he yielded to the temptation to picture the kind of society in which he would have men live. He had doubtless read More's *Utopia* (1516); Campanella had just published his *City of the Sun* (1623); now (1624) Bacon wrote *The New Atlantis*. "We sailed from Peru (where we had continued for the space of one whole year) for China and Japan by the South Sea." A long calm, failing rations, a providential isle, a people living happily under laws made for them by a late King Salomon. Instead of a parliament, a Salomon's House—an aggregation of observatories, laboratories, libraries, zoological and botanical gardens—manned by scientists, economists, technicians, physicians, psychologists, and philosophers, chosen (as in Plato's *Republic*) by equal tests after equal educational opportunity, and then (without elections) governing the state, or, rather, ruling nature in the interest of man. "The end of our Foundation," one of these rulers explains to the barbarians from Europe, "is the knowledge of causes and secret motions of things, and the enlarging of the bounds of Human Empire, to the effecting of all things possible."[70] Already, in this South Pacific enchantment, the Salomonic wizards have invented microscopes, telescopes, self-winding clocks, submarines, automobiles, and airplanes; they have discovered anesthetics, hypnosis, and ways of preserving health and lengthening life; they have found ways of grafting plants, generating new species, transmuting metals, and transmitting music to distant places. In Salomon's House government and science are bound together, and all the tools and organization of research that Bacon had begged James to provide are there part of the equipment of the state. The island is economically independent; it avoids foreign trade as a snare to war; it imports knowledge, but not goods. So the humbled philosopher replaces the proud statesman, and the same man who had advised an occasional war as a social tonic now in his closing years dreams of a paradise of peace.

VI. *The Chanticleer of Reason*

He continued working to the end. A year after his retirement he published a *History of the Reign of Henry VII*. It set a new standard for historiography: a clear account, in fine, strong prose, of issues, policies, and events; a just, impartial, penetrating sketch of a ruler unidealized, illuminatingly real.[71] A medley of treatises followed: *History* [i.e., a study] *of Winds, History of Density and Rarity, History of Life and Death, Sylva Sylvarum*, and further essays. He had unexpected leisure now—no place, no children, no friends, for the place seekers who had crowded about him in his days of power were scraping before other doors. "What comrades have you in your work?" he asked a correspondent. "As for me, I am in the completest solitude."[72]

Seeking to test how long snow could keep flesh from putrefaction, he interrupted a journey one day in spring to buy a fowl. He killed it and stuffed it with snow, then found himself chilled. He went to the nearby home of Lord Arundel and was there put to bed. He thought the trouble would soon pass; he wrote that the experiment had "succeeded excellently well." He had preserved the fowl—but he lost his life. Fever consumed him, phlegm choked him; on April 9, 1626, he died, aged sixty-five, the glowing candle suddenly snuffed out.

———————————

He was not, as Pope thought, "the wisest, brightest, meanest of mankind."[73] Montaigne was wiser, Voltaire brighter, Henry VIII meaner; and Bacon's enemies called him kindly, helpful, and quick to forgive. He was self-seeking to the verge of servility, and proud enough to anger the gods; but we share these faults sufficiently to pardon his humanity for the light that he shed. His egotism was the wind in his sails. To see ourselves as others see us would be crippling.

He was not a scientist, but a philosopher of science. His range of observation was immense, but his field of speculation was too vast to allow him much time for special investigations; he attempted some, with little result. He fell far behind the progress of contemporary science. He rejected the Copernican astronomy, but gave excellent reasons for doing so.[74] He ignored Kepler, Galileo, and Napier. He often noted (as in *The New Atlantis*), but still underrated, the role of imagination, hypothesis, and deduction in scientific research. His proposal for a patient collection and classification of facts worked well in astronomy, where the stellar observations and records of thousands of students gave Copernicus inductive material for his revolutionary deductions; but it bore small resemblance to the actual methods that in his time discovered the laws of planetary motions, the satellites of Jupiter, the magnetism of the earth, and the circulation of the blood.

He did not claim to have discovered induction; he knew that many men had practiced it before him. He was not the first to "overthrow Aristotle"; men like Roger Bacon and Petrus Ramus had been doing this for centuries past. And the Aristotle whom they deposed was not (as Francis Bacon sometimes realized) the Greek who had often used and praised induction and experiment, but the transmogrified *ille philosophus* of the Arabs and the Scholastics. What Bacon wanted to overthrow was the mistaken attempt to deduce medieval creeds from ancient metaphysics. In any event, he helped to free Renaissance Europe from too cramping a deference to antiquity.

He was not the first to emphasize knowledge as the road to power; Roger Bacon had done it, and Campanella had said, with Baconian pithiness, "*Tantum possumus quantum scimus*"—Our power is proportioned to our knowledge.[75] Perhaps the statesman stressed unduly the utilitarian ends of science. Yet he recognized the value of "pure" as compared with "applied" science—of "light" as distinct from "fruits." He urged a study of ends as well as of means, and knew that a century of inventions would create greater problems than it solved if it left human motives unchanged. He might have discovered in his own moral laxity the abyss created by the progress of knowledge beyond the discipline of character.

What remains after all these hindsight deductions? This: that Francis Bacon was the most powerful and influential intellect of his time. Shakespeare, of course, stood above him in imagination and literary art; but Bacon's mind ranged over the universe like a searchlight peering and prying curiously into every corner and secret of space. All the exhilarating enthusiasm of the Renaissance was in him, all the excitement and pride of a Columbus sailing madly into a new world. Hear the joyful cry of this Cock Robin announcing the dawn:

> Thus have I concluded this portion of learning touching Civil Knowledge; and with civil knowledge have concluded Human Philosophy; and with human philosophy, Philosophy in General. And being now at some pause, looking back into that I have passed through, this writing

seemeth to me, as far as a man can judge of his own work, not much better than that noise or sound which musicians make while they are tuning their instruments; which is nothing pleasant to hear, but yet is a cause why the music is sweeter afterwards. So have I been content to tune the instruments of the muses that they may play that have better hands. And surely, when I set before me the condition of these times, in which learning hath made her third visitation or circuit, in all the qualities thereof; as the excellency and vivacity of the wits of this age; the noble helps and lights which we have by the travails of ancient writers; the art of printing, which communicateth books to men of all fortunes; the openness of the world by navigation, which hath disclosed multitudes of experiments, and a mass of natural history; . . . I cannot but be raised to this persuasion, that this third period of time will far surpass that of the Græcian and Roman learning. . . . As for my labours, if any man shall please himself or others in the reprehension of them, they shall make that ancient and patient request, *Verbere sed audi* [Strike me if you will, only hear me]; let men reprehend them, so they observe and weigh them.[76]

Because he expressed the noblest passion of his age—for the betterment of life through the extension of knowledge—posterity raised to his memory a living monument of influence. Scientists were stirred and invigorated not by his method but by his spirit. How refreshing, after centuries of minds imprisoned in their roots or caught in webs of their own wishful weaving, to come upon a man who loved the sharp tang of fact, the vitalizing air of seeking and finding, the zest of casting lines of doubt into the deepest pools of ignorance, superstition, and fear! Some men in that age, like Donne, thought the world was decaying, hastening to a consumed or shattered end; Bacon announced to his times that they were the youth of a world rampant with effervescent life.

Men would not listen to him at first; in England, France, and Germany they preferred to carry the competition of faiths to the arbitrament of arms; but when that fury had cooled, those who were not fettered with certainties organized themselves in the spirit of Bacon for the enlargement of man's empire not over men but over the conditions and hindrances of human life. When Englishmen founded the Royal Society of London for Improving Natural

Knowledge (1660), it was Francis Bacon who was honored as its inspiration, and Salomon's House in *The New Atlantis* probably pointed the goal.[77] Leibniz hailed Bacon as the regenerator of philosophy.[78] And when the *philosophes* of the Enlightenment put together their world-shaking *Encyclopédie* (1751), they dedicated it to Francis Bacon. "If," said Diderot in the prospectus, "we have come to it successfully, we shall owe most to the Chancellor Bacon, who proposed the plan of a universal dictionary of sciences and arts at a time when, so to speak, neither arts nor sciences existed. That extraordinary genius, at a time when it was impossible to write a history of what was known, wrote one of what it was necessary to learn." And d'Alembert, in a frenzy of enthusiasm, called Bacon "the greatest, the most universal, and the most eloquent of philosophers." When the Enlightenment had burst into the French Revolution the Convention had the works of Bacon published at the expense of the state.[79] The tenor and career of British thought from Hobbes to Spencer—excepting Berkeley and Hume and the English Hegelians—followed Bacon's line. His tendency to conceive the external world in Democritean terms gave Hobbes the impetus to materialism; his emphasis on induction spurred Locke to an empirical psychology in which the study of the mind would be freed from the metaphysics of the soul; and his stress on "commodities" and "fruits" shared with the philosophy of Helvétius in leading Bentham to identify the useful and the good. The Baconian spirit prepared England for the Industrial Revolution.

Therefore we may place Francis Bacon at the head of the Age of Reason. He was not, like some of his successors, an idolator of reason; he distrusted all cogitations unchecked by actual experience, and all conclusions tainted with desire. "The human understanding is no dry light, but receives an infusion from the will and affections; whence proceed sciences which may be called 'sciences as one would.' For what a man had rather were true he more readily believes."[80] Bacon preferred "that reason which is elicited from facts. . . . From a closer and purer league between these two faculties, the experimental and the rational . . . much may be hoped."[81]

Nor did he, like the *philosophes* of the eighteenth century, propose reason as an enemy of religion or as a substitute for it; he made room for both of them in philosophy and life. But he repudiated the reliance upon traditions and authorities; he required rational and natural explanations instead of emotional presumptions, supernatural interventions, and popular mythology. He raised a banner for all the sciences, and drew to it the most eager minds of the succeeding centuries. Whether he willed it or not, the enterprise that he called for—the comprehensive organization of scientific research, the ecumenical expansion and dissemination of knowledge—contained in itself the seeds of the profoundest drama of modern times: Christianity, Catholic or Protestant, fighting for its life against the spread and power of science and philosophy. That drama had now spoken its prologue to the world.

CHAPTER VIII

THE GREAT REBELLION

1625–49

I. The Changing Economy

The revolution that enthroned Parliament and killed a king—144 years before Louis XVI atoned for his ancestry—had its roots in economic conflict and religious rivalry.

Feudalism was an organization and dependency of agriculture; monarchy, in Western Europe, was an organization and culmination of feudalism; it was tied by its roots to an economy of landlords and land. In England two economic developments cut these feudal roots. One was the growth of the "gentry," the untitled owners of minor estates, who, on the land, ranked between the titled nobility and the yeomanry, or peasant proprietors. They fretted under a king, a court, and a code of laws still thinking or fashioned in feudal terms; they bought or captured seats in the House of Commons; they longed for a government submissive to a Parliament submissive to themselves. The other development was the expanding wealth of the bourgeoisie—bankers, merchants, manufacturers, lawyers, physicians—and its demand for political representation commensurate with its economic power. These revolutionary factors had no common interest; they collaborated only in the attempt to check the pedigreed landlords, the snobbish court, and a king who considered a hereditary aristocracy the necessary source of economic and political order and stability.

Year by year the English economy was changing its base and fulcrum from static land to movable money. Before 1540 a brass factory required an investment of $300 (in United States currency of 1958); in 1620, $125,000. By 1650 capitalistic undertakings involving large outlays of funds had developed alum factories in Yorkshire, paper manufactures at Dartford, cannon foundries at Brendeley, and deep-level mines that were called upon for more and more coal, copper, tin, iron, and lead. In 1550 only a few English mines produced more than 300 tons a year; in 1640 several gave 20,000 tons each. Artisans using metal depended on mining and metallurgical industries concentrated under capitalistic control. Textile organizations furnished material to shops employing 500 to 1,000 workers, and to weavers and sewers scattered among thousands of houses in towns and villages. Agriculture itself was sharing in the capitalistic conversion of production: capitalists bought and enclosed large tracts of land to provide meat for the towns and wool for factories at home and abroad. England's foreign commerce grew tenfold between 1610 and 1640.

Not in England's memory had the gap been so wide between rich and poor. "The laborer's service sank to the worst scale of remuneration during the first half of the seventeenth century, for the price of food increased while wages remained stationary."[1] Taking 100 as a base, the real wages of English carpenters stood at 300 about 1380, at 370 in 1480, at 200 under Elizabeth, at 120 under Charles I—the lowest in four hundred years.[2] Unemployment was so great in 1634 that Charles compelled the demolition of a newly erected mechanical sawmill because it threw so many sawyers out of work.[3] War with France raised taxes, war in France disrupted the export trade, bad harvests (1629–30) inflated prices to the verge of starvation;[4] the swelling economy burst in depressions (1629–32, 1638). All these factors collaborated with religious strife to drive many English families to America, and to plunge England into a civil war that changed the face and destiny of the nation.

The class war became also a conflict of regions and moral codes. The north was overwhelmingly agricultural and largely Catholic, however clandestinely; London and the south were increasingly industrial and Protestant. The new business class, while cherishing its monopolies and protective tariffs, demanded a free economy, in which wages and prices would be determined by the supply of labor and goods; in which there would be no feudal or governmental control of production, distribution, profit, or property; and in which no stigma would be attached to commercial occupations, the charging of interest, or the manipulation of wealth. The barons and their peasants clung to the feudal concept of mutual obligation and group responsibility, of state regulation of wages and prices, of limits by custom and law to conditions of employment and profit. The barons protested that the new mercantile economy, producing for a national or international market, was disrupting class relations and social stability. They (and the gentry and the government) felt their own solvency threatened by the effects of inflation on the value of the traditional dues, rents, or taxes upon which they depended. They looked with angry disdain upon the lawyers who shared so prominently in administration, and the merchants who ruled the cities. They dreaded the power of mercantile London, which, with a population of some 300,000 out of England's 5,000,000, was able to finance an army and a revolution.

II. The Religious Caldron: 1624–49

The new King, raised in the old feudal and social code of the land, and lost in the London of merchants and Puritans, was troubled beyond patience by the variety and the intensity of religious beliefs. The right of individual judgment, which every new opinion preached until it came to power, united with the spread of the Bible to encourage the diversity of sects. One pamphleteer (1641) listed twenty-nine; another (1646), 180. Besides the cleavage between Catholics and Protestants, there was the tense division of Protestants into Anglicans, Presbyterians, and Puritans, and of Puritans into Independents who dreamed of a republic, Quakers who opposed war, violence, and oaths, Millenarians— or Fifth Monarchy Men—who believed that Jesus would soon come to establish His personal rule on earth, Antinomians who argued that the elect of God were exempt from human laws, and Brownist Separatists, and Seekers, and Ranters. A member of Parliament complained that "mechanical men" (artisans) were setting up pulpits and preaching their own hot brands of faith, many of them clothing economic or political demands in Scriptural texts. And there were Anabaptists, who administered baptism only to adults; and Baptists, who separated from the Separatists (1606) and divided (1633) into General Baptists rejecting, and Particular Baptists accepting, the Calvinist doctrine of predestination.

The multiplication of sects, and their spirited debates, led a small minority to doubt all forms of Christianity. Bishop Fotherby mourned (1622) that "the Scriptures (with many) have lost their authority, and are thought only fit for the ignorant and the idiotic."[5] And the Reverend James Cranford (1646) spoke of "multitudes" who "have changed their faith either to Skepticism . . . or Atheism, to believe nothing."[6] A pamphlet entitled *Hell Broke Loose: A Catalogue of the Many Spreading Errors, Heresies, and Blasphemies of These Times* (1646) cited, as the first heresy, the opinion "that the Scripture, whether a true manuscript [an authentic text] or no . . . is but humane [man-made], and not able to discover [reveal] a divine God."[7] Another heresy declared that "right Reason is the rule of Faith, and . . . we are to believe the Scriptures, and the doctrines of the Trinity, Incarnation, Resurrection, so far as we see them agreeable to reason, and no further."[8] A large number of doubters denied hell and the divinity of Christ. A growing number of thinkers, who came to be called deists, sought a compromise between skepticism and religion by proposing a Christianity confined to the belief in God and immortality. Edward, Lord Herbert of Cherbury, gave this *via media* a philosophical formulation in a remarkable essay on truth, *De veritate* (1624). Truth, said Herbert, is independent of Scripture, and cannot be decreed by a church or any other authority. The best test of truth is universal assent. Consequently the wisest religion would be a "natural" rather than a revealed religion, and would limit itself to doctrines generally accepted by the different creeds: that there is a Supreme Being, that He should be worshiped chiefly by virtuous living, and that good conduct will be rewarded, and bad conduct punished, either here or in a life hereafter. Herbert, says Aubrey, died "serenely," after being refused the sacraments.[9]

Parliament was more worried about Catholicism than about heresy. In 1634 the Catholics in England were probably a quarter of the population,[10] and, despite all laws and perils, there were still some 335 Jesuits there.[11] Prominent nobles accepted the old faith. George Calvert, Lord Baltimore, announced his conversion in 1625; in 1632 Charles gave him a charter to found the colony that became Maryland. The Catholic Queen, Henrietta Maria, sent an emissary to Rome (1633) to solicit a cardinal's hat for a British subject. The Anglican King offered to allow a Catholic bishop to reside in England if Urban VIII would support Charles's plan for some diplomatic marriages (1634); the Pope refused. The Catholics called for religious tolerance, but Parliament—remembering Catholic intolerance, the Massacre of St. Bartholomew, and the Gunpowder Plot, and loath to risk inquiry into Protestant titles to once Catholic property—demanded instead the full enforcement of the anti-Catholic laws. A strong "no popery" sentiment, especially in the gentry and the middle class, opposed alike the influx of Catholic priests into England and the growing approximation of Anglican to Catholic ritual and thought.

The Established Church enjoyed the full protection of the state. The Anglican creed and worship were legally compulsory; even the Thirty-nine Articles were made law of the land (1628). The Anglican bishops claimed the Apostolic

Succession—that is, that they had been ordained by an Apostle; and they rejected the Presbyterian and Puritan assertion that others than bishops might validly ordain a minister. Many Anglican ecclesiastics in this age were men of great learning and good will. James Ussher, Archbishop of Armagh, was a real scholar despite his famous calculation (in his *Annales Veteris Testamenti,* 1650) that God had created the world on October 22, 4004 B.C.—a chronological slip that was made semiofficial in editions of the Authorized Version.[12] John Hales, chaplain to an English embassy in Holland, preached doubt, reason, and toleration:

> The ways that lead us to . . . any knowledge . . . are but two: first, experience, secondly ratiocination. They that come and tell you what to believe, what you are to do, and tell you not why, they are not physicians but leeches . . . The chiefest sinew and strength of wisdom is not easily to believe. . . . Those things which we reverence for antiquity, what were they at their first birth? Were they false? Time cannot make them more true. The circumstance of time . . . is merely impertinent . . . It is not the variety of opinions but our own perverse wills—who think it meet that all should be conceited [of the same thought] as ourselves are—which hath so inconvenienced the Church. Were we not so ready to anathematize each other where we concur not in opinion, we might in hearts be united . . . Two parts there are that do completely make up a Christian man—a true faith and an honest conversation [conduct]. The first, though it seems the worthier, and gives us the name of Christians, yet the second, in the end, will prove the surer . . . There is no kind of man . . . though he be an heathen and idolater, unto whom the skirts of Christian compassion do not reach.[13]

Hale's generosity was not reciprocated by some "idolators." A Jesuit, writing under the name "Edward Knott" a tract entitled *Charity Mistaken* (1630), maintained that, barring accidents, no Protestant could be saved.[14] The condemned were reassured by William Chillingworth, whose *The Religion of Protestants a Safe Way to Salvation* (1637) was the outstanding theological treatise of the time. Chillingworth knew both sides: he had been converted to Catholicism, had returned to Protantism, and still had his reservations; he had, said

Clarendon, "contracted such a habit of doubting that by degrees he grew confident of nothing, and a skeptic, at least, in the greatest mysteries of religion."[15]

The most eloquent of these Caroline Anglicans was Jeremy Taylor. His sermons are still readable, and more moving than Bossuet's; even a Frenchman has been stirred by them.[16] Taylor was an ardent Royalist, a chaplain in the army of Charles I. When the Presbyterians and the Puritans controlled Parliament and abused the once intolerant Anglicans intolerantly, he issued *The Liberty of Prophesying* (1646), a timid call for toleration: any Christian who accepted the Apostles' Creed should be received within the amity of the Church, and Catholics were to be left free unless they insisted on papal sovereignty over England and kings.* Taylor was captured and imprisoned by the Parliamentary party in the Civil War, but after the Restoration he was raised to the episcopacy, and his ardor for toleration cooled.

The growing influence of Catholicism appeared in the predominant Anglican of the age. William Laud was a man of ideas and will, born to rule or die, strictly virtuous, severely strict, and resolute to the point of irascible inflexibility. Like a good churchman, he took it for granted that a unified religious belief was indispensable to successful government, and that a complex ceremonial was necessary for a tranquilizing and effectual faith. To the sorrow of Presbyterians and Puritans, he proposed to recall the arts to the service of the Church, to beautify the altar, the pulpit, and the baptismal font, to restore the cross to the ritual and the surplice to the priest. As a special mountain of offense, he ordered the Communion table, which heretofore had been placed in the center of the chancel (where it had sometimes served as a hat stand), to be put behind a railing at the eastern end of the church. These changes were mostly a revival of Elizabethan customs and laws, but to the Puritans, who loved simplicity, they represented a backsliding to Catholicism and the renewal of a class separation between priest and congregation. Laud seems to have felt that the Catholic Church was right in surrounding religion with ceremony and endowing the priest with an aura of sanctity.[17] The Roman Church appreciated his views, even to offering him a cardinal's hat.[18] He courteously refused, but the offer appeared to support the reproaches of the Puritans. They called him the forerunner of Antichrist. Charles made him Archbishop of Canterbury (1633)

---

* In 1631, in Massachusetts Bay Colony, Roger Williams advocated unlimited toleration for Catholics, Jews, and infidels.

and a commissioner of the treasury. Another archbishop was made Chancellor of Scotland. People complained that ecclesiastics were returning to political power, as in the heyday of the medieval Church.

From his Lambeth Palace the new Primate of All England set himself to remolding English ritual and morals. He made a hundred new enemies by levying, through the Court of High Commission (a judiciary body set up by Elizabeth, and now predominantly ecclesiastical), severe fines from persons convicted of adultery; and the victims found little comfort in his devoted use of the fines to repair the decaying St. Paul's Cathedral and to drive lawyers, hucksters, and gossipers from its naves.[19] Ministers who rejected the new ritual were deprived of their benefices; writers and speakers who repeatedly criticized it, who questioned the Christian creed, or who opposed the institution of bishops were to be excommunicated, and were to stand in the stocks and perhaps lose their ears.

The brutality of the punishments exacted under Laud's regime must be visualized to understand his fate. In 1628, at his instigation, a Puritan minister, Alexander Leighton, was indicted before the Star Chamber as the admitted author of a book that called the institution of bishops anti-Christian and satanic. He was put in irons and was kept in solitary confinement for fifteen weeks in an unheated cell "full of rats and mice, and open to snow and rain." His hair fell out, his skin peeled off. He was tied to a stake and received thirty-six stripes with a heavy cord upon his naked back; he was placed in the pillory for two hours in November's frost and snow; he was branded in the face, had his nose slit and his ears cut off, and was condemned to life imprisonment.[20] In 1633 Ludowyc Bowyer, who had charged Laud with being a Catholic at heart, was fined, branded, mutilated, and sentenced to imprisonment for life.[21] William Prynne, firebrand of the Puritans, in *News from Ipswich* (1636) denounced Laud's bishops as servants of the pope and the Devil, and recommended hanging for bishops; he was branded on both cheeks, had his ears cut off, and was jailed till the Long Parliament freed him (1640). A woman who insisted on keeping Saturday as the Sabbath was imprisoned for eleven years.[24]

Laud's chief enemies, the Puritans, agreed with him on the necessity of intolerance. They thought it a reasonable conclusion from the divine origin of Christianity and the Scriptures; anyone who opposed a faith so founded must be a criminal or a fool, and society should be protected from the many damnations that would follow from his teaching. The Presbyterians pleaded with

Parliament (1648) to legislate life imprisonment for all who continued to teach Catholic, Arminian, Baptist, or Quaker views, and death for all who denied the doctrines of the Trinity or the Incarnation. Cromwell's Independents, however, offered toleration to all who would accept the fundamentals of Christianity, but they excluded Catholics, Unitarians, and defenders of prelacy.[25]

There were so many parties among the Puritans that it is a rare generalization that can hold of them all. Most of them adhered to a strict Calvinism, to individual political liberty, to the right of congregations to run their own affairs without episcopal supervision, and to a worship unceremonious, egalitarian, and divorced from the distractions of religious art. They agreed with the Presbyterians in theology, but rejected presbyteries as tending to exercise episcopal power. They insisted on a literal interpretation of Scripture, and condemned the pretense of reason to sit in judgment on revealed truth. They attached as much reverence to the Old Testament as to the New; they applied to themselves the Judaic conception of the chosen people; they baptized their children with the names of Old Testament patriarchs and heroes; they thought of God in terms of a stern Yahveh, and added the Calvinistic conviction that most men were the "children of wrath," doomed before their birth, by the arbitrary will of a relentless deity, to everlasting hell; and they ascribed the salvation of the few "elect" not to good works but to divine grace granted at divine whim. Some of them thought they talked to God; some, thinking themselves damned, went about the streets groaning in anticipation of their eternal sufferings. The thunderbolts of God seemed always to hang over the heads of men.

In this self-imposed Terror "Merrie England" almost disappeared. The humanism of the Renaissance, the lusty naturalism of the Elizabethans, yielded to a sense of sin, a fear of divine vengeance, which looked upon most pleasures as wiles of Satan and challenges to God. The old monastic fears of the flesh returned, perhaps to a larger proportion of the people than ever in known history before. Prynne declared all embraces "lewd," all mixed dancing "lascivious."[26] To most Puritans music, stained glass, religious images, surplices, anointed priests were obstacles to direct communion with God. They studied the Bible with devoted diligence and quoted its phrases in nearly every speech, in almost every paragraph; some zealots embroidered their clothing with Scriptural texts; the especially godly added "Verily" or "Yea, verily" to attest sincerity or truth. Good Puritans prohibited the use of cosmetics and banned hairdressing as vanity; they earned the nickname "Roundheads" because they cut their hair close to the head.

They denounced the theater as scandalous (it was), the baiting of bears and bulls as barbarous, the morals of the court as pagan. They condemned festival jollities, ringing bells, gathering around the Maypole, drinking healths, playing cards. They forbade all games whatever on the Sabbath; that day was to be kept for God, and it was no longer to bear the heathen name Sunday. They—Milton among them—cried out in anger when Charles I and Laud, renewing an edict of James I, issued (1633) a "Declaration of Sports" sanctioning Sunday games after Sunday prayers. The Puritans extended their Sabbatarianism—the advocacy of blue Sundays—to Christmas; they lamented the style of celebrating the birth of Christ with merrymaking, dancing, and games; they rightly ascribed many Christmas customs to pagan origins; they demanded that Christmas should be made a solemn day of fasting and atonement; and in 1644 they prevailed upon Parliament to sanction this view by law.

As Protestantism had stressed the sermon beyond Catholic precedent, so Puritanism expanded it even beyond Protestant custom. A hunger for sermons gnawed at some hearts; the mayor of Norwich moved to London to hear more preaching; a mercer resigned from a congregation because it provided only one sermon per Sunday. Special "lecturers" arose to ease this hunger—laymen hired by a parish to preach a Sunday sermon additional to what the regular minister offered. Most Puritan preachers took their function with high seriousness; they terrified their audiences with descriptions of hell; some of them denounced sinners publicly by name; one pointed out the drunkards in his congregation and, talking of whores, specified as an example the wife of a chief parishioner; another told his auditors that if adultery, swearing, cheating, and Sabbath breaking could lead a man to heaven, the whole parish would be saved.[27] The Puritan ministers felt it their duty to prescribe or proscribe the conduct, dress, studies, and amusements of the people. They forbade the observance of the holydays established by pagan custom or the Catholic Church, and so added some fifty working days to the year.[28] A call to duty sounded throughout the Puritan ethic, and with it a stern inculcation of courage, self-reliance, prudence, thrift, and work. It was an ethic congenial to the middle class; it made for industrious workers and gave a religious sanction to mercantile enterprise and private property. Poverty, not wealth, was a sin; it revealed lack of personal character and divine grace.[29]

Politically, the Puritans aspired to a democratic theocracy in which there would be none but moral and religious distinctions among men, no ruler but Christ, no law but God's Word. They resented the heavy taxes that supported the Anglican Church; their businessmen felt themselves milked by that expensive and superior Establishment; the "trading part of a nation," said one pamphleteer, "is devoured in this Prelatical Gulph."[30] The Puritans defended wealth, but scorned the idle luxury of the nobility. They carried morality to excess, as later ages carried liberty; but perhaps their inhuman code was a necessary corrective to the loose morals of Elizabethan England. They produced some of the strongest characters in history—Cromwell and Milton, and the men who conquered the American wilderness. They defended and transmitted to us parliamentary government and trial by jury. To them, in part, England owes the solid sobriety of the British character, the stability of the British family, and the integrity of Britain's official life. Nothing is lost.

III. The Puritans and the Theater

The first victory of the Puritans was in their war against the theater. Everything that distinguished them—their theology of "elect" and "reprobate," their strict morality, their solemn mood and Biblical speech—had been ridiculed on the stage with gross and unforgivable caricature. And in 1629 came the culminating crime: a French actress dared to replace a boy in taking a female part in a play at the Blackfriars. She was pelted with apples and rotten eggs.

The new dramatists might have appeased the Puritan party, for, though now and then they stooped to conquer the groundlings with ribaldry, by and large they were gentlemen. Philip Massinger's *A New Way to Pay Old Debts* (1625) satirized not prim virtue but monopolistic greed; there was no soaring poetry in it, no crackling wit, no winging imagery; but the unscrupulous extortioner was brought to justice in the end, and five acts transpired without a trull. John Ford angled for an audience by entitling a play *'Tis Pity She's a Whore,* but this and *The Broken Heart* (both 1633) kept a decent pitch, and might still hold the boards if modern audiences could stomach the holocausts of their denouements.

The Puritans fired their hottest shot against the theater when their most fearless protagonist, William Prynne, sent to the press (1632) his *Histriomastix, the Players Scourge.* Prynne was a lawyer and made no claim to impartiality; he presented a thousand-page brief for the plaintiff. By quotations from the Bible, from the Fathers of the Church, and even from the pagan philosophers, he proved that the drama had been invented by Satan and had begun as a form of devil worship. Most plays are blasphemous and obscene, full of amorous embraces, wanton gestures, and lust-arousing music, song, and dance; all dancing is devilish, and its every pace is a step to hell; most actors are profane and godless criminals. "The Church of God, not the playhouse, is the only 'proper' school; the Scriptures, sermons, and devout and pious books . . . are the only lectures" (reading) fit for Christians. And if they need diversion,

> they have the several prospects of the sun, the moon, the planets, the stars, with all the infinite variety of creatures, to delight their eyes. They have music of all birds . . . to please their ears; the incomparably delicate odoriferous scents and perfumes of all herbs, all flowers, fruits to refresh their noses; the savoury tastes of all edible creatures . . . the pleasures that orchards, rivers, gardens, ponds, woods . . . can afford them; the comfort of friends, kindred, husbands, wives, children, possessions, wealth, and all other external blessings that God hath bestowed upon them.[31]

The argument was learned and eloquent, but it called all actresses whores, and the Queen had just imported some actresses from France and was herself rehearsing a part in a court masque. Henrietta Maria took offense, and Laud indicted Prynne for seditious libel. The author protested that he had had no intention of libeling the Queen; he apologized for the intemperance of his book; nevertheless, with a severity which the Puritans long remembered, he was debarred from the practice of law, was fined the impossible sum of £5,000 ($250,000?), and was sentenced to life imprisonment. He was placed in the pillory, and both his ears were cut off.[32] From his prison he issued *News from Ipswich* (1636), in which he denounced Anglican prelates as devilish traitors and ravenous wolves, and recommended that these bishops be hanged. He was pilloried again, and the stumps of his ears were shorn away. He remained in jail until the Long Parliament freed him in 1640.

In 1642 the Parliament ordered all the theaters of England closed. This was at first a war measure, apparently limited to "these calamitous times," but it remained in force till 1656. The long career of the Elizabethan drama came to an end amid a drama greater than any that the English stage had ever played.

IV. Caroline Prose

There were at least two men in England who could look out upon the seething scene with perspective and calm. John Selden was so learned that men said, *"Quod Seldenus nescit nemo scit"*—What Selden does not know, nobody knows. As an antiquarian he collected state records of pre-Norman England and compiled an authoritative *Titles of Honor* (1614); as an Orientalist he made a European reputation with his study of polytheism, *De diis Syris* (1617); as a jurist he expounded rabbinical law and wrote a *History of Tythes* refuting the claim of the divine origin of tithes; as an M.P. he took part in impeaching Buckingham and Laud and in drawing up the Petition of Right; he was twice imprisoned. He attended the Westminster Assembly as a lay delegate "to see wild asses fight," and pleaded for moderation in religious disputes. After his death his *Table Talk,* recorded by his secretary, became an English classic. Shall we sample him?

> 'Tis a vain thing to talk of an heretic, for a man can think no otherwise than he does think. In the primitive times there were many opinions. One of these being embraced by some prince . . . the rest were condemned as heresies . . . No man is the wiser for his learning; it may administer matter to work in . . . but wit [intelligence] and wisdom are born with a man . . . Wise men say nothing in dangerous times. The lion . . . called the sheep to ask her if his breath smelled; she said Yes; he bit off her head for a fool. He called the wolf and asked him; he said No; he tore him to pieces for a flatterer. At last he called the fox, and asked him. Why [said the fox], he had got a cold and could not smell.[33]

Sir Thomas Browne was a fox. Born in London (1605), educated at Winchester School, Oxford, Montpellier, Padua, and Leiden, absorbing arts and sciences and history at every turn, he resigned himself to the practice of medicine at Norwich. He sublimated his uroscopies by jotting down his ideas *de omnibus rebus et quibusdam aliis* ("on all things and a few others"), and eloquently concealed his theology in *Religio medici* (1642), one of the milestones in English prose. Here is a British Montaigne, quite as quaint and fanciful, as undulant and diverse, perhaps borrowing from him in the pages of friendship,[34] subordinating his skepticism to conformity, relishing reason and professing faith, congested with classical allusions and derivatives, but loving the art and the music of words, and using style as "the antiseptic of decay."

He was by education inclined to doubt. His longest work, *Pseudodoxia epidemica* (1646), explained and chastised hundreds of "false opinions epidemic" in Europe—that a carbuncle gives light in the dark, that an elephant has no joints, that the phoenix regenerates itself from its own ashes, that the salamander can live in fire, that the unicorn has a horn, that swans sing before their death, that the forbidden fruit was an apple, that "the toad pisseth and this way diffuseth its venom."[35] But, like every iconoclast, he had his icons. He accepted angels, demons, palmistry, and witches;[36] in 1664 he shared in the condemnation as witches of two women, who were soon thereafter hanged protesting their innocence.[37]

He had no fancy for women, and thought sex ridiculous:

> I was never yet once, and commend their resolutions who never marry twice . . . I could be content that we might procreate like trees, without conjunction, or that there were any way to perpetuate the world without this trivial and vulgar way of union; it is the foolishest act a wise man commits in all his life; nor is there anything that will more deject his cool'd imagination, when he shall consider what an odd and unworthy piece of folly he hath committed.[38]

As to his titular topic, he is apologetically Christian:

> For my religion, though there be several circumstances that might persuade the world I have none at all (as the general scandal of my profession, the natural course of my studies, the indifferency of my behavior and discourse in matters of religion, neither violently defending one, nor with that common ardor and contention opposing another), yet, in despite hereof, I dare without usurpation the honorable style of Christian. Not that I merely owe this title to the font, my education, or the clime wherein I was born . . . but having in my riper years and confirmed judgment seen and examined all.[39]

He feels that the marvels and the order of the world declare a divine mind—"nature is the art of God."[40] He confesses to having entertained some heresies, and he slips into some doubts about the Biblical account of Creation;[41] but now he feels the need of an established religion to guide wondering, wandering men; and he deplores the vanity of heretics who disturb the social order with their hot infallibilities.[42] Puritans were not to his taste; he remained quietly faithful to the first Charles during the Civil War and was knighted for his pains by the second.

In his later years he was moved to meditation on death by the unearthing of some ancient sepulchral urns in Norfolk, and he recorded his thoughts in a desultory masterpiece of English prose, *Hydriotaphia, Urne-Buriall* (1658). He recommends cremation as the least vain method of disencumbering the earth of ourselves. "Life is a pure flame, and we live by an invisible Sun within us"; but we flicker out with ignominious haste. "Generations pass while some trees stand, and old families last not three oaks."[43] The world itself is probably nearing its end in "this setting part of time." We need the hope of immortality to gird us against this brevity; it is a precious prop to feel ourselves immortal—but a great pity that we must be scared into decency by visions of hell.[44] Heaven is no "empyreal vacuity" but "within the circle of this sensible world," in a condition of mental content and peace. Then, hurrying back from the verge of heresy, he ends his *Religio* with a modest prayer to God:

> Bless me in this life with but peace of my conscience, command of my affections, the love of Thyself and my dearest friends, and I shall be happy enough to pity Caesar. These are, O Lord, the humble desires of my most reasonable ambition, and all I dare call happiness on earth; wherein I set no rule or limit to thy Hand or Providence. Dispose of me according to the wisdom of Thy pleasure. Thy will be done, though in my undoing.[45]

V. Caroline Poetry

Meanwhile a bevy of minor bards—each of whom is someone's major love—amused the leisurely with amorous rhymes and tuneful piety; and because the King liked them and they sang his cause through all vicissitudes, history knows them as the Cavalier Poets. Robert Herrick apprenticed his pen to Ben Jonson, and thought for a time that a bowl of wine would make a book of verse; he drank to Bacchus for hours on end, and then studied for the ministry. He took courses in love, pledged himself to prefer mistresses to marriage,[46] and counseled virgins to "gather rosebuds" while they bloomed. His "Corinna" received further prodding:

> Get up, get up for shame! The blooming morn
> Upon her wings presents the god unshorn.
>> See how Aurora throws her fair
>> Fresh-quilted colors through the air;
>> Get up, sweet Slug-a-bed, and see
>> The dew bespangling herb and tree . . .
> Come, let us go, while we are in our prime,
> And take the harmless folly of the time!
>> We shall grow old apace, and die
>> Before we know our liberty . . .
> Then while time serves, and we are but decaying,
> Come, my Corinna, come, let's go a-Maying.[47]

And so in many of the wanton poems that he published in 1648 in the collection *Hesperides*; even in our loose days they need expurgation to suit Everyman. But eating is also necessary, so Herrick left his beloved London (1629), and—taking Catullus with him—went sorrowfully to be vicar of a modest parsonage in distant Devonshire. Soon he began to write *Noble Numbers, or Pious Pieces*, and first a prayer for absolution:

> For those my unbaptised rhymes,
> Writ in my wild unhallowed times,
> For every sentence, clause, and word,
> That's not inlaid with Thee (my Lord),
> Forgive me, God, and blot each line
> Out of my book that is not Thine.[48]

In 1647 the Puritans deprived him of his benefice. He starved loyally through the dour days of the Commonwealth, but was restored by the Restoration to his vicarage, and died there at eighty-four, Corinna lost in the dusk of memory.

Thomas Carew did not live so long, but he too found time for mistresses. Drunk with the inexplicable charms of woman, he sang them in such rapt detail ("A Rapture"), and with such cavalier contempt for chastity, that other poets reproved him for his licentious exactitude. The Puritans could not forgive Charles I for making him a gentleman of the privy chamber, but perhaps the King pardoned the matter for the form; in these Caroline poets all the Gallic finesse of Ronsard and the Pléiade is imported to grace with delicate art the indelicacies of desire.

Sir John Suckling crowded much living into his thirty-three years. Born in 1609, he inherited a great fortune at eighteen, made the Grand Tour, was knighted by Charles I, fought under Gustavus Adolphus in the Thirty Years' War, returned to England (1632) to become by his good looks, his wit, and his generous wealth a favorite at the court. He was, says Aubrey, "the greatest gallant of his time, and the greatest gamester, both for bowling and cards . . . His sisters would come to the . . . bowling green, crying for fear he should lose all their portions."[49] He invented cribbage. He never married, but entertained "a great number of ladies of quality"; at one party he served the ladies, as dessert, silk stockings, then a great luxury.[50] His play *Aglaura* was produced with lavish scenery, paid for from his purse. He raised his own troops to fight for the King and risked his life in an attempt to rescue the King's minister, Sir Thomas Wentworth, Earl of Strafford, from the Tower. Frustrated, he fled to the Continent, and there, deprived of his fortune, he took poison and died.

Richard Lovelace too served the King in war and verse, and he too was rich and handsome, "the most amiable and beautiful person that ever eye beheld"[51]—so Anthony à Wood saw him at Oxford. In 1642 he headed a delegation from Kent to petition the Long Parliament (transiently Presbyterian) for the restoration of the Anglican liturgy. For this audacious orthodoxy he was imprisoned for seven weeks. His Althea came to comfort him, and he made her immortal with a line:

> When Love with unconfined wings
>   Hovers within my gates,
> And my divine Althea brings
>   To whisper at the grates;
> When I lie tangled in her hair
>   And fettered to her eye,
> The birds that wanton in the air

Know no such liberty. . . .

> Stone walls do not a prison make,
>   Nor iron bars a cage;
> Minds innocent and quiet take
>   That for an hermitage;
> If I have freedom in my love
>   And in my soul am free,
> Angels alone, that soar above,
>   Enjoy such liberty.[52]

He went off to the wars again in 1645—and apologized to his betrothed (Lucy Sacheverell) in "To Lucasta, Going to the Wars":

> Tell me not, sweet, I am unkind
>   That from the nunnery
> Of thy chaste breast and quiet mind
>   To war and arms I fly. . . .

> Yet this inconstancy is such
>   As thou too shalt adore;
> I could not love thee, dear, so much,
>   Loved I not honour more.[53]

On the false report of his death in battle, Lucasta (chaste Lucy) married another suitor. Having lost both his lady and his fortune in the Royalist cause, Lovelace was reduced to depend upon the charity of his friends for food, and he who had worn cloth of silver and gold now dressed in rags and lived in slums. He died of consumption in 1658, aged forty.

He might have learned the art of survival from Edmund Waller, who managed to be active for sixty years on both sides of the Great Rebellion, became the most popular poet of his time, outlived Milton, and died in bed at eighty-one (1687). He entered Parliament at sixteen, went mad at twenty-three, recovered, married a London heiress at twenty-five, buried her three years later, and soon wooed "Sacharissa" (Lady Dorothy Sidney) with a fresh variant of an ancient theme:

Go, lovely Rose!
Tell her, that wastes her time and me,
That now she knows,
When I resemble her to thee,
How sweet and fair she seems to be.

Tell her, that's young,
And shuns to have her graces spied,
That hadst thou sprung
In deserts, where no men abide,
Thou must have unrecommended died. . . .

Then die! that she
The common fate of all things rare
May read in thee;
How small a part of time they share
That are so wondrous sweet and fair!

One other hardly minor poet enters this period. Richard Crashaw burned with religious ardor rather than with the fevers of the flesh. His father, an Anglican clergyman, wrote tracts against Catholicism and filled his son with fears of popery; Richard became a Catholic. He was expelled from Cambridge (1644) for supporting the King; he fled from England to Paris, where he consoled his poverty with visions of God. The Spanish mystics were to him a revelation of religious intensity and devotion. Standing before a picture of St. Teresa, he envied her transfixion by the dart of Christ, and begged her to accept him as her selfless disciple:

By the full kingdom of that final kiss
That seized thy parting soul, and sealed thee His;
By all the heavens thou hast in Him
(Fair sister of the seraphim);
By all of Him we have in thee,
Leave nothing of myself in me.
Let me so read thy life that I
Unto all life of mine may die.

This and other poems he gave to the world in *Steps to the Temple* (1646), an ambivalent mixture of pious ecstasies and poetic conceits. Through him and a like but later poet, Henry Vaughan, we perceive that not all England was in those hectic days divided into Puritans and Cavaliers, but that amid the fury of poetical and theological war some spirits found religion neither in massive shrines and hypnotic ritual, nor in fearful dogmas and proud election, but in the childlike, trustful communion of the baffled and surrendering soul with a humane and forgiving God.

VI. Charles I Versus Parliament: 1625–29

And now this tragic King over whom all England was to fight, what sort of man and monarch was he? Before the storm soured the milk of human kindness in him, he was a reasonably good man—a loving son, an unusually faithful husband, a loyal friend, a father idolized by his children. He had begun the struggle of life by fighting a congenital weakness of physique; he could not walk till he was seven. He overcame this defect by resolute pursuit of vigorous sports, until in maturity he could ride and hunt with the best. He suffered from an impediment of speech; until ten he could hardly speak intelligibly; his father thought of having an operation performed on the boy's tongue. Charles gradually improved, but to the end of his life he stammered and had to counter his difficulty by speaking slowly.[54] When his popular brother Henry died, leaving him heir apparent, Charles was suspected of complicity in the death; the charge was unjust, but it shared in darkening the Prince's mood. He preferred a studious solitude to the bibulous hilarity of his father's court. He became proficient in mathematics, music, and theology, learned something of Greek and Latin, spoke French, Italian, and a little Spanish. He loved art; he cherished and expanded the collection left by his brother; he became a discriminating collector, and a generous patron of artists, poets, and musicians. He invited the Italian painter Orazio Gentileschi to his court, then Rubens, Vandyck, and Frans Hals; Hals declined, and Rubens came chiefly as ambassador; but all the world knows Charles as the proud and handsome king, with Vandyke beard, repeatedly painted by Vandyck. William Dobson, pupil of Vandyck, continued the idealization of the royal family.

Charles's parentage and marriage contributed to his ruin. He inherited his father's conception of the royal prerogative as absolute, with power to make as well as administer laws, to rule without Parliament, and to override laws enacted by Parliament. This view seemed justified by precedents and was taken for granted in France and Spain; it was encouraged in Charles by Buckingham, the court, and the Queen. Henrietta Maria had been reared at the French court in the very days when Richelieu was making her brother Louis XIII absolute over everybody but Richelieu. She had come to England as an avowed Catholic, bringing priests in her bridal train, and her faith had been made more intense by the disabilities she saw it suffer there. She had all the allure of beauty, vivacity, and wit, and the full Medicean flair for politics. Inevitably she urged her devoted husband to alleviate the lot of English Catholics; doubtless she dreamed of converting the King himself. She gave him six children; it must have cost him many a struggle to resist her wish that they might be brought up Catholic. But he had developed a sincere attachment to the Anglican Church, and he realized that his England was predominantly Protestant and hostile to a threatening papacy.

Charles's first Parliament met on June 18, 1625. One hundred lords—peers and bishops—sat in the upper house; five hundred men, three fourths of them Puritan,[55] had been elected to the Commons by various forms of financial or political skulduggery;[56] there was no pretense of democracy. Probably the level of ability in this Parliament was higher than an adult suffrage would have returned; here were Coke, Selden, Pym, Sir John Eliot, Sir Thomas Wentworth, and others marked for history. The total wealth of the Commoners exceeded threefold the wealth of the lords.[57] The Commons showed its temper by demanding the full enforcement of the anti-Catholic laws. The King asked for an appropriation for governmental expenses and the war with Spain; Parliament granted him £140,000 ($7,000,000?), which was purposely inadequate; the fleet alone required twice that sum. For two centuries the English monarchs had been granted, for the duration of their reigns, the right to levy export and import duties, usually of two to three shillings per tun (a large cask), and six to twelve pence per pound; now the Parliament's "tonnage and poundage" bill allowed Charles this right for one year only. It argued that previous appropriations had been squandered in the extravagance of James's court; it complained that taxes had been levied without its consent; it was resolved to compel hereafter an annual summoning of Parliament and an annual examination, by Parliament, of governmental expenditures. Charles took umbrage at these economics and intentions, and when plague threatened London he seized the excuse to dissolve the Parliament (August 12, 1625).

The government was now in the hands of Buckingham. Charles had not merely inherited the amiable, reckless Duke from his father; he had been brought up with him, had traveled with him, in a companionship that made it difficult for the King to see in his friend an unwise and disastrous counselor. Buckingham, with the support of Parliament, had led James into war with Spain; Parliament now refused to finance the war. The Duke organized an armada to go out and capture Spanish spoils or ports; it failed utterly, and the returning soldiers, unpaid and demoralized, spread rape, robbery, and defeatism in the coastal towns.

Desperate for funds, Charles resigned himself to calling his second Parliament. The opposition grew stronger with his needs. The House warned him not to levy taxes without parliamentary sanction. Eliot, once a friend of the Duke, excoriated him as a corrupt incompetent who had grown richer with each failure of strategy or policy. Parliament appointed a committee to investigate Buckingham; Charles rebuked it, saying, "I would not have the House to question my servants, much less one that is so near me." Eliot advised Parliament to withhold any grant of funds until the King admitted its right to demand the removal of a minister; Charles angrily reminded Parliament that he could at any time dismiss it; the Commons replied by formally impeaching Buckingham—accusing him of treason and demanding his dismissal (May 8, 1626); it informed the King that until this was done it would grant no funds. The King dissolved the Parliament (June 15). The issue of ministerial responsibility was left to the future.

But Charles was again destitute. A large quantity of royal plate was sold. "Free benevolences"—gifts to the King—were asked of the country; the yield was slight; British money was pro-Parliament. Charles ordered his agents to collect tonnage and poundage dues despite lack of Parliamentary consent, and to seize the goods of merchants who failed to pay; he commanded the ports to maintain the fleet; he allowed his agents to impress men into military service. English and Danish troops, fighting for Protestantism in Germany, were being overwhelmed by the Imperialists; England's Danish allies demanded the subsidy she had promised them. Charles ordered a forced loan—every taxpayer was to lend the government one percent of the value of his land, five percent of the worth of his personal property. Rich opponents were jailed, poor opponents were hustled into the army or the navy. Meanwhile English merchants delivered materials at Bordeaux and La Rochelle to Huguenots embattled with

Richelieu; France declared war on England (1627). Buckingham led a fleet to attack the French at La Rochelle; the expedition failed. The £200,000 raised by the loan was soon spent, and Charles was again at his money's end. He summoned his third Parliament.

It met on March 17, 1628. Coke, Eliot, Wentworth, and John Hampden were returned, and, for the first time, Huntingdon Borough sent up a sturdy squire named Oliver Cromwell. Charles, in his speech from the throne, sternly called for funds, and added, with reckless insolence, "Take not this as threatening; I scorn to threaten any but my equals."[58] Parliament proposed £350,000, but, before voting it, required the King's consent to a "Petition of Right" (May 28, 1628) which became a historic landmark in the rise of Parliament to mastery:

> TO THE KING'S MOST EXCELLENT MAJESTY:
> We humbly show unto our sovereign lord the King . . . that whereas it is declared and enacted by a statute . . . of Edward I . . . that no tallage or aid shall be laid or levied by the King . . . without the good will and assent of the archbishops, bishops, earls, barons, knights, burgesses, and other the freemen of the commonalty . . . your subjects have inherited this freedom, that they should not be compelled to contribute to any tax, tallage, aid, or other like charge not set by common consent in Parliament.

The petition went on to protest against forced loans, and the King's violation of the rights of habeas corpus and trial by jury as embodied in the Magna Charta of 1215. "We shall know by this [petition] if Parliaments live or die," said Coke. Charles gave it an ambiguous consent; Parliament demanded a clearer reply, and still held up the appropriation; Charles gave formal consent. London felt the significance of the surrender; there broke out such ringing of bells as had not been heard there for years.

Parliament, moving forward, requested the King to dismiss Buckingham; Charles refused. Suddenly both sides were startled to find this issue taken out of their hands. John Felton, a wounded ex-soldier weighed down with debts, angry at the arrears of his pension, and inflamed by pamphlets, bought a butcher's knife, walked sixty miles from London to Portsmouth, plunged the weapon into Buckingham's breast, and yielded himself to the authorities (August 23,

1628). Buckingham's wife, soon to give birth, collapsed at sight of the corpse. Felton, overcome with remorse, sent her his apologies and begged her forgiveness; she gave it. He was executed without torture.

The Parliament admonished the King that his continued collection of tonnage and poundage dues violated the Petition of Right; Charles replied that such dues had not been mentioned in the document; Parliament encouraged merchants to refuse to pay them.[59] Reasserting its right to legislate for religion despite the ecclesiastical supremacy of the king, it proclaimed a strictly Calvinist, anti-Arminian interpretation of the Thirty-nine Articles as the law of England; it proposed, of its own authority, to enforce religious conformity on this basis, and to deal out penalties to Catholics and Arminians alike.[60] Charles ordered the Parliament to adjourn; the Speaker, obeying, left the chair; but Parliament refused to adjourn, and members compelled the Speaker to resume the chair. Sir John Eliot now (March 2, 1629) offered three resolutions which made it a capital crime to introduce "Popery, or Arminianism, or other opinions disagreeing from the true and orthodox Church," to counsel, or take any share in, the collection of tonnage or poundage dues not sanctioned by Parliament, or to pay such unsanctioned dues. The Speaker refused to put the motions to a vote; a member put them; the House acclaimed and passed them. Then, learning that the King's troops were about to enter and dismiss the Parliament, it moved its own adjournment and dispersed.

On March 5 Charles ordered the imprisonment of Eliot, Selden, and seven other members of Parliament on charges of sedition. Six of them were soon released; three were condemned to heavy fines and long imprisonment; Eliot died in the Tower, aged thirty-eight (1632).

VII. Charles Absolute: 1629–40

Eleven years—the longest such interval in English history—were to pass without the assembling of Parliament. Charles was now free to be an absolute king. Theoretically he was claiming no more than James, Elizabeth, and Henry VIII; practically he was claiming more, for they had never stretched the royal prerogative so near the breaking point as Charles was doing by levying unsanctioned taxes, forcing loans, billeting soldiers on citizens, making arbitrary arrests, denying prisoners the rights of habeas corpus and trial by jury, extending the tyranny and severity of the Star Chamber in political, and of the Court of High

Commission in ecclesiastical, trials. But Charles's basic mistake was his failure to recognize that the wealth now represented by the House of Commons was much greater than that wielded by or loyal to the King, and that the power of Parliament must be increased accordingly.

Amid this crisis, before it drew the nation's blood, the economy prospered, for Charles, like his father, was a man of peace and, through most of his reign, kept England out of war, while Richelieu exhausted France and Germany became a wilderness. The harassed King did what he could to mitigate the natural concentration of wealth. He ordered a halt to enclosures, annulled all those made in five Midland counties between 1625 and 1630, and fined six hundred recalcitrant landlords.[61] He had the wages of textile workers raised in 1629, 1631, 1637; he bade the justices of the peace exercise better control over prices; he appointed commissions to protect the wage scale and supervise poor relief; and Laud made new enemies by warning employers not to "grind the faces of the poor."[62] But at the same time the government granted, and profited from, monopolies in soap, salt, starch, beer, wine, and hides; it kept to itself a monopoly in coal, buying it at eleven shillings a caldron and selling it for seventeen in summer and nineteen in winter;[63] and these monopolies too ground the faces of the poor. During this period over twenty thousand Puritans emigrated to New England.

Charles pleaded that he had to find some ways to pay the costs of government. In 1634 he tried, disastrously, a new tax. Precedents existed for requiring coastal cities, in return for the protection afforded them by the navy, to fit out vessels for it in time of war, or, instead, to contribute "ship money" to the government for the maintenance of the fleet. Charles now (1635), without precedent, exacted this ship money from all England in time of peace, alleging the (quite real) need to rebuild the dilapidated navy for emergency and to protect British commerce from Channel piracy. Many resisted the new levy. To test its legality John Hampden refused to pay it; he was indicted, but was left free. He was a well-to-do Puritan of Buckinghamshire, no firebrand, but a quiet man (said the Royalist Clarendon) of "extraordinary sobriety and strictness,"[64] who hid firmness in courtesy and leadership in modesty.

His trial was long delayed, but came to court at last in November 1637. The lawyers for the Crown cited precedents for the ship-money tax, and held that the king, in time of peril, had the right to call for financial aid without waiting to assemble Parliament. Hampden's attorneys replied that there was no emergency, there had been plenty of time to call Parliament, and the exaction violated the Petition of Right accepted by the King. The judges voted seven to five for the Crown, but public sentiment supported Hampden, and questioned the impartiality of judges subject to royal retaliation; Hampden was soon released. Charles continued till 1639 to collect ship money, and he used most of it to build the navy that fought victoriously against the Dutch in 1652.

Meanwhile he had extended his blunders to Scotland. He shocked the Presbyterian Scots by marrying a Catholic and extending the authority of the bishops over the presbyteries of the Kirk. He alarmed half the nobility by an "Act of Revocation" (1625) revoking all grants of Church or Crown lands made to Scottish families since the accession of Mary Stuart. He named to the Privy Council of Scotland five bishops and an archbishop, John Spottiswoode, and (1635) made this prelate Chancellor—the first churchman to be appointed to that office since the Reformation. When, after irritating delays, he came to Scotland to be crowned (1633), he allowed the bishops to carry out the ritual with the almost Catholic ceremonies of the Anglican Church—vestments, candles, altar, and crucifix. Determined to enforce their authority over the presbyteries, the Scottish bishops drew up a set of liturgical rules, which, because emended and approved by the Archbishop of Canterbury, came to be known as "Laud's Canons." These gave the king full jurisdiction over all ecclesiastical matters, forbade assemblies of the clergy except at the king's call, restricted the right of teaching to persons licensed by a bishop, and limited ordination to candidates accepting these canons.[65] Charles sanctioned the canons and ordered them proclaimed in all Scottish churches. The Presbyterian ministers protested that half the Reformation was thereby annulled, and they warned that Charles was preparing to submit Britain to Rome. When an attempt was made, in St. Giles's Church, Edinburgh, to conduct a service according to the new formulas, a riot broke out; sticks and stones were hurled at the officiating dean; Jenny Geddes flung her stool at his head, crying, "Thou foul thief, wilt thou say Mass at my lug [ear]?"[66] Petitions from all classes were sent to Charles to revoke the canons; he replied by branding such petitions treasonable. Scotland now set the pace in revolt against the King.

On February 28, 1638, representatives of the Scottish ministry and laity signed at Edinburgh the National Covenant, reaffirming the Presbyterian faith and ritual, rejecting the new canons, and pledging themselves to defend the Crown and the "true religion." Nearly all Scotland, urged on by the ministers, subscribed to this covenant. Spottiswoode and all but four of the bishops fled to England. The General Assembly of the Kirk at Glasgow repudiated all bishops, and declared the

Kirk to be independent of the state. Charles sent orders to the Assembly to disperse or be charged with treason; it continued its sittings. The King mustered an unenthusiastic army of 21,000 men and advanced toward Scotland; the "Covenanters" raised 26,000 men aflame with patriotic and religious fervor. When the two forces came face to face Charles agreed to submit the issues to a free Scottish Parliament and an unhindered Assembly of the Kirk; a truce was signed at Berwick (June 18, 1639), and the "First Bishops' War" ended without shedding blood. But the new Assembly, convened at Edinburgh (August 12, 1639), confirmed the "treasonable" decisions of the Glasgow conference, and the Scottish Parliament ratified the acts of the Assembly. Both sides prepared for the "Second Bishops' War."

In this crisis Charles called to his aid a man as resolute and thorough (this word was his motto) as the King was vacillating and incompetent. Thomas Wentworth had reached Parliament at twenty-one (1614), and had often voted against the King. Charles won him over by making him president of the Council of the North, rewarded his vigorous enforcement of the royal policies by appointing him to the Privy Council, and sent him as Lord Deputy to Ireland (1632), where his "Thorough" policy of merciless efficiency stamped out rebellion and created an angry peace. In 1639 he was made Earl of Strafford and chief counselor to Charles. He advised the King to raise a large army, suppress the Covenanters, and face a recalcitrant Parliament with an irresistible force. But a large army required large funds, which could hardly be raised without Parliament. Reluctantly, Charles summoned his fourth Parliament. When this "Short Parliament" met (April 13, 1640), he displayed to it an intercepted letter in which Covenanters had solicited the aid of Louis XIII;[67] against such treason, argued the King, he had the right to organize an army. John Pym secretly communicated with Covenanters, decided that their cause was akin to Parliament's case against the King, and persuaded the Parliament to deny the King the subsidies and arrange an alliance with the Scots. Charles dissolved the Short Parliament as traitorous (May 5, 1640). Riots broke out in London; a mob attacked the palace of Archbishop Laud; not finding him, it killed a Catholic who refused to join in Protestant worship.[68]

Charles moved north with an improvised army. The Scots came down over the border, defeated the English (August 20, 1640), and took possession of northern England. The helpless monarch agreed to pay them £850 a day until a satisfactory treaty could be concluded; he could not pay, and the Scottish army remained around Newcastle as a decisive ally of the English Parliament in its war with the King. Bewildered and desperate, Charles called a council of peers to meet him at York. They advised him that his authority was on the verge of collapse, and that he must find some accommodation with his enemies. For the last time he summoned a Parliament, the longest and most fateful in English history.

VIII. *The Long Parliament*

It assembled at Westminster November 3, 1640. The House was composed of some five hundred men, the "flower of the English gentry and the educated laity . . . an aristocratic and not a popular house,"[69] representing the wealth rather than the people of England, but standing clearly for the future against the past. The majority of the Short Parliament were returned, brooding revenge. Selden, Hampden, and Pym were again on hand, and Oliver Cromwell, though not yet a leader, was a man of mark.

It is impossible, at this distance, to picture him objectively, for since his rise and till today historians have described him as an ambitious hypocrite[70] or a statesman-saint.[71] A personality so ambivalent probably encloses—sometimes he harmonizes—in his character the opposite qualities that beget such contradictory estimates. This may be the key to Cromwell.

He was one of those landowners without pedigree who stood outside the glamour of government, but paid uncomfortably for its maintenance. And yet he too had ancestors. His father, Robert Cromwell, had a modest estate in Huntingdon, worth three hundred pounds a year; his great-grandfather, Richard Williams, the nephew of Henry VIII's minister Thomas Cromwell, changed his name to Cromwell, and received, from minister or King, manors and revenues confiscated from the Catholic Church.[72] Oliver was one of ten children and was the only one who survived infancy. His grammar-school instructor was a fervent preacher who wrote a treatise proving the pope to be Antichrist, and another recording the divine punishment of notorious sinners. In 1616 Oliver entered Sidney Sussex College, Cambridge, where the headmaster was Samuel Ward, who died in prison (1643) for taking a strong Puritan stand against Laud's innovations and Charles's "Declaration of Sports." Apparently Oliver left Cambridge without graduating. Later (1638) he accused himself of some youthful wickedness:

> You know what my manner of life hath been. Oh, I have lived in a loved darkness, and hated light; I was a chief, the chief, of sinners.

This is true: I hated godliness; yet God had mercy on me. Oh, the riches of His mercy! Praise Him for me—pray for me, that He who hath begun a good work would perfect it in the day of Christ.[73]

He experienced all the ecstasies of repentance; he had hallucinations of death and other mental terrors that left him permanently touched with melancholy, and for the rest of his life he spoke in terms of Puritan piety. He settled down, married, had nine children, and became so model a citizen that in 1628, aged twenty-eight, he was chosen to represent Huntingdon in Parliament. He sold his Huntingdon property for £1,800 in 1631 and moved to St. Ives, later to Ely. When Cambridge returned him to Parliament in 1640 he was described by another member as "very ordinarily appareled" in "a plain cloth suit. . . His linen not very clean . . . a speck or two of blood upon his little [neck] band," his face "swollen and reddish," his voice "sharp and untunable," his temper "exceeding fiery," but under firm control.[74] He bided his time, talked with God, and had the strength of ten. As yet, however, God chose other instruments.

It was John Pym who revealed the angry mood of the Parliament by denouncing Strafford as a secret papist plotting to bring in an army from Ireland, to overthrow Parliament, and to "alter law and religion."[75] On November 11, 1640, the House of Commons—which had never forgiven his desertion to the King—impeached the Earl as a traitor and had him sent to the Tower. On December 16, having declared the new Anglican canons illegal, it impeached Archbishop Laud on grounds of "popery" and treason, and had him too sent to the Tower. Selden later confessed, "We charge the prelatical clergy with popery to make them odious, though we know they are guilty of no such thing."[76] Charles was so bewildered by these uncompromising moves that he took no action to protect his aides. The Queen justified the Parliament's fears by asking her confessor to solicit aid from the Pope.[77]

Excitement and passion mounted on both sides. A "Root and Branch" faction among the London radicals—which included Milton—petitioned Parliament to abolish episcopacy and restore the government of the Church to the people; it branded as abominable the opinion of some bishops "that the pope is not Antichrist . . . and that salvation is attainable in that [Catholic] religion."[78] The House rejected the petition, but voted the debarment of the clergy from all legislative and judicial functions. The Lords agreed, with the proviso that bishops should retain their seats in the upper house. This, however, was precisely what the Commons wished to end, for it expected that the bishops in the Lords would always vote for the King. Pamphlets defending or attacking episcopacy made the issue boil. Bishop Joseph Hall claimed divine right for it on the ground that it had been established by the Apostles or Christ; five Presbyterian publicists replied in a famous pamphlet under the pseudonym "Smectymnuus," composed of their initials; five later blasts were contributed by Milton. On May 27, 1641, Cromwell again proposed the total abolition of the episcopacy; the bill was passed by the House, rejected by the Lords. On September 1 the Commons resolved that "scandalous pictures" of the Trinity, all images of the Virgin Mary, all crosses and "superstitious figures" should be removed from English churches, and that all "dancing and other sports" were to be avoided on the Lord's Day. Another wave of iconoclasm swept over England; altar rails and screens were taken down, stained-glass windows were smashed, statues were demolished, pictures were cut to shreds.[79] The House again passed a bishops' exclusion bill on October 23. The King appealed to the Lords, declaring that he was resolved to die in the maintenance of the existing doctrine and discipline of the Anglican Church; he did. His intervention secured the defeat of the bill, but hostile crowds prevented the bishops from attending Parliament. Twelve of them signed a protest, declaring that any legislation passed in their absence would be null and void. Parliament impeached and imprisoned them. Finally the Lords ratified the exclusion bill (February 5, 1642), and bishops no longer sat in Parliament.

The victorious Commons proceeded to consolidate its power. It borrowed money from the city of London to finance its maintenance. It passed bills requiring triennial Parliaments and forbidding the dissolution of any Parliament within fifty days of its convening, or of the present Parliament without its consent. It reformed taxation and the judiciary. It abolished the Star Chamber and the Court of High Commission. It ended monopolies and the levy of ship money, and rescinded the verdict against Hampden. It granted the King the right to collect tonnage and poundage dues, but only for periods specified by Parliament. Charles agreed to these measures, and the Parliament passed from reform to revolution.

In March 1641 it brought Strafford to trial; in April it pronounced him guilty of treason and sent the bill of attainder to the King for signature. Against Laud's advice, Charles appeared in the Lords and declared that though he was ready to disqualify Strafford from office he would never consent to condemn him for treason. The Commons pronounced this royal appearance a violation of parliamentary privilege and freedom. On the next day "great multitudes" gathered about the House of Lords and the palace of the King, crying "Justice! justice!" and demanding Strafford's death. The frightened Privy Council begged Charles to yield; he refused. The

Archbishop of York added his plea for signature; nobles warned the King that his own life and the lives of the Queen and his children were in danger; he still refused. Finally the condemned man himself sent him a message advising him to sign, as the only alternative to mob violence.[80] Charles signed and never forgave himself. On May 12, 1641, Strafford was led out to execution. Laud stretched out his hands through the bars of his cell window to bless him as he passed. "Thorough" died without whimpering, before a hostile crowd.

His execution sharpened the division of the House into what later came to be the rival parties of Whigs and Tories—those who favored and those who opposed the further transference of power from king to Parliament. Men like Lucius Cary (Viscount Falkland) and Edward Hyde (future Earl of Clarendon), both of whom had supported Parliament, wondered now whether the King, having been so severely chastened, might not be a desirable bulwark against mob rule in London, Puritan rule in religion, and a runaway Parliament that would disestablish the Church, threaten private property, and imperil the whole class structure of British life. Pym, Hampden, and Cromwell might have admitted these dangers, but there was another that touched them more closely: they had gone so far that they feared for their lives if Charles should recover power. At any moment the King might bring over a half-Catholic army from Ireland as Strafford had proposed to do. For its own safety Parliament decided to maintain the friendly army of Scots in the north of England. It sent the Scots an initial gift of £300,000 and pledged a monthly subsidy of £25,000.[81]

The fears of the Parliament were sharpened by the sudden outbreak of a wild revolt in Ireland (October 1641). Phelim O'Neill, Rory O'More III, and other leaders called for a war of liberation—of Ulster from its English colonists, of Catholics from oppression, of Ireland from England. Inflamed by the memory of merciless persecutions and brutal evictions, the rebels fought with a fury that made them barbarous; the English in Ireland, defending what now seemed to them their legitimate property as well as their lives, returned barbarity with ferocity, and every victory became a massacre. The English Parliament wrongly suspected the King of having fomented the revolt to restore Catholicism in Ireland and later in England; it refused his request for funds to raise an army to rescue the English in the Pale; such an army might be turned against Parliament itself. The Irish revolt continued throughout the English revolution.

The revolution took a further step when Charles advanced two of the excluded and impeached bishops to higher place. Indignant Commoners proposed a "Grand

Remonstrance" which would summarize and publicize the case of Parliament against the King, and would compel him to give Parliament the right to veto his appointments to important posts. Many conservatives felt that the measure would transfer executive power to the Parliament and reduce the King to impotence. The division of parties became acute, the debate more violent; members clutched their swords to emphasize their words; Cromwell later declared that if the bill had lost he would have taken ship to America.[82] It passed by eleven votes, and on December 1, 1641, it was presented to the King. It began by affirming its loyalty to the Crown. It proceeded to list in detail the offenses which the King had given Parliament and the injuries he had inflicted upon the country. It reviewed the abuses which parliamentary reforms had corrected; it charged "papists . . . bishops, and the corrupt part of the clergy," and self-seeking councilors and courtiers, with plotting to make England Catholic. It pointed to repeated violations of the Petition of Right and to highhanded dissolutions of elected Parliaments. It asked the King to call an assembly of divines to restore the Anglican worship to its pre-Laudian form. It proposed that he remove from his Council all opponents of the Parliament's policies, and employ hereafter only "such counselors, ambassadors, and other ministers . . . as the Parliament have cause to confide in; without which they could not give his Majesty such supplies for his own support, or such assistance for the Protestant party beyond the seas, as was desired."[83]

Charles took his time answering this ultimatum. On December 15 Parliament went over his head to the people by ordering publication of the Grand Remonstrance. Charles then replied. He agreed to call a synod to repress all invasions of "popery"; he refused to deprive the bishops of their votes in Parliament; he insisted on his right to call to his Council, and to public employment, such men as he thought fit; and he again asked for funds. Instead, the Commons proposed a "Militia Bill" which would give it control of the army.

Charles, so regularly irresolute, now rushed into a bold stroke that Parliament denounced as an act of war. On January 3, 1642, his attorney general, before the Lords, indicted, in the King's name, five members of the lower house—Pym, Hampden, Holles, Heselrige, Strode—on a charge of treason for seeking to turn the army from obedience to the King and for encouraging a "foreign power" (Scotland) to invade England and make war upon the King. On the next day Charles, supported by three hundred soldiers whom he left at the door, entered the House of Commons to arrest the five men; they were not there, having taken refuge in friendly homes; "I see," said the baffled King, "all the birds are flown."

As he walked out he was rebuked with cries of "Privilege!"; for such royal and armed invasion of Parliament was manifestly illegal. In fear of wholesale arrest, the Commons moved to the Guildhall, under protection of the citizens. When Charles left London for Hampton Court, the Commons, including the five indicted men, returned to Westminster. Queen Henrietta fled secretly to France with the Crown jewels to buy aid for the King. Charles left for the north with the Great Seal. He tried to enter Hull and secure the military supplies there; the town refused to admit him; he moved on to York. Parliament ordered all armed forces to obey only Parliament (March 5, 1642). Thirty-five peers and sixty-five Commoners seceded from Parliament and joined Charles at York. Edward Hyde now became chief adviser to the King.

On June 2 Parliament transmitted to Charles nineteen propositions whose acceptance it held to be essential to peace. He was to turn over to Parliament control of the army and all fortified places. Parliament was to revise the liturgy and the government of the Church. It was to appoint and dismiss all ministers of the Crown and the guardians of the King's children, and was to have authority to exclude from the upper house all peers hereafter created. Charles rejected the proposals as in effect a destruction of the monarchy. As if rehearsing the French Revolution, Parliament appointed a Committee of Public Safety, and ordered that "an army shall be forthwith raised" (July 12). Cromwell and others left for their home boroughs to organize volunteers. In an appeal to the nation (August 2), Parliament based its revolt not on the desirability of parliamentary sovereignty, but on the imminence of a Catholic uprising in England; and it warned the country that victory for the King would be followed by a general massacre of Protestants.[84] On August 17 its agents seized the military stores at Hull. On August 27, 1642, Charles unfurled his standard at Nottingham and began the Civil War.

IX. The First Civil War: 1642–46

England was now divided as seldom in known history before. London, the ports, the manufacturing towns, in general the south and the east, most of the middle class, part of the gentry, and practically all Puritans were for Parliament. Oxford and Cambridge, the west and the north, most of the aristocracy and the peasantry, and nearly all Catholics and episcopalian Anglicans stood with the King. The House of Commons was itself divided: some 300 members were on the rebel side, some 175 were Royalists. In the Lords 30 of the 110 peers sided at first with

Parliament. The balance of wealth fell against the King; London had half the money of the nation and lent heavily to the revolution; Charles could not borrow anywhere; the navy was against him, and it blocked foreign aid; he had to rely upon gifts and men from the great estates, whose owners felt that their landed interest depended on his victory. Some chivalric virtues and sentiment survived in the old families; they gave their loyalty to the King without stint; they fought and died like gentlemen. The colorful Cavaliers, their hair in ringlets, their horses in gay accouterment, had all the romance of the war on their side, and all the poets but Milton. The money was with Parliament.

The gauge of blood began at Edgehill (October 23, 1642). Each army had some 14,000 men. The Royalists were led by Prince Rupert, the twenty-two-year-old son of Charles's sister, Elizabeth of Bohemia; the "Roundheads," by Robert Devereux, third Earl of Essex. The result was indecisive, but Essex withdrew his forces, and the King marched on to make Oxford his headquarters. Nehemiah Wallington, a fervent or politic Puritan, called it a great victory for Parliament and God:

> Herein we see God's great mercy . . . for, as I hear, the slaughter was in all 5,517; but ten of the enemy's side were slain to one of ours. And observe God's wonderful works, for those that were slain of our side were mostly of them that ran away; but those that stood most valiantly to it, they were most preserved. . . .
>
> If I could relate how admirably the hand of Providence ordered our artillery and bullets for the destruction of the enemy! . . . Oh, how God did guide their bullets . . . that some fell down before them [of our side], some grazed along, some bullets went over their heads, and some one side of them! Oh, how seldom or never were they hurt, that stood valiant to it, by their bullets! . . . This is the Lord's doing, and it is marvelous in my eyes.[85]

However, matters went poorly for Parliament in the ensuing spring. Queen Henrietta stole back to England with arms and ammunition and joined Charles at Oxford. Essex dallied while his army was eroded by desertion and disease. Hampden was mortally wounded in a skirmish at Chalgrove Field. A Parliamentary force was defeated at Adwalton Moor (June 30, 1643), another was destroyed at Roundway Down (July 13); Bristol fell to the King. In this nadir of its fortunes, Parliament turned to Scotland for help. On September 22 it signed with Scottish commissioners a "Solemn League and Covenant" which pledged the Scots to send an army to Parliament's aid in return for £30,000 a month, on condition that Parliament establish in England and Ireland the Presbyterian form of Protestantism—church government by presbyteries free from episcopal control. In the same month Charles made peace with the Irish insurgents, and imported some of them to fight for him in England. English Catholics rejoiced, Protestants turned increasingly against the King. In January 1644 the Irish invaders were defeated at Nantwich, and the Scottish invaders advanced into England. The Civil War now involved three nations and four faiths.

On July 1, 1643, the Westminster Assembly—121 English divines, thirty English laymen, and (later) eight Scottish delegates—met to define the new Presbyterian Protestantism of England. Hampered by Parliamentary domination, it dragged out its conferences through six years. A few members, favoring episcopacy, withdrew; a small group of Puritan Independents demanded that each congregation should be free from presbyteries as well as from bishops; the majority, following the pledge and the will of Parliament, favored the rule of religion in England and Ireland, as in Scotland, by presbyters, presbyteries, provincial synods, and general assemblies. Parliament abolished the Anglican episcopacy (1643), adopted and legislated the Presbyterian organization and creed (1646), but gave itself a veto power over all ecclesiastical decisions. In 1647 the Assembly issued the Westminster Confession of Faith, Larger Catechism, and Smaller Catechism, reaffirming the Calvinistic doctrine of predestination, election, and reprobation.* The decisions of the Westminster Assembly were set aside by the restoration of the Stuart dynasty and the Anglican Church, but the confession and the catechisms have remained in theoretical force in the Presbyterian churches of the English-speaking world.

---

* Excerpts from the Westminster Confession, ch. iii: "By the decree of God, for the manifestation of His glory, some men and angels are predestined unto everlasting life, and others foreordained to everlasting death. . . . Those of mankind that are predestined unto life, God, before the foundation of the world was laid, according to His eternal and immutable purpose, and the secret counsel and good pleasure of His will, hath chosen in Christ unto everlasting glory, out of His mere free grace and love, without any foresight of faith or good works, or perseverance in either of them . . . and all to the praise of His glorious grace . . . The rest of mankind God was pleased, according to the unsearchable counsel of His own will, whereby He extendeth or withholdeth mercy as He pleaseth, for the glory of His sovereign power over His creatures, to pass by, and to ordain them to dishonour and wrath for their sin, to the praise of His glorious justice."[86]

The Assembly and the Parliament agreed in rejecting the plea of the minor sects for religious toleration. The incorporated city of London petitioned Parliament to suppress all heresies. In 1648 the Commons passed bills punishing with life imprisonment the opponents of infant baptism, and with death those who denied the Trinity, or the Incarnation, or the divine inspiration of the Bible, or the immortality of the soul.[87] Several Jesuits were executed between 1642 and 1650; and on January 10, 1645, Archbishop Laud, aged seventy-two, was led from the Tower to the block. Parliament felt that it was engaged in a war to the death and that it was no time for amenities. Cromwell, however, stood out for some measure of toleration. In 1643 he organized at Cambridge a regiment which came to be called the Ironsides—a name originally given by Prince Rupert to Cromwell himself. Into this company he welcomed men of any faith—except Catholics and Episcopalians—"who had the fear of God before them and made some conscience of what they did."[88] When a Presbyterian officer wished to cashier a lieutenant colonel as an Anabaptist, Cromwell protested, "Sir, the state, in choosing men to serve it, takes no notice of their opinions; if they be willing to serve it faithfully, that suffices."[89] He asked Parliament (1644) to "endeavour the finding out some way how far tender consciences, who cannot in all things submit to the common [ecclesiastical] rule . . . may be borne with according to the Word."[90] Parliament ignored the request, but he continued to practice a comparative toleration in his regiments, and during his ascendancy in England.

Cromwell's development as a general was one of the surprises of the war. He shared with Lord Ferdinando Fairfax the honors of a victory at Winceby (October 11, 1643). At Marston Moor (July 2, 1644) Fairfax was routed, but Cromwell's Ironsides saved the day. Other Parliamentary leaders, the earls of Essex and Manchester, suffered reverses or failed to follow up their successes; Manchester frankly admitted his unwillingness to overthrow the King. To get rid of these titled generals, Cromwell proposed a "Self-denying Ordinance" (December 9, 1644) by which all members of Parliament were to resign their commands. The proposal was defeated; it was revived and passed (April 3, 1645); Essex and Manchester retired; Sir Thomas Fairfax, son of Ferdinando, was made commander in chief, and he soon appointed Cromwell lieutenant general in charge of the cavalry. Parliament ordered the formation of a "New Model" army of 22,000 men. Cromwell undertook to train it.

He had had no military experience before the war, but his force of character, his steadiness of purpose and will, his skill in playing upon the religious and political feelings of men, enabled him to mold his regiments into a unique discipline and loyalty. The Puritan faith equaled the Spartan ethic in making invincible soldiers. These men did not "swear like a trooper"; on the contrary, no oaths were heard in their camp, but many sermons and prayers. They stole not, nor raped, but they invaded churches to rid them of religious images and "prelatical" or "papistical" clergymen.[91] They shouted with joy or fury when they encountered the enemy. And they were never beaten. At Naseby (June 14, 1645), when the Royalists were routing Sir Thomas Fairfax's infantry, Cromwell with his new cavalry turned the defeat into so thorough a victory that the King lost all his infantry, all his artillery, half his cavalry, and copies of his correspondence, which were published to show that he planned to bring more Irish troops into England and to repeal the laws against Catholics.

From that time Charles's affairs rapidly worsened. The Marquis of Montrose, his heroic general in Scotland, after many victories, was routed at Philiphaugh and fled to the Continent. On July 30, 1645, the Parliamentary army took Bath; on August 23 Rupert surrendered Bristol to Fairfax. The King turned in all directions for help, in vain. On every side and pretext his troops, feeling their cause hopeless, went over to the enemy. By separate and devious negotiations he tried to divide his foes—the Independents from the Parliament, Parliament from the Scots—and failed. He had already sent his pregnant wife across hostile country to find ship for France; now he bade Prince Charles escape from England by whatever possible means. He himself, disguised and with but two attendants, made his way to the north and surrendered to the Scots (May 5, 1646). The First Civil War was in effect at an end.

X. The Radicals: 1646–48

Charles had been led to hope that the Scots would treat him as still their King; they preferred to consider him their prisoner. They offered to help him regain his throne if he would sign the Solemn League and Covenant making the Presbyterian form of Christianity compulsory throughout the British Isles; he refused. The English Parliament sent commissioners to the Scots at Newcastle, proposing to accept Charles as King on condition that he accept the Covenant, consent to the proscription of leading Royalists, and allow Parliament to control all armed forces and name all high officials of the state; he refused. Parliament offered the Scots £400,000 to pay their arrears and expenses if they would return to Scotland and surrender the King to English commissioners. The Scottish Parliament agreed. It accepted the money not as a price for the King, but as just reimbursement for its outlay in the war; Charles, however, felt that he had been bartered for gold. He was removed to Holmby House in Northamptonshire (January 1647) as prisoner of the English Parliament.

The English army, now encamped at Saffron Walden, forty miles from London, reviewed its victories and called for commensurate rewards. The cost of maintaining these thirty thousand men had compelled Parliament to raise taxes to twice their maximum under Charles; even so it owed the soldiers from four to ten months of back pay. Moreover, the Puritan Independents, defeated in Parliament, were gaining the upper hand in the army, and Cromwell, their leader, was suspected of ambitions inconsistent with the sovereignty of Parliament. Worse yet, there were in his regiment "Levelers" who rejected all distinctions of rank in Church and state, and who called for manhood suffrage and religious liberty. A few of them were anarchist communists; William Walwyn declared that all things should be in common; then "there would be no need for government, for there would be no thieves or criminals."[92] John Lilburne, the most un-discourageable of the Levelers after every arrest and punishment, was "the most popular man in England" (1646).[93] Cromwell was attacked as a Leveler, but, though sympathetic with them, he was hostile to their ideas, feeling that in the England of that day democracy would lead to chaos.

Parliament, now Presbyterian, resented the threat implied in the nearness of so large and troublesome an army so potently Independent. It passed a bill to disband half of it and to enroll the rest as volunteers for service in Ireland. The soldiers demanded their arrears; Parliament voted them a part in cash, the remainder in promises. The army refused to disband until fully paid. Parliament reopened negotiations with the King, and nearly reached an agreement with him to restore him on his consenting to accept the Covenant for three years. Warned of this, a squad of cavalry raided Holmby House, captured the King, and took him to Newmarket (June 3–5, 1647). Cromwell hurried to Newmarket and made himself head of a Council of the Army. On January 10 the army began a leisurely march upon London. En route it sent to Parliament a declaration formulated chiefly by Cromwell's able son-in-law Henry Ireton, which condemned the absolutism of Parliament as no better than the King's, and demanded the election of a new Parliament by a wider suffrage. Parliament was between two fires, for the merchants, the manufacturers, and the populace of London, fearing occupation by the army, clamored for the restoration of the King on almost any terms. A city crowd invaded Parliament (July 26), and compelled it to invite the King to London and to put the militia under Presbyterian command. Sixty-seven Independents left Parliament for the army.

On August 6 the troops entered London, bringing the King with them. The sixty-seven Independents were escorted back to their places in Parliament. From that time until Cromwell took supreme authority, the army dominated Parliament. It was not chaotic or unprincipled; it maintained order in the city and within its own ranks; and its demands, though probably impracticable at the time, were sanctioned by posterity. In the pamphlet *The Case of the Army Truly Stated* (October 9, 1647) it called for freedom of trade, abolition of monopolies, and restoration of common lands to the poor, and urged that no man be forced to testify against himself in court.[94] In *An Agreement of the People* (October 30) it proclaimed that "all power is originally and essentially in the whole body of the people"; that the only just government is through representatives freely chosen by manhood suffrage; that therefore kings and lords, if allowed to exist, should be subordinate to the House of Commons; that no man should be exempt from the laws; and that all should enjoy full religious liberty.[95] "Every man born in England, the poor man, the meanest man in the kingdom," said Colonel Rainsborough, ought to have a voice in choosing those who made the laws of the land by which he was to live and die.[96]

Cromwell quieted the debate by summoning its leaders to prayer. The Levelers charged him with hypocrisy and with secret negotiations for restoring the King, and he confessed that he still believed in monarchy. He explained to the democrats that the resistance to their proposals would be too formidable to be overcome by mere "fleshly strength," and after long argument he persuaded the leaders to reduce their demand for universal suffrage to a request for an extension of the franchise. Some soldiers refused to compromise; they wore the *Agreement* in their hats, and ignored Cromwell's command to remove it. He had three ringleaders arrested; they were tried by court-martial and condemned to death; he ordered them to throw dice for their lives; the one who lost was shot. Discipline revived.

Meanwhile the King escaped from his army captors, made his way to the coast and the Isle of Wight, and found friendly lodging in Carisbrooke Castle (November 14, 1647). He was heartened by news of Royalist rebellions against Parliament in the countryside and in the fleet. Scottish commissioners in London secretly offered a Scottish army to re-enthrone him if he would adopt Presbyterian Christianity and suppress other forms of religion. He accepted this "engagement," but limited it to three years. The commissioners left London to raise an army. The Scottish Parliament ratified their plan for an invasion of England, and issued a manifesto (May 3, 1648) requiring all Englishmen to take the Covenant, to suppress all forms of religion except the Presbyterian, and to disband the Independent army. The English Parliament saw itself superseded and England subordinated to Scotland if these proposals came into force. It hurriedly made its peace with Cromwell and persuaded him to lead his troops against the Scots; doubtless it was glad to put him at a distance and in peril. After three days of pleading he prevailed upon the army to follow him back to battle. It went reluctantly, and some leaders vowed that if they again saved England, it would be their "duty . . . to call Charles Stuart, that man of blood, to account for the blood he had shed."[97]

XI. Finis: 1648–49

Cromwell's energy made short work of the Second Civil War. While Fairfax put down Royalist revolts in Kent, Oliver turned west and captured a Royalist stronghold in Wales. The Scots crossed the Tweed on July 8 and moved with alarming speed to within forty miles of Liverpool. At Preston, in Lancashire, Cromwell's nine thousand men met twice that number of Scots and Cavaliers and overwhelmed them (August 17).

While Cromwell and his army were saving Parliament, it plotted to protect itself from them by reopening negotiations for the restoration of the King. But it insisted that he should sign and enforce the Covenant; he would not. The returning army offered to support his restoration with severe limitations on the royal prerogative; he refused (November 17). To prevent his being restored by Parliament, the army captured him again and lodged him in Hurst Castle, opposite the Isle of Wight. Parliament condemned the action and voted to accept the King's latest terms as a basis for settlement. The army leaders, anticipating death if Charles were restored, declared that none might be permitted to pass into the House but such as had continued "faithful to the public interest." Early on December 6 Colonel Thomas Pride and a troop of soldiers surrounded and invaded the House of Commons and barred or expelled 140 Royalist and Presbyterian members; forty who resisted were jailed.[98] Cromwell approved the action, and joined in voting for the speedy trial and execution of the King.

Of the five hundred members who in 1640 had composed the House of Commons only fifty-six now remained. This "Rump Parliament," by a majority of six, passed an ordinance declaring it treason for a king to make war upon Parliament. The Lords rejected the ordinance as beyond the authority of the Commons; the Commons thereupon (January 4, 1649) resolved that the people were, "under God, the original of all just power"; that the Commons, as representing the people, had "the supreme power in this nation"; and that therefore its enactments, without the consent of the Lords or the king, had the force of law. On January 6 they named 135 commissioners to try the King. One commissioner, Algernon Sidney, told Cromwell they had no legal authority to try a king. Cromwell lost his temper. "I tell you," he cried, "we will cut off his head with the crown upon it."[99] The army leaders made a last attempt to avoid regicide; they offered to acquit Charles if he would agree to the sale of the bishops' lands and resign the power to veto the ordinances of Parliament. He said he could not, for he had sworn to be faithful to the Church of England. There was no question of his courage.

The trial began on January 19, 1649. The sixty or seventy impromptu judges who consented to act sat on a raised dais at one end of Westminster Hall, soldiers stood at the other, spectators thronged the galleries; Charles was seated in the center, alone. The presiding officer, John Bradshaw, stated the charge and asked the King to answer. Charles denied the authority of the court to try him, or that it represented the people of England, and claimed that government by a Rump Parliament dominated by the army was a worse tyranny than any he had ever shown. The galleries cried, "God save the King!" The pulpits condemned the trial; Bradshaw feared for his life in the streets. Prince Charles dispatched from Holland a sheet bearing only his signature, and promised the judges to abide by any terms they would write over his name if they would spare his father's life.[100] Four nobles offered to die in Charles's stead; they were refused.[101] Fifty-nine judges, including Cromwell, signed the death sentence. On January 30, before a vast and horror-stricken crowd, the King went quietly to his death. His head was severed with one blow of the executioner's ax. "There was such a groan by the thousands then present," wrote an eyewitness, "as I never heard before and desire I may never hear again."[102]

Was the execution legal? Of course not. On the basis of existing law, the Parliament progressively and rudely appropriated royal rights sanctioned by the precedents of a hundred years. By definition a revolution is illegal; it can advance to the new only by violating the old. Charles was sincere in defending the powers he had inherited from Elizabeth and James; he was sinned against as well as sinning; his fatal error lay in not recognizing that the new distribution of wealth required, for social stability, a new distribution of political power.

Was the execution just? Yes, so far as war is just. Once law is set aside by trial at arms, the defeated may ask for mercy, but the victor may exact the ultimate penalty if he judges it necessary as a preventive of renewed resistance, or as a deterrent to others, or as protection for the lives of himself and his followers. Presumably a triumphant King would have hanged Cromwell, Ireton, Fairfax, and many more, perhaps with the tortures regularly allotted to persons convicted of treason.

Was the execution wise? Probably not. Cromwell apparently believed that a live king, no matter how securely imprisoned, would be a stimulus to repeated Royalist revolts. But so would the King's son, unreachable in France or Holland, as yet unblemished with his father's faults, and soon to be glorified with romance. The execution of Charles I led to a foreseeable revulsion of national feeling, which in eleven years restored his line. Subsequent history suggests that mercy would have been wisdom. When Charles's son James II gave equally great offense, the Glorious Revolution of 1688, managed with aristocratic finesse, deliberately allowed him to escape to France; and the results of that deposition were permanent. However, it was the earlier Rebellion that made the later Revolution possible in all its swift effectiveness.

The Great Rebellion corresponded both to the Huguenot uprisings in sixteenth-century France and, despite many differences, to the French Revolution of 1789—in the first case the insurrection of a stern and simple Calvinism, sinewed by mercantile wealth, against a ritualistic Church and an absolutist government; in the second case the revolt of a national assembly, expressing the power of the purse and the middle class, against a landed aristocracy led by a well-meaning but blundering ruler. By 1789 the English had digested their two rebellions, and could look with horror and eloquence upon a revolution that, like its own, incarnadined a country and killed a king because the past had tried to stand still.

FRANCIS BACON

I. From Aristotle to the Renaissance

When Sparta blockaded and defeated Athens towards the close of the fifth century B.C., political supremacy passed from the mother of Greek philosophy and art, and the vigor and independence of the Athenian mind decayed. When, in 399 B.C., Socrates was put to death, the soul of Athens died with him, lingering only in his proud pupil, Plato. And when Philip of Macedon defeated the Athenians at Chæronea in 338 B.C., and Alexander burned the great city of Thebes to the ground three years later, even the ostentatious sparing of Pindar's home could not cover up the fact that Athenian independence, in government and in thought, was irrevocably destroyed. The domination of Greek philosophy by the Macedonian Aristotle mirrored the political subjection of Greece by the virile and younger peoples of the north.

The death of Alexander (323 B.C.) quickened this process of decay. The boy-emperor, barbarian though he remained after all of Aristotle's tutoring, had yet learned to revere the rich culture of Greece, and had dreamed of spreading that culture through the Orient in the wake of his victorious armies. The development of Greek commerce, and the multiplication of Greek trading posts throughout Asia Minor, had provided an economic basis for the unification of this region as part of an Hellenic empire; and Alexander hoped that from these busy stations Greek thought, as well as Greek goods, would radiate and conquer. But he had underrated the inertia and resistance of the Oriental mind, and the mass and depth of Oriental culture. It was only a youthful fancy, after all, to suppose that so immature and unstable a civilization as that of Greece could be imposed upon a civilization immeasurably more widespread, and rooted in the most venerable traditions. The quantity of Asia proved too much for the quality of Greece. Alexander himself, in the hour of his triumph, was conquered by the soul of the East; he married (among several ladies) the daughter of Darius; he adopted the Persian diadem and robe of state; he introduced into Europe the Oriental notion of the divine right of kings; and at last he astonished a sceptic Greece by announcing, in magnificent Eastern style, that he was a god. Greece laughed; and Alexander drank himself to death.

This subtle infusion of an Asiatic soul into the wearied body of the master Greek was followed rapidly by the pouring of Oriental cults and faiths into Greece along those very lines of communication which the young conqueror had opened up; the broken dykes let in the ocean of Eastern thought upon the lowlands of the still adolescent European mind. The mystic and superstitious faiths which had taken root among the poorer people of Hellas were reinforced and spread about; and the Oriental spirit of apathy and resignation found a ready soil in decadent and despondent Greece. The introduction of the Stoic philosophy into Athens by the Phoenician merchant Zeno (about 310 B.C.) was but one of a multitude of Oriental infiltrations. Both Stoicism and Epicureanism—the apathetic acceptance of defeat, and the effort to forget defeat in the arms of pleasure—were theories as to how one might yet be happy though subjugated or enslaved; precisely as the pessimistic Oriental stoicism of Schopenhauer and the despondent epicureanism of Renan were in the nineteenth century the symbols of a shattered Revolution and a broken France.

Not that these natural antitheses of ethical theory were quite new to Greece. One finds them in the gloomy Heraclitus and the "laughing philosopher" Democritus; and one sees the pupils of Socrates dividing into Cynics and Cyrenaics under the lead of Antisthenes and Aristippus, and extolling, the one school apathy, the other happiness. Yet these were even then almost exotic modes of thought: imperial Athens did not take to them. But when Greece had seen Chæronea in blood and Thebes in ashes, it listened to Diogenes; and when the glory had departed from Athens she was ripe for Zeno and Epicurus.[1]

Zeno built his philosophy of *apatheia* on a determinism which a later Stoic, Chrysippus, found it hard to distinguish from Oriental fatalism. When Zeno, who did not believe in slavery, was beating his slave for some offense, the slave pleaded, in mitigation, that by his master's philosophy he had been destined from all eternity to commit this fault; to which Zeno replied, with the calm of a sage, that on the same philosophy he, Zeno, had been destined to beat him for it. As Schopenhauer deemed it useless for the individual will to fight the universal will, so the Stoic argued that philosophic indifference was the only reasonable attitude to a life in which the struggle for existence is so unfairly doomed to inevitable defeat. If victory is quite impossible it should be scorned. The secret of peace is not to make our achievements equal to our desires, but to lower our desires to the level of our achievements. "If what you have seems insufficient to you," said the Roman Stoic Seneca (d. 65 A.D.), "then, though you possess the world, you will yet be miserable."

Such a principle cried out to heaven for its opposite, and Epicurus, though himself as Stoic in life as Zeno, supplied it. Epicurus, says Fenelon,[2] "bought a fair garden, which he tilled himself. There it was he set up his school, and there he lived a gentle and agreeable life with his disciples, whom he taught as he walked and worked. . . . He was gentle and affable to all men . . . He held there was nothing nobler than to apply one's self to philosophy." His starting point is a conviction that apathy is impossible, and that pleasure—though not necessarily sensual pleasure—is the only conceivable, and quite legitimate, end of life and action. "Nature leads every organism to prefer its own good to every other good";—even the Stoic finds a subtle pleasure in renunciation. "We must not avoid pleasures, but we must select them." Epicurus, then, is no epicurean; he exalts the joys of intellect rather than those of sense; he warns against pleasures that excite and disturb the soul which they should rather quiet and appease. In the end he proposes to seek not pleasure in its usual sense, but *ataraxia*—tranquillity, equanimity, repose of mind; all of which trembles on the verge of Zeno's "apathy."

The Romans, coming to despoil Hellas in 146 B.C., found these rival schools dividing the philosophic field; and having neither leisure nor subtlety for speculation themselves, brought back these philosophies with their other spoils to Rome. Great organizers, as much as inevitable slaves, tend to stoic moods: it is difficult to be either master or servant if one is sensitive. So such philosophy as Rome had was mostly of Zeno's school, whether in Marcus Aurelius the emperor or in Epictetus the slave; and even Lucretius talked epicureanism stoically (like Heine's Englishman taking his pleasures sadly), and concluded his stern gospel of pleasure by committing suicide. His noble epic "On the Nature of Things,"[3] follows Epicurus in damning pleasure with faint praise. Almost contemporary with Cæsar and Pompey, he lived in the midst of turmoil and alarms; his nervous pen is forever inditing prayers to tranquillity and peace. One pictures him as a timid soul whose youth had been darkened with religious fears; for he never tires of telling his readers that there is no hell, except here, and that there are no gods except gentlemanly ones who live in a garden of Epicurus in the clouds, and never intrude in the affairs of men. To the rising cult of heaven and hell among the people of Rome he opposes a ruthless materialism. Soul and mind are evolved with the body, grow with its growth, ail with its ailments, and die with its death. Nothing exists but atoms, space, and law; and the law of laws is that of evolution and dissolution everywhere.

> No single thing abides, but all things flow.
>   Fragment to fragment clings; the things thus grow
>   Until we know and name them. By degrees
>   They melt, and are no more the things we know.
>
> Globed from the atoms, falling slow or swift
>   I see the suns, I see the systems lift
>   Their forms; and even the systems and their suns
>   Shall go back slowly to the eternal drift.
>
> Thou too, O Earth—thine empires, lands and seas—
>   Least, with thy stars, of all the galaxies,
>   Globed from the drift like these, like these thou too
>   Shalt go. Thou art going, hour by hour, like these.
>
> Nothing abides. Thy seas in delicate haze
>   Go off; those moonèd sands forsake their place;
>   And where they are shall other seas in turn
>   Mow with their scythes of whiteness other bays.[4]

To astronomical evolution and dissolution add the origin and elimination of species.

> Many monsters too the earth of old tried to produce, things of strange face and limbs; . . . some without feet, some without hands, some without mouth, some without eyes. . . . Every other monster . . . of this kind earth would produce, but in vain; for nature set a ban on their increase, they could not reach the coveted flower of age, nor find food, nor be united in marriage; . . . and many races of living things must then have died out and been unable to beget and continue their breed.

For in the case of all things which you see breathing the breath of life, either craft or courage or speed has from the beginning of its existence protected and preserved each particular race. . . . Those to whom nature has granted none of these qualities would lie exposed as a prey and booty to others, until nature brought their kind to extinction.[5]

Nations, too, like individuals, slowly grow and surely die: "some nations wax, others wane, and in a brief space the races of living things are changed, and like runners hand over the lamp of life." In the face of warfare and inevitable death, there is no wisdom but in *ataraxia*—"to look on all things with a mind at peace." Here, clearly, the old pagan joy of life is gone, and an almost exotic spirit touches a broken lyre. History, which is nothing if not humorous, was never so facetious as when she gave to this abstemious and epic pessimist the name of Epicurean.

And if this is the spirit of the follower of Epicurus, imagine the exhilarating optimism of explicit Stoics like Aurelius or Epictetus. Nothing in all literature is so depressing as the "Dissertations" of the slave, unless it be the "Meditations" of the emperor. "Seek not to have things happen as you choose them, but rather choose that they should happen as they do; and you shall live prosperously."[6] No doubt one can in this manner dictate the future, and play royal highness to the universe. Story has it that Epictetus' master, who treated him with consistent cruelty, one day took to twisting Epictetus' leg to pass the time away. "If you go on," said Epictetus calmly, "you will break my leg." The master went on, and the leg was broken. "Did I not tell you," Epictetus observed mildly, "that you would break my leg?"[7] Yet there is a certain mystic nobility in this philosophy, as in the quiet courage of some Dostoievskian pacifist. "Never in any case say, I have lost such a thing; but, I have returned it. Is thy child dead?—it is returned. Is thy wife dead?—she is returned. Art thou deprived of thy estate?—is not this also returned?"[8] In such passages we feel the proximity of Christianity and its dauntless martyrs; indeed were not the Christian ethic of self-denial, the Christian political ideal of an almost communistic brotherhood of man, and the Christian eschatology of the final conflagration of all the world, fragments of Stoic doctrine floating on the stream of thought? In Epictetus the Greco-Roman soul has lost its paganism, and is ready for a new faith. His book had the distinction of being adopted as a religious manual by the early Christian Church. From these "Dissertations" and Aurelius' "Meditations" there is but a step to "The Imitation of Christ."

Meanwhile the historical background was melting into newer scenes. There is a remarkable passage in Lucretius[9] which describes the decay of agriculture in the Roman state, and attributes it to the exhaustion of the soil. Whatever the cause, the wealth of Rome passed into poverty, the organization into disintegration, the power and pride into decadence and apathy. Cities faded back into the undistinguished hinterland; the roads fell into disrepair and no longer hummed with trade; the small families of the educated Romans were outbred by the vigorous and untutored German stocks that crept, year after year, across the frontier; pagan culture yielded to Oriental cults; and almost imperceptibly the Empire passed into the Papacy.

The Church, supported in its earlier centuries by the emperors whose powers it gradually absorbed, grew rapidly in numbers, wealth, and range of influence. By the thirteenth century it owned one-third of the soil of Europe,[10] and its coffers bulged with donations of rich and poor. For a thousand years it united, with the magic of an unvarying creed, most of the peoples of a continent; never before or since was organization so widespread or so pacific. But this unity demanded, as the Church thought, a common faith exalted by supernatural sanctions beyond the changes and corrosions of time; therefore dogma, definite and defined, was cast like a shell over the adolescent mind of medieval Europe. It was within this shell that Scholastic philosophy moved narrowly from faith to reason and back again, in a baffling circuit of uncriticized assumptions and pre-ordained conclusions. In the thirteenth century all Christendom was startled and stimulated by Arabic and Jewish translations of Aristotle; but the power of the Church was still adequate to secure, through Thomas Aquinas and others, the transmogrification of Aristotle into a medieval theologian. The result was subtlety, but not wisdom. "The wit and mind of man," as Bacon put it, "if it work upon the matter, worketh according to the stuff, and is limited thereby; but if it work upon itself, as the spider worketh his web, then it is endless, and bringeth forth indeed cobwebs of learning, admirable for the fineness of thread and work, but of no substance or profit." Sooner or later the intellect of Europe would burst out of this shell.

After a thousand years of tillage, the soil bloomed again; goods were multiplied into a surplus that compelled trade; and trade at its cross-roads built again great cities wherein men might coöperate to nourish culture and rebuild civilization.[11] The Crusades opened the routes to the East, and let in a stream of luxuries

TABLE OF PHILOSOPHIC AFFILIATIONS

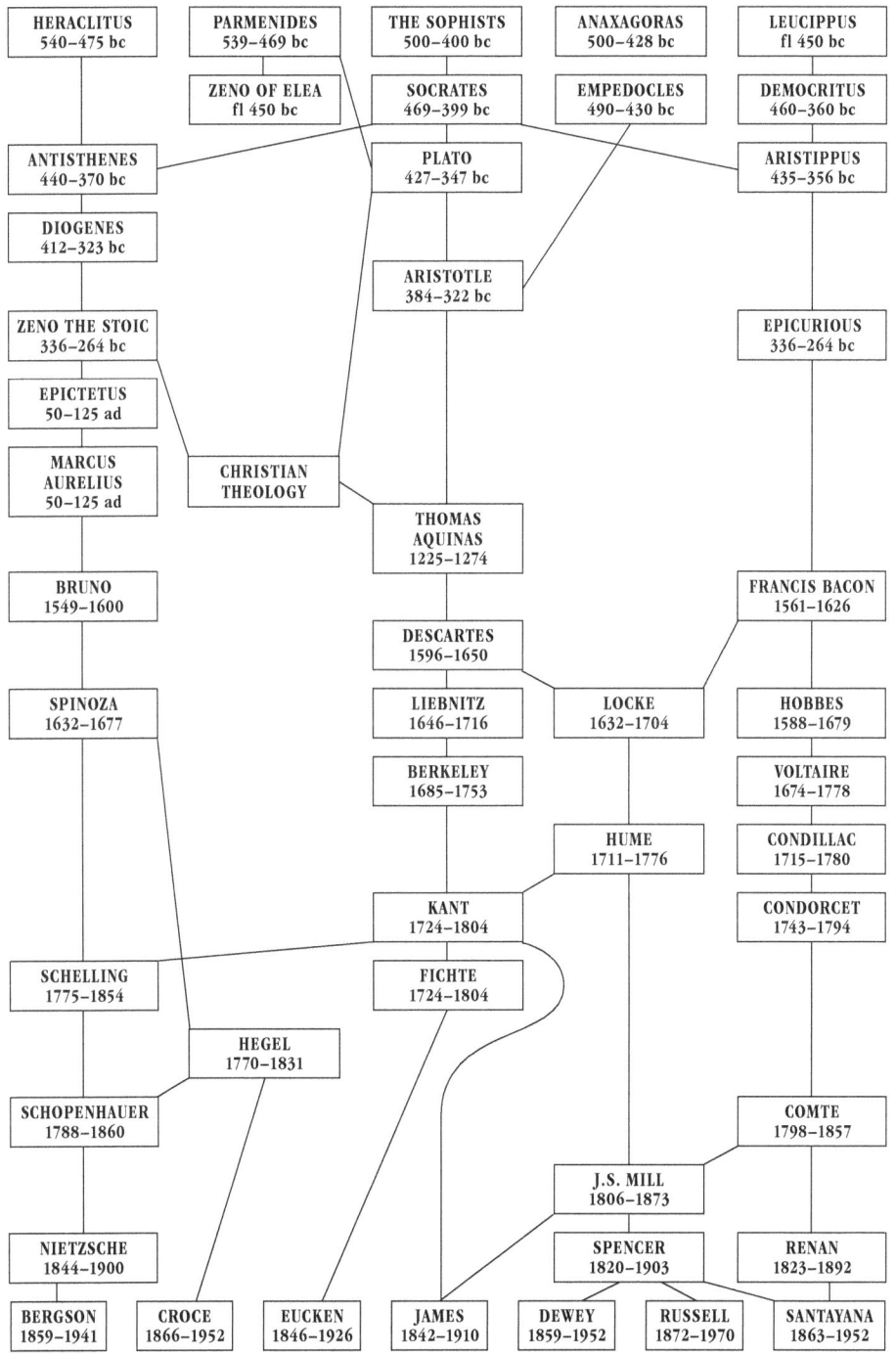

and heresies that doomed asceticism and dogma. Paper now came cheaply from Egypt, replacing the costly parchment that had made learning the monopoly of priests; printing, which had long awaited an inexpensive medium, broke out like a liberated explosive, and spread its destructive and clarifying influence everywhere. Brave mariners armed now with compasses, ventured out into the wilderness of the sea, and conquered man's ignorance of the earth; patient observers, armed with telescopes, ventured out beyond the confines of dogma, and conquered man's ignorance of the sky. Here and there, in universities and monasteries and hidden retreats, men ceased to dispute and began to search; deviously, out of the effort to change baser metal into gold, alchemy was transmuted into chemistry; out of astrology men groped their way with timid boldness to astronomy; and out of the fables of speaking animals came the science of zoology. The awakening began with Roger Bacon (d. 1294); it grew with the limitless Leonardo (1452–1519); it reached its fulness in the astronomy of Copernicus (1473–1543) and Galileo (1564–1642), in the researches of Gilbert (1544–1603) in magnetism and electricity, of Vesalius (1514–1564) in anatomy, and of Harvey (1578–1657) on the circulation of the blood. As knowledge grew, fear decreased; men thought less of worshiping the unknown, and more of overcoming it. Every vital spirit was lifted up with a new confidence; barriers were broken down; there was no bound now to what man might do. "But that little vessels, like the celestial bodies, should sail round the whole globe, is the happiness of our age. These times may justly use *plus ultra*"—more beyond—"where the ancients used *non plus ultra*."[12] It was an age of achievement, hope and vigor; of new beginnings and enterprises in every field; an age that waited for a voice, some synthetic soul to sum up its spirit and resolve. It was Francis Bacon, "the most powerful mind of modern times,"[13] who "rang the bell that called the wits together," and announced that Europe had come of age.

II. The Political Career of Francis Bacon

Bacon was born on January 22, 1561, at York House, London, the residence of his father, Sir Nicholas Bacon, who for the first twenty years of Elizabeth's reign had been Keeper of the Great Seal. "The fame of the father," says Macaulay, "has been thrown into the shade by that of the son. But Sir Nicholas was no ordinary man."[14] It is as one might have suspected; for genius is an apex, to which a family builds itself through talent, and through talent in the genius's offspring subsides again towards the mediocrity of man. Bacon's mother was Lady Anne Cooke, sister-in-law of Sir William Cecil, Lord Burghley, who was Elizabeth's Lord Treasurer, and one of the most powerful men in England. Her father had been chief tutor of King Edward VI; she herself was a linguist and a theologian, and thought nothing of corresponding in Greek with bishops. She made herself instructress of her son, and spared no pains in his education.

But the real nurse of Bacon's greatness was Elizabethan England, the greatest age of the most powerful of modern nations. The discovery of America had diverted trade from the Mediterranean to the Atlantic, had raised the Atlantic nations—Spain and France and Holland and England—to that commercial and financial supremacy which had been Italy's when half of Europe had made her its port of entry and exit in the Eastern trade; and with this change the Renaissance had passed from Florence and Rome and Milan and Venice to Madrid and Paris and Amsterdam and London. After the destruction of the Spanish naval power in 1588, the commerce of England spread over every sea, her towns throve with domestic industry, her sailors circumnavigated the globe and her captains won America. Her literature blossomed into Spenser's poetry and Sidney's prose; her stage throbbed with the dramas of Shakespeare and Marlowe and Ben Jonson and a hundred vigorous pens. No man could fail to flourish in such a time and country, if there was seed in him at all.

At the age of twelve Bacon was sent to Trinity College, Cambridge. He stayed there three years, and left it with a strong dislike of its texts and methods, a confirmed hostility to the cult of Aristotle, and a resolve to set philosophy into a more fertile path, to turn it from scholastic disputation to the illumination and increase of human good. Though still a lad of sixteen, he was offered an appointment to the staff of the English ambassador in France; and after careful casting up of *pros* and *cons*, he accepted. In the Proem to *The Interpretation of Nature,* he discusses this fateful decision that turned him from philosophy to politics. It is an indispensable passage:

> Whereas, I believed myself born for the service of mankind, and reckoned the care of the common weal to be among those duties that are of public right, open to all alike, even as the waters and the air, I therefore asked myself what could most advantage mankind, and for the performance of what tasks I seemed to be shaped by nature. But when I searched, I found no work so meritorious as the discovery

and development of the arts and inventions that tend to civilize the life of man. . . . Above all, if any man could succeed—not merely in bringing to light some one particular invention, however useful—but in kindling in nature a luminary which would, at its first rising, shed some light on the present limits and borders of human discoveries, and which afterwards, as it rose still higher, would reveal and bring into clear view every nook and cranny of darkness, it seemed to me that such a discoverer would deserve to be called the true Extender of the Kingdom of Man over the universe, the Champion of human liberty, and the Exterminator of the necessities that now keep men in bondage. Moreover, I found in my own nature a special adaptation for the contemplation of truth. For I had a mind at once versatile enough for that most important object—I mean the recognition of similitudes—and at the same time sufficiently steady and concentrated for the observation of subtle shades of difference. I possessed a passion for research, a power of suspending judgment with patience, of meditating with pleasure, of assenting with caution, of correcting false impressions with readiness, and of arranging my thoughts with scrupulous pains. I had no hankering after novelty, no blind admiration for antiquity. Imposture in every shape I utterly detested. For all these reasons I considered that my nature and disposition had, as it were, a kind of kinship and connection with truth.

But my birth, my rearing and education, had all pointed, not toward philosophy, but towards politics: I had been, as it were, imbued in politics from childhood. And as is not unfrequently the case with young men, I was sometimes shaken in my mind by opinions. I also thought that my duty towards my country had special claims upon me, such as could not be urged by other duties of life. Lastly, I conceived the hope that, if I held some honorable office in the state, I might have secure helps and supports to aid my labors, with a view to the accomplishment of my destined task. With these motives I applied myself to politics.[15]

Sir Nicholas Bacon died suddenly in 1579. He had intended to provide Francis with an estate; but death overreached his plans, and the young diplomat, called hurriedly to London, saw himself, at the age of eighteen, fatherless and penniless. He had become accustomed to most of the luxuries of the age, and he found it hard to reconcile himself now to a forced simplicity of life. He took up the practice of law, while he importuned his influential relatives to advance him to some political office which would liberate him from economic worry. His almost begging letters had small result, considering the grace and vigor of their style, and the proved ability of their author. Perhaps it was because Bacon did not underrate this ability, and looked upon position as his due, that Burghley failed to make the desired response; and perhaps, also, these letters protested too much the past, present and future loyalty of the writer to the honorable Lord: in politics, as in love, it does not do to give one's self wholly; one should at all times give, but at no time all. Gratitude is nourished with expectation.

Eventually, Bacon climbed without being lifted from above; but every step cost him many years. In 1583 he was elected to Parliament for Taunton; and his constituents liked him so well that they returned him to his seat in election after election. He had a terse and vivid eloquence in debate, and was an orator without oratory. "No man," said Ben Jonson, "ever spoke more neatly, more (com)pressedly, more weightily, or suffered less emptiness, less idleness in what he uttered. No member of his speech but consisted of its own graces. His hearers could not cough or look aside from him without loss. He commanded where he spoke. . . . No man had their affections more in his power. The fear of every man that heard him was lest that he should make an end."[16] Enviable orator!

One powerful friend was generous to him—that handsome Earl of Essex whom Elizabeth loved unsuccessfully, and so learned to hate. In 1595 Essex, to atone for his failure in securing a political post for Bacon, presented him with a pretty estate at Twickenham. It was a magnificent gift, which one might presume would bind Bacon to Essex for life; but it did not. A few years later Essex organized a conspiracy to imprison Elizabeth and select her successor to the throne. Bacon wrote letter after letter to his benefactor, protesting against this treason; and when Essex persisted, Bacon warned him that he would put loyalty to his Queen above even gratitude to his friend. Essex made his effort, failed, and was arrested. Bacon pled with the Queen in his behalf so incessantly that at last she bade him "speak of any other subject." When Essex, temporarily freed, gathered armed forces about him, marched into London, and tried to rouse its populace to revolution, Bacon turned against him angrily. Meanwhile he had been given a place in the prosecuting office of the realm; and when Essex, again arrested, was tried for treason, Bacon took active part in the prosecution of the man who had been his unstinting friend.[17]

Essex was found guilty, and was put to death. Bacon's part in the trial made him for a while unpopular; and from this time on he lived in the midst of enemies watching for a chance to destroy him. His insatiable ambition left him no rest; he was ever discontent, and always a year or so ahead of his income. He was lavish in his expenditures; display was to him a part of policy. When, at the age of forty-five, he married, the pompous and costly ceremony made a great gap in the dowry which had constituted one of the lady's attractions. In 1598 he was arrested for debt. Nevertheless, he continued to advance. His varied ability and almost endless knowledge made him a valuable member of every important committee; gradually higher offices were opened to him: in 1606 he was made Solicitor-General; in 1613 he became Attorney-General; in 1618, at the age of fifty-seven, he was at last Lord Chancellor.

III. The Essays[18]

His elevation seemed to realize Plato's dreams of a philosopher-king. For, step by step with his climb to political power, Bacon had been mounting the summits of philosophy. It is almost incredible that the vast learning and literary achievements of this man were but the incidents and diversions of a turbulent political career. It was his motto that one lived best by the widest life—*bene vixit qui bene latuit.* He could not quite make up his mind whether he liked more the contemplative or the active life. His hope was to be philosopher and statesman, too, like Seneca; though he suspected that this double direction of his life would shorten his reach and lessen his attainment. "It is hard to say," he writes,[19] "whether mixture of contemplations with an active life, or retiring wholly to contemplations, do disable or hinder the mind more." He felt that studies could not be either end or wisdom in themselves, and that knowledge unapplied in action was a pale academic vanity. "To spend too much time in studies is sloth; to use them too much for ornament is affectation; to make judgment wholly by their rules is the humor of a scholar. . . . Crafty men condemn studies, simple men admire them, and wise men use them; for they teach not their own use; but that is a wisdom without them, and above them, won by observation."[20] Here is a new note, which marks the end of scholasticism—i. e., the divorce of knowledge from use and observation—and places that emphasis on experience and results which distinguishes English philosophy, and culminates in pragmatism. Not that Bacon for a moment ceased to love books and meditation; in words reminiscent of Socrates he writes, "without philosophy I care not to live";[21] and he describes himself as after all "a man naturally fitted rather for literature than for anything else, and borne by some destiny, against the inclination of his genius" (i.e., character), "into active life."[22] Almost his first publication was called "The Praise of Knowledge" (1592); its enthusiasm for philosophy compels quotation:

> My praise shall be dedicate to the mind itself. The mind is the man, and knowledge mind; a man is but what he knoweth. . . . Are not the pleasures of the affections greater than the pleasures of the senses, and are not the pleasures of the intellect greater than the pleasures of the affections? Is not that only a true and natural pleasure whereof there is no satiety? Is not that knowledge alone that doth clear the mind of all perturbations? How many things be there which we imagine are not? How many things do we esteem and value more than they are? These vain imaginations, these ill-proportioned estimations, these be the clouds of error that turn into the storms of perturbations. Is there then any such happiness as for a man's mind to be raised above the confusion of things, where he may have a respect of the order of nature and the error of men? Is there but a view only of delight and not of discovery? Of contentment and not of benefit? Shall we not discern as well the riches of nature's warehouse as the beauty of her shop? Is truth barren? Shall we not thereby be able to produce worthy effects, and to endow the life of man with infinite commodities?

His finest literary product, the *Essays* (1597–1623), show him still torn between these two loves, for politics and for philosophy. In the "Essay of Honor and Reputation" he gives all the degrees of honor to political and military achievements, none to the literary or the philosophical. But in the essay "Of Truth" he writes: "The inquiry of truth, which is the love-making or wooing of it; the knowledge of truth, which is the praise of it; and the belief of truth, which is the enjoying of it, is the sovereign good of human natures." In books "we converse with the wise, as in action with fools." That is, if we know how to select our books. "Some books are to be tasted," reads a famous passage, "others to be swallowed, and some few to be chewed and digested"; all these groups forming, no doubt, an infinitesimal portion of the oceans and cataracts of ink in which the world is daily bathed and poisoned and drowned.

Surely the *Essays* must be numbered among the few books that deserve to be chewed and digested. Rarely shall you find so much meat, so admirably dressed and flavored, in so small a dish. Bacon abhors padding, and disdains to waste a word; he offers us infinite riches in a little phrase; each of these essays gives in a page or two the distilled subtlety of a master mind on a major issue of life. It is difficult to say whether the matter or the manner more excels; for here is language as supreme in prose as Shakespeare's is in verse. It is a style like sturdy Tacitus', compact yet polished; and indeed some of its conciseness is due to the skillful adaptation of Latin idiom and phrase. But its wealth of metaphor is characteristically Elizabethan, and reflects the exuberance of the Renaissance; no man in English literature is so fertile in pregnant and pithy comparisons. Their lavish array is the one defect of Bacon's style: the endless metaphors and allegories and allusions fall like whips upon our nerves and tire us out at last. The *Essays* are like rich and heavy food, which cannot be digested in large quantities at once; but taken four or five at a time they are the finest intellectual nourishment in English.[23]

What shall we extract from this extracted wisdom? Perhaps the best starting point, and the most arresting deviation from the fashions of medieval philosophy, is Bacon's frank acceptance of the Epicurean ethic. "That philosophical progression, 'Use not that you may not wish, wish not that you may not fear,' seems an indication of a weak, diffident and timorous mind. And indeed most doctrines of the philosophers appear to be too distrustful, and to take more care of mankind than the nature of the thing requires. Thus they increase the fears of death by the remedies they bring against it; for whilst they make the life of man little more than a preparation and discipline for death, it is impossible but the enemy must appear terrible when there is no end of the defense to be made against him."[24] Nothing could be so injurious to health as the Stoic repression of desire; what is the use of prolonging a life which apathy has turned into premature death? And besides, it is an impossible philosophy; for instinct will out. "Nature is often hidden; sometimes overcome; seldom extinguished. Force maketh nature more violent in the return; doctrine and discourse maketh nature less importune; but custom only doth alter or subdue nature. . . . But let not a man trust his victory over his nature too far; for nature will lay buried a great time, and yet revive upon the occasion or temptation. Like as it was with Æsop's damsel, turned from a cat to a woman, who sat very demurely at the board's end, till a mouse ran before her. Therefore let a man either avoid the occasion altogether, or put himself often to it, that he may be little moved with it."[25] Indeed Bacon thinks the body should be inured to excesses as well as to restraint; else even a moment of unrestraint may ruin it. (So one accustomed to the purest and most digestible foods is easily upset when forgetfulness or necessity diverts him from perfection.) Yet "variety of delights rather than surfeit of them"; for "strength of nature in youth passeth over many excesses which are owing a man till his age";[26] a man's maturity pays the price of his youth. One royal road to health is a garden; Bacon agrees with the author of *Genesis* that "God Almighty first planted a garden"; and with Voltaire that we must cultivate our back yards.

The moral philosophy of the *Essays* smacks rather of Machiavelli than of the Christianity to which Bacon made so many astute obeisances. "We are beholden to *Machiavel*, and writers of that kind, who openly and unmasked declare what men do in fact, and not what they ought to do; for it is impossible to join the wisdom of the serpent and the innocence of the dove, without a previous knowledge of the nature of evil; as, without this, virtue lies exposed and unguarded."[27] "The Italians have an ungracious proverb, *Tanto buon che val niente*,"—so good that he is good for nothing.[28] Bacon accords his preaching with his practice, and advises a judicious mixture of dissimulation with honesty, like an alloy that will make the purer but softer metal capable of longer life. He wants a full and varied career, giving acquaintance with everything that can broaden, deepen, strengthen or sharpen the mind. He does not admire the merely contemplative life; like Goethe he scorns knowledge that does not lead to action: "men ought to know that in the theatre of human life it is only for Gods and angels to be spectators."[29]

His religion is patriotically like the King's. Though he was more than once accused of atheism, and the whole trend of his philosophy is secular and rationalistic, he makes an eloquent and apparently sincere disclaimer of unbelief. "I had rather believe all the fables in the Legend, and the Talmud and the Alcoran, than that this universal frame is without a mind. . . . A little philosophy inclineth a man's mind to atheism; but depth in philosophy bringeth men's minds about to religion. For while the mind of man looketh upon second causes scattered, it may sometimes rest in them and go no further; but when it beholdeth the chain of them, confederate and linked together, it must needs fly to Providence and Deity."[30] Religious indifference is due to a multiplicity of factions. "The causes of atheism are, divisions in religion, if they be many;

for any one division addeth zeal to both sides; but many divisions introduce atheism. . . . And lastly, learned times, especially with peace and prosperity; for troubles and adversities do more bow men's minds to religion."[31]

But Bacon's value lies less in theology and ethics than in psychology. He is an undeceivable analyst of human nature, and sends his shaft into every heart. On the stalest subject in the world he is refreshingly original. "A married man is seven years older in his thoughts the first day."[32] "It is often seen that bad husbands have good wives." (Bacon was an exception.) "A single life doth well with churchmen, for charity will hardly water the ground where it must first fill a pool. . . . He that hath wife and children hath given hostages to fortune; for they are impediments to great enterprises, either of virtue or mischief."[33] Bacon seems to have worked too hard to have had time for love, and perhaps he never quite felt it to its depth. "It is a strange thing to note the excess of this passion. . . . There was never proud man thought so absurdly well of himself as the lover doth of the person beloved. . . . You may observe that amongst all the great and worthy persons (whereof the memory remaineth either ancient or recent), there is not one that hath been transported to the mad degree of love; which shows that great spirits and great business do keep out this weak passion."[34]

He values friendship more than love, though of friendship too he can be sceptical. "There is little friendship in the world, and least of all between equals, which was wont to be magnified. That that is, is between superior and inferior, whose fortunes may comprehend the one the other. . . . A principal fruit of friendship is the ease and discharge of the fullness and swellings of the heart, which passions of all kinds do cause and induce." A friend is an ear. "Those that want friends to open themselves unto are cannibals of their own hearts. . . . Whoever hath his mind fraught with many thoughts, his wits and understanding do clarify and break up in the communicating and discoursing with another; he tosseth his thoughts more easily; he marshaleth them more orderly; he seeth how they look when they are turned into words; finally, he waxeth wiser than himself; and that more by one hour's discourse than by a day's meditation."[35]

In the essay "Of Youth and Age" he puts a book into a paragraph. "Young men are fitter to invent than to judge, fitter for execution than for counsel, and fitter for new projects than for settled business; for the experience of age in things that fall within the compass of it, directeth them; but in new things abuseth them. . . . Young men, in the conduct and management of actions, embrace more than they can hold, stir more than they can quiet; fly to the end without consideration of the means and degrees; pursue absurdly some few principles which they have chanced upon; care not to" (i.e., how they) "innovate, which draws unknown inconveniences. . . . Men of age object too much, consult too long, adventure too little, repent too soon, and seldom drive business home to the full period, but content themselves with a mediocrity of success. Certainly it is good to compel employments of both, . . . because the virtues of either may correct the defects of both." He thinks, nevertheless, that youth and childhood may get too great liberty, and so grow disordered and lax. "Let parents choose betimes the vocations and courses they mean their children should take, for then they are most flexible; and let them not too much apply themselves to the disposition of their children, as thinking they will take best to that which they have most mind to. It is true that, if the affections or aptness of the children be extraordinary, then it is good not to cross it; but generally the precept" of the Pythagoreans "is good, *Optimum lege, suave et facile illud faciet consuetudo*,"—choose the best; custom will make it pleasant and easy.[36] For "custom is the principal magistrate of man's life."[37]

The politics of the *Essays* preach a conservatism natural in one who aspired to rule. Bacon wants a strong central power. Monarchy is the best form of government; and usually the efficiency of a state varies with the concentration of power. "There be three points of business" in government: "the preparation; the debate or examination; and the perfection" (or execution). "Whereof, if you look for dispatch, let the middle only be the work of many, and the first and last the work of a few."[38] He is an outspoken militarist; he deplores the growth of industry as unfitting men for war, and bewails long peace as lulling the warrior in man. Nevertheless, he recognizes the importance of raw materials: "Solon said well to Crœsus (when in ostentation Crœsus showed him his gold), 'Sir, if any other come that hath better iron than you, he will be master of all this gold."[39]

Like Aristotle, he has some advice on avoiding revolutions. "The surest way to prevent seditions . . . is to take away the matter of them; for if there be fuel prepared, it is hard to tell whence the spark shall come that shall set it on fire. . . . Neither doth it follow that the suppressing of fames" (i.e., discussion) "with too much severity should be a remedy of troubles; for the despising of them many times checks them best, and the going about to stop them but makes a wonder long-lived. . . . The matter of sedition is of two kinds: much poverty and much discontentment. . . . The causes and motives of seditions are, innovation in religion; taxes; alteration of laws and customs; breaking of privileges; general oppression; advancement of unworthy persons, strangers; dearths; disbanded soldiers; factions grown desperate; and whatsoever in offending a people joineth them in a common cause." The cue of every leader, of course, is to divide his enemies and to unite his friends. "Generally, the dividing and breaking of all factions . . . that are adverse to the state, and setting them at a distance, or at least distrust, among themselves, is not one of the worst remedies; for it is a desperate case, if those that hold with the proceeding of the state be full of discord and faction, and those that are against it be entire and united."[40] A better recipe for the avoidance of revolutions is an equitable distribution of wealth: "Money is like muck, not good unless it be spread."[41] But this does not mean socialism, or even democracy; Bacon distrusts the people, who were in his day quite without access to education; "the lowest of all flatteries is the flattery of the common people";[42] and "Phocion took it right, who, being applauded by the multitude, asked, What had he done amiss?"[43] What Bacon wants is first a yeomanry of owning farmers; then an aristocracy for administration; and above all a philosopher-king. "It is almost without instance that any government was unprosperous under learned governors."[44] He mentions Seneca, Antoninus Pius and Aurelius; it was his hope that to their names posterity would add his own.

IV. The Great Reconstruction

Unconsciously, in the midst of his triumphs, his heart was with philosophy. It had been his nurse in youth, it was his companion in office, it was to be his consolation in prison and disgrace. He lamented the ill-repute into which, he thought, philosophy had fallen, and blamed an arid scholasticism. "People are very apt to contemn truth, on account of the controversies raised about it, and to think those all in a wrong way who never meet."[45] "The sciences . . . stand almost at a stay, without receiving any augmentations worthy of the human race; . . . and all the tradition and succession of schools is still a succession of masters and scholars, not of inventors. . . . In what is now done in the matter of science there is only a whirling about, and perpetual agitation, ending where it began."[46] All through the years of his rise and exaltation he brooded over the restoration or reconstruction of philosophy; *"Meditor Instaurationem philosophiae."*[47]

He planned to centre all his studies around this task. First of all, he tells us in his "Plan of the Work," he would write some *Introductory Treatises,* explaining the stagnation of philosophy though the posthumous persistence of old methods, and outlining his proposals for a new beginning. Secondly he would attempt a new *Classification of the Sciences,* allocating their material to them, and listing the unsolved problems in each field. Thirdly, he would describe his new method for the *Interpretation of Nature.* Fourthly, he would try his busy hand at actual natural science, and investigate the *Phenomena of Nature.* Fifthly, he would show the *Ladder of the Intellect,* by which the writers of the past had mounted towards the truths that were now taking form out of the background of medieval verbiage. Sixthly, he would attempt certain *Anticipations* of the scientific results which he was confident would come from the use of his method. And lastly, as *Second* (or *Applied*) *Philosophy,* he would picture the utopia which would flower out of all this budding science of which he hoped to be the prophet. The whole would constitute the *Magna Instauratio,* the Great Reconstruction of Philosophy.[48]

It was a magnificent enterprise, and—except for Aristotle—without precedent in the history of thought. It would differ from every other philosophy in aiming at practice rather than at theory, at specific concrete goods rather than at speculative symmetry. Knowledge is power, not mere argument or ornament; "it is not an opinion to be held . . . but a work to be done; and I . . . am laboring to lay the foundation not of any sect or doctrine, but of utility and power."[49] Here, for the first time, are the voice and tone of modern science.

1. THE ADVANCEMENT OF LEARNING

To produce works, one must have knowledge. "Nature cannot be commanded except by being obeyed."[50] Let us learn the laws of nature, and we shall be her masters, as we are now, in ignorance, her thralls; science is the road to utopia. But in what condition this road is—tortuous, unlit, turning back upon itself, lost in useless by-paths, and leading not to light but to chaos. Let us then begin by making a survey of the state of the sciences, and marking out for them their proper and distinctive fields; let us "seat the sciences each in its proper place";[51] examine their defects, their needs, and their possibilities; indicate the new problems that await their light; and in general "open and stir the earth a little about the roots" of them.[52]

This is the task which Bacon set himself in *The Advancement of Learning.* "It is my intention," he writes, like a king entering his realm, "to make the circuit of knowledge, noticing what parts lie waste and uncultivated, and abandoned by the industry of man; with a view to engage, by a faithful mapping out of the deserted tracts, the energies of public and private persons in their improvement."[53] He would be the royal surveyor of the weed-grown soil, making straight the road, and dividing the fields among the laborers. It was a plan audacious to the edge of immodesty; but Bacon was still young enough (forty-two is young in a philosopher) to plan great voyages. "I have taken all knowledge to be my province," he had written to Burghley in 1592; not meaning that he would make himself a premature edition of the *Encyclopedia Britannica*, but implying merely that his work would bring him into every field, as the critic and coördinator of every science in the task of social reconstruction. The very magnitude of his purpose gives a stately magnificence to his style, and brings him at times to the height of English prose.

So he ranges over the vast battle-ground in which human research struggles with natural hindrance and human ignorance; and in every field he sheds illumination. He attaches great importance to physiology and medicine; he exalts the latter as regulating "a musical instrument of much and exquisite workmanship easily put out of tune."[54] But he objects to the lax empiricism of contemporary doctors, and their facile tendency to treat all ailments with the same prescription—usually physic. "Our physicians are like bishops, that have the keys of binding and loosing, but no more."[55] They rely too much on mere haphazard, uncoördinated individual experience; let them experiment more widely, let them illuminate human with comparative anatomy, let them dissect and if necessary vivisect; and above all, let them construct an easily accessible and intelligible record of experiments and results. Bacon believes that the medical profession should be permitted to ease and quicken death (euthanasy) where the end would be otherwise only delayed for a few days and at the cost of great pain; but he urges the physicians to give more study to the art of prolonging life. "This is a new part" of medicine, "and deficient, though the most noble of all; for if it may be supplied, medicine will not then be wholly versed in sordid cures, nor physicians be honored only for necessity, but as dispensers of the greatest earthly happiness that could well be conferred on mortals."[56] One can hear some sour Schopenhauerian protesting, at this point, against the assumption that longer life would be a boon, and urging, on the contrary, that the speed with which some physicians put an *end* to our illnesses is a consummation devoutly to be praised. But Bacon, worried and married and harassed though he was, never doubted that life was a very fine thing after all.

In psychology he is almost a "behaviorist": he demands a strict study of cause and effect in human action, and wishes to eliminate the word *chance* from the vocabulary of science. "*Chance* is the name of a thing that does not exist."[57] And "what chance is in the universe, so will is in man."[58] Here is a world of meaning, and a challenge of war, all in a little line: the Scholastic doctrine of free will is pushed aside as beneath discussion; and the universal assumption of a "will" distinct from the "intellect" is discarded. These are leads which Bacon does not follow up;[59] it is not the only case in which he puts a book into a phrase and then passes blithely on.

Again in a few words, Bacon invents a new science—social psychology. "Philosophers should diligently inquire into the powers and energy of custom, exercise, habit, education, example, imitation, emulation, company, friendship, praise, reproof, exhortation, reputation, laws, books, studies etc.; for these are the things that reign in men's morals; by these agents the mind is formed and subdued."[60] So closely has this outline been followed by the new science that it reads almost like a table of contents for the works of Tarde, Le Bon, Ross, Wallas, and Durkheim.

Nothing is beneath science, nor above it. Sorceries, dreams, predictions, telepathic communications, "psychical phenomena" in general must be subjected to scientific examination; "for it is not known in what cases, and how far, effects attributed to superstition participate of natural causes."[61] Despite his strong naturalistic bent he feels the fascination of these problems; nothing human is alien to him. Who knows what unsuspected truth, what new science, indeed, may grow out of these investigations, as chemistry budded out from alchemy? "Alchemy may be compared to the man who told his sons he had left them gold buried somewhere in his vineyard; where they, by digging, found no gold, but by turning up the mould about the roots of the vines, procured a plentiful vintage. So the search and endeavors to make gold have brought many useful inventions and instructive experiments to light."[62]

Still another science grows to form in Book VIII: the science of success in life. Not yet having fallen from power, Bacon offers some preliminary hints on how to rise in the world. The first requisite is knowledge: of ourselves and of others. *Gnothe seauton* is but half; know thyself is valuable chiefly as a means of knowing others. We must diligently inform ourselves of the particular persons we have to deal with—their tempers, desires, views, customs, habits; the assistances, helps and assurances whereon they principally rely, and whence they received their power; their defects and weaknesses, whereat they chiefly lie open and are accessible; their friends, factions, patrons, dependants, enemies, enviers, rivals; their times and manners of access. . . . But the surest key for unlocking the minds of others turns upon searching and sifting either their tempers and natures, or their ends and designs; and the more weak and simple are best judged by their temper, but the more prudent and close by their designs. . . . But the shortest way to this whole inquiry rests upon three particulars; viz.—1. In procuring numerous friendships. . . . 2. In observing a prudent mean and moderation between freedom of discourse and silence. . . . But above all, nothing conduces more to the well-representing of a man's self, and securing his own right, than not to disarm one's self by too much sweetness and good-nature, which exposes a man to injuries and reproaches; but rather . . . at times to dart out some sparks of a free and generous mind, that have no less of the sting than the honey.[63]

Friends are for Bacon chiefly a means to power; he shares with Machiavelli a point of view which one is at first inclined to attribute to the Renaissance, till one thinks of the fine and uncalculating friendships of Michelangelo and Cavalieri, Montaigne and La Boetie, Sir Philip Sidney and Hubert Languet.[64] Perhaps this very practical assessment of friendship helps to explain Bacon's fall from power, as similar views help to explain Napoleon's; for a man's friends will seldom practice a higher philosophy in their relations with him than that which he professes in his treatment of them. Bacon goes on to quote Bias, one of the Seven Wise Men of ancient Greece: "Love your friend as if he were to become your enemy, and your enemy as if he were to become your friend."[65] Do not betray even to your friend too much of your real purposes and thoughts; in conversation, ask questions oftener than you express opinions; and when you speak, offer data and information rather than beliefs and judgments.[66] Manifest pride is a help to advancement; and "ostentation is a fault in ethics rather than in politics."[67] Here again one is reminded of Napoleon; Bacon, like the little Corsican, was a simple man enough within his walls, but outside them he affected a ceremony and display which he thought indispensable to public repute.

So Bacon runs from field to field, pouring the seed of his thought into every science. At the end of his survey he comes to the conclusion that science by itself is not enough: there must be a force and discipline outside the sciences to coördinate them and point them to a goal. "There is another great and powerful cause why the sciences have made but little progress, which is this. It is not possible to run a course aright when the goal itself has not been rightly placed."[68] What science needs is philosophy—the analysis of scientific method, and the coördination of scientific purposes and results; without this, any science must be superficial. "For as no perfect view of a country can be taken from a flat; so it is impossible to discover the remote and deep parts of any science by standing upon the level of the same science, or without ascending to a higher."[69] He condemns the habit of looking at isolated facts out of their context, without considering the unity of nature; as if, he says, one should carry a small candle about the corners of a room radiant with a central light.

Philosophy, rather than science, is in the long run Bacon's love; it is only philosophy which can give even to a life of turmoil and grief the stately peace that comes of understanding. "Learning conquers or mitigates the fear of death and adverse fortune." He quotes Virgil's great lines:

> Felix qui potuit rerum cognoscere causas,
> Quique metus omnes, et inexorabile fatum,
> Subjecit pedibus, strepitumque Acherontis avari—

"happy the man who has learned the causes of things, and has put under his feet all fears, and inexorable fate, and the noisy strife of the hell of greed." It is perhaps the best fruit of philosophy that through it we unlearn the lesson of endless acquisition which an industrial environment so insistently repeats. "Philosophy directs us first to seek the goods of the mind, and the rest will either be supplied, or not much wanted."[70] A bit of wisdom is a joy forever.

Government suffers, precisely like science, for lack of philosophy. Philosophy bears to science the same relationship which statesmanship bears to politics: movement guided by total knowledge and perspective, as against aimless and individual seeking. Just as the pursuit of knowledge becomes scholasticism when divorced from the actual needs of men and life, so the pursuit of politics becomes a destructive bedlam when divorced from science and philosophy. "It is wrong to trust the natural body to empirics, who commonly have a few receipts whereon they rely, but who know neither the cause of the disease, nor the constitution of patients, nor the danger of accidents, nor the true methods of cure. And so it must needs be dangerous to have the civil body of states managed by empirical statesmen, unless well mixed with others who are grounded in learning. . . . Though he might be thought partial to his profession who said, 'States would then be happy, when either kings were philosophers or philosophers kings,' yet so much is verified by experience, that the best times have happened under wise and learned princes."[71] And he reminds us of the great emperors who ruled Rome after Domitian and before Commodus.

So Bacon, like Plato and us all, exalted his hobby, and offered it as the salvation of man. But he recognized, much more clearly than Plato (and the distinction announces the modern age), the necessity of specialist science, and of soldiers and armies of specialist research. No one mind, not even Bacon's, could cover the whole field, though he should look from Olympus' top itself. He knew he needed help, and keenly felt his loneliness in the mountain-air of his unaided enterprise. "What comrades have you in your work?" he asks a friend. "As for me, I am in the completest solitude."[72] He dreams of scientists coördinated in specialization by constant communion and coöperation, and by some great organization holding them together to a goal. "Consider what may be expected from men abounding in leisure, and from association of labors, and from successions of ages; the rather because it is not a way over which only one man can pass at a time (as is the case with that of reasoning), but within which the labors and industries of men (especially as regards the collecting of experience) may with the best effort be collected and distributed, and then combined. For then only will men begin to know their strength when, instead of great numbers doing all the same things, one shall take charge of one thing, and another of another."[73] Science, which is the organization of knowledge, must itself be organized.

And this organization must be international; let it pass freely over the frontiers, and it may make Europe intellectually one. "The next want I discover is the little sympathy and correspondence which exists between colleges and universities, as well throughout Europe as in the same state and kingdom."[74] Let all these universities allot subjects and problems among themselves, and coöperate both in research and in publication. So organized and correlated, the universities might be deemed worthy of such royal support as would make them what they shall be in Utopia—centers of impartial learning ruling the world. Bacon notes "the mean salaries apportioned to public lectureships, whether in the sciences or the arts";[75] and he feels that this will continue till governments take over the great tasks of education. "The wisdom of the ancientest and best times always complained that states were too busy with laws, and too remiss in point of education."[76] His great dream is the socialization of science for the conquest of nature and the enlargement of the power of man.

And so he appeals to James I, showering upon him the flattery which he knew his Royal Highness loved to sip. James was a scholar as well as a monarch, prouder of his pen than of his sceptre or his sword; something might be expected of so literary and erudite a king. Bacon tells James that the plans he has sketched are "indeed *opera basilica*,"—kingly tasks—"towards which the endeavors of one man can be but as an image on a cross-road, which points out the way but cannot tread it." Certainly these royal undertakings will involve expense; but "as the secretaries and spies of princes and states bring in bills for intelligence, so you must allow the spies and intelligencers of nature to bring in their bills if you would not be ignorant of many things worthy to be known. And if Alexander placed so large a treasure at Aristotle's command for the support of hunters, fowlers, fishers, and the like, in much more need do they stand of this beneficence who unfold the labyrinths of nature."[77] With such royal aid the Great Reconstruction can be completed in a few years; without it the task will require generations.

What is refreshingly new in Bacon is the magnificent assurance with which he predicts the conquest of nature by man: "I stake all on the victory of art over nature in the race." That which men have done is "but an earnest of the things they shall do." But why this great hope? Had not men been seeking truth, and exploring the paths of science, these two thousand years? Why should one hope now for such great success where so long a time had given so modest a result?— Yes, Bacon answers; but what if the methods men have used have been wrong and useless? What if the road has been lost, and research has gone into by-paths ending in the air? We need a ruthless revolution in our methods of research and thought, in our system of science and logic; we need a new Organon, better than Aristotle's, fit for this larger world.

And so Bacon offers us his supreme book.

2. THE NEW ORGANON

"Bacon's greatest performance," says his bitterest critic, "is the first book of the *Novum Organum*."[78] Never did a man put more life into logic, making induction an epic adventure and a conquest. If one must study logic, let him begin with this book. "This part of human philosophy which regards logic is disagreeable to the taste of many, as appearing to them no other than a net, and a snare of thorny subtlety. . . . But if we would rate things according to their real worth, the rational sciences are the keys to all the rest."[79]

Philosophy has been barren so long, says Bacon, because she needed a new method to make her fertile. The great mistake of the Greek philosophers was that they spent so much time in theory, so little in observation. But thought should be the aide of observation, not its substitute. "Man," says the first aphorism of the *Novum Organum,* as if flinging a challenge to all metaphysics—"Man, as the minister and interpreter of nature, does and understands as much as his observations on the order of nature . . . permit him; and neither knows nor is capable of more." The predecessors of Socrates were in this matter sounder than his followers; Democritus, in particular, had a nose for facts, rather than an eye for the clouds. No wonder that philosophy has advanced so little since Aristotle's day; it has been using Aristotle's methods. "To go beyond Aristotle by the light of Aristotle is to think that a borrowed light can increase the original light from which it is taken."[80] Now, after two thousand years of logic-chopping with the machinery invented by Aristotle, philosophy has fallen so low that none will do her reverence. All these medieval theories, theorems and disputations must be cast out and forgotten; to renew herself philosophy must begin again with a clean slate and a cleansed mind.

The first step, therefore, is the Expurgation of the Intellect. We must become as little children, innocent of isms and abstractions, washed clear of prejudices and preconceptions. We must destroy the Idols of the mind.

An idol, as Bacon uses the word (reflecting perhaps the Protestant rejection of image-worship), is a picture taken for a reality, a thought mistaken for a thing. Errors come under this head; and the first problem of logic is to trace and dam the sources of these errors. Bacon proceeds now to a justly famous analysis of fallacies; "no man," said Condillac, "has better known than Bacon the causes of human error."

These errors are, first, *Idols of the Tribe*—fallacies natural to humanity in general. "For man's sense is falsely asserted" (by Protagoras' "Man is the measure of all things") "to be the standard of things: on the contrary, all the perceptions, both of the senses and the mind, bear reference to man and not to the universe; and the human mind resembles those uneven mirrors which impart their own properties to different objects . . . and distort and disfigure them."[81] Our thoughts are pictures rather of ourselves than of their objects. For example, "the human understanding, from its peculiar nature, easily supposes a greater degree of order and regularity in things than it really finds. . . . Hence the fiction that all celestial bodies move in perfect circles."[82] Again,

> the human understanding, when any proposition has been once laid down (either from general admission and belief, or from the pleasure it affords), forces everything else to add fresh support and confirmation: and although most cogent and abundant instances may exist to the contrary, yet either does not observe, or despises them, or it gets rid of and rejects them by some distinction, with violent and injurious prejudice, rather than sacrifice the authority of its first conclusions. It was well answered by him who was shown in a temple the votive tablets suspended by such as had escaped the peril of shipwreck, and was pressed as to whether he would then recognize the power of the gods. . . . "But where are the portraits of those that have perished in spite of their vows?" All superstition is much the same, whether it be that of astrology, dreams, omens, retributive judgment, or the like, in all of which the deluded believers observe events which are fulfilled, but neglect and pass over their failure, though it be much more common.[83]

"Having first determined the question according to his will, man *then* resorts to experience; and bending her into conformity with his placets, leads her about like a captive in a procession."[84] In short, "the human understanding is no dry light, but receives an infusion from the will and affections, whence proceed sciences which may be called 'sciences as one would.' . . . For what a man had rather were true, he more readily believes."[85] Is it not so?

Bacon gives at this point a word of golden counsel. "In general let every student of nature take this as a rule—that whatever his mind seizes and dwells upon with peculiar satisfaction, is to be held in suspicion; and that so much the more care is to be taken, in dealing with such questions, to keep the understanding even and clear."[86] "The understanding must not be allowed to jump

and fly from particulars to remote axioms and of almost the highest general-
ity; . . . it must not be supplied with wings, but rather hung with weights to
keep it from leaping and flying."[87] The imagination may be the greatest enemy
of the intellect, whereas it should be only its tentative and experiment.

A second class of errors Bacon calls *Idols of the Cave*—errors peculiar to the
individual man. "For every one . . . has a cave or den of his own, which refracts
and discolors the light of nature"; this is his character as formed by nature
and nurture, and by his mood or condition of body and mind. Some minds,
e.g., are constitutionally analytic, and see differences everywhere; others are
constitutionally synthetic, and see resemblances; so we have the scientist and
the painter on the one hand, and on the other hand the poet and the philosopher. Again, "some dispositions evince an unbounded admiration for antiquity,
others eagerly embrace novelty; only a few can preserve the just medium, and
neither tear up what the ancients have correctly established, nor despise the just
innovations of the moderns."[88] Truth knows no parties.

Thirdly, *Idols of the Market-place,* arising "from the commerce and association of men with one another. For men converse by means of language; but
words are imposed according to the understanding of the crowd; and there
arises from a bad and inapt formation of words, a wonderful obstruction to the
mind."[89] Philosophers deal out infinites with the careless assurance of gram-
marians handling infinitives; and yet does any man know what this "infinite"
is, or whether it has even taken the precaution of existing? Philosophers talk
about "first cause uncaused," or "first mover unmoved"; but are not these again
fig-leaf phrases used to cover naked ignorance, and perhaps indicative of a
guilty conscience in the user? Every clear and honest head knows that no cause
can be causeless, nor any mover unmoved. Perhaps the greatest reconstruction
in philosophy would be simply this—that we should stop lying.

"Lastly, there are idols which have migrated into men's minds from the
various dogmas of philosophers, and also from wrong laws of demonstration.
These I call *Idols of the Theatre,* because in my judgment all the received systems
of philosophy are but so many stage-plays, representing worlds of their own
creation after an unreal and scenic fashion. . . . And in the plays of this philosophic theater you may observe the same thing which is found in the theater
of the poets—that stories invented for the stage are more compact and elegant,
and more as we would wish them to be, than true stories out of history."[90] The

world as Plato describes it is merely a world constructed by Plato, and pictures Plato rather than the world.

We shall never get far along towards the truth if these idols are still to trip us up, even the best of us, at every turn. We need new modes of reasoning, new tools for the understanding. "And as the immense regions of the West Indies had never been discovered, if the use of the compass had not first been known, it is no wonder that the discovery and advancement of arts hath made no greater progress, when the art of inventing and discovering of the sciences remains hitherto unknown."[91] "And surely it would be disgraceful, if, while the regions of the material globe . . . have been in our times laid widely open and revealed, the intellectual globe should remain shut up within the narrow limits of old discoveries."[92]

Ultimately, our troubles are due to dogma and deduction; we find no new truth because we take some venerable but questionable proposition as an indubitable starting-point, and never think of putting this assumption itself to the test of observation or experiment. Now "if a man will begin with certainties, he shall end in doubts; but if he will be content to begin in doubts he shall end in certainties" (alas, it is not quite inevitable). Here is a note common in the youth of modern philosophy, part of its declaration of independence; Descartes too would presently talk of the necessity of "methodic doubt" as the cobweb-clearing pre-requisite of honest thought.

Bacon proceeds to give an admirable description of the scientific method of inquiry. "There remains *simple experience; which,* if taken as it comes, is called accident" ("empirical"), "if sought for, experiment. . . . The true method of experience first lights the candle" (hypothesis), "and then by means of the candle shows the way" (arranges and delimits the experiment); "commencing as it does with experience duly ordered and digested, not bungling nor erratic, and from it educing axioms, and from established axioms again new experiments."[93] (We have here—as again in a later passage[94] which speaks of the results of initial experiments as a "first vintage" to guide further research—an explicit, though perhaps inadequate, recognition of that need for hypothesis, experiment and deduction which some of Bacon's critics suppose him to have entirely overlooked.) We must go to nature instead of to books, traditions and authorities; we must "put nature on the rack and compel her to bear witness" even against herself, so that we may control her to our ends. We must gather together from every quarter a "natural history" of the world, built by the united research of Europe's scientists. We must have induction.

But induction does not mean "simple enumeration" of all the data; conceivably, this might be endless, and useless; no mass of material can by itself make science. This would be like "chasing a quarry over an open country"; we must narrow and enclose our field in order to capture our prey. The method of induction must include a technique for the classification of data and the elimination of hypotheses; so that by the progressive canceling of possible explanations one only shall at last remain. Perhaps the most useful item in this technique is the "table of more or less," which lists instances in which two qualities or conditions increase or decrease together, and so reveals, presumably, a causal relation between the simultaneously varying phenomena. So Bacon, asking, What is heat?—seeks for some factor that increases with the increase of heat, and decreases with its decrease; he finds, after long analysis, an exact correlation between heat and motion; and his conclusion that heat is a form of motion constitutes one of his few specific contributions to natural science.

By this insistent accumulation and analysis of data we come, in Bacon's phrase, to the *form* of the phenomenon which we study—to its secret nature and its inner essence. The theory of forms in Bacon is very much like the theory of ideas in Plato: a metaphysics of science. "When we speak of forms we mean nothing else than those laws and regulations of simple action which arrange and constitute any simple nature. . . . The form of heat or the form of light, therefore, means no more than the law of heat or the law of light."[95] (In a similar strain Spinoza was to say that the law of the circle is its *substance*.) "For although nothing exists in nature except individual bodies exhibiting clear individual effects according to particular laws; yet, in each branch of learning, those very laws—their investigation, discovery and development—are the foundation both of theory and of practice."[96] Of theory and of practice; one without the other is useless and perilous; knowledge that does not generate achievement is a pale and bloodless thing, unworthy of mankind. We strive to learn the forms of things not for the sake of the forms but because by knowing the forms, the laws, we may remake things in the image of our desire. So we study mathematics in order to reckon quantities and build bridges; we study psychology in order to find our way in the jungle of society. When science has sufficiently ferreted out the forms of things, the world will be merely the raw material of whatever utopia man may decide to make.

3. THE UTOPIA OF SCIENCE

To perfect science so, and then to perfect social order by putting science in control, would itself be utopia enough. Such is the world described for us in Bacon's brief fragment and last work, *The New Atlantis,* published two years before his death. Wells thinks it Bacon's "greatest service to science"[97] to have drawn for us, even so sketchily, the picture of a society in which at last science has its proper place as the master of things; it was a royal act of imagination by which for three centuries one goal has been held in view by the great army of warriors in the battle of knowledge and invention against ignorance and poverty. Here in these few pages we have the essence and the "form" of Francis Bacon, the law of his being and his life, the secret and continuous aspiration of his soul.

Plato in the *Timaeus*[98] had told of the old legend of Atlantis, the sunken continent in the Western seas. Bacon and others identified the new America of Columbus and Cabot with this old Atlantis; the great continent had not sunk after all, but only men's courage to navigate the sea. Since this old Atlantis was now known, and seemed inhabited by a race vigorous enough, but not quite like the brilliant Utopians of Bacon's fancy, he conceived of a new Atlantis, an isle in that distant Pacific which only Drake and Magellan had traversed, an isle distant enough from Europe and from knowledge to give generous scope to the Utopian imagination.

The story begins in the most artfully artless way, like the great tales of Defoe and Swift. "We sailed from Peru (where we had continued for the space of one whole year), for China and Japan by the South Sea." Came a great calm, in which the ships for weeks lay quietly on the boundless ocean like specks upon a mirror, while the provisions of the adventurers ebbed away. And then resistless winds drove the vessels pitilessly north and north and north, out of the island-dotted south into an endless wilderness of sea. The rations were reduced, and reduced again, and again reduced; and disease took hold of the crew. At last, when they had resigned themselves to death, they saw, almost unbelieving, a fair island looming up under the sky. On the shore, as their vessel neared it, they saw not savages, but men simply and yet beautifully clothed, clean, and manifestly of developed intelligence. They were permitted to land, but were told that the island government allowed no strangers to remain. Nevertheless, since some of the crew were sick, they might all stay till these were well again.

During the weeks of convalescence the wanderers unraveled, day by day, the mystery of the New Atlantis. "There reigned in this island about nineteen hundred years ago," one of the inhabitants tells them, "a King whose memory above all others we most adore. . . . His name was Solamona, and we esteem him as the Law-giver of our nation. This King had a large heart . . . and was wholly bent to make his kingdom and people happy."[99] "Among the excellent acts of that King one above all hath the preëminence. It was the creation and institution of the Order, or Society, which is called Solomon's House; the noblest foundation, as we think, that was ever upon the earth; and the lantherne of this kingdom."[100]

There follows a description of Solomon's House, too complicated for a quoted abstract, but eloquent enough to draw from the hostile Macaulay the judgment that "there is not to be found in any human composition a passage more eminently distinguished by profound and serene wisdom."[101] Solomon's House takes the place, in the New Atlantis, of the Houses of Parliament in London; it is the home of the island government. But there are no politicians there, no insolent "elected persons," no "national palaver," as Carlyle would say; no parties, caucuses, primaries, conventions, campaigns, buttons, lithographs, editorials, speeches, lies, and elections; the idea of filling public office by such dramatic methods seems never to have entered the heads of these Atlantans. But the road to the heights of scientific repute is open to all, and only those who have traveled the road sit in the councils of the state. It is a government of the people and for the people by the selected best of the people; a government by technicians, architects, astronomers, geologists, biologists, physicians, chemists, economists, sociologists, psychologists and philosophers. Complicated enough; but think of a government without politicians!

Indeed there is little government at all in the New Atlantis; these governors are engaged rather in controlling nature than in ruling man. "The End of Our Foundation is the Knowledge of Causes and secret motions of things; and the enlarging of the bounds of human empire, to the effecting of all things possible."[102] This is the key-sentence of the book, and of Francis Bacon. We find the governors engaged in such undignified tasks as studying the stars, arranging to utilize for industry the power of falling water, developing gases for the cure of various ailments,[103] experimenting on animals for surgical knowledge, growing new varieties of plants and animals by cross-breeding, etc. "We imitate the flights of birds; we have some degree of flying in the air. We have ships and boats for going under water." There is foreign trade, but of an unusual sort; the island produces what it consumes, and consumes what it produces; it does not go to war for foreign markets. "We maintain a trade, not of gold, silver, or jewels, nor for silks, nor for spices, nor for any other commodity or matter; but only for God's first creature, which was light; to have light of the growth of all parts of the world."[104] These "Merchants of Light" are members of Solomon's House who are sent abroad every twelve years to live among foreign peoples of every quarter of the civilized globe; to learn their language and study their sciences and industries and literatures; and to return, at the end of the twelve years, to report their findings to the leaders of Solomon's House; while their places abroad are taken by a new group of scientific explorers. In this way the best of all the world comes soon to the New Atlantis.

Brief as the picture is, we see in it again the outline of every philosopher's utopia—a people guided in peace and modest plenty by their wisest men. The dream of every thinker is to replace the politician by the scientist; why does it remain only a dream after so many incarnations? Is it because the thinker is too dreamily intellectual to go out into the arena of affairs and build his concept into reality? Is it because the hard ambition of the narrowly acquisitive soul is forever destined to overcome the gentle and scrupulous aspirations of philosophers and saints? Or is it that science is not yet grown to maturity and conscious power?—that only in our day do physicists and chemists and technicians begin to see that the rising rôle of science in industry and war gives them a pivotal position in social strategy, and points to the time when their organized strength will persuade the world to call them to leadership? Perhaps science has not yet merited the mastery of the world; and perhaps in a little while it will.

V. Criticism

And now how shall we appraise this philosophy of Francis Bacon's?

Is there anything new in it? Macaulay thinks that induction as described by Bacon is a very old-fashioned affair, over which there is no need of raising any commotion, much less a monument. "Induction has been practiced from morning till night by every human being since the world began. The man who infers that mince pies disagreed with him because he was ill when he ate them, well when he ate them not, most ill when he ate most and least ill when he ate least, has employed, unconsciously but sufficiently, all the tables of the *Novum Organum*."[105] But John Smith hardly handles his "table of more or less" so accurately, and more probably will continue his mince-pies despite the seismic disturbances of his lower strata. And even were John Smith so wise, it would not shear Bacon of his merit; for what does logic do but formulate the experience and methods of the wise?—what does any discipline do but try by rules to turn the art of a few into a science teachable to all?

But is the formulation Bacon's own? Is not the Socratic method inductive? Is not Aristotle's biology inductive? Did not Roger Bacon practise as well as preach the inductive method which Francis Bacon merely preached? Did not Galileo formulate better the procedure that science has actually used? True of Roger Bacon, less true of Galileo, less true yet of Aristotle, least true of Socrates. Galileo outlined the aim rather than the method of science, holding up before its followers the goal of mathematical and quantitative formulation of all experience and relationships; Aristotle practised induction when there was nothing else for him to do, and where the material did not lend itself to his penchant for the deduction of specific conclusions from magnificently general assumptions; and Socrates did not so much practise induction—the gathering of data—as analysis—the definition and discrimination of words and ideas.

Bacon makes no claim to parthenogenetic originality; like Shakespeare he takes with a lordly hand, and with the same excuse, that he adorns whatever he touches. Every man has his sources, as every organism has its food; what is his is the way in which he digests them and turns them into flesh and blood. As Rawley puts it, Bacon "contemned no man's observations, but would light his torch at every man's candle."[106] But Bacon acknowledges these debts: he refers to "that useful method of Hippocrates,"[107]—so sending us at once to the real source of inductive logic among the Greeks; and "Plato," he writes (where less accurately we write "Socrates"), "giveth good example of inquiry by induction and view of particulars; though in such a wandering manner as is of no force or fruit."[108] He would have disdained to dispute his obligations to these predecessors; and we should disdain to exaggerate them.

But then again, is the Baconian method correct? Is it the method most fruitfully used in modern science? No: generally, science has used, with best result, not the accumulation of data ("natural history") and their manipulation by the complicated tables of the *Novum Organum,* but the simpler method of hypothesis, deduction and experiment. So Darwin, reading Malthus' *Essay on Population*, conceived the idea of applying to all organisms the Malthusian hypothesis that population tends to increase faster than the means of subsistence; deduced from this hypothesis the probable conclusion that the pressure of population on the food-supply results in a struggle for existence in which the fittest survive, and by which in each generation every species is changed into closer adaptation to its environment; and finally (having by hypothesis and deduction limited his problem and his field of observation) turned to "the unwithered face of nature" and made for twenty years a patient inductive examination of the facts. Again, Einstein conceived, or took from Newton, the hypothesis that light travels in curved, not straight lines; deduced from it the conclusion that a star appearing to be (on the straight-line theory) in a certain position in the heavens is really a little to one side of that position; and he invited experiment and observation to test the conclusion. Obviously the function of hypothesis and imagination is greater than Bacon supposed; and the procedure of science is more direct and circumscribed than in the Baconian scheme. Bacon himself anticipated the superannuation of his method; the actual practice of science would discover better modes of investigation than could be worked out in the interludes of statesmanship. "These things require some ages for the ripening of them."

Even a lover of the Baconian spirit must concede, too, that the great Chancellor, while laying down the law for science, failed to keep abreast of the science of his time. He rejected Copernicus and ignored Kepler and Tycho Brahe; he depreciated Gilbert and seemed unaware of Harvey. In truth, he loved discourse better than research; or perhaps he had no time for toilsome investigations. Such work as he did in philosophy and science was left in fragments and chaos at his death; full of repetitions, contradictions, aspirations, and introductions. *Ars longa, vita brevis*—art is long and time is fleeting: this is the tragedy of every great soul.

To assign to so overworked a man, whose reconstruction of philosophy had to be crowded into the crevices of a harassed and a burdened political career, the vast and complicated creations of Shakespeare, is to waste the time of students with the parlor controversies of idle theorists. Shakespeare lacks just that which distinguishes the lordly Chancellor—erudition and philosophy. Shakespeare has an impressive smattering of many sciences, and a mastery of none; in all of them he speaks with the eloquence of an amateur. He accepts astrology: "This huge state . . . whereon the stars in secret influence comment."[109] He is forever making mistakes which the learned Bacon could not possibly have made: his Hector quotes Aristotle and his Coriolanus alludes to Cato; he supposes the Lupercalia to be a hill; and he understands Cæsar about as profoundly as Cæsar is understood by H. G. Wells. He makes countless references to his early life and his matrimonial tribulations. He perpetrates vulgarities, obscenities and puns natural enough in the gentle roisterer who could not quite outlive the Stratford rioter and the butcher's son, but hardly to be expected in the cold and calm philosopher. Carlyle calls Shakespeare the greatest of intellects; but he was rather the greatest of imaginations, and the keenest eye. He is an inescapable psychologist, but he is not a philosopher: he has no structure of thought unified by a purpose for his own life and for mankind. He is immersed in love and its problems, and thinks of philosophy, through Montaigne's phrases, only when his heart is broken. Otherwise he accepts the world blithely enough; he is not consumed with the reconstructive vision that ennobled Plato, or Nietzsche, or Bacon.

Now the greatness and the weakness of Bacon lay precisely in his passion for unity, his deside to spread the wings of his coördinating genius over a hundred sciences. He aspired to be like Plato, "a man of sublime genius, who took a view of everything as from a lofty rock." He broke down under the weight of the tasks he had laid upon himself; he failed forgivably because he undertook so much. He could not enter the promised land of science, but as Cowley's epitaph expressed it, he could at least stand upon its border and point out its fair features in the distance.

His achievement was not the less great because it was indirect. His philosophical works, though little read now, "moved the intellects which moved the world."[110] He made himself the eloquent voice of the optimism and resolution of the Renaissance. Never was any man so great a stimulus to other thinkers. King James, it is true, refused to accept his suggestion for the support of science, and said of the *Novum Organum* that "it was like the peace of God, which passeth all understanding." But better men, in 1662, founding that Royal Society which was to become the greatest association of scientists in the world, named Bacon as their model and inspiration; they hoped that this organization of English research would lead the way toward that Europe-wide association which the *Advancement of Learning* had taught them to desire. And when the great minds of the French Enlightenment undertook that masterpiece of intellectual enterprise, the *Encylopédie*, they dedicated it to Francis Bacon. "If," said Diderot in the Prospectus, "we have come of it successfully, we shall owe most to the Chancellor Bacon, who threw out the plan of an universal dictionary of sciences and arts, at a time when, so to say, neither arts nor sciences existed. That extraordinary genius, when it was impossible to write a history of what was known, wrote one of what it was necessary to learn." D'Alembert called

Bacon "the greatest, the most universal, and the most eloquent of philosophers." The Convention published the works of Bacon at the expense of the state.[111] The whole tenor and career of British thought have followed the philosophy of Bacon. His tendency to conceive the world in Democritean mechanical terms gave to his secretary, Hobbes, the starting-point for a thorough-going materialism; his inductive method gave to Locke the idea of an empirical psychology, bound by observation and freed from theology and metaphysics; and his emphasis on "commodities" and "fruits" found formulation in Bentham's identification of the useful and the good.

Wherever the spirit of control has overcome the spirit of resignation, Bacon's influence has been felt. He is the voice of all those Europeans who have changed a continent from a forest into a treasure-land of art and science, and have made their little peninsula the center of the world. "Men are not animals erect," said Bacon, "but immortal gods." "The Creator has given us souls equal to all the world, and yet satiable not even with a world." Everything is possible to man. Time is young; give us some little centuries, and we shall control and remake all things. We shall perhaps at last learn the noblest lesson of all, that man must not fight man, but must make war only on the obstacles that nature offers to the triumph of man. "It will not be amiss," writes Bacon, in one of his finest passages, "to distinguish the three kinds, and as it were grades, of ambition in mankind. The first is of those who desire to extend their power in their native country; which kind is vulgar and degenerate. The second is of those who labor to extend the power of their country and its dominion among men; this certainly has more dignity, but not less covetousness. But if a man endeavor to establish and extend the power and dominion of the human race itself over the universe, his ambition is without doubt both a more wholesome thing and a nobler than the other two."[112] It was Bacon's fate to be torn to pieces by these hostile ambitions struggling for his soul.

VI. Epilogue

"Men in great place are thrice servants; servants to the sovereign or state, servants of fame, and servants of business, so as they have no freedom, neither in their persons nor in their action, nor in their time. . . . The rising unto place is laborious, and by pains men come to greater pains; and it is sometimes base, and by indignities men come to dignities. The standing is slippery, and the regress is either a downfall or at least an eclipse."[113] What a wistful summary of Bacon's epilogue!

"A man's shortcomings," said Goethe, "are taken from his epoch; his virtues and greatness belong to himself." This seems a little unfair to the *Zeitgeist*, but it is exceptionally just in the case of Bacon. Abbott,[114] after a painstaking study of the morals prevalent at Elizabeth's court, concludes that all the leading figures, male and female, were disciples of Machiavelli. Roger Ascham described in doggerel the four cardinal virtues in demand at the court of the Queen:

> Cog, lie, flatter and face,
> Four ways in Court to win men grace.
> If thou be thrall to none of these,
> Away, good Piers! Home, John Cheese!

It was one of the customs of those lively days for judges to take "presents" from persons trying cases in their courts. Bacon was not above the age in this matter; and his tendency to keep his expenditure several years in advance of his income forbade him the luxury of scruples. It might have passed unnoticed, except that he had made enemies in Essex' case, and by his readiness to sabre foes with his speech. A friend had warned him that "it is too common in every man's mouth in Court that . . . as your tongue hath been a razor to some, so shall theirs be to you."[115] But he left the warnings unnoticed. He seemed to be in good favor with the King; he had been made Baron Verulam of Verulam in 1618, and Viscount St. Albans in 1621; and for three years he had been Chancellor.

Then suddenly the blow came. In 1621 a disappointed suitor charged him with taking money for the despatch of a suit; it was no unusual matter, but Bacon knew at once that if his enemies wished to press it they could force his fall. He retired to his home, and waited developments. When he learned that all his foes were clamoring for his dismissal, he sent in his "confession and humble submission" to the King. James, yielding to pressure from the now victorious Parliament against which Bacon had too persistently defended him, sent him to the Tower. But Bacon was released after two days; and the heavy fine which had been laid upon him was remitted by the King. His pride was not quite broken. "I was the justest judge that was in England these fifty years," he said; "but it was the justest judgment that was in Parliament these two hundred years."

He spent the five years that remained to him in the obscurity and peace of his home, harassed by an unwonted poverty, but solaced by the active pursuit of philosophy. In these five years he wrote his greatest Latin work, *De Augmentis Scientiarum,* published an enlarged edition of the Essays, a fragment called *Sylva Sylvarum*, and a *History of Henry VII*. He mourned that he had not sooner abandoned politics and given all his time to literature and science. To the very last moment he was occupied with work, and died, so to speak, on the field of battle. In his essay "Of Death" he had voiced a wish to die "in an earnest pursuit, which is like one wounded in hot blood, who for the time scarce feels the hurt." Like Cæsar, he was granted his choice.

In March, 1626, while riding from London to Highgate, and turning over in his mind the question how far flesh might be preserved from putrefaction by being covered with snow, he resolved to put the matter to a test at once. Stopping off at a cottage, he bought a fowl, killed it, and stuffed it with snow. While he was doing this he was seized with chills and weakness; and finding himself too ill to ride back to town, he gave directions that he should be taken to the nearby home of Lord Arundel, where he took to bed. He did not yet resign life; he wrote cheerfully that "the experiment . . . succeeded excellently well." But it was his last. The fitful fever of his varied life had quite consumed him; he was all burnt out now, too weak to fight the disease that crept up slowly to his heart. He died on the ninth of April, 1626, at the age of sixty-five.

He had written in his will these proud and characteristic words: "I bequeath my soul to God. . . . My body to be buried obscurely. My name to the next ages and to foreign nations." The ages and the nations have accepted him.

ENDNOTES

CHAPTER I

1. Froude, *Reign of Elizabeth*, I, 11.
2. Neale, *Queen Elizabeth*, 26.
3. Ibid., 37.
4. Froude, I, Introd., vii.
5. Read, C., *Mr. Secretary Cecil and Queen Elizabeth*, 32.
6. Ibid., 119.
7. Hughes, P., *The Reformation in England*, III, 46.
8. Froude, *Elizabeth*, III, 306.
9. Froude, I, 448.
10. Barnes, H. E., *Economic History of the Western World*, 205.
11. Hallam, *Constitutional History of England*, I, 245.
12. Lingard, J., *History of England*, VI, 324.
13. Christopher Hatton in *Shakespeare's England*, I, 80.
14. Neale, 61.
15. Ibid., 75-6.
16. *Shakespeare's England*, I, 5.
17. Neale, 386.
18. Froude, I, 120.
19. *Cambridge Modern History*, III, 289.
20. Froude, IV, 62.
21. Thornton, *Table Talk from Ben Jonson to Leigh Hunt*, 9.
22. Hallam, I, 133.
23. Neale, 80.
24. Read, 363.
25. Froude, II, 84.
26. *Camb. Mod. History*, II, 582.
27. Froude, I, 300.
28. Ibid., 103.
29. Ibid., 491.
30. Creighton, *Queen Elizabeth*, 254.
31. Church, R. W., *Spenser*, 116.
32. Lingard, VI, 321.
33. Aubrey, *Brief Lives*, 305.
34. Chute, *Shakespeare of London*, 145.
35. Bacon, Fr., *Philosophical Works*, 869; Apophthegm 55.
36. Froude, V, 206.
37. Sir John Hayward in Muir, K., *Elizabethan and Jacobean Prose*, 1.
38. Chute, *Ben Jonson*, 164.
39. Froude, I, 8, 14.
40. Ibid. and 145; II, 338; Allen, J. W., *History of Political Thought in the Sixteenth Century*, 199-200.
41. Ascham, *The Scholemaster*, 81.
42. Froude, III, 4.
43. Taine, *English Literature*, 160.
44. Smith, Preserved, *The Age of the Reformation*, 634.
45. Robertson, J. M., *Short History of Freethought*, II, 5, 6.
46. Bradbrook, *The School of Night*, 7; Boas, *Marlowe and His Circle*, 90; and the ed. of *Love's Labour's Lost* by A. T. Quiller Couch and J. Dover Wilson, London, 1923.
47. Bradbrook, 39.
48. Ibid., 12.
49. Robertson, *Freethought*, II, 10.
50. Green, J. R., *Short History of the English People*, ch. vii, sect. 3.
51. Froude, I, 183; IV, 65; V, 228.
52. Ibid., IV, 385-6.
53. *Camb. Mod. History*, II, 562.
54. Chute, *Ben Jonson*, 79.

55. Roeder, *Catherine de' Medici*, 492.

56. Froude, IV, 119; Neale, 215.

57. Payne, E. A., *The Anabaptists of the 16th Century*, 19; Lingard, VI, 170.

58. Pastor, *History of the Popes*, XVI, 250.

59. McCabe, *Candid History of the Jesuits*, 150.

60. Froude, I, 329.

61. Ibid., II, 345; Hughes, III, 159.

62. Macaulay, *Critical and Historical Essays*, I, 6; *Camb. Mod. History*, III, 349.

63. Lingard, VI, 122.

64. Hughes, III, 289.

65. Pastor, XIX, 441-2.

66. Ibid.

67. McCabe, *Candid History*, 148.

68. Ibid., 150.

69. Froude, IV, 284.

70. Ibid., 294-5.

71. Lngard, VI, 165; Froude, IV, 297.

72. Pastor, XIX, 458.

73. Hughes, III, 325-6.

74. Neale, 265.

75. Hughes, III, 363; Williams, F. B., *Elizabethan England*, 10.

76. Froude, V, 238.

77. Hughes, III, 380; Neale, 299.

78. Hallam, I, 169; Lingard, VI, 257.

79. Hughes, III, 392-6.

80. Allen, J. W., *History of Political Thought in the Sixteenth Century*, 216-7; Hallam, I, 190.

81. Hallam, I, 198.

82. Hughes, III, 408.

83. Lea, H. C., *Studies in Church History*, 508.

84. Neale, 178.

85. Hallam, I, 205.

86. *Camb. Mod. History*, III, 345.

87. Walton, Izaak, *Life of Richard Hooker*, in Clark, B. H., *Great Short Biographies of the World*, 556.

88. Hooker, Richard, *Works: Laws of Ecclesiastical Polity*, I, x, 4, 8.

89. Ibid., VIII, vi, 11.

90. Ibid., I, i, 1.

91. Froude, IV, 237.

92. Ibid., 191.

93. D'Alton, E. A., *History of Ireland*, III, 199.

94. Froude, IV, 233, 236.

95. Ibid., 233.

96. Froude, II, 466.

97. *Encyclopaedia Britannica*, 14th ed., XV, 778b.

98. Froude, II, 211.

99. Nussbaum, F. L., *History of the Economic Institutions of Modern Europe*, 122; Froude, II, 468.

100. Barnes, *Economic History*, 265.

101. Acton, J. E., *Lectures on Modern History*, 152; Davies, E. Trevor, *The Golden Age of Spain*, 212; Froude, III, 309; V, 37.

102. Froude, V, 344.

103. Ibid., 400.

104. Michelet, Jules, *Histoire de France*, IV, 4.

105. Froude, V, 413.

106. Ibid., 430-1.

107. Spedding, J., *Life and Times of Francis Bacon*, I, 56.

108. Strachey, *Elizabeth and Essex*, 173.

109. In Eddy, Sherwood, *The Challenge of Europe*, 205n.

110. Strachey, *Elizabeth and Essex*, 6.

111. Clarendon, *Robert Devereux and George Villiers*, in Clark, *Great Short Biographies*, 603.

112. Spedding, I, 21.

113. Ibid., 179.

114. Ibid., 56.

115. Strachey, 65.

116. Spedding, I, 231.

117. Spedding, note to Rawley's *Life of Bacon*, in Bacon, *Philosophical Works*, 3.

118. Strachey, 172; Spedding, *Life of Bacon*, I, 227; Creighton, *Queen Elizabeth*, 279.

119. Holzknecht, *Backgrounds of Shakespeare's Plays*, 301; Chambers, E. K., *William Shakespeare*, I, 354; Strachey, 241.

120. Spedding, I, 343-8.

121. Strachey, 264-5.

122. Creighton, 295.

123. Strachey, 279.

124. In Muir, *Elizabethan and Jacobean Prose*, 39.

125. Ibid., 40.

126. *Hamlet*, III. iii, 15-23.

127. Bacon, *Advancement of Learning*, Preface to the King.

128. *Henry VIII*, V, v, 18.

CHAPTER II

1. A phrase of unknown origin, as old as 1300.—Mencken, H. L., *New Dictionary of Quotations*, 343.

2. Bernal, *Science in History*, 284; Wolf, A., *History of Science in the Eighteenth Century*, 630.

3. Trevelyan, *English Social History*, 191.

4. Rogers, *Economic Interpretation of History*, 38; Traill, *Social England*, III, 365; Froude, *Henry VIII*, I, 19; Lipson, *Growth of English Society*, 157f.

5. *Shakespeare's England*, I, 320.

6. Rogers, *Economic Interpretation*, 37; Rogers, *Six Centuries of Work and Wages*, 84, 88, 100.

7. Renard and Weulersce, *Life and Work in Modern Europe*, 94; *Shakespeare's England*, I, 331.

8. Creighton in Traill, III, 373.

9. Gasquet, *Henry VIII and the English Monasteries*, II, 515n.

10. Smith, P., *Age of the Reformation*, 476.

11. Beard, Chas., *Toward Civilization*, 227.

12. Trevelyan, *Social History*, 160-1.

13. Wolf, *History of Science in the Sixteenth and Seventeenth Centuries*, 614.

14. Thompson, J. W., *Economic and Social History of Europe in the Later Middle Ages*, 497.

15. Sée, H., *Modern Capitalism*, 55.

16. Trevelyan, *Social History*, 120.

17. Sarton, G., *Introduction to the History of Science*, IIIa, 324.

18. Addison, J. D., *Arts and Crafts in the Middle Ages*, 26.

19. Froude, *Elizabeth*, II, 88.

20. Chute, *Shakespeare of London*, 63.

21. Ascham, *Scholemaster*, 71-8 and end.

22. Einstein, Lewis, *Italian Renaissance in England*, 160.

23. Hughes, III, 137.

24. Goethe, *Faust*, Part II, lines 616-18, quoted in Haydn, H., *The Counter-Renaissance*, 362.

25. *Camb. Mod. History*, III, 362.

26. Chute, *Ben Jonson*, 41.

27. Trend, J. B., *Civilization of Spain*, 110.

28. Hughes, III, 144.

29. *Shakespeare's England*, I, 416.

30. Froude, *Elizabeth*, V, 462.

31. Trevelyan, *Social History*, 140.

32. Lingard, VI, 323.

33. *King Lear*, IV, vi.

34. Lingard, VI, 323.

35. Hallam, I, 35.

36. *Shakespeare's England*, I, 398.

37. Froude, *Elizabeth*, IV, 122-3; *Shakespeare's England*, I, 400.

38. Hallam, I, 234; Spenser, E., *Poetical Works*, Introd., xxiii.

39. Browne, Sir Thos., *Religio Medici*, Introd., x.

40. Garrison, *History of Medicine*, 819.

41. Bacon, Essay "Of Gardens," in *Philosophical Works*, 791.

42. *Merchant of Venice*, I, ii.

43. *Much Ado about Nothing*, III, iv.

44. Holzknecht, 44.

45. Philip Stubbs in James, B. B., *Women of England*, 250.

46. Wright, Thomas, *Womankind in Western Europe*, 334.

47. *Merchant of Venice*, III, ii, 89.

48. *Shakespeare's England*, II, 94.

49. Wright, Thomas, *History of Domestic Manners and Sentiments in England*, 456.

50. James I, *A Counterblast to Tobacco* (1604), in Muir, 89.

51. McKinney and Anderson, *Music in History*, 278.

52. *Oxford History of Music*, II, 221.

53. Ibid., 208.

54. Haydn, H., *The Portable Elizabethan Reader*, 666.

55. Burney, C., *General History of Music*, II, 306.

56. In the National Portrait Gallery, London.

57. Blomfield, R., *Short History of Renaissance Architecture in England*, 37.

58. Bishop, A. T., *Renaissance Architecture of England*, 34; Blomfield, 86.

59. Ibid.

60. Haydn, *Counter-Renaissance*, 13.

CHAPTER III

1. Burton, Robert, *Anatomy of Melancholy*, 7.

2. *Shakespeare's England*, II, 183.

3. Putnam, G. H., *Censorship of the Church of Rome*, II, 258.

4. *Shakespeare's England*, II, 217.

5. Cambridge *History of English Literature*, III, 369.

6. Garnett and Gosse, *English Literature*, II, 68.

7. Camb. *History of English Literature*, III, 372.

8. Ascham, *Scholemaster*, 17-23.

9. Haydn, *Portable Elizabethan Reader*, 183.

10. Lyly, *Euphues: The Anatomy of Wit*, 33.

11. Greene, Robert, *A Groats-worth of Wit Bought with a Million of Repentance*, in Taine, *English Literature*, 168.

12. In Muir, 28.

13. Symonds, J. A., *Shakespeare's Predecessors*, 435.

14. Saintsbury, *History of Elizabethan Literature*, 233.

15. Bourne, *Sir Philip Sidney*, 75.

16. Aubrey's *Brief Lives*, 278.

17. Bourne, 115.

18. Ibid., 27-30.

19. Ibid., 277.

20. Sidney, Philip, *Works: Defense of Poetry*, 9.

21. Sidney, *Works*, III, 14.

22. Ibid., I, 7.

23. Ibid., I, 16.

24. *Defense of Poetry*, 41.

25. Sidney, Sonnet xxxi.

26. Bourne, 326.

27. In Haydn, *Elizabethan Reader*, 394.

28. Bourne, 349.

29. Spenser, *Poetical Works*, 559.

30. Prefatory *Letter to Raleigh*, in *Poetical Works*, 407.

31. *Faerie Queene*, II, xii, 78.

32. Thornton, *Table Talk*, 1.

33. Van Doren, *Anthology of World Poetry*, 1026.

34. Aristotle, *Poetics*, 1449-50.

35. *Defense of Poetry*, 38.

36. Mantzius, *History of Theatrical Art*, III, 11.

37. *Shakespeare's England*, II, 241.

38. Chambers, E. K., *The Elizabethan Stage*, I, 255.

39. Holzknecht, 110.

40. Chambers, *Elizabethan Stage*, I, 258.

41. Shakespeare, *Twelfth Night*, II, iii.

42. *Pericles*, IV, ii.

43. Chambers, *Elizabethan Stage*, IV, 273-5.

44. *Henry V*, I, i, 13.

45. *Hamlet*, III, ii, 10.

46. Holzknecht, 153.

47. *Shakespeare's England*, II, 277.

48. *Hamlet*, II, ii, 354.

49. Mantzius, III, 228.

50. Marlowe, *Works*, Appendix, 428-30.

51. Bakeless, John, *Tragicall History of Christopher Marlowe*, 112.

52. Symonds, *Shakespeare's Predecessors*, 437.

53. Bakeless, 113.

54. Marlowe, *Tamburlane*, Part I, Act II, vii.

55. France, A., *The Gods Are Athirst*, 57.

56. Ecclesiastes, i, 18.

57. Marlowe, *Faustus*, I, i.

58. *The Jew of Malta*, II, iii.

59. Ibid., I, i.

60. Ibid., II, i.

61. *Tamburlane*, Part I, Act I, i.

62. Bakeless, 156; *Esquire Magazine*, December 1954.

CHAPTER IV

1. Chambers, *William Shakespeare*, II, 264.

2. Ibid., 257.

3. Lee, Sidney, *Life of William Shakespeare*, 22.

4. Chambers, *Shakespeare*, II, 188.

5. Ibid., 189.

6. Ibid., 259, 265.

7. Shakespeare, Sonnet xxix.

8. Sonnet CX.

9. Chute, *Shakespeare*, 269.

10. Sonnet CLII.

11. Lee, 68.

12. Raleigh, W., *Shakespeare*, 150.

13. Chambers, *Shakespeare*, I, 434.

14. *As You Like It*, II, vii.

15. *King Lear*, IV, vi, 120.

16. *Timon of Athens*, IV, i, 35.

17. Ibid., IV, iii, 54.

18. Ibid., IV, iii, 151f.

19. *Troilus and Cressida*, II, ii, 166.

20. *Coriolanus*, I, iv, 57.

21. Thornton, *Table Talk*, 5.

22. *Encycl. Brit.*, III, 781b.

23. *Two Gentlemen of Verona*, I, i, 71.

24. *The Tempest*, I, ii, 129.

25. *Midsummer Night's Dream*, II, iii, 61.

26. *Hamlet*, II, ii, 310.

27. *Romeo and Juliet*, , ii, 139

28. *Julius Caesar*, I, ii, 139.

29. *Tempest*, II, i, 47.

30. Hauser, A., *Social History of Art*, I, 422.

31. *Love's Labour's Lost*, I, i, 166.

32. *Richard III*, 1, i, 1.

33. Ibid., I, i, 24.

34. *2 Henry IV*, IV, iv.

35. *1 Henry IV*, III, i.

36. *Much Ado about Nothing*, II, iii.

37. *2 Henry IV*, III, i.

38. *King John*, IV, ii.

39. *Troilus and Cressida*, III, iii.

40. *Midsummer Night's Dream*, I, iii.

41. *Merchant of Venice*, I, iii.

42. *Twelfth Night*, III, iv.

43. *Mid. Night's Dream*, I, i.

44. *Othello*, I, i.

45. *King Lear*, IV, vi.

46. *Hamlet*, I, iv.

47. Ibid., II, ii.

48. *Mid. Night's Dream*, II, i.

49. *Two Gentlemen of Verona*, IV, ii.

50. *Cymbeline*, II, iii.

51. *Measure for Measure*, IV, ii.

52. *Mid. Night's Dream*, V, i, 7.

53. Examples in Chambers, *Shakespeare*, 228-30.

54. *Comedy of Errors*, III, i, 76.

55. *Tempest*, IV, i, 199.

56. *As You Like It*, III, ii.

57. Shaw, Bernard, *Man and Superman*, Preface, xxviii.

58. *Hamlet*, I, v.

59. *Much Ado about Nothing*, V, i.

60. *Hamlet*, III, iv, 88.

61. Ibid., II, ii.

62. *Coriolanus*, IV, vii.

63. *Hamlet*, I, iv, 25.

64. *Richard III*, V, iii.

65. *Richard II*, III, iii.

66. *1 Henry IV*, III, i; cf. Haydn, *Counter-Renaissance*, 602f.

67. *Troilus and Cressida*, I, iii.

68. *King Lear*, V, ii, 9.

69. *Twelfth Night*, II, iii.

70. *King Lear*, IV, vi, 112f.

71. *Pericles*, II, i.

72. *Tempest*, II, i, 147-64.

73. *Hamlet*, IV, iv, 35.

74. Raleigh, *Shakespeare*, 61.

75. *King John*, III, i.

76. *Henry VIII*, II, ii; *Romeo and Juliet*, IV, ii.

77. *King Lear*, IV, i, 36.

78. Ibid., V, iii, 169.

79. V, ii, 10.

80. *King John*, III, iv, 108.

81. *Hamlet*, I, iii, 126-28.

82. *Macbeth*, V, v, 23.

83. *Merchant of Venice*, V, i.

84. *Measure for Measure*, III, i, 118.

85. *Hamlet*, I, iv, 67.

86. Chambers, *Shakespeare*, II, 194.

87. In Lee, *Shakespeare*, 179.

88. Jonson, *Timber*, in Chute, *Ben Jonson*, 340.

89. Lee, 177.

90. Ibid., 178.

91. Aubrey, 275.

92. Jonson, *Timber*, in Lee, 277.

93. Chambers, *Shakespeare*, I, 84.

94. Lee, 203.

95. Aubrey, 275.

96. Ibid., 85.

97. *Tempest*, I, ii, 5.

98. Ibid., IV, i, 148.

99. V, i, 48.

100. V, i, 181.

101. Chambers, *Shakespeare*, I, 89.

102. Holzknecht, 380-1.

103. Voltaire, Letter of July 19, 1776, in Denoiresterres, G., *Voltaire et la société française au xviiime siècle*, VIII, 108.

104. In Croce, B., *Ariosto, Shakespeare, and Corneille*, 284.

105. Voltaire, article on Dramatic Art, in Holzknecht, 387.

106. Goethe, *Wilhelm Meister*, Book II, chs. xiii-xvi.

CHAPTER V

1. Brantôme, *Book of the Ladies*, 92.

2. Ibid., 124.

3. Sainte-Beuve, *English Portraits*, 6.

4. Pastor, XVI, 283.

5. Lingard, VI, 12.

6. *Book of Discipline*, Heads I and III, in Knox, *History of the Reformation in Scotland*, II, 281-3.

7. Knox, *History*, II, 321-2.

8. In National Portrait Gallery, London, and in Uffizi Gallery, Florence.

9. Lang, Andrew, *Mystery of Mary Stuart*, 13, 61.

10. Knox, *History*, II, 10; Froude, *Elizabeth*, I, 255.

11. Knox, II, 8.

12. Ibid., 12.

13. Ibid., 13f.

14. Lang, *History of Scotland*, II, 107.

15. Ibid.

16. Muir, Edwin, *John Knox*, 240.

17. Knox, *History*, II, 29.

18. Lang, *History*, II, 110.

19. Fosdick, *Great Voices of the Reformation*, xxix.

20. Knox, *History*, II, 44-6.

21. Lang, *History*, II, 126.

22. Knox, II, 71-7; Lang, II, 127; Muir, *Knox*, 253.

23. Knox, II, 81.

24. Ibid., 83.

25. Ibid., 93.

26. Zweig, *Mary Queen of Scots*, 108.

27. Neale, *Queen Elizabeth*, 141.

28. Lang, *History*, II, 160.

29. Ibid.; Froude, *Elizabeth*, II, 50.

30. Lang, II, 162.

31. *Camb. Mod. History*, III, 272.

32. Lang, *Mystery*, 75.

33. Ibid., 108-11.

34. *Camb. Mod. History*, III, 273.

35. Lang, *History*, II, 171; Lingard, VI, 67.

36. Lang, II, 170-2.

37. Ibid.; Knox, *History*, lxxiii.

38. Zweig, 158.

39. Lang, *Mystery*, 236.

40. Acton, *Lectures*, 150-2; Lang, *Mystery*, 295, 353, 362.

41. Ibid., 133.

42. Lang, *History*, II, 188.

43. Neale, 161.

44. Lang, *Mystery*, 194.

45. Froude, *Elizabeth*, II, 307, 310.

46. Brockway and Winer, *Second Treasury of the World's Great Letters*, 112.

47. Hallam, I, 167.

48. Froude, *Elizabeth*, II, 407.

49. Ibid., 404; Lang, II, 200.

50. Lang, II, 203.

51. Lang, *Mystery*, 286.

52. Lingard, VI, 97.

53. Froude, III, 110.

54. Muir, *Knox*, 282.

55. Knox, *History*, I, vii.

56. Lingard, VI, 126.

57. Ibid., 128; Hughes, III, 278.

58. Roeder, *Catherine de' Medici*, 491.

59. Neale, 263.

60. Pastor, XIX, 450-2.

61. Lingard, VI, 187.

62. Ibid., 205-6; Pastor, XXI, 7-19.

63. Ibid., 25; Froude, V, 259-61.

64. Williams, Chas., *James I*, 76, 80-3; Froude, V, 294.

65. Zweig, 291.

CHAPTER VI

1. Fontenoy in Froude, V, 74.

2. Lang, *History*, 276, 294-6, 305, 395; Lingard, VI, 183.

3. Lea, *Studies in Church History*, 502-8.

4. Ibid., 500.

5. Lang, *History*, II, 243.

6. James I, *Basilikon Doron*, in Gooch, *English Democratic Ideas in the Seventeenth Century*, 41.

7. Lang, *History*, II, 278.

8. *History Today*, March 1956, 159.

9. Buckle, *History of Civilization*, IIa, 199.

10. Williams, *James I*, 132.

11. *Encycl. Brit.*, IV, 310.

12. Allen, J. W., *History of Political Thought*, 339-40; cf. Carlyle, R. W., *History of Medieval Political Theory*, 332f; Figgis, J. N., *From Gerson to Grotius*, 167-72.

13. Allen, op. cit., 342.

14. Quoted by Oliver Dick in Introduction to Aubrey's *Brief Lives*, xxx.

15. In Chute, *Ben Jonson*, 249.

16. Ibid., 268.

17. Ibid., 217.

18. Bowen, C. D., *The Lion and the Throne*, 315.

19. Aubrey, 67.

20. In Robinson, J. H., *Readings in European History*, 349; Allen, 254; Dunning, W. A., *History of Political Theories*, II, 217.

21. Allen, J. W., *English Political Thought*, 26.

22. Ibid., 124.

23. Lingard, VII, 17.

24. Allen, *English Political Thought*, 223.

25. Williams, *James I*, 192-3.

26. Lingard, VII, 19-22.

27. Ibid., 29.

28. Ibid., 40-3.

29. Ibid., 46-8.

30. Ibid., 50, 96.

31. McCabe, *Candid History of the Jesuits*, 198.

32. Lang, *History*, II, 508.

33. Aubrey, 21.

34. Hallam, H., *Literature of Europe*, III, 324.

35. Webster, *The White Devil*, in Webster and Ford, *Plays*, p. 91.

36. Webster, *Duchess of Malfy*, in Webster and Ford, p. 145.

37. Ibid., IV, ii.

38. Thornton, *Table Talk*, 15.

39. Thomas Fuller in Chute, *Ben Jonson*, 37.

40. Jonson, *Every Man out of His Humour*, Induction.

41. Thornton, 7.

42. Jonson, Every *Man out of His Humour*, Induction.

43. Thornton, 8.

44. Chute, *Ben Jonson*, 161.

45. Jonson, *The Alchemist*, II, i.

46. Baskerville, Read, etc., *Elizabethan and Stuart Plays*, 1077.

47. Herrick, *Poems*, 241.

48. Chute, *Ben Jonson*, 310.

49. Williams, *James I*, 189.

50. Introduction to Burton, *Anatomy of Melancholy*, p. x.

51. Ibid.

52. Burton, *Anatomy of Melancholy*, 8.

53. Ibid., 3.

54. Ibid., 79-80.

55. Donne, *Poems*, 83.

56. Ibid., 26.

57. Elegy XIII; Elegy II.

58. *Poems*, 182.

59. Ibid., 180.

60. Thornton, 4.

61. *Poems*, 253.

62. In Peterson, *Treasury of the World's Great Speeches*, 91.

63. Ibid., 92.

64. Walton, *Life of Dr. Donne*, in Peterson, 95.

65. Hallam, *Constitutional History*, I, 347; *Encycl. Brit.*, XVIII, 961b; Lingard, VII, 7.

66. Text in Schuster, M. L., *Treasury of the World's Great Letters*, 82-4.

67. Raleigh, Sir Walter, *Selections*, 61.

68. Ibid., 117.

69. Lingard, VII, 101.

70. Spedding, *Life of Fr. Bacon*, II, 288-9; Wallace, *Sir Walter Raleigh*, 261f.

71. Lingard, VII, 102.

72. *Encycl. Brit.*, XVIII, 961b.

73. Wallace, *Raleigh*, 315.

74. Raleigh, *Selections*, Introduction, 28.

75. Lingard, VII, 117.

76. Williams, *James I*, 258.

77. Hallam, *Constitutional History*, 109.

78. Ibid., 122.

79. MacLaurin, C., *Mere Mortals*, 137.

CHAPTER VII

1. Browne, Sir Thomas, *Pseudodoxia Epidemica*, in *Works*, Vols. II and III.

2. Thorndike, Lynn, *History of Magic and Experimental Science*, VI, 548-9.

3. Lecky, *Rationalism in Europe*, I, 38n; Williams, *James I,* 106-10.

4. Lang, *History*, II, 434.

5. Hughes, *Reformation*, II, 286n.

6. Ibid., 285.

7. Thorndike, VI, 550; Chute, *Ben Jonson*, 229.

8. Trevelyan, *English Social History*, 232.

9. Smith, Preserved, *History of Modern Culture*, I, 97.

10. Ibid., 95.

11. Robertson, *History of Freethought*, II, 13.

12. Huntington Library Bulletin, April 1934, p. 99.

13. Wolf, *History of Science*, I, 292.

14. Ibid., 426.

15. John, Evan, *King Charles I*, 153; Kellogg, *The New Dietetics*, 847.

16. Garrison, *History of Medicine*, 248.

17. Sigerist, *The Great Doctors*, 141.

18. Harvey, *Exercitatio anatomica de motu cordis et sanguinis*, in Hammerton, *Great Books*, 273.

19. Walsh, J. J., *The Popes and Science*, 396.

20. Aubrey, 131.

21. Prinzmetal, *Heart Attack*, 121-2.

22. Aubrey, 128.

23. Ibid., 130.

24. Ibid., 11.

25. Gardiner, S. R., in Garnett and Gosse, *English Literature*, II, 12.

26. Spedding, *Life of Bacon*, I, 542.

27. Aubrey, 9.

28. Macaulay, *Critical and Historical Essays*, II, 326-8.

29. Bowen, *The Lion and the Throne*, 428; *Camb. Mod. History*, III, 571.

30. Spedding, *Life*, II, 463.

31. Ibid., 633.

32. Ibid., I, 563.

33. Ibid., 569.

34. Bacon, *Philosophical Works*, 241.

35. Ibid.

36. Ibid., 244.

37. Ibid., 247.

38. Aubrey, 130.

39. Bacon, *Phil. Works*, 167.

40. Ibid., 76, 78; *De Augmentis scientiarum*, Preface.

41. *Philosophical Works*, 76.

42. *Advancement of Learning*, ch. 8.

43. Bacon, *Works*, ed. Spedding and Ellis, VII, 241.

44. *Novum organum*, i, 97.

45. Ibid., i, 82; and "Plan of the Work" in *Philosophical Works*, 250.

46. *Novum organum*, ii, 13, 17.

47. *Philosophical Works*, 144.

48. Ibid., 77.

49. Ibid., 50.

50. Spedding, *Life*, I, 111.

51. *Novum organum*, ii, 2.

52. Ibid., ii, 8.

53. Ibid.

54. *De Augmentis*, iv, 3.

55. *Novum organum*, i, 66.

56. De *Augmentis*, end.

57. Essay "Of Atheism."

58. Ibid.; *Advancement of Learning*, in *Philosophical Works*, 45; *De Augmentis*, iii, 2.

59. Essay "Of Atheism."

60. *Valerius Terminus*, ch. i, in *Philosophical Works*, 186.

61. Rawley's *Life*, in *Phil. Works,* 9.

62. *De Augmentis*, ix, 1.

63. Essay "Of Goodness."

64. Ibid.

65. "Of Marriage and Single Life."

66. Essays "Of Empire" and "Of the True Greatness of Kingdoms."

67. *De Augmentis*, viii, 3, in *Phil. Works*, 610-11.

68. "Of Vicissitude of Things."

69. "Of Seditions and Troubles."

70. *Phil. Works*, 727.

71. *History of Henry VII*, in *Works*, VI, 238-45.

72. In Nichol, J., *Fr. Bacon*, II, 4.

73. Pope's *Essay on Man*, line 282.

74. *Thema coeli*, in *Phil. Works*, 705; *Descriptio globi intellectualis*, ibid., 685.

75. In Friedell, *Cultural History of the Modern Age*, I, 335.

76. *The Advancement of Learning*, in *Phil. Works*, 167.

77. Wolf, *Science in the Sixteenth Century*, 640; Bernal, *Science in History*, 305.

78. Hallam, *Literature of Europe*, III, 72.

79. Nichol, J., II, 235.

80. *Novum organum*, i, 49.

81. Ibid., i, 26, 95.

CHAPTER VIII

1. Rogers, *Six Centuries of Work and Wages*, 103.

2. Ibid., table at p. 73.

3. John, *Charles I*, 167.

4. French, Allen, *Charles I and the Puritan Upheaval*, 100-2.

5. Robertson, J. M., *Freethought*, II, 24.

6. Ibid., 77.

7. Ibid., 76.

8. Ibid.

9. Aubrey, 135.

10. Belloc, H., *Richelieu*, 49.

11. McCabe, *Candid History*, 202.

12. Toynbee, A., *Study of History*, IX, 178.

13. Allen, *English Political Thought*, 237.

14. Ibid., 242.

15. Ibid.

16. Taine, *English Literature*, 259-62.

17. Hume, D., *History of England*, IV, 183.

18. Gardiner, S. R., *History of England 1603–42*, VII, 302.

19. French, *Charles I*, 281.

20. Lingard, VII, 181; Taine, *English Literature*, 265.

21. *Camb. Mod. History*, IV, 279.

22. Allen, *English Thought*, 194.

23. Carlyle, T., *Oliver Cromwell*, I, 93.

24. French, 306.

25. Schaff, *History of the Christian Church: The German Reformation*, I, 79.

26. Allen, *English Thought*, 283.

27. French, 281.

28. Markun, L., *Mrs. Grundy*, 114.

29. Weber, Max, *The Protestant Ethic*, 177.

30. Beard, Miriam, *History of the Business Man*, 387.

31. Allen, *English Thought*, 279f; Lingard, VIII, 190.

32. Ibid., 191n.

33. Thornton, *Table Talk*, 72, 106.

34. Browne, *Religio Medici*, 77.

35. Browne, *Works*, II, 226.

36. *Religio Medici*, 70, 34.

37. Singer, *Studies in the History of Science*, 222.

38. *Religio Medici*, 82.

39. Ibid., 1.

40. Ibid., 18.

41. Ibid., 25.

42. Ibid., 10.

43. Ibid., 179.

44. Ibid., 60.

45. Ibid., 92.

46. Herrick, *Poems*, 181.

47. Ibid., 178.

48. Ibid., 398.

49. Aubrey, 287.

50. Ibid., 289.

51. Ibid., 192.

52. Lovelace, *Poems*, 78.

53. Ibid., 18.

54. MacLaurin, *Mere Mortals*, 143-4; John, *Charles I*, 4; French, 16.

55. Bishop, *Renaissance Architecture*, 25.

56. John, *Charles I*, 65.

57. Ibid., 66.

58. Ibid., 133; Lingard, VII, 164.

59. Gardiner, S. R., *History of England 1603–42,* VII, 1.

60. Ibid., 41-3.

61. Tawney, *Religion and the Rise of Capitalism*, 173.

62. Ibid., 174; Allen, *English Thought*, 360.

63. Rickard, *Man and Metals*, II, 799.

64. Clarendon, *History of the Rebellion*, I, 323.

65. Ibid., 188f.

66. Carlyle, *Oliver Cromwell*, I, 94.

67. Lang, *History of Scotland*, III, 71.

68. John, *Charles I*, 207.

69. Morley, *Oliver Cromwell*, 72.

70. Clarendon, *passim*; Hume, D., *History of England*, IV, 174, 401.

71. Carlyle, *Oliver Cromwell*; Firth, *Oliver Cromwell*; Buchan, *Oliver Cromwell*.

72. Morley, *Cromwell*, 9.

73. Carlyle, *Cromwell*, I, 98.

74. Ibid., 108.

75. Clarendon, I, 300; Gardiner, *History of England*, IX, 230.

76. Thornton, *Table Talk*, 108.

77. Gardiner, IX, 251-2.

78. Allen, *English Thought*, 346f.

79. Morley, *Cromwell*, 91; Hallam, *Constitutional History*, II, 119; Allen, 354.

80. Clarendon, I, 452.

81. Ibid., 466.

82. Firth, *Cromwell*, 61.

83. Clarendon, II, 49 f.

84. Allen, *English Thought*, 313, 403-4.

85. Robinson, J. H., *Readings*, 356.

86. Schaff, *History of the Christian Church: The Swiss Reformation*, II, 565.

87. Firth, 149; Bury, J. B., *History of Freedom of Thought*, 86; Robertson, J. M., *Freethought*, II, 76.

88. *Camb. Mod. History*, IV, 312.

89. Firth, 147.

90. Ibid.

91. Macaulay, *History of England*, I, 100.

92. Gooch, *English Democratic Ideas*, 119, 179.

93. Ibid., 124.

94. Ibid., 128.

95. *Camb. Mod. History*, IV, 345.

96. Firth, 175.

97. Morley, *Cromwell*, 240.

98. Lingard, VIII. 110.

99. Morley, 267.

100. John. *Charles I*, 294.

101. Hume, *History*, IV, 485.

102. Churchill, W. S., *History of the English-Speaking Peoples*, II, 223.

103. Robinson, *Readings*, 359.

BONUS (FRANCIS BACON)

1. The table on pages 000–000 indicates approximately the main lines of philosophical development in Europe and America.

2. Quoted as motto on the title-page of Anatole France's *Garden of Epicurus*.

3. Professor Shotwell (*Introduction to the History of History*) calls it "the most marvelous performance in all antique literature."

4. Paraphrase by Mallock: *Lucretius on Life and Death*, pp. 15–16.

5. V., 830 f., translation by Munro.

6. *Enchiridion and Dissertations of Epictetus;* ed. Rolleston; p. 81.

7. *Ibid.,* xxxvi.

8. *Ibid.,* 86.

9. II, 1170. This oldest is also the latest theory of the decline of Rome; cf. Simkhovitch: *Toward the Understanding of Jesus;* New York, 1921.

10. Robinson and Beard: *Outlines of European History;* Boston, 1914, i, 443.

11. The render probably knows that *city, civility, culture,* and *civilization* have all one Identical Latin root; just as one Greek word gives us *polity, politics,* and *policemen.*

12. Bacon: *The Advancement of Learning;* bk. ii, ch, 10. A medieval motto showed a ship turning back at Gibraltar into the Mediterranean, with the inscription, *Non plus ultra*—go no farther.

13. E. J. Payne in *The Cambridge Modern History,* i, 65.

14. *Essays:* New York, 1850: iii, 342.

15. Translation by Abbott: *Francis Bacon;* London, 1885; p. 37.

16. Nichol: *Francis Bacon;* Edinburgh, 1907; i, 37.

17. Hundreds of volumes have been written on this aspect of Bacon's career. The case against Bacon, as "the wisest and meanest of mankind" (so Pope called him), will be found in Macaulay's essay, and more circumstantially in Abbott's *Francis Bacon;* these would apply to him his own words: "Wisdom for a man's self is the wisdom of rats, that will be sure to leave a house somewhat before it falls" (Essay "Of Wisdom for a Man's Self"). The case for Bacon is given in Spedding's *Life and Times of Francis Bacon,* and in his *Evenings with a Reviewer* (a detailed reply to Macaulay). *In medio veritas.*

18. The author has thought it better in this section to make no attempt to concentrate further the already compact thought of Bacon, and has preferred to put the philosopher's wisdom in his own incomparable English rather than to take probably greater space to say the same things with less clarity, beauty, and force.

19. *Valerius Terminus, ad fin.*

20. "Of Studies."

21. Dedication of *Wisdom of the Ancients.*

22. *De Augmentis,* viii, 3.

23. The author's preference is for Essays 2, 7, 8, 11, 12, 16, 18, 20, 27, 29, 38, 39, 42, 46, 48, 50, 52, 54.

24. *Adv. of L.,* vii, 2. Certain passages from this book are brought in here, to avoid a repetition of topics under each work.

25. "Of Nature in Men."

26. "Of Regiment of Health."

27. *Adv. of L.,* xii, 2.

28. "Of Goodness."

29. *Adv. of L.,* vii, 1.

30. "Of Atheism."

31. *Ibid.*

32. Letter to Lord Burghley, 1606.

33. "Of Marriage and Single Life." Contrast the more pleasing phrase of Shakespeare, that "Love gives to every power a double power."

34. "Of Love."

35. "Of Followers and Friends"; "Of Friendship."

36. "Of Parents and Children."

37. "Of Custom."

38. "Of Dispatch."

39. "Of the True Greatness of Kingdoms."

40. "Of Seditions and Troubles."

41. *Ibid.*

42. In Nichol, ii, 149.

43. *Adv. of L.,* vi, 3.

44. *Ibid.,* i.

45. *Ibid.*

46. Preface to *Magna Instauratio.*

47. *Redargutio Philosophiarum.*

48. Bacon's actual works under the foregoing heads are chiefly these:

    I. *De Interpretations Naturae Proemium* (Introduction to the Interpretation of Nature, 1603); *Redargutio Philosophiarum* (A Criticism of Philosophies, 1609).

    II. *The Advancement of Learning* (1603–5); translated as *De Augmentis Scientiarum,* 1622).

    III. *Cogitata et Visa* (Things Thought and Seen, 1607); *Filum Labyrinthi* (Thread of the Labyrinth, 1606); *Novum Organum* (The New Organon, 1608–20).

    IV. *Historia Naturalis* (Natural History, 1622); *Descriptio Globi Intellectualis* (Description of the Intellectual Globe, 1612).

    V. *Sylva Sylvarum* (Forest of Forests, 1624).

    VI. *De Principiis* (On Origins, 1621).

    VII. *The New Atlantis* (1624).

Note.—All of the above but *The New Atlantis* and *The Advancement of Learning* were written in Latin; and the latter was translated into Latin by Bacon and his aides, to win for it a European audience. Since historians and critics always use the Latin titles in their references, these are here given for the convenience of the student.

49. Preface to *Magna Instauratio.*

50. "Plan of the Work."

51. *Adv. of L.,* iv, 2.

52. *Ibid.,* vi, 3.

53. *Ibid.,* ii, 1.

54. *De Aug.,* iv.

55. *Adv. of L.,* iv, 2.

56. *Ibid.*

57. *Novum Organum,* i, 60.

58. *De Interpretatione Naturae,* in Nichol, ii, 118.

59. They are developed in Spinoza's *Ethics,* Appendix to Book I.

60. *Adv. of L.,* vii, 3.

61. *De Aug.,* ix, in Nichol, ii, 129.

62. *Adv. of L.,* i.

63. *Ibid.,* viii, 2.

64. Cf. Edward Carpenter's delightful *Iolaüs:* an *Anthology of Friendship.*

65. *Adv. of L.,* viii, 2.

66. Essays "Of Dissimulation" and "Of Discourse."

67. *Adv. of L.,* viii, 2.

68. *Adv. of L.,* i, 81.

69. *Ibid.,* i.

70. *Ibid.,* viii, 2.

71. *Ibid.,* i.

72. In Nichol, ii, 4.

73. *Nov. Org.,* i, 118.

74. *Ibid.*

75. *Adv. of L.,* ii, 1.

76. *Ibid.,* i.

77. *Ibid.,* ii, 1.

78. Macaulay, *op. cit.,* p. 92

79. *Adv. of L.,* v, 1.

80. *Valerius Terminus.*

81. *Nov. Org.,* i, 41.

82. *Ibid.,* i, 45.

83. *Ibid.,* i, 46.

84. *Ibid.,* i, 63.

85. *Ibid.,* i, 49.

86. *Ibid.,* i, 58.

87. *Ibid.,* i, 104.

88. *Ibid.* i. 56.

89. *Ibid.,* i, 43.

90. *Ibid.,* i, 44.

91. *Adv. of L.,* v, 2.

92. *Nov. Org.,* i, 84.

93. *Ibid.,* i, 82.

94. *Ibid.,* ii, 20.

95. *Ibid.,* ii, 13, 17.

96. *Ibid.,* ii, 2.

97. *Outline of History,* ch. xxxv, sect. 6.

98. Sect. 25.

99. *The New, Atlantis,* Cambridge University Press, 1900; p. 20.

100. *Ibid.,* p. 22.

101. *Ibid.,* p. xxv.

102. *Ibid.,* p. 34.

103. Cf. The New York *Times* of May 2, 1928, for a report of War Department chemists on the use of war gases to cure diseases.

104. *New Atlantis,* p. 24.

105. *Op. cit.,* p. 471.

106. Quoted by J. M. Robertson, Introduction to *The Philosophical Works of Francis Bacon;* p. 7.

107. *Adv. of L.,* iv, 2.

108. *Fil. Lab., ad fin.*

109. Sonnet xv.

110. Macaulay, p. 491.

111. Nichol, ii. 235.

112. *Nov. Org.,* i, 129.

113. Essay "Of Great Place."

114. *Francis Bacon,* ch. i.

115. *Ibid.,* p. 13 note.

www.ingramcontent.com/pod-product-compliance
Lightning Source LLC
Chambersburg PA
CBHW071710120626
46550CB00001B/177